Date Due

Apr 8 '47	Mar 14 '57	
May 27 '47	Apr 8 '57	
Jul 14 '47	Oct 21 '57	
Oct 24 '47	Nov 13 '57	
Feb 23 '48	Dec 14 '57	
Mar 19 '48	Jan 7 '58	
	Jan 22 '58	
Ma. 31 '48	Apr 17 '58	
Apr 7 '48	May 9 '60	
May 22 '50	May 25 '60	
Jun 26 '50	Dec 5 '61	
Mar 5 '51	Jan 3 '62	
	Nov 27 '62	
Dec 3 '54		
Mar 28		
Apr 2 '55		
Apr 16 '55		
Aug 16 '55		

Behold the Man

THE MACMILLAN COMPANY
NEW YORK · BOSTON · CHICAGO
DALLAS · ATLANTA · SAN FRANCISCO

MACMILLAN AND CO., LIMITED
LONDON · BOMBAY · CALCUTTA
MADRAS · MELBOURNE

**THE MACMILLAN COMPANY
OF CANADA, LIMITED**
TORONTO

Behold the Man

AN ANTHOLOGY OF JESUS CHRIST

EDITED BY RALPH L. WOODS

THE MACMILLAN COMPANY · NEW YORK

1944

First Printing

A WARTIME BOOK

THIS COMPLETE EDITION IS PRODUCED
IN FULL COMPLIANCE WITH THE GOVERN-
MENT'S REGULATIONS FOR CONSERVING
PAPER AND OTHER ESSENTIAL MATERIALS

PRINTED IN THE UNITED STATES OF AMERICA
BY THE VAIL-BALLOU PRESS, INC., BINGHAMTON, N. Y.

TO
MARY ELIZABETH WOODS

What Think Ye of Christ?

—Matt. 22: 42.

Introduction

Perhaps it is in order for the editor briefly to discuss the purpose and plan of this collection and to suggest its scope by mentioning the standards established for the inclusion of material.

The purpose of the book is simply to bring together, in an orderly and interesting way, what outstanding men and women, of the past and present, have written and said about Jesus Christ.

As each of innumerable passages on Christ was encountered three questions were asked:

(1) Is or was the person who said this an *outstanding* person?
(2) Is what he has said about Christ *interesting?*
(3) Has this *outstanding* person put these *interesting* comments in *readable* prose?

When passages met these specifications they were nominated for the anthology. But before gaining actual admission to the collection they had to pass a few more tests.

For example, any selection that might give offense to anyone accepting the divine nature of Christ was ruled out of the book. This does not mean, of course, that every person quoted accepts the divinity of Christ. It does mean that the passages used from those not believing in Christ's divinity nevertheless respect the feelings and faith of those who do accept Christ as God. Of course, a great number of the selections are from men and women who accept the divinity of Christ.

Another and sometimes more difficult test applied to all selections is that they should be of such nature as neither to plead for nor condemn or speak offensively of any creed, doctrine, church or faith.

Finally, selections that discussed Christ exclusively in terms of a particular Church's doctrines and creeds were rejected as not belonging in a non-sectarian book designed to show what great men and women throughout the ages have thought of Jesus as Man, Teacher, God, Reformer, Redeemer, Leader, Prophet and Messiah.

In short, the editor has been careful to avoid proving anything about Christ except that for nearly two thousand years His life, character and work have fascinated succeeding generations, inspired great writers, thinkers, philosophers, theologians, scholars, publicists, statesmen and churchmen to make many unusual and often brilliant and beautiful observations and interpretations of Him, and that Christ's many-sidedness and universal appeal are without parallel in all history.

The reader will no doubt agree that these standards for the inclusion of material are not the kind of restrictions that often and deservedly provoke quarrelsome criticism. On the contrary, they broaden the scope and enlarge the appeal of the book, because they keep out sectarian theological discussions and exegetical excesses— of which there is a plethora elsewhere.

Consequently, Jesus Christ is here interpreted, observed and commented upon in an atmosphere free of theological fog.

R. L. W.

Port Washington, N.Y.
June 1944.

CONTENTS

Page

GOD

TEACHER

Page

REDEEMER

LEADER

MESSIAH

PROPHET

MAN

KARL ADAM   (1876–   )

"THE CAPTAIN OF HIS SOUL"

Translated by Dom Justin McCann, O.S.B.

Away then with Nietzsche's supposition, that Jesus never laughed.
How is it possible that He should not Himself have known a deep
and pure joy, who was preaching the glad gospel of the Father, and
who in all joy and in all sorrow recognized God's infinite power and
goodness? Jesus loved men and loved their life in the will of His
Father. He was drawn to man not merely by His tears, but by His
laughter also. . . .

There was in Him no world-weariness, no strengthless melancholy,
no timid shrinking from the fray. He looked reality full in the face,
and gripped it with both His hands, and with His whole heart accepted it. There was no part of reality which He tried violently to
explain away, or to shut His eyes to. Jesus was no dreamer. He was a
realist, utterly alive to all the facts, to the full, complete reality,
whether that reality were light or darkness. Nor was His devotion
to natural things and to man any mere "love to order," any mere act
of obedience to God which left His heart indifferent.

For the will of God and natural things were not for Jesus two separate and disjointed factors, only conjoined in a purely external manner. On the contrary the will of God was manifested in things and
through them. Therefore, in loving the will of God, He was loving
things also, in the very centre of their being. He felt Himself one
with all reality, in a union that was formed and maintained by that
living might of God's will which was manifest in all. . . .

His life-zest was ennobled and transfigured by a marvellous steadi-
ness of soul, a sure loftiness of sentiment and thought. His long fast
in the wilderness, His vigils, the poverty of His wandering life, the
labours of His preaching, His ministry to the poor and outcast, the
maturity and distinction of His manner towards His malicious opponents, above all the heroism of His life and of His death—these

3

things can be understood only if we realize that He was ever and in all circumstances the captain of His soul. . . .

Jesus did not flee from life, nor yet was He subject to life: Jesus mastered life.

MARY AUSTIN   (*1868–1934*)

A MAN WISE IN LIFE

He was a small-town man and no world-builder. He preached the Kingdom of God, knowing God for a spirit and having an increasing realization of the kingdom as a state of being. But he had no program. He followed the inward voice, and followed it instinctively with the freedom of a river in its natural channel, with no fretting of the flesh. But where the voice left him uninformed he was simply a man from Nazareth; his social outlook was the outlook of the villager.

Formerly, great prophets of Israel had come out of the Wilderness; their words were full of the terrible things—thunders, earthquakes, fire on the mountains. But the words of Jesus are all of the small town; the candle and the bushel, the housewife's measure of yeast, the children playing in the street. The rich he knew only as the poor and the oppressed know them; the kings of his parables were the kings of fairy-tale and legend, such kings and potentates as make the stock of the village story-teller. His very way of speaking was a folkway, the pithy sentence, the pregnant figure. He saw God reflected in every surface of the common life, and taught in parables which are, after all, but a perfected form of the quizzes and riddles dear to the unlettered wit. That is why so many of them are remembered while his profounder sayings escaped his hearers. It is evident from the form of these, blunted as they are by retranslation, that they were, many of them, cast in the matched and balanced sentences of Hebrew verse, which accounts in part for their easy retention.

He was a man wise in life, but unlearned. He read no books but the

Scriptures, wrote nothing, took the folk way of transmitting his teaching from mouth to mouth and trusted God for the increase; and he had the folk way in his profoundest speech of identifying himself with the Power that used him. He dramatized all his relations to the Invisible. With it all he was a Jew of the circumcision. He grew up beyond Judaism as a stalk of grain from its sheath, but never out of it. Always to his death, it was there about the roots of his life. At Capernaum, when the Centurion had come to him, touching the illness of his servant, it had been thought necessary to explain that the soldier had been good to the Jews and had built them a synagogue. In the sending of his disciples he had explicitly directed them not to go into Samaria. His final illumination on this point he took with that extraordinary spiritual efficiency which distinguished him; equally with John the Baptist he understood that many should come in from strange lands and sit down with the children of Abraham and Isaac and Jacob. But the stalk had not yet overtopped its sheath when the returning twelve met him at the appointed rendezvous, which was probably Capernaum.

HARRY ELMER BARNES   (*1889–*   )

EVIDENCES OF HISTORICITY

In the light of the multiplicity of books which have been written about the life and teachings of Jesus, some of them devoted to a minute analysis of his views on some specific topic or to an elaborate description of a particular period of his life or phase of his personality, it may surprise some readers to learn that anyone has ever seriously questioned the actual historicity of Jesus. Even well-known historical scholars have frequently revealed curious misconceptions about the actual evidence for the life and teaching of Jesus. . . . As a matter of fact, the evidence for the point of view that Jesus was actually an historic character is so slight that a considerable number of the most distinguished students of New Testament times have declared Jesus to be a mythological personage, the outgrowth of the myth-making tendencies common to religious peoples of all ages and particularly prevalent in the period of the early Roman Empire. . . .

The actual documentary evidence for the life of Jesus . . . may be divided into two classes; non-Christian and Christian. Of the former, next to nothing exists. In all, this evidence mounts up to some twenty-four lines, not a single one of which is of admitted authenticity. There are four references altogether in non-Christian sources, three from Roman writers and one from the Jewish historian Josephus. . . .

We may now pass to a discussion of the Christian sources relative to the life of Jesus. The earliest New Testament documents are the Epistles of St. Paul written between 47 and 54 A.D. In these Epistles there are frequent references to Jesus and his doctrines, but they are of practically no historical value as bearing upon the life of Jesus. There is no evidence that Paul ever saw or listened to Jesus during his ministry. Further, Paul was not friendly with or sympathetic toward the actual Apostles, and hence made no effort to exploit his opportunities to learn about Jesus after his conversion to Christianity. Again, Paul was not interested in the historical Christ. He formulated his doctrines in isolation upon the basis of his own theology and religious program, assigning the origin of his views to Jesus occasionally, only for the purpose of giving them greater prestige. When he refers to Jesus it is more a theological gesture than a literal historical reference. . . . In short, Paul . . . apparently knew little or nothing about the real life of Jesus. . . .

We come next to the four Gospels. The Gospel of St. John may be eliminated at once as an historical document. No serious scholar contends for a moment that it presents a real historical account of the life and doctrines of Jesus. . . . The three Synoptic Gospels, Mark, Matthew and Luke, represent our only actual Christian sources for Jesus' life and teachings. . . . No one of the three Synoptic Gospels was written by an eye-witness of the events recounted in the Gospels. There is a legend to the effect that Mark wrote in part from the reminiscences of St. Peter, but there is no positive proof of this contention. At any rate, the story in Mark is the most direct and straight-forward account we have of the life of Jesus. . . .

There is, therefore, a very slender body of original independent material on the life of Jesus contained in the three Synoptic Gospels. . . . It is most reasonable to suppose that the Gospels represent a composite set of reminiscences about Jesus which were gradually accumulated in the decades preceding the compilation of the Gospels.

In spite of the slim body of documentary material bearing upon Jesus and his teachings, and conceding the plausibility of the thesis that he was not actually a historic character, it seems to the writer more consonant with probability to conclude that Jesus was a historic personage, concerning whom we have an unfortunately small body of authentic and dependable information.

ALBERT J. BEVERIDGE   (1862-1927)

NEEDS NO INTERPRETER

This little book draws rapidly to a close and yet I have said almost nothing about the Saviour. Somehow or other I couldn't bring myself to it. The story of our Lord, as a mere matter of reading is above the charm of any narrative you will find. His divinity aside, the practical wisdom of his sayings exceeds those of Solomon. But what he did, what he lived and what he said cannot be retold with an infinitesimal part of the entertainment which the gospels themselves give. That is true, of course, of the whole Bible—true of Moses, of Joshua and David and the rest—but with the Master, somehow "it's different."

I never read an essay upon our Lord but with a certain kind of repulsion. He needs no interpreter; comment and commentary on him seem sacrilege—of course, such a view is undoubtedly unreasonable and unintelligent, but I just feel that way about it.

SHIRLEY JACKSON CASE   (*1872*-   )

SOME CHARACTERISTICS EXPLAINED BY EARLY ENVIRONMENT

Jesus had grown up in the village of Nazareth a member of the artisan class. Through parental training and synagogue attendance he had acquired the common man's knowledge of Jewish religion. To this he added a further discipline in the practical school of real life. Here he made various contacts with different types of people, as the circles of his activity gradually widened. First in the home, then in the immediate vicinity, then in the life of Palestine at large he was disciplined in the school of experience. Even during the "hidden" years of his career he was not merely a citizen of Nazareth; he was also a resident in the Holy Land.

The significance of Jesus' wider contacts with the life of his day has not always been fully appreciated. Nazareth has commonly been assigned the role of a secluded village, almost lost behind the surrounding hills. It is assumed to have been so cut off from the rest of the country that its inhabitants had no immediate contact with the varied interests of contemporary Galilean society in the larger centers of population. Sometimes Jesus is permitted a wider outlook as he makes imagined ascents to the top of the encircling hills where the panorama might refresh his memory of Old Testament history. Or his imagination might have been stirred by sight of the peoples and caravans moving along the busy highways of Galilee. But even so, he remains detached, an individual apart, contemplating the passing scene from a position of isolation. That he himself actively participated in the life of a going society, which included in its maelstrom many diverse currents, is rarely or never imagined. . . .

Jesus was a lad perhaps between five and ten years of age when the Romans wreaked on Sepphoris their vengeance for its connection with the revolution of Judas. Apparently Antipas began the work of reconstruction about ten years later, but at what date it was completed is unknown. A heap of ruins could not be converted into the "ornament of all Galilee" in a single day. One may surmise that the task was not finished until about the year 25 A.D. and that its completion, and the accomplishment of a similar rebuilding program at Betharamatha, released laborers who could now be employed upon the new foundation at Tiberias.

That a vigorous building enterprise was in progress at Sepphoris while Jesus was still a youth, and at the same time the main support of a family of at least six younger children and a widowed mother, suggests the probability that he may have plied his carpenter's trade in the city. Very likely "carpenter" as applied to Jesus meant not simply a worker in wood but one who labored at the building-trade in general, and it requires no very daring flight of the imagination to picture the youthful Jesus seeking and finding employment in the neighboring city of Sepphoris. But whether or not he actually labored there, his presence in the city on various occasions can scarcely be doubted; and the fact of such contacts during the formative years of his young manhood may account for attitudes and opinions that show themselves conspicuously during his public ministry. Had his earlier experience been confined within the narrow limits of a secluded village, certain traits of his character are exceedingly difficult to explain. They become more readily understandable when we assume that in his youth and early manhood his outlook had been shaped by wider contacts with a more varied environment.

The unconventionality of Jesus in mingling freely with the common people, his generosity toward the stranger and the outcast, and his conviction of the equality of all classes before God, perhaps owe their origin in no slight degree to the proximity of Nazareth to Sepphoris. Had Jesus spent his youth exclusively in a small village amid strictly Jewish surroundings, he would have been less likely to acquire the generous attitudes which later characterized his public career. But if in Sepphoris he had come into contact not only with Jewish fellow-laborers but also with artisans of other nationalities, or if only on brief but numerous visits to the city he frequently encountered a mixed population on the streets and in the shops, and thus grew accustomed to freedom of intercourse, one can a little better understand the genesis of that spirit of toleration which caused him to be called the friend of publicans and sinners.

Still another distinctive feature about the career of Jesus was his method of procedure. He quite reversed the program of the contemporary Jewish reformer, such as one meets in the Zadokite sectary, the Essene, a Bannus, or a John the Baptist. The representatives of these movements summoned people to separate themselves from their customary pursuits as a condition for realizing a better righteousness. In order to be especially pleasing to God, one must withdraw from the ordinary contacts of daily life. Jesus, on the other hand, did not call upon his followers to sever relations with their fellows, nor did he perpetuate in his own practice even the distinguishing mark of the Johannine baptismal rite. In his view religion was something that could function to the full while people were engaged in their normal activities. His ideals of righteousness were realizable and to be realized in close contact with society in the actual process of everyday living. Had he arrived at his convictions in the seclusion of a small village, from which occasionally he withdrew to the quiet of the surrounding hills to perfect his meditations, probably he would have demanded of his disciples a similar isolation as the condition necessary for attaining true righteousness. If, on the contrary, his own deepest religious experiences had been evolved amid the multifarious contacts of a complex society, such as residence in the neighborhood of Sepphoris provided, one can the more readily understand why he was no voice crying in the wilderness, but was the companionable teacher equally at home in the crowded streets of Capernaum, among the fishermen on the shore of the lake, among the laborers in the fields, or with the travelers on the highways. They had all been a part of his earlier experiences, and nothing about these relations seemed strange or unnatural to him now or inconsistent with genuine piety.

Perhaps the influence of Sepphoris is to be seen even more effectively in the shaping of Jesus' attitude toward the Roman government. The people of Sepphoris and its vicinity were three-quarters of a century earlier than the people of Jerusalem in learning by sad experience the utter futility of a revolution against Rome. When at the time of his first insurrection Judas had taken possession of the royal treasures and arms at Sepphoris, evidently the citizens were not unsympathetic with his action, for when the Romans suppressed the revolution they burned the city and enslaved the inhabitants. But the residents of the new city were distinctly opposed to all revolutionary movements. Not even its Jewish population could be persuaded to take up arms against Rome. . . .

Similarly, Jesus, living in the environment of Sepphoris and facing life's problems in the light of its experiences, shared the conviction that the Kingdom of God was not to be established by the use of the sword. Deliverance for the chosen people was to come in some other way. Throughout his career he maintained this attitude of non-resistance toward Rome. But this was not the characteristic psychology of other parts of the country. When his enemies induced him to admit the propriety of paying tribute to Caesar, they executed a skilful maneuver for undermining the loyalty of his followers from Galilee (Mark 12: 13 ff.). His state of mind was hard even for his most devoted followers to comprehend. Up to the very end they were expecting him to restore the Kingdom of David and give them positions of honor in his cabinet. The hope that Jesus would ultimately effect Israel's deliverance by assuming the role of a new and more successful revolutionist clung to his disciples until the crucifixion. When this took place, they fled from Jerusalem with the conviction that God had forsaken him. But Peter, James, and John were from that region of Galilee where the psychology of revolution still flourished. As yet they had not learned the lesson that had been taught Sepphoris and its neighborhood a generation earlier, and had not appreciated the full measure of Jesus' inherited conviction that God had no intention of asking his people to initiate their own desired redemption by a revolt against Rome.

Lord Charnwood (Godfrey Rathbone Benson, 1st Baron) (*1864–*)

ALL THINGS TO ALL MEN

Great numbers of ordinary readers have derived, mainly from the first three Gospels, a knowledge of Jesus Christ, amounting to what, though my own phrase jars on me a little, I can only call personal acquaintance. People have remarked lately that we know very little about our Lord. That is true of a part of the details which biographers generally labor to tell us, but this sense of acquaintance with His person, which those of us who are interested in Him at all possess, really far exceeds anything similar that we possess in regard to any other historical figure. In occasional moments of confidence two of us could discuss together what Jesus Christ would have said or done in any given circumstances. We should do so with a reality of interest, and what is more, with a prospect of fairly definite result, to which there is certainly no parallel. To suppose that this figure we know is a creation either of art or of accident would be absurd. Yet if corroboration is wanted for the idea which we thus draw from the Gospels, corroboration is ready. In early writers so different as Clement of Rome, St. James, the author of the Epistle to the Hebrews, St. Peter, the author of the Acts, and St. Paul with the peculiar and penetrating knowledge which he gained as a persecutor, we find concordant testimony to what might loosely be called the Christian rule of conduct accepted from the first, or rather to the Christian pattern of manhood and womanhood. The traits of this pattern are those of the historic Jesus. The only rule is "the measure of the stature of the fullness of Christ." The pattern has, above all, this utterly singular feature which again we can hardly ascribe either to art or to accident: it is originally the type of man with the intellect and temperament of genius, and with will and nerves of steel, engaged upon a strange, tremendous enterprise, yet it is without hesitation taken home for personal use by people, whom differences of intellect, temperament, circumstance, vocation, strength, race, age, sex, would seem to place immeasurably far from Him.

G. K. CHESTERTON   (1874–1936)

A WISE AND GOOD JUDGE

If Christ was simply a human character, he really was a highly complex and contradictory character. For he combined exactly the two things that lie at the two extremes of human variation. He was exactly what the man with a delusion never is; he was wise; he was a good judge. What he said was always unexpected; but it was always unexpectedly magnanimous and often unexpectedly moderate. Take a thing like the point of the parable of the tares and the wheat. He has the quality that unites sanity and subtlety. It has not the simplicity of the madman. It has not even the simplicity of a fanatic. It might be uttered by a philosopher a hundred years old, at the end of a century of Utopias. Nothing could be less like this quality of seeing beyond and all around obvious things, than the condition of the egomaniac with the one sensitive spot on his brain. . . . Divinity is great enough to be divine; it is great enough to call itself divine. But as humanity grows greater, it grows less and less likely to do so. God is God, as the Moslems say; but a great man knows he is not God, and the greater he is the better he knows it. . . .

Even on the purely human and sympathetic side, therefore, the Jesus of the New Testament seems to me to have in a great many ways the note of something superhuman; that is of something human and more than human.

JAMES FREEMAN CLARKE   (1810–1888)

A LIFE OF ALL-SIDED DEVELOPMENT

From the fullness of life in the soul of Jesus has proceeded the fullness of life in his religion. If Christianity does justice to the different sides of human nature, and meets the various needs of the soul, it is because the same all-sided development was in the life of Jesus himself. When he said: "I am not come to destroy, but to fulfill," he indicated the large character of his influence and work. He was able to sympathize with all forms of goodness, to accept truth from all quarters. His work was not to destroy anything, but to fulfill everything by supplying its deficiencies.

In the records of the life and teachings of Jesus, we see a union of those elements usually separated in men. He united love to God with love to man; courage and caution; perfect freedom from forms, and reverence for the substance in all forms; hatred of sin, and love for the sinner.

SAMUEL L. CLEMENS   (1835–1910)

A STUPEFYING FACT

The longest journey our Saviour ever performed was from here [Capernaum] to Jerusalem—about one hundred to one hundred and twenty miles. The next longest was from here to Sidon—say about sixty or seventy miles. Instead of being wide apart—as American appreciation of distances would naturally suggest—the places made most particularly celebrated by the presence of Christ are nearly all right here in full view, and within cannon-shot of Capernaum. Leaving out two or three short journeys of the Saviour, he spent his life, preached his gospel, and performed his miracles within a compass no larger than an ordinary county in the United States. It is as much as I can do to comprehend this stupefying fact.

Irvin S. Cobb   (*1876–1944*)

"GREATEST GENTLEMAN THAT EVER LIVED"

If . . . there was a determination to practice the sectless preachments and the teachings of Jesus Christ, Who was the first true gentleman of recorded history and the greatest gentleman that ever lived, I might not have joined the fold, but certainly I'd have stood on the side lines and cheered for it.

By the way, have you ever noticed that in time of war not the most passionate partisan dares to ask the Prince of Peace to bless his bloody arms and forward his bloody deeds? He invokes the aid of the god of unjustified battles as created by the ancient Hebrews.

*   *   *   *

Out of all history you'll find but one world conqueror who came with clean hands—and those hands the soldiers pierced with iron spikes when they nailed the Nazarene to the cross.

William H. Crawshaw   (*1861–1940*)

HIS GENIUS MANIFESTED

When human power becomes so great and original that we can account for it only as a kind of divine inspiration, we call it genius. If we discover in Christ the exhibition of a similar greatness and originality, why should we not seek reverently to contemplate this higher side of his human nature? Such an endeavor can only serve to exalt his name and leads us to a more complete understanding of his personality. It may also impress us with the conviction that these powers which are the glory of man emanate, like all other human powers, from the divine nature, and are a faint shadow of the working of the divine mind. Perhaps it may lead us to find unexpected depths of meaning in the conception that man is made in the image of God. It should certainly teach us that Christ is our brother through all the range of human experience and thought and activity—on the heights of human intelligence as well as on the common levels of human living and in the depths of human sorrow. Perhaps genius is only the exaltation and refinement of powers which are more or less common to all men: but if so, Christ possessed this exaltation and refinement, and is in a very true sense to be numbered among the men of genius who are thus the representatives of their fellows in the world's witenagemot. As we seek to know what are the qualities of true manhood, and then search the record of his life in order to see how these are illustrated in his every purpose and action, so we may ask what is implied by genius and in what sense and degree genius is manifested in the personality of Christ.

When we speak of Christ's manhood, we do not assume that he displayed absolutely every manly quality, but only such as are essential to the manly spirit. Likewise in the matter of genius, we need not assume that we shall find it displayed in every possible form, but only in its essential power and in such measure as was consistent with the purpose of his great mission. His manifestation of genius was not an end in itself, except as it served to show his possession of the higher qualities of human nature. In its details it was purely incidental to the working out of a larger purpose and entirely subservient to the attainment of that purpose. It was determined by his own individual personality, as in the case of every other man of genius, and perhaps still more by the immediate objects which he had in view. To most men, the possession of genius is a sufficient reason for spending all the energies of the being and using all the opportunities of the lifetime in cultivating that genius, in providing channels for its operation, and in realizing all its possibilities. To Christ, genius was simply an instrument for service, to be displayed only so far as it might be useful—along with other means—for accomplishing the tasks which were before him. . . . The fact that these exhibitions of genius were merely the incidental workings of his mind and personality increases our sense of their greatness and our sense of Christ's majestic powers. They were manifestations of his human nature, essentially the same in their quality as other exhibitions of genius, and they justify the attempt to understand them and to estimate their value by comparison with the best powers and achievements of other men of genius. . . .

Christ was the great worker of miracles, not because he exercised a superhuman and arbitrary power to overrule the common law of nature, but because he thought in the divine way and had the divine attitude toward all created things.

JOHN H. DIETRICH (*1878–*)

"HIS STRANGE POTENCY"

We are to contemplate this morning the problem of Jesus' historical existence, and we are moved to think of the power of the ideal that accompanies his name. How tremendous his influence in the lives of men, and yet how infinitesimal the details of his existence. Millions, yes hundreds of millions, first around the Mediterranean, then throughout the continent of Europe, now over the whole Western world, have fallen under his strange potency.

For his sake men have loved and hated one another, massacred and helped one another, known the extremes of passion and of sacrifice. By him some have been raised to heights of ecstasy and others plunged to depths of despair. By him they have been mellowed, fortified, comforted, exalted, stirred in every way. He was the mirage toward which rushed the mad squadrons of the Crusaders. He was the mystic lover inviting docile processions of virgins to take the veil. In his name the Holy Inquisition tortured and killed and in his name hospitals have soothed and healed.

Did he actually live on earth, or only in the minds of men? What manner of man was he—wise or foolish, humble or powerful? It matters not, he is the highest aspiration of human souls beneath the Western sky, an inward force that the centuries have been powerless to exhaust. There never was such a stupendous event as that which introduced the ideal of Jesus into the world.

WILL DURANT   (*1885–*   )

GOD'S HIGHEST INCARNATION

PAUL. Forget Wagner, and remember Christ. My religion would have in it these two elements—the Living God and the human Christ; for Christ, as the old theology symbolically understood, was the highest incarnation of God. The greatest creation of life is not thought, but love; and the greatest triumph of human genius is not the plays of Shakespeare, nor the marbles of the Parthenon, but the ethics of Christ; next to parental care, this is the finest force for good that ever came into the world. I know, Philip, that you consider Christ's moral doctrine as impracticable. But I have heard you quote with approval the last line of Spinoza's *Ethics*—that "all excellent things are as difficult as they are rare." To say that something is difficult is no objection to it; it is the function of an ethical ideal to lift us, against all the weight of instincts made rapacious by the struggle for existence, to levels of consideration and courtesy where civilization and the cooperative life become possible. So long as the counsels of Christ are within the limits of our ideal strength, it is good that they should hold up to us the perfection towards which we should grow, and which we may keep perpetually in mind. What is the doctrine of Christ but the Golden Rule—and is the Golden Rule quite impracticable? On the contrary it is the essence of wisdom in our relations with men. I have found that where I have fought back I multiplied resistance and raised new obstacles against myself; where I did kindnesses they came back to me a hundredfold; where I loved I won. If I could have my way I would define an atheist as one who is disloyal to life or irreverent to growth; and I would define a Christian as a man who accepts, and sincerely tries to practice, the ethics of Christ.

PHILIP. Splendid, Paul. I will join your church at once, if you won't insist on personal immortality.

PAUL. Why should we not differ on some things and work together where we can? After all, we differ only in phrases; the older generation meant what we mean—reverence for all life, and loyalty to the largest whole; they merely used other symbols and other words. Now that the battle is over we see how close we were, how we are all members of one another still. In my ideal church all would be welcome who accepted the Golden Rule; there would be no other test. You would all be eligible—even Philip, who thinks Christ unpractical, and Andrew, who considers himself a machine, and Clarence, who doubts everything but loves all. I vision a Church as all-embracing as Christ's affection, accepting all and rejecting none. It would honor truth and beauty as well as goodness, this Church of mine; it would nourish every art, and make its every chapel and cathedral a citadel of adult education, bringing science and history, literature and philosophy, music and art to those too old for school, and yet young enough to learn. But it would hold knowledge barren without brotherhood; it would allow every division, and every doubt, except that in the end love is the highest wisdom.

ARIEL. Let us end there. Here among these books, coming to us from the genius of a hundred lands, we may admit that we are brothers, that religion and brotherhood ought to be one, that Confucius and Buddha, Isaiah and Christ, Spinoza and Whitman, are prophets of one faith. If we can agree on what these men held in common, it is enough.

SIR JAMES. Madame, I know your religion well; for here in your copy of Whitman I find a poem marked that might be the guide and motto of us all. It is called "To Him That Was Crucified."

ARIEL. Read it to us; perhaps it will cool our nerves after this argument.

(*Sir James reads.*)

ARIEL. It is very beautiful.

MATTHEW. It is beautiful, but conceited and impious.

PHILIP. If that is Christianity, I'm a Christian.

PAUL. No one ever caught better the essence of Christianity.

WILLIAM. It satisfies me.

KUNG. I understand your Christ much better now.

SIDDHA. I accept him gladly as a great Buddhist.

ESTHER. I accept him as a great Jew.

CLARENCE. And a thorough-going anti-clerical.

THEODORE. I will accept him if you will make *Leaves of Grass* a part of the Scriptures.

SIR JAMES. He is the most lovable of the gods.

ANDREW. I trust that he existed. Let us go to bed.

HAVELOCK ELLIS   (*1859–1939*)

A LOVELY CRYSTAL FIGURE

There was a real Jesus, impossible as it will ever be even for the concentrated vision of a Binet-Sanglé to discern all his features. Yet around that concealed human person it is really the Imagination of Man which has built up the lovely crystal figure we see. An innumerable company of men, who had a few of them seen Jesus and most of them only heard of him, aided in this task. Each threw into it his highest inspiration, his deepest insight, with the sublime faith —based on that deep human impulse, seen even in our dreams, to exteriorise our own feelings—that this divine moment of his own soul could only be the truthful expression of a Saviour and liberator of Man.

It was the peculiar virtue of the personality of Jesus that all these inspirations and insights could adhere to it and drew together into a congruous whole. At the same time a reversed process was evidently in movement. All the facts of the hero's life, actual or alleged, and all his sayings, real or apocryphal, were sifted and filtered through the human imagination, so purged that not a single trivial, ignoble, or even ordinary crude unpleasing statement has come down to us. At once by putting in and taking out, with an art like that of the painter and the sculptor in one, under some rare combination of favouring conditions, the human imagination, out of the deepest impulses of the human heart, has unconsciously wrought this figure of Jesus, purified of dross and all gold, tragic in its sublimity and tremendously tender in its loving-kindness. So that now when I open and turn over with reverent joy the leaves of the Gospels, I feel that here is enshrined the highest achievement of Man the Artist, a creation to which nothing can be added, from which nothing can be taken away.

Canon Frederic W. Farrar   (*1831–1903*)

"ONE WHO REJOICED IN SPIRIT"

But Christ came to convince us that a *relative* insignificance may be an *absolute* importance. He came to teach that continual excitement, prominent actions, distinguished services, brilliant success, are no essential elements of true and noble life, and that myriads of the beloved of God are to be found among the insignificant and the obscure. . . . The calmest and most unknown lot is often the happiest, and we may safely infer that these years in the home and trade of the carpenter of Nazareth were happy years in our Saviour's life. Often, even in his later days, it is clear that His words are the words of one who rejoiced in spirit; they are words which seem to flow from the full river of an abounding happiness. But what must that happiness have been in those earlier days before the storms of righteous anger had agitated His unruffled soul, or His heart burned hot with terrible indignation against the sins and hypocrisies of men? . . . In the case of many myriads, and assuredly not least in the case of the saints of God, a sorrowful and stormy manhood has often been preceded by a calm and rosy dawn.

HILARIN FELDER   (*1867–*)

HIS UNLIMITED PERFECTION

Translated by John L. Stoddard

In the first place, we naturally stand under the spell of that all-commanding quality which we have discovered everywhere in Christ, a quality unique in the history of mankind—we mean the absolutism of his character. Every revelation of the divinely human life of Jesus, every one of its negative and positive perfections, and its abounding virtue and perfect sinlessness in their manifold manifestations are all marked by the stamp of unlimited perfection.

On this absolutism are based that harmony and universality of Christ which captivate us with a power that is as winning as it is majestic. All other characters are lacking in these qualities and have the disadvantage of possessing much narrow-mindedness and many incongruities. One-sided talents, one-sided development and one-sided activities are characteristic of everything human. . . .

In Jesus, on the contrary, harmony and universality emanate from his absolutism. Because all high qualities are to be found in him in their highest perfection, they all possess the most complete symmetry. Thus we find in him ardent zeal and inexhaustible patience, noble fervour and indulgent leniency, holy seriousness and sunny cheerfulness, an impulse to solitude and yet world publicity, majestic greatness and the deepest humility, inflexible determination and the sweetest gentleness, powerful energy and quiet self-possession, the warmest love for sinners and invincible hatred of sin, compassionate sympathy and strictest justice; irresistible attractiveness and fearless frankness, incorruptible truthfulness and extreme forbearance, mildness and force, resignation and resistance, adamantine strength and motherly tenderness, indefatigable outward activity and inward contemplation, childlike confidence in God and manly self-consciousness. . . . In him combine in wonderful harmony all the higher and lower powers of his soul, his feelings and sentiments, understanding and will, idealism and realism, an intense sense of reality as regards the things of this world, and a ceaseless striving to promote the kingdom of heaven.

GEORGE WALTER FISKE   (*1872–*   )

INFLUENCES OF ENVIRONMENT

Most writers have neglected to note the influence of Jesus' trade as a carpenter upon his growing religious experience as youth and man. That it furnished an ideal laboratory for his experiments in personal relations and Christian good will cannot be doubted. If he had been born in a rich man's palace, what chance would he have had to discover first hand the experiences and needs of the average man, and what appeal would he ever have made to such people? If he had been reared in comfort, spending his life as a professional man, he would have missed the practical experience of working with tools and materials, and the problems and simple joys involved in producing tangible results of his manual skill. Such things loom large in the daily experience of the common man, whom Jesus had to understand in order to help.

It has often been noted that although Nazareth for some reason had a bad reputation, it was at the cross-roads of the busiest part of

Palestine, and was therefore an ideal home village for an alert boy to grow up in who desired many contacts with life. The great caravan routes to Damascus, to Tyre, to Arabia, and to Egypt passed through or near it, and a garrison of Roman soldiers was only five miles to the westward. So a Nazareth boy did not need to travel to see the world. Much of the world came to his door. From the hilltop three minutes' walk back of his home he could see more than half of Palestine, from the gleaming shore line of the Mediterranean on the west to the Midian plateau and the eastern desert; and southward across the historic plain of Esdraelon to the Samarian hill and the mountains north of the Holy City.

What a vantage point of vision for the dreams of youth! The panorama of his country's history lay before him. It must have been a daily inspiration, challenging him to make his life count, to live up to the noble record of his forefathers. The ancient Hebrews, unlike their neighbors, the Phoenicians, took little interest in life upon the sea. The only "sea" mentioned in the Gospels is the little lake of Galilee. Yet when the Boy of Nazareth saw ships but sixteen miles away on the Great Sea, his imagination must sometimes have leaped to the great world of the Roman Empire beyond his ken.

On his return from that first wonderful journey to Jerusalem with his deepened sense of responsibility and life's meaning, Jesus without doubt welcomed the chance to help in the home carpenter shop. As the oldest son that career was his destiny, and for some twenty years he made it the work of his life.

HARRY EMERSON FOSDICK   (*1878–*)

HIS BALANCED QUALITIES

In the course of our studies on the character of Jesus, we have been compelled continually to notice the remarkable poise in which the Master holds opposing virtues that with us are most difficult of combination. No sooner have we emphasized one quality in him, such as his amazing self-assurance, than we must balance our thought by laying stress upon the contrasting quality, his profound humility. We have noted his severity in moral standards and his sternness in judgment coupled with an unfailing appreciation of even faint beginnings of genuine goodness in any man; we have noted his intense susceptibility to sorrow, his heart quick as the apple of an eye to feel the hurt of others' misery and of his own, but yet joined with it his exhaustless cheer and joy; we have noted his combination of ambition, that included God's eternal purpose for the world, with devoted interest in apparently insignificant persons. This spherical balance in the Master's character has always attracted the attention of those who studied him. . . .

This study of the balanced qualities in the Master's character could be extended almost without limit. We undertake to exalt the gentleness of Jesus to whom mothers brought their children that he might lay his hands on them and pray and we are at once compelled to note his fiery indignation also as he drives the money-changers from the Temple. We undertake an appreciation of the liberality of Jesus, who broke down racial and sectarian boundaries in his sympathy, and extended welcome to the gentiles, and we are compelled to stress upon the other side, the strictness of Jesus who would not abate for compassion's sake one least emphasis upon the requirements of righteousness, and who said, "Narrow is the gate and straitened the way that leadeth unto life, and few are they that find it" (Matt. 7:14). But perhaps the most illuminating way in which we may perceive the completeness of the Master's character is to note the universality of his appeal, the manner in which his character has overpassed and comprehended all the deep divisions of our human life.

Herbert F. Gallagher   (*1898*–   )

HE WILLED TO LIVE UNKNOWN

Really to know the life of Christ is to have seen, behind the veil of
His active ministry, the secret recesses of His spirit, in the long years
of His hidden life in Nazareth. Thirty-three years He dwelt among
us. All that He cared to manifest concerning thirty of those years is
the fact that they were hidden. . . .

To the wisdom of the world, the hidden life of Christ would
appear to be a grave mistake. If He had so important a mission to
accomplish, to free a world lying prostrate under the yoke of sin
and error, to reconstruct human society on new and solid foundations of supernatural faith and grace, to establish a kingdom as vast
as the world itself and more lasting than time, why did He spend
so many years in a town of uncultured peasants, and so short a time
in the active ministry? . . . We know that Christ's brief public
ministry was not a failure. Indeed it was in the very seclusion of
Nazareth that He made His plans to establish His kingdom, and
began there the victory that overcame the world. He who came to
redeem the world wills to begin its salvation by a life that was
hidden from the world. Men had to be taught by example how to
lead the life which Christ came to restore.

Our Lord was not idle during those thirty years. The work He
came to do was going on in that quiet village. The treasury of His
merits that was to enrich mankind was growing daily and hourly.
In seclusion, the hidden acts of the Heart of Christ were already
beginning the work of Redemption, the same work that would later
be furthered by His sermons and miracles.

*   *   *   *

Our Divine Lord wished to be like His brethren, to share our lot
as He shared our nature. Now the vast majority of men live in obscurity. It was for this reason that Christ willed to live unknown.
To the many men and women who lead quite ordinary Christian

lives, who seem to have no vocation to any special heroism in God's service, yet who walk in His presence and in the way of His commandments, seeing Christ in their fellowmen and serving Him in His creatures, and to the shut-ins who have entered the home of Nazareth with the golden key of suffering, whose own hidden life is tabernacled with Christ in God—to all these the hidden life of Christ is an example and an inspiration!

Only three years of action; yet full thirty years of silence and labor, of docile obedience to His very own creatures, and submission to the circumstances directed by His own hand. Full thirty years of detachment from the world, from its opinions, and its passing glories. This was Christ's vocation, and it is ours.

George Holley Gilbert   (*1854–1930*)

MAN AND NATURE HIS STUDY

Jesus never refers in a direct manner to his earthly father, but it seems natural to suppose that the fatherhood which He had known in the home in Nazareth was to him a stepping-stone to the conception and the experience of the heavenly fatherhood; and if so, it must have been rich in love and wisdom. Again, it may be allowable to think that Jesus' appreciation of childhood, His love for children, and His sympathy with them, argue sweet memories of His own childhood, and hence throw a gracious light upon Joseph and Mary (Mark x. 13–16; ix. 36; Matthew xviii. 10). From the glimpses which we have into the early life of Jesus, and from His work as a teacher, we derive the impression that the development of His inner life had been normal, an even and beautiful growth; and this, especially when we think of the childhood of Jesus, is most easily understood if the influence of Joseph and Mary was even and beautiful, and the home life in Nazareth a normal home life. . . .

Mary was of a thoughtful and contemplative spirit, as is indicated by the statements that she kept the various incidents regarding Jesus, pondering them in her heart (Luke ii. 19, 51). The fact that Mary did not fully realize what Jesus was, either in His childhood or in His ministry (Luke ii. 33; Mark iii. 21, 31; John ii. 3, 4), is not strange, but perfectly natural. In the long years spent in Nazareth, Jesus had appeared to her as one of her other children, except in His spotless purity. There was no other indication of His Messianic character and mission. This failure to realize fully what Jesus was, made it possible for the mother to treat Him in a natural way. Nor is it strange that Mary did not fully understand Jesus after He began His Messianic work. His ideal of the Messiaship was widely different from the popular thought, and so, doubtless, from her thought; and even the disciples, who were constantly with Him, came but slowly to understand Him. Therefore Mary's attitude toward Jesus is neither an indication of intellectual poverty or of spiritual narrowness. . . .

Such was the home of which Jesus was a member until about thirty years of age. All that we know suggests that it was a pure and noble family, in which were manifest the best spiritual characteristics of an ancestral line that included some of the greatest names in Israel's history. Both Joseph and Mary, according to tradition, belonged to the lineage of David (Matthew i. 20; Luke i. 27, 32, 69).

THE STUDY OF THE LAW

Jesus grew in wisdom as He grew in stature (Luke ii. 40, 52). He had a child's knowledge of the law when He was a child, and that was followed by a youth's knowledge, and that in turn by the mature knowledge of a man. In a home like that of Joseph and Mary a child began to learn the law as soon as it began to speak. This was in accord with the word of Scripture (Deut. vi. 6, 7), which commands parents to teach the law diligently to their children. . . . It is probable that the parents taught Jesus verses out of the law long before He had learned to read. It is probable that He learned to read at home, but uncertain whether He learned to read the law in Hebrew or in Aramaic. If He knew Hebrew, which seems probable in view of the fact that it was cherished as the sacred tongue and studied by all the rabbis, then He doubtless learned it as a child at home and as an attendant on the services of the synagogue. There is no evidence that He ever attended a school; indeed, it is quite uncertain whether there were village schools in the time of Jesus. Keim thinks the first were established about 64 A.D., while Schurer is of the opinion that they may have existed in the time of Christ. But there was a synagogue in Nazareth which Jesus doubtless attended, and where through many years He heard the law read (Mark vi. 2), first in Hebrew, then in Aramaic, and where He heard the sacred language also in certain parts of the liturgical service. When Jesus at the age of twelve was in the temple, He entered into conversation with the scribes, and they were amazed at His understanding and His answers. From this incident it seems allowable to infer that the scribes in Nazareth were interested in Jesus, and that He had discussed the law with them. It is not improbable that some Nazarene scribe helped Him to learn Hebrew. How much help He may have received from the synagogue in understanding the Old Testament, we cannot say. Certain it is that His accurate and comprehensive knowledge of the law implies that He studied it long and patiently for Himself. It is possible that there was a copy of the Old Testament in His home, or at least of the chief parts of the Old Testament. His spiritual understanding of the law was doubtless due in the main to His own purity and spirituality, yet as a child He may have been greatly helped by His parents to a true apprehension of the meaning of Scripture. They had a vital piety, and that piety must have been sustained by their feeding on the word of God. So their teaching would naturally lead their children into the inner sense of Scripture. . . .

Though Jesus in His childhood and youth may have been helped by the scribes in Nazareth, it is certain that He did not take up a formal course of study with them, or attend a rabbinical school elsewhere. His townspeople knew Him only as a carpenter, and were surprised that He should come forward in the synagogue as a teacher (Mark vi. 2, 3). In Jerusalem it seems to have been well known that Jesus had not learned the law from the recognized teachers (John vii. 15). He was called *rabbi*, but this does not imply that He had received rabbinical ordination. It was simply an expression of His disciples' reverence for Him as their teacher, called forth by His surpassing knowledge of the law.

THE STUDY OF NATURE

The development of Jesus was influenced by the world around Him as well as by the record of God's revelation contained in the Old Testament. It is plain from the Gospels that Jesus was a close observer of nature, and had pondered much on the meaning of natural phenomena. This is shown by the aptness of His many illustrations drawn from nature, and also by the fact that a large number of His parables are based on natural phenomena. He saw an analogy between the visible world and the invisible, and taught truths of His kingdom from what He observed in the field and by the wayside. To Him, nature was full of spiritual meaning. It spoke to Him of the goodness of God and the minuteness of His tender care. He admired the beauty of the lilies, but the thought that especially impressed Him was that *God* had clothed them, *God* had given them this raiment which surpassed in glory the raiment of Solomon (Matt. vi. 28–30). He watched the birds of the air, and thought how the heavenly Father fed them, and how not one of the least of them could fall to the ground without His notice (Matt. vi. 26; x. 29). When the sun arose and shined on the evil and the good, and when the rain came down upon the just and unjust, it was to Him a parable of the divine love (Matt. v. 44, 45). The tares in the wheat were like the children of the evil one, and the birds catching away the seed before it sprouted were like Satan who takes away the good word from the heart (Matt. xiii. 19, 38). The book of nature had its mystery for Jesus as it has for every thoughtful observer. He recognized that a man cannot tell whence the wind comes and whither it goes (John iii. 8); and cannot tell how the seed germinates, and grows until the full corn appears in the ear (Mark iv. 27).

The fact that Jesus, in His teaching, drew so constantly and widely from the treasury of nature, and always with wondrous propriety, shows that He had looked upon the earth and the heaven with an observant, sympathetic eye. His reading of nature, like His reading of the Old Testament, was altogether different from that of the scribes of His day. It was deeply spiritual, and full of hope because full of the thought of the heavenly Father.

THE STUDY OF MAN

But Jesus, while studying in the book of nature and in the Old Testament, surely did not keep aloof from men or ignore any human interest. What characterized His ministry we may suppose characterized also His earlier years in the quiet of Nazareth, namely, a genuine sympathy with men. He was no Essene, withdrawing from His fellow-men to live a narrow self-centred life. He may have loved the solitude of the mountain top, but only that He might there commune with God, and receive wisdom and grace for the service of men. With the common life of the peasant and artisan He had such familiarity as can have been gained only by close observation. He was acquainted with the work of the tailor (Mark ii. 21) and the vine dresser (Mark ii. 22; Matt. xx. 1–16; John xv. 1–10), the gardener and the carpenter (Matt. vii. 16–21; 24–26; Luke viii. 6–9), the housewife and the pearl-merchant (Matt. xiii. 33, 44), the shepherd and the fisherman (Matt. vii. 15; Luke xv. 3–7; Matt. xxv. 31–46; John x. 1–16; Matt. xiii. 47–50; Luke v. 1–11). He was acquainted also with current history, at least as far as could be expected of one who lived in a small provincial town. He knew of the embassy that had been sent after Archelaus (Luke xix. 12), and the mode of capital punishment followed by the Romans in dealing with the Galilean Zealots (Mark ix. 42); He knew of the high-handed acts of Pilate (Luke xiii. 1), and the tragedy in Siloam (Luke xiii. 4); He had thought of the relations of the Jews to Rome, and had reached conclusions widely different from those of the Pharisees (Mark xii. 16–17; Luke xix. 1–10); He knew that those who had been condemned to be crucified bore their crosses to the place of execution (Mark viii. 34), and He knew the character and life of the Pharisees through and through (Matt. xxiii, etc.).

In His contact with men He discovered good where others saw only evil, as in publicans, profligates, and the robber on the cross. Since it was true in His ministry, that He came close to the lowest and the worst, we may think that in His earlier life also He had felt a genuine sympathy with these classes and had seen that there was hope for them. He doubtless saw the wretchedness of their estate as no one else, but He did not despair. While His own inner purity made Him uniquely appreciative of the sinfulness of men, His sense of the fatherliness of God and of God's power made Him uniquely hopeful. What He said on a certain occasion in defense of His Sabbath miracle, we may suppose that He had long seen and felt, namely, that the Father is constantly at work among men in their behalf.

Jesus then, we remark in conclusion, when He went forth from Nazareth to His brief public ministry, knew the nature and needs of man with whom He was to deal. He was also enriched by the possession of the deepest truths of the word of God, and by an intimate acquaintance with the world of nature, not such as is had by a man of science, but rather that of a poet and prophet. It was the religious meaning and value of history and life which He, as no other, saw and interpreted.

George Holley Gilbert   (*1854–1930*)

THE POWER OF HIS PRESENCE

It is needful to say but few words in regard to the personal appearance of Jesus. All representations are purely imaginary, and express the ideas, artistic or religious, of the various ages in which they have been produced. At one time, under the influence of the fifty-third of Isaiah, He had been thought of as without form or comeliness, having no beauty that we should desire Him; and again, the words of the Psalmist have been applied to Him and understood literally, "Thou art fairer than the children of men." We have no definite knowledge, and inferences which seem valid to one, another may question. The Jews once said to Jesus, "Thou art not yet *fifty* years old" (John viii. 57); and it may perhaps be inferred from this that He looked somewhat older than He really was. It is natural, in view both of His holiness and of the unparalleled physical strain that He endured, to think that He was free from disease, full of physical vigor, and that all the faculties of body as of mind were unimpaired. It is natural also to think that the majesty and greatness and gentleness of His spirit were reflected on His features and in His bearing. When He passed through the midst of His enraged townspeople, the force that awed them and made them for the moment powerless against Him may have been naught but the outflashing of His mighty will (Luke iv. 30). We can hardly believe otherwise than that His features were capable of expressing in a remarkable degree the tenderness of His love, and that thus there was manifested a power which drew outcasts to His feet and broke the heart of Peter in the midst of his denials.

CHARLES GUIGNEBERT   (*1867–*   )

AN INSPIRED GALILEAN

It was commonly said that the Galileans were unmanageable, doubtless because in the early times of the Roman domination some very resolute nationalistic gangs had taken refuge in their mountains. Fun was made, too, of them on account of their provincial accent. As a matter of fact, their piety retained, it seems, a spontaneity, ardor and profundity which testified to an intensely fervent religious life which was missing in the scrupulosity of Judean Pharisaism.

Jesus, therefore, was born and grew up in a district in which the majority of minds were preoccupied with religious interests. He sprang from a sphere in which the habit of life was one of simple hope and of anxious expectation of a certain miraculous event, procurable by the Jews, through their piety alone, which would render them masters of the world. But this people is governed by priests who do not share this hope and are mistrustful of the difficulties it may create for them with their foreign political masters. It is to some extent hemmed in by teachers of the stamp that can say that no ignorant person could be pious, and who feel scarcely any sympathy for a popular movement.

We have given, therefore, a profoundly pious man of the people whose mentality has not been withered in any way by the doctrine of the scribes, but from earliest childhood has been imbued with the prevailing ideas of his milieu, one who has acquired no intellectual or religious or moral life save through them. If he is also endowed with that singularly marvelous faculty of mustering within himself thoughts which are floating in the air he breathes and re-creating them, as it were, by his meditation upon them (and that must be the case with all who are inspired), it is easy to understand how he should come to translate his convictions into actions. An inspired Galilean of that epoch could not fail to announce in a more or less personal and original way the imminent realization of the hopes of the age. And such appears to have been, in fact, the origin of the "rise" of Jesus.

Documents which would enable us to explore the material of details of his intellectual development and grasp the precise determining causes of the path taken by his initiative are lacking. It is not necessary, however, to assume that there was anything complicated about either. All our Gospels note an ill-defined but real relation between the opening of his public life and the preaching of another inspired layman who proclaimed the necessity for repentance in view of the near approach of the promised era. It may be that Jesus had known John the Baptist and had been to hear him, and that through his example the vocation slowly and mysteriously preparing in the depths of his consciousness was irresistibly imposed upon his will. It may be that at the news of the imprisonment of John by Herod Antipas Jesus began to preach, in order that the Kingdom should not lack a herald. . . .

Whether he knew from the very beginning what he really wanted,

or even what he represented, may be doubted. Proceeding on different lines from the Baptist, for he had entirely renounced the ascetic
life and the menacing language of his predecessor, Jesus developed
the same main themes: The Kingdom is at hand, that great transformation which shall rid the world of injustice and evil; repent, if
you would have a place among the elect. Why did he say this? He
said it because he was urged thereto by a secret force, because he felt
the Lord within him, as had all the inspired Jewish prophets. And
what did he mean by it? How did he picture the Kingdom and its
coming, in his own mind? We do not know; for our texts date from
a time when the delay in the coming of the Kingdom had already
modified the portrait of it in the minds of Christians. He doubtless
imagined it in conformity with what was said about it around himself as the advent of the materialized joy for Israel and a dazzling
manifestation of the benediction of Jahveh, the form of which popular imagination had never really determined exactly and which he
himself, possibly, did not strictly define. There is nothing to assure
us that in the beginning he did not make allusions to Messianic upheavals of the warfare which, according to majority opinion, the
Messiah was to bring upon the world. Our Gospels carry some traces
of this frame of mind, but it is natural that these features should have
gradually disappeared and little be left of them in the writings designed to prove that in him, so mild and peace-loving, would be
found he "who should come." . . .

The Gospel passages which are available, therefore, leave us in a
state of uncertainty as to what Jesus himself thought about the guiding principle of his mission, and the nature of his own personality
and the scope of his own part. On the other hand, they make it clear
that he was unsuccessful and that his Palestinian compatriots did not
believe him in regard to his mission nor did they conform to the
moral appeals made by him. During the time—a very brief one moreover—that he spent among them, they looked upon his comings and
goings with curiosity or with indifference, but no attempt to follow
him took place. At the most, perhaps, he won over a few hundreds of
simple Galileans. Although the Gospels portray crowds fascinated

by his discourses thronging around him, that does not cause us to forget what they tell us elsewhere, with much more truth, of the hard hearts of the Jews. Indeed, Jesus himself seems to have despaired of softening them. The reasons for his failure are self-evident.

To the populace he did not speak in the terms they had anticipated. He preached self-examination, love of one's neighbor, humbleness of heart and a son's faith in God to people who were expecting an appeal to arms and the announcement of the final struggle preceding an everlasting triumph. He did not say to them: "Arise! the Messiah of Jahveh is in your midst," but: "Prepare yourselves by repentance to make a good showing in the Judgment which is at hand." He did not ask them to act, but merely to mark time in a specified moral and religious attitude, which changed expectation into constraint. Though a son of Israel, he probably displayed a comparatively mild exclusiveness only. The heartfelt piety and the confiding faith of the Roman centurion or the woman of Canaan seemed to him to be worth as much as pure Jewish descent. Or rather, a heathen who believed through his words was considered by him as far superior to a well-born Jew who was an unbeliever. He said a good deal about justice, peace, devotion to the Father, and also spoke of resignation and patience. But of rebellion and of the triumph of the chosen people over other nations he never said a word. And although all this constitutes for us his originality and his charm, it could in no way please the ardent Messianists of Palestine.

To the Scribes he appeared to be an ignorant pretender, who naively assumed that good sense could take the place of learning and the heart act as a substitute for the reason. He spoke "with authority" although he had not frequented the schools, because he felt within himself the inspiration of the Father. Their spirit was a trial to him; the spontaneity characteristic of his religion felt itself under constraint face to face with the formalism of theirs, and this antipathy could not fail to be mutual. Surely we ought not to forget that our Gospels reflect the ideas and prepossessions of a time when Jewish legalism was no longer considered binding by Christians. They even regarded it as their chief foe, and this would consequently incline them to attribute to the Master the same aversion which they themselves felt toward it. Nevertheless, from the numerous passages in which Christ takes the scribes to task, and, conversely, from those in which they seek to entrap him by insidious questions, it is scarcely possible not to obtain a distinct impression that a dormant conflict existed between them and him. According to all the evidence, he respected the Law and paid attention to its demands, but he did not pay them exclusive attention, and he showed himself disposed to give his own pious inspirations precedence over rabbinical injunctions.

And as for the priests of Jerusalem and the Sadducean aristocracy, to them he seemed to be the most dangerous and embarrassing of agitators. He was dangerous, because in the end he might incite the people to one of those violent and irrational revolts which the Roman authorities were always rigorously repressing. The commotions connected with it would also disturb the peace of the Temple hierarchy. He was embarrassing, because he went so far as inconsiderately to parade before the populace comparisons and expostulations which were definitely to the disadvantage of the priesthood.

ADOLF VON HARNACK (1851–1930)

THE GREATEST FACT ABOUT HIM

Translated by Thomas Bailey Saunders

He lived in religion, and it was breath to him in the fear of God; his whole life, all his thoughts and feelings, were absorbed in the relation to God, and yet he did not talk like an enthusiast and a fanatic, who sees only one red-hot spot, and so is blind to the world and all that it contains. He spoke his message and looked at the world with a fresh and clear eye for the life, great and small, that surrounded him. He proclaimed that to gain the whole world was nothing if the soul were injured, and yet he remained kind and sympathetic to every living thing. That is the most astonishing and the greatest fact about him! His discourses, generally in the form of parables and sayings, exhibit every degree of human speech and the whole range of the emotions. The sternest tones of passionate accusation and indignant reproof, nay, even irony, he does not despise; but they must have formed the exception with him. He is possessed of a quiet, uniform, collected demeanour, with everything directed to one goal. He never uses any ecstatic language, and the tone of stirring prophecy is rare. Entrusted with the greatest of all missions, his eye and ear are open to every impression of the life around him—a proof of intense calm and absolute certainty. "Mourning and weeping, laughing and dancing, wealth and poverty, hunger and thirst, health and sickness, children's play and politics, gathering and scattering, the leaving of home, life in the inn and the return, marriage and funeral, the splendid house of the living and the grave of the dead, the sower and the reaper in the field, the lord of the vintage among his vines, the idle workman in the marketplace, the shepherd searching for the sheep, the dealer in pearls on the sea, and, then again, the woman at home anxious over the barrel of meal and the leaven, or the lost piece of money, the widow's complaint to the surly official, the earthly food that perishes, the mental relation of the teacher and pupil, on the one side regal glory and the tyrant's lust of power, on the other childish innocence and the industry of the servant—all these pictures enliven his discourse and make it clear even to those who are children in mind." They do more than tell us that he spoke in picture and parable. They exhibit an inner freedom and a cheerfulness of soul in the midst of the greatest strain, such as no prophet ever possessed before him. His eye rests kindly upon the flowers and the children, on the lily of the field—"Solomon in all his glory is not clothed like one of them"—on the birds in the air and the sparrows on the house-top. The sphere in which he lived, above the earth and its concerns, did not destroy his interest in it; no! he brought everything in it into relation with the God whom he knew, and he saw it as protected in him: "Your Father in heaven feeds them." The parable is his most familiar form of speech. Insensibly, however, parable and sympathy pass into each other. Yet he who had not where to lay his head does not speak like one who has broken with everything, or like an heroic penitent, or like an ecstatic prophet, but like a man who has rest and peace for his soul, and is able to give life and strength to others. He strikes the mightiest notes; he offers men an inexorable alternative; he leaves them no escape; and yet the strongest emotion seems to come naturally to him, and he expresses it as something natural; he clothes it in the language in which a mother speaks to her child.

GEORG WILHELM FRIEDRICH HEGEL   (*1770–1831*)

THE MAN-GOD CONSIDERED

Translated by Rev. E. B. Spiers and J. Burton Sanderson

In the Church Christ has been called the God-Man. This is the extraordinary combination which directly contradicts the Understanding; but the unity of the divine and human natures has here been brought into human consciousness and has become a certainty for it, implying that the otherness, or as it is also expressed, the finitude, the weakness, the frailty of human nature is not incompatible with this unity, just as in the eternal Idea otherness in no way detracts from the unity which God is.

This is the extraordinary combination the necessity of which we have seen. It involves the truth that the divine and human natures are not implicitly different. God in human form. The truth is that there is only one reason, one Spirit, that Spirit as finite has no true existence. . . .

By faith this individual is known to possess divine nature, whereby God ceases to be a Being beyond this world. When Christ is looked at in the same way as Socrates, He is looked at as an ordinary man, just as the Mohammedans consider Christ as God's ambassador in the general sense in which all great men are God's ambassadors or messengers. If we say nothing more of Christ than that He was a teacher of humanity, a martyr for the truth, we do not occupy the Christian standpoint, the standpoint of the true religion.

The one side is this human side, this appearance of one who was a living man. As an immediate or natural man he is subject to the contingency which belongs to outward things, to all temporal relations and conditions; he is born, as Man he has the needs which all other men have except that he does not share in the corruption, the passions, the particular inclinations of men, in the special interests of the worldly life in connection with which uprightness and moral teaching may also find a place; on the contrary, he lives only for the truth and the proclamation of the truth, his activity consists simply in fulfilling the higher consciousness of men.

GRANVILLE HICKS   (*1901–*   )

HIS FIGURE LAID HOLD OF MEN

Most men find in Jesus a reflection of their own ideals. Take any number of recent biographies. For Bruce Barton Jesus is a modern business man, the he-man type, an advertiser, a Rotary Club speaker, and the like. For Mary Austin he is a mystic. For Klausner and Jacobs he is a Jew. For Upton Sinclair he is a socialist. And I might go on. What is the significance of this? To me it is simply that . . . the figure of Jesus has laid hold of men. At first they thought of him as the Son of Man, then Paul thought of him more or less as the risen god of a cult of salvation, then the author of the fourth gospel identified him with the Logos, then the theologians battled for centuries as to how his nature could be both human and divine. Always he was the instrument of salvation, whether in the terms of the mysteries, in the crude barter theory of the Middle Ages, or in the atonement theory of Anselm. Always the man himself was obscured. And then suddenly men became interested in the man himself. They wanted the historical Jesus, but they couldn't find him. All that was left was the mythical figure in what Santayana calls "the Christian epic." The scholars went to the Gospels, and some of them admitted that their research was fruitless. Other men and women, not scholars, went to the Gospels, and finally they brought forth a man in their own image. So many recent biographers, as I have said, have simply embodied their own ideals in Jesus. So we have on the one hand the historical Jesus, whom we can but vaguely discern and who is not particularly important for our day. On the other hand we have a multitude of figures, the mythological Christs, not only of the churches but of groups of men and women outside the churches. Each figure represents a body of ideals that were vital at the time and in the place of its creation, and each figure is therefore important. But none of these figures is the Jesus who was born in Palestine and died there some nineteen centuries ago.

John Haynes Holmes   (*1879-*   )

ALWAYS A MAN OF POWER

I would impress upon you the wonder of Jesus's personality. In him, as in few men who have ever lived, do we find a perfect combination of that sweetness and strength which invariably make up the ideal human character.

How admirable was the charm of this man—his gentleness, sensitiveness, poise, and purity. See him as he walks in the fields, by the lakesides, in the olive groves, and loses himself in rapture over the birds of the air and the flowers of the field. Behold him as he opens his arms to little children, and holds them in close affection to his breast. Watch him as he talks with women, and treats them, in this age when the "female of the species" was either a slave or a toy, with a reverence as touching as it was unexampled. Note how he looked upon the rich young ruler to love him, received the prostitute to forgive her, and dined with publicans and sinners to bring them healing. Never was there a kindlier, more compassionate man. "Tenderness of heart," says Renan, "was in him transformed into infinite sweetness, poetry, and universal charm."

These qualities are beautiful, but may easily fall into weakness or even frailty. It is only when we see sweetness united with the antithetical quality of strength that we begin to appreciate the real greatness of the Nazarene's personality. He was throughout his career a man of power. It is overwhelmingly impressive to note how often this word "power" is applied in the New Testament to the word and work of Jesus. Throughout his career, he was an overwhelmingly dominant factor in the life of his time, and in the lives of the individuals whom he touched. The healing of the sick, the calling of the disciples, indictment of the Pharisees, the stirring of Pilate, the conversion of the soldier at the foot of the cross—all these testify to the potency of Jesus's spirit. He spoke as one having authority, acted as one chosen to rule, and lived and died as one in touch with God.

GERARD MANLEY HOPKINS   (*1844–1889*)

ALL THE WORLD'S HERO

Our Lord Jesus Christ, my brethren, is our hero, a hero all the world wants. You know how books of tales are written, that put one man before the reader and shews him off handsome for the most part and brave and call him My Hero or Our Hero. Often mothers make a hero of a son; girls of a sweetheart and good wives of a husband. Soldiers make a hero of a great general, a party of its leader, a nation of any great man that brings it glory, whether king, warrior, statesman, thinker, poet, or whatever it shall be. But Christ, he is the hero. He too is the hero of a book or books, of the divine Gospels. He is a warrior and a conqueror. He is a king, Jesus of Nazareth king of the Jews, though when he came to his own kingdom his own did not receive him, and now, his people having cast him off, we Gentiles are his inheritance. He is a statesman, that drew up the New Testament in his blood . . . He is a thinker, that taught us divine mysteries. He is an orator and a poet, as in his eloquent words and parables appears. He is all the world's hero, the desire of nations. But besides he is the hero of single souls; his mother's hero, not out of motherly foolish fondness but because he was, as the angel told her, great and the Son of the Most High and all that he did and said and was done and said about him she laid up in her heart. He is the truelove and the bridegroom of men's souls: the virgins follow him whithersoever he goes; the martyrs follow him through a sea of blood, through great tribulation; all his servants take up their cross and follow him. And those even that do not follow him, yet they look wistfully after him, own him a hero, and wished they dared answer his call. Children as soon as they can understand him ought to be told about him, that they make him the hero of their young hearts. . . .

There met in Jesus Christ all things that can make man lovely and loveable. In his body he was most beautiful. This is known first by the tradition in the Church that it was so and by holy writers agreeing to suit those words to him/Thou art beautiful in mould above the sons of men; we have even accounts of him written in early times. They tell us that he was moderately tall, well built and slender in frame, his features straight and beautiful, his hair inclining to auburn, parted in the midst, curling and clustering about the ears and neck as the leaves of a filbert, so they speak, upon the nut. He wore also a forked beard and this as well as the locks upon his head were never touched by razor or shears; neither, his health being perfect, could a hair ever fall to the ground. The account I have been quoting (it is from memory, for I cannot now lay my hands upon it) we do not indeed know for certain to be correct, but it has been current in the Church and many generations have drawn our Lord accordingly either in their own minds or in his images. Another proof of his beauty may be drawn from the words *proficiebat sapienta et aetate et gratia apud Deum et homines* (Luc. ii. 52)/he went forward in wisdom and bodily frame and favour with God and men; that is/he pleased both God and men daily more and more by his growth of mind and body. But he could not have pleased by growth of body unless the body was strong, healthy, and beautiful that grew. But the best proof of all is this, that his body was the special work of the Holy Ghost. He was not born in nature's course, no man was his father; had he been born as others are he must have inherited some defect of figure or constitution, from which no man born as fallen men are born is wholly free unless God interfere to keep him so. But his body was framed directly from heaven by the power of the Holy Ghost, of whom it would be unworthy to leave any the least blotch or failing in his work. So the first Adam was moulded by God himself and Eve built up by God too out of Adam's rib and they could not but be pieces, both, of faultless workmanship; the same then and much more must Christ have been. His constitution too was tempered perfectly, he had neither disease nor the seeds of any: weariness he felt when he was wearied, hunger when he fasted, thirst when he had long gone without drink, but to the touch of sickness he was stranger. I leave it to you, brethren, then to picture him, in whom the fulness of the godhead dwelt bodily, in his bearing how majestic, how strong and yet how lovely and lissom in his limbs, in his look how earnest, grave but kind. In his Passion all this strength was spent, this lissomeness crippled, this beauty wrecked, this majesty beaten down. But now it is more than all restored, and for myself I make no secret that I look forward with eager desire to seeing the matchless beauty of Christ's body in the heavenly light.

I come to his mind. He was the greatest genius that ever lived. You know what genius is, brethren—beauty and perfection in the mind. For perfection in the bodily frame distinguishes a man among other men his fellows: so may the mind be distinguished for its beauty above all other minds and that is genius. Then when this genius is duly taught and trained, that is wisdom; for without training genius is imperfect and again wisdom is imperfect without genius. But Christ, we read, advanced in wisdom and in favour with God and men: now this wisdom, in which he excelled all men, had to be founded on an unrivalled genius. Christ then was the greatest genius that ever lived. You must not say, Christ needed no such thing as genius; his wisdom came from heaven, for he was God. To say so is to speak like the heretic Apollinaris, who said that Christ had indeed a human body but no soul, he needed no mind and soul, for his godhead, the Word of God, that stood for mind and soul in him. No, but Christ was perfect man and must have mind as well as body and that mind was, no question, of the rarest excellence and beauty; it was genius. As Christ lived and breathed and moved in a true and not phantom human body and in that laboured, suffered, was crucified, died, and was buried; as he merited by acts of his human will; so he reasoned and planned and invented by acts of his own human genius, genius made perfect by wisdom of its own, not the divine wisdom only.

A witness to his genius we have in those men who being sent to arrest him came back empty handed, spellbound by his eloquence, saying/Never man spoke like this man.

A better proof we have in his own words, his sermon on the mount, his parables, and all his sayings recorded in the Gospel. My brethren we are so accustomed to them that they do not strike us as they a stranger that hears them first, else we too should say/Never man etc. No stories or parables are like Christ's, so bright, so pithy, so touching; no proverbs or sayings are such jewellery: they stand off from other men's thoughts like stars, like lilies in the sun; nowhere in literature is there anything to match the Sermon on the Mount: if there is let men bring it forward. Time does not allow me to call your minds to proofs or instances. Beside Christ's sayings in the Gospels a dozen or so more have been kept by tradition and are to be found in the works of the Fathers and early writers and one even in the Scripture itself: It is more blessed etc. When these sayings are gathered together, though one cannot feel sure of everyone, yet reading all in one view they make me say/These must be Christ's, never man etc. One is: Never rejoice but when you look upon your brother in love. Another is: My mystery is for me and for the children of my house. . . .

Now in the third place, far higher than beauty of the body, higher than genius and wisdom the beauty of the mind, comes the beauty of his character, his character as a man. For the most part his very enemies, those that do not believe in him, allow that a character so noble was never seen in human mould. Plato the heathen, the greatest of the Greek philosophers, foretold of him: he drew by his wisdom a picture of the just man in his justice crucified and it was fulfilled in Christ. Poor was his station, laborious his life, bitter his ending: through poverty, through labour, through crucifixion his majesty of nature more shines. No heart as his was ever so tender, but tenderness was not all: this heart so tender was as brave, it could be stern. He found the thought of his Passion past bearing, yet he went through with it. He was feared when he chose: he took a whip and singlehanded cleared the temple. The thought of his gentleness towards children, towards the afflicted, towards sinners, is often dwelt on; that of his courage less. But for my part I like to feel I should have feared him. We hear also of his love, as for John and Lazarus; and even love at first sight, as of the young man that had kept all the commandments from his childhood. But he warned or rebuked his best friends when need was, as Peter, Martha, and even his mother. For, as St. John says, he was full both of grace and of truth.

But, brethren, from all that might be said of his character I single out one point and beg you to notice that. He loved to praise, he loved to reward. He knew what was in man, he best knew men's faults and yet he was the warmest in their praise. When he worked a miracle he would grace it with/Thy faith hath saved thee, that it might almost seem the receiver's work, not his. He said of Nathanael he was an Israelite without guile; he that searches hearts said this, and yet what praise that was to give! He called the two sons of Zebedee Sons of Thunder, kind and stately and honourable name! We read of nothing thunderlike that they did except, what was sinful, to wish fire down from heaven on some sinners, but they deserved the name or he would not have given it, and he has given it to them for all time. Of John the Baptist he said that his greater was not born of woman. He said to Peter/Thou art Rock/and rewarded a moment's acknowledgment of him with the lasting headship of his Church. He defended Magdalen and took means that the story of her generosity should be told for ever. And though he bids *us* say we are unprofitable servants, yet he himself will say to each of us/Good and faithful servant, well done.

And this man whose picture I have tried to draw for you, brethren, is your God. He was your maker in time past; hereafter he will be your judge. Make him your hero now. Take some time to think of him; praise him in your hearts.

ROBERT G. INGERSOLL   (*1833–1899*)

THE UNBELIEVER'S TRIBUTE

For the man Christ—for the reformer who loved his fellow-men— for the man who believed in an Infinite Father, who would shield the innocent and protect the just—for the martyr who expected to be rescued from the cruel cross, and who at last, finding that his hope was dust, cried out in the gathering gloom of death: "My God! My God! Why hast thou forsaken me?"—for that great and suffering man, mistaken though he was, I have the highest admiration and respect.

THOMAS JEFFERSON   (*1743–1826*)

A STATESMAN'S VIEW

To the corruptions of Christianity I am, indeed, opposed; but not to the genuine precepts of Jesus himself. I am a Christian, in the only sense in which he wished anyone to be; sincerely attached to his doctrines, in preference to all others; ascribing to himself every *human* excellence and believing he never claimed any other. . . .

His parentage was obscure; his condition poor; his education null; his natural endowments great; his life correct and innocent; he was meek, benevolent, patient, firm, disinterested, and of the sublimest eloquence. . . .

According to the ordinary fate of those who attempt to enlighten and reform mankind, he fell an early victim of the jealousy and combination of the altar and the throne, at about thirty-three years of age, his reason having not yet attained the *maximum* of its energy, nor the course of his preaching, which was but of three years, at most, presented occasions for developing a complete system of morals.

*   *   *   *

Notwithstanding these disadvantages, a system of morals is presented to us, which, if filled up in the style and spirit of the rich fragments he left us, would be the most perfect and sublime that has ever been taught by man.

JEROME K. JEROME   (*1859–1927*)

HIS SPIRIT IN ALL MEN

Of all who have been given power to help man in his struggle for spiritual existence, one must place Jesus Christ as the highest. As a child, I had been taught that Christ was really God. There was some mystery about a Trinity, which I did not understand—which no one has ever understood, which the early Church wisely forbade its votaries from even trying to understand. Christ, himself I could have loved. I doubt if any human being has ever read or heard his story without coming to love him—certainly no child. It was thinking of him as God that caused me to turn away from him. If all the time he was God then there had been no reality in it. It had all been mere play-acting. If Christ was God, what help to me the example of his life?

But Christ my fellow-man—however far above me—was still my brother, sharer of my bonds and burthens. From his sufferings, I could learn courage. From his victory, I could gather hope. What he demanded of me, that I could give. Where he led, I too might follow.

The Christ spirit is in all men. It is the part of man that is akin to God. By listening to it, by making it our guide, we can grow like God—fit ourselves to become His comrade, His fellow-labourer.

CARL G. JUNG $(1875-$ $)$

HE FOLLOWED THE INNER VOICE

Translated by Stanley Dell

One of the most shining examples of the life and meaning of personality that history has preserved for us is the life of Christ. In Christianity, which—it may be mentioned in passing—was the only religion really persecuted by the Romans, there appeared a direct opponent of the Caesarean madness of Rome, a trait that distinguished not only the emperor, but every Roman as well: *civis Romanus sum*. The opposition showed itself wherever the cult of Caesar and Christianity clashed. But as we know from what the Evangelists intimate as to the psychic evolution of the personality of Christ, this opposition also played the decisive role in the soul of the founder of the Christian religion. The story of the temptation clearly shows us with what kind of psychic power Jesus had collided: it was the power-devil of the contemporary mind that led him into serious temptation in the wilderness. This devil was the objective-psychic that held all the people of the Roman imperium under its spell; this is why it promised to Jesus also all the kingdoms of earth, as if it desired to make a Caesar of him.

Following the inner voice, his vocation and his calling, Jesus freely exposed himself to the attack of the imperialistic delusion that filled everyone, conqueror and conquered alike. In this way he recognized the nature of the objective-psychic, which had plunged the whole world into a state of suffering and had produced a yearning for salvation that found its expression even in the heathen poets. He did not suppress this psychic onslaught, but consciously let it act upon him; nor did he allow himself to be suppressed by it, but assimilated it. And so world-conquering Caesarism was changed into a spiritual kingship, and the *imperium Romanum* became a universal and unworldly kingdom of God. While the Jewish people as a whole was expecting an imperialistic and politically active hero, Jesus fulfilled the Messianic vocation less for his nation than for the Roman world, and pointed out to humanity the old truth that, where force rules, there is no love, and where love rules, force does not count. The religion of love was the exact psychological counterpart to the Roman bedevilment with power.

The example of Christianity perhaps best illustrates the abstract discussions I have presented above. This apparently unique life has become a sacred symbol because it is the prototype of the only meaningful life, that is, a life that strives for the individual realization of its own particular law, such realization being absolute and unconditional. In this sense one may exclaim with Tertullian: *anima naturaliter christiana!*

The deification of Jesus as well as of Buddha is not surprising, but strikingly shows the enormous valuation that humanity puts upon these heroes, and so upon the ideal of the development of personality. Though it seems at present as if the blind and destructive prevalence of senseless, collective force would thrust the ideal of personality into the background, yet this is only a passing revolt against the ascendancy of the past.

Robert Keable *(1887–1927)*

"COMPLETE IN LOVELINESS"

You cannot find anywhere, in the whole range of literature or art, any story so complete in loveliness and pathos as this story of the traditional Jesus. Words fail as one contemplates it. It has taken to itself perhaps the one magic that is left to the world. The very words in which it is enshrined are of incomparable beauty and moving power. Delete that traditional figure, and all the best and happiest of our life becomes a hollow sham. You can see it in little things as well as great, even down to a Christmas festival, which is all tinsel and electric light without the manger of Bethlehem, without the littered straw, the ox and the sheep and the ass crowding in in adoration, the shepherds listening to the song of the angels, and the three kings coming from afar. . . .

You cannot pare the traditional Christ theologically to suit your convenience. You cannot identify him with an historical Jesus. The two figures are eternally separate, and in a sense irreconcilable. And it is even well that it is so. The main power and charm of the traditional Jesus lie in the fact that he is not historical, that he is not mummified in any Gospel, and that he can be seen from many angles. He does not belong to the study, and he is not the creation of understanding. His ancestry is a far more beautiful one than that. . . .

We ask men to believe in a traditional Jesus, but we do not mean by "believe" that we ask them to accept as history his traditional story, or to accept as science his theological sin-bearing. It would be easier, probably, if we asked them instead to glory in the traditional Jesus.

JOHN KEATS   (*1795–1821*)

HIS SPLENDOUR UNOBSCURED

I have no doubt that thousands of people never heard of have had hearts completely disinterested: I can remember but two—Socrates and Jesus— Their histories evince it. What I heard a little time ago, Taylor observes with respect to Socrates, may be said of Jesus— That he was so great a man that though he transmitted no writing of his own to posterity, we have his Mind and his sayings and his greatness handed to us by others. It is to be lamented that the history of the latter was written and revised by Men interested in the pious frauds of Religion. Yet through all this I see his splendour.

COUNT HERMAN A. VON KEYSERLING   (*1880–   *)

THE INNER CHRIST REMAINS

Translated by J. Holroyd Reece

It is highly interesting and characteristic, what is happening to Christ in the course of his most recent development. The historical Jesus is receding into the background; there is no more talk of objective salvation, and the whole theodicy of the Middle Ages is ignored. What remains is the inner Christ, whom Jesus was the first man to call to life within himself, and whom every one is to make supreme within himself in his own personal way. The man who disregards Christ as an individual will hardly recognise a new saviour. There can be no doubt whatever that the future belongs to these independent spirits.

Joseph Klausner   (*1874–*   )

THE WORK OF THE DISCIPLES

Translated by W. S. Stinespring

If Jesus had not been a remarkable personality, who did remarkable
deeds and spoke remarkable words, he would have faded from the
memory of his disciples after his shameful death on the cross as faded
the memory of the rest of the "false Messiahs," that is to say, the
saviors who did not succeed in saving. The very fact that his disciples, both male and female, cherished his memory even after the
crucifixion, reaching the point where they saw him in their imagination as risen and alive—this very fact proves that the influence of
Jesus upon the little group brought about wonderment and adoration. And without certain deeds of healing the sick, the distressed,
and the hysterical, without the formulation of a new prayer, without a distinctive attitude toward the ritual requirements as over
against the ethical, without opposition toward the Pharisees and Sadducees, without the choosing of disciples and the sending out of
apostles (preachers), without all these things it is impossible to
imagine such adoration lasting after the crucifixion and beyond the
time of burial. However, Jesus himself did not deliver a single word
with intent to found a new religion or a new religious community;
he laid down a number of precepts for his disciples only, and it was
they alone who made of these precepts ritual requirements in com-
memoration of him, or by imitation of his deeds and words. Thus
they built up ritual requirements for a new church which was in
process of formation.

Jean Baptiste Henri-Dominique Lacordaire   (*1802–1861*)

"THE FIRST GENTLEMAN IN THE WORLD"

Translator Anonymous

Every being, save God, pre-exists in its germ, and man in particular pre-exists in his ancestors. No one appears here below whose reign has not been prepared long beforehand; and the more important the destiny designed for him by Providence, the more important also is the preparatory action of his ancestors. Jesus Christ, as man, should therefore have pre-existed after the manner of men; and, inasmuch as he was greater than all men by his destiny, he should also have pre-existed in a manner peculiar to himself alone. I remark then, in the first place, that alone amongst all the great names, he possesses authentic genealogy which remounts from him even to the father of the human race, and that he is thus, undoubtedly, the first gentleman in the world.

Jean Baptiste Henri-Dominique Lacordaire   (*1802–1861*)

HISTORY'S MOST VENERABLE FORM

Translator Anonymous

Whatever motives Jesus Christ might have had against calling himself God, he did call himself God; such is the fact . . . Did Jesus Christ believe in his divinity? Was he convinced of the truth of that vital dogma which he laid down as the basis of his teaching and for which he died? Was he sincere, or—pardon the expression—was he an impostor? We cannot advance a step further in his life before we solve this doubt. What think you, Must we place him with the impostors or with the sincere? . . .

It is answered by the character of the man, and hence I may conclude that the cause is judged in favour of Jesus Christ; for no more venerable form has dawned upon the horizon of history. The simple course of time has placed him above all, leaving nothing visible that can approach it. By the consent of all, even of those who do not believe in him, Jesus Christ is a good man, a sage, an elect, an incomparable personage. He has done such great, such holy things, that even his enemies pay constant homage to his work and to his person.

John LaFarge, S.J. (*1880–*)

THE RESURRECTION AS HISTORY

Some years ago a capable lawyer wrote a little book on the Resurrection, treating the historical fact from the standpoint of legal evidence. The result was a convincing argument for the truth of the Gospel narrative. An interesting study could be made of the Resurrection as an example of publicity. What means did the Saviour use, and under what circumstances, to promote the knowledge of this most astounding news item that the world has ever seen?

From a merely human angle, the circumstances were anything but favorable for spreading the news that Christ had come back to life. The public mind was under the spell of a general belief that the Nazarene had failed. People were prepared for such a belief by constant propaganda from the enemies of the Saviour. They had been told that He must fail, that His was a losing cause, that He could not possibly fulfil His promises. As a blatant fact, the entire projects of the Nazarene had collapsed. His organization of disciples, such as it was, had completely broken up. His multitude of one-time followers had deserted Him and were turned into his bitterest opponents. With the Leader dead and buried as a convicted criminal, all that remained of his great religious and social movement was the small original directing committee of twelve, headed by Simon Peter. Yet even this inner body was disrupted. One of its most important and educated members had attempted to do some profiteering. When his conduct was observed, he had dickered with the enemy, and finally betrayed the Leader Himself. The others had lost their bearings and were sunk in a stupor of bewilderment bordering on despair. Hence the great News had to make headway against an overwhelming presumption of improbability not from the nature of the event alone, but from the painful circumstances that surrounded the death of Christ.

As we study the plan that met these obstacles and overcame them, we notice some distinctive features. First, there was little if any mass publicity. The only step that the Saviour seems to have taken in this direction was His appearance, towards the close of His forty days of risen life on earth, to 500 persons in Galilee. Though nothing further is told of this public apparition, it appears to have been a sort of extension of the private interviews which, in His risen capacity, He granted to His chosen intimates after the great event had taken place.

On the other hand, the utmost care was evident in the choice of those who were privileged to be the direct witnesses of the Resurrection. They were those men and women who were least disposed to imagine this very thing. Indeed, the Saviour Himself had considerable difficulty in convincing them of the reality of His own Person. Yet they were those persons who, when they did once realize the fact as a fact, were the best qualified, by their previous training, their personal moral character, and their intense affection for the Leader, to act as the initial agents and officially commissioned leaders in the vast plan of publicity that was to follow.

If the Resurrection had been an event which would lose its urgent significance with the lapse of time, there would have been reason for giving it an immediate and widely diffused publicity. But it was unique in the fact that the event itself was to continue forever, and therefore would need to be publicized just as much a couple of thousand years hence as a week after its initial occurrence. So that the problem was the establishment of a continuing organization that would carry on the campaign of publicity until the end of time.

D. H. Lawrence   (*1885–1930*)

PUZZLE OF THE RESURRECTION

The Churches loudly assert: We preach Christ crucified!—But in so doing, they preach only half of the Passion, and do only half their duty. The Creed says: "Was crucified, dead, and buried . . . the third day He rose again from the dead." And again, "I believe in the resurrection of the body . . ." So that to preach Christ Crucified is to preach Christ born among men—which is Christmas; Christ Crucified, which is Good Friday; and Christ Risen, which is Easter. And after Easter, till November and All Saints, and till Annunciation, the year belongs to the Risen Lord: that is, all the full-flowering spring, all summer, and the autumn of wheat and fruit, all belong to Christ Risen. . . .

And the Churches, instead of preaching the Risen Lord, go on preaching the Christ-child and Christ Crucified. Now man cannot live without some vision of himself. But still less can he live with a vision that is not true to his inner experience and inner feeling. And the vision of Christ-child and Christ Crucified are both untrue to the inner experience and feeling of the young. They don't feel that way. They show the greatest forbearance and tolerance of their elders, for whom the two images *are* livingly true. But for the post-war young, neither the Christ-child nor Christ Crucified means much. . . .

Christ risen in the flesh! We must accept the image complete, if we accept it at all. We must take the mystery in its fulness and in fact. It is only the image of our own experience. Christ rises, when He rises from the dead, in the flesh, not merely as spirit. He rises with hands and feet, as Thomas knew for certain: and if with hands and feet, then with lips and stomach and genitals of a man. Christ risen, and risen in the whole of His flesh, not with some left out.

Christ risen in the full flesh! What for? It is here the Gospels are all vague and faltering, and the Churches leave us in the lurch. Christ risen in the flesh in order to lurk obscurely for six weeks on earth, then be taken vaguely up into heaven in a cloud? Flesh, solid flesh, feet and bowels and teeth and eyes of a man, taken up into heaven in a cloud, and never put down again?

It is the only part of the great mystery which is all wrong. The virgin birth, the baptism, the temptation, the teaching, Gethsemane, the betrayal, the crucifixion, the burial and resurrection, these are all true according to our inward experience. They are what men and women go through, in their different ways. But floated up into heaven as flesh-and-blood, and never set down again—this nothing in all our experience will ever confirm. If aeroplanes take us up, they bring us down, or let us down. Flesh and blood belong to the earth, and only to the earth. We know it.

And Jesus was risen flesh-and-blood. He rose a man on earth to live on earth. The greatest test was still before Him: His life as a man on earth. Hitherto He had been a sacred child, a teacher, a messiah, but never a full man. Now, risen from the dead. He rises to be a man on earth, and live His life of the flesh, the great life, among other men. This is the image of our inward state to-day.

This is the image of the young: the Risen Lord. The teaching is over, the crucifixion is over, the sacrifice is made, the salvation is accomplished. Now comes the true life, man living his full life on earth, as flowers live their full life, without rhyme or reason except the magnificence of coming forth into fulness.

If Jesus rose from the dead in triumph, a man on earth triumphant in renewed flesh, triumphant over the mechanical anti-life convention of Jewish priests, Roman despotism, and universal money-lust; triumphant above all over His own self-absorption, self-consciousness, self-importance; triumphant and free as a man in full flesh and full, final experience, even the accomplished acceptance of His own death; a man at last full and free in flesh and soul, a man at one with death; then He rose to become at one with life, to live the great life of the flesh and soul together, as peonies or foxes do, in their lesser way.

LIN YUTANG (*1895–*)

CHRIST AND CONFUCIUS CONTRASTED

Jesus was a romanticist, Confucius a realist; Jesus was a mystic, Confucius a positivist; Jesus was a humanitarian, Confucius a humanist. In these two personalities we see typified the contrast between Hebrew religion and poetry and Chinese realism and common sense. Confucianism, strictly speaking, was not a religion; it had certain feelings toward life and the universe that bordered on the religious feeling, but it was not a religion. There are such great souls in the world who cannot get interested in the life hereafter or in the question of immortality or in the world of spirits in general. That type of philosophy could never satisfy the Germanic races, and certainly not the Hebrews, but it satisfied the Chinese race—in general.

MARQUESS OF LOTHIAN (Philip Henry Kerr) (*1882–1940*)

CONQUEROR OF ROME

It is certainly not the duty of the church, as the vehicle through which Spirit reaches man, to advocate the creation of a federation of nations today. But the effective growth of Christianity in the minds and hearts of mankind will inevitably tend to bring such a consummation, with its ending of war and the demonism which springs from anarchy, into being. We have already once in history witnessed the power of Christianity to begin to do this very thing. At the outset Jesus refused to lend himself to the movement among the Jews which sought to break up the Roman Empire, and it was his refusal to surrender to nationalism which enabled the priests to rally the populace to the demand for the release of Barabbas and his own crucifixion. Thus when asked whether his disciples should pay tribute to Caesar, he replied, "Render unto Caesar the things that are Caesar's, and to God the things that are God's." It is not un-reasonable to infer that Jesus understood the advantage of a universal empire which, for all its ruthlessness, gave peace and the reign of a fairly advanced system of law to the then civilized world, apart from India, China, and the Far East, and considered that it was the duty of Christians to transform it by the Spirit they manifested rather than to destroy it. Paul certainly thought so. And Christianity, not Judaism, eventually did conquer Rome, and in doing so tempered its brutality with tolerance and humanity.

EMIL LUDWIG   (*1881–*   )

ON THE HILL OF CALVARY

Translated by Eden and Cedar Paul

How heavy the cross is, and the way seems long. Death will be easy enough. Indeed, it will not be death at all, for the Father will hold out loving arms, and the glories of heaven will be opened!

The day is hot, and this cedar wood is heavy. The crosspiece and the upright are hollowed out, so as to dovetail into one another. Roughly done, but strong enough to bear a man's weight.

*   *   *   *

The cross is too heavy for him; the sap is still in the wood. That young fellow passing by is vigorous. Let him carry it for the con-demned man—not very far, now. A kindly-looking fellow, he car-ried another's cross, and has received the new message in his heart though he has never heard it with his ears. Thus in the last hour there comes a new disciple. . . .

While the cross is thus borne forwards on a young man's powerful shoulders, there totters behind it the pale figure of the prophet, sud-denly grown old, pushed and jostled by the soldiers of the escort.

*   *   *   *

Up there on the hill, more legionnaires are already at work hammering and delving, for there are two other crucifixions to-day, Jews expiating the crimes of theft and murder. While some of the soldiers are digging holes in the ground, others are nailing the criminals to the crosses as these lie flat upon the soil. One of them resists; but strong hands hold him fast, his yells are ignored, and the huge nails are driven home, one through each hand, and one through both feet. Nail them firmly, so that no cord need be wasted on the malefactors! Now, up with the cross! . . . Thus almost simultaneously the two crosses with the thieves nailed to them are set up in the scorching sunlight, and the air is rent with the screams of the tortured men.

He whose turn is now to come sees all this as if in a dream. "Murderers and thieves," he thinks; "poor men, led astray, sentenced, and hurried off to their doom!" Above the head of each a placard has been affixed, declaring in three languages the nature of the offenders' crimes. There must be such a placard for him, too. Yes, that thickset little soldier, the one who had kicked him just now, is nailing it to his cross. "Rex Judaeorum." . . .

He suddenly becomes aware that his arms have been seized by pitiless hands, and that he has been stretched on the cross. He watches a nail, which looms gigantic before his eyes. Horror overwhelms him; pain racks him; he faints.

When he comes to his senses again, and grows aware of the fiery smart in his wounds, he turns his head to right and to left, and the sight of the other crosses recalls him to an understanding of what has happened.

* * * *

As the slow minutes ebb away, pain chases pain through his tortured frame, as if it were being seared with fire, devoured by beasts of prey.

At length, when ages, as it seems, have passed, when he feels that the heart in his frail body is breaking; when intelligence and imagination are clouded, and faith and hope are obscured; when all his consciousness is filled with pain—he breaks the silence he has kept throughout these dreadful hours. The torment of mind and body finds vent in a heart-rending cry.

*   *   *   *

This cry of agony and despair ends a life which for thirty years has expressed itself in the gentle tones of love that brings solace to others, in the voiceless song of an affectionate human heart.

EVERETT DEAN MARTIN   (*1880–1941*)

HISTORY'S SYMBOLIC FIGURE

The Christ of the New Testament is a symbolic figure, whether or not he ever existed as an historical character. Many elements of the Gospel narrative are held to be unhistorical by Christian scholars who have given the subject serious study. A courageous attempt has been made during the last seventy-five years, chiefly by German scholars, to reconstruct out of what was recognized to be an accumulation of myth and legend a true historical Jesus. But the problem is of intellectual interest chiefly; and even so, the difficulties have been so great, and the data so small, that the work done has necessarily contained much material that was purely conjectural. The beauty and wonder of the Gospel story had for the most part to be stripped off. Such a person as the man Jesus, whose dim historic outlines are seemingly restored by this long labor of critical analysis, may perhaps once have lived, but this is not the Christ of the Christian faith.

According to the working hypothesis of New Testament criticism, the fictitious figure of the Christ developed in spite of those actions and sayings of Jesus which are held to be historical. Historical scholarship may perhaps be the gainer by this research, but as the religious emotion once created the Christ symbol, it may be expected to cling to it. And if, after so many years of strenuous study and effort, the attempt to locate the person of Jesus in history leaves the believer with only a martyred and mistaken idealist, a moralistic and somewhat revolutionary Hebrew prophet—from whom we may derive inspiration, doubtless, though with some difficulty; and if, as we are told, the historical existence of even this far-away figure is still open to serious question, why not abandon the whole search for historical fact so far as it concerns the story of Christ, and treat the narrative as pure symbol? It has that value, at any rate; and on the authority of the best scholarship, that which has really had a dominant place in Christian faith is held to be unhistorical. It would seem that criticism had started out to demonstrate the historicity of Jesus and had, in fact, succeeded in leading us to the rediscovery of the symbolic Christ of religious experience.

JAMES MARTINEAU   (1805–1900)

AN ACCEPTABLE INTERPRETER

We conceive that Jesus of Nazareth lived and died, not to *persuade* the Father, not to *appease* the Father, not to make a sanguinary *purchase* from the Father, but simply to *"show* us the Father"; to leave upon the human heart a new, deep, vivid impression of what God is in himself, and of what he designs for his creature, man; to become, in short, the accepted interpreter of heaven and life. And this he achieved, in the only way of which we can conceive as practicable, by a new disclosure in his own person of all that is holy and godlike in character—startling the human soul with the sudden apparition of a being diviner far than it had yet beheld, and lifting its faith at once into quite another and purer region. . . . And so Christ, standing in solitary greatness, opens at once the eye of conscience to perceive and know the pure and holy God the Father that dwelt in him and made him so full of truth and grace. . . . Of anything *more perfect* than the meek yet majestic Jesus, no heart can ever dream.

B. W. MATURIN (*1847–1915*)

POWER OF THE HIDDEN LIFE

There were two sides to the life of our Lord. To those who saw Him in His public ministry during the last three years of His life, it seemed one of constant and unceasing labour. He "went about doing good." He was ever at the call of any who needed Him; He gave Himself no rest, so that He had not so much time as to eat bread. As we read the Gospels, we read of days crowded with work of the most trying kind, dealing constantly with all sorts of people, addressing crowds and then meeting the needs of individuals, and never apparently alone, the Apostles always with Him. His life was almost lived in public. Almost the whole Gospel is taken up with the events of about three years. To those who saw Him and heard Him, it is as if His life seemed to be without rest, a life of unsparing energy and toil.

But there was another side which they could not see—the hidden life. His public life was built upon and rested upon a life of thirty years of hiddenness and preparation. For every year in public there were ten years in private. In the solitude and retirement of Nazareth He grew up; there His human character formed and developed, far from the noise and excitement of the world; thirty years out of thirty-three He lived there, almost His whole life. What does three years count for in many a man's life? And He spent His whole life except three years at Nazareth.

And even after that long period of preparation, He retired into deeper solitude before His public ministry began. He spent forty days in the wilderness in absolute solitude, except for the presence of visitors from the world of spirits. And again and again we read of His withdrawing in the midst of His life of active work for prayer.

"In the morning, rising up a great while before day, He went out and departed into a solitary place, and there prayed."

Yes, there was the hidden life from which the public life gained all its power. All His actions were rooted in God; He never forgot Himself, never got carried away by the interest or excitement of the multitudes with whom He had to deal, never swerved from the purpose and Will of God.

The hidden life *is* hidden, we know almost nothing about it; if it were known, and could be described, it would not be hidden. Now and again, in the thick and pressure of His work, the veil is lifted for a moment, and we are allowed to see those nights of prayer; but men could feel and see the mysterious power in His words and acts and bearing that were the outward manifestations of that inner life, but that was all. His life—that out of which all this public life grew —was hidden.

FRANÇOIS MAURIAC   (*1885–*   )

"A MAN AMONG MANY"

Translated by Julie Kernan

Jesus of the Gospels is the contrary of an artificial and composite being. Here is the most moving of the great figures of history, and of all the great characters history places before us, the least logical because he is the most living. It is for us to understand him in what is most peculiar and essential to ourselves.

Before we think of him as God, we must think of him as a man in an epoch fairly near to our own; a definite man belonging to his own country, his own clan, a man among many, one of them—so much, indeed, that to distinguish him from the eleven poor people about him, the kiss of Judas must point him out. This journeyman carpenter speaks and acts as God. This Galilean of the lower classes, member of a very poor family, which family, moreover, mocks him and believes him mad, possesses such power over matter, over bodies and over hearts that he stirs up the people to a fresh hope of the coming of the Messiah; and the priests, to put down the impostor, must have recourse to their worst enemy, the Roman.

JOHN STUART MILL   (*1806–1873*)

UNTOUCHED BY RATIONAL CRITICISM

Whatever else may be taken away from us by rational criticism, Christ is still left a unique figure, not more unlike all His precursors than all His followers, even those who had the direct benefit of His personal teaching. It is of no use to say that Christ as exhibited in the Gospels is not historical, and that we know not how much of what is admirable has been superadded by the tradition of His followers. The tradition of followers suffices to insert any number of marvels, and may have inserted all the miracles which He is reputed to have wrought. But who among His followers, or among their proselytes, was capable of inventing the sayings ascribed to Jesus, or of imagining the life and character revealed in the Gospels? Certainly not the fishermen of Galilee, as certainly not St. Paul, whose character and idiosyncracies were of a totally different sort; still less the early Christian writers, in whom nothing is more evident than that the good which was in them was all derived, as they always professed it was derived, from the higher source. . . . About the life and sayings of Jesus, there is a stamp of personal originality combined with profundity of insight, which if we abandon the idle expectation of finding scientific precision where something very different was aimed at, must place the Prophet of Nazareth, even in the estimation of those who have no belief in his inspiration, in the very first rank of the men of sublime genius of whom our species can boast. When this preeminent genius is combined with the qualities of probably the greatest moral reformer, and martyr to that mission, who ever existed upon earth, religion cannot be said to have made a bad choice in pitching on this man as the ideal representative and guide of humanity; nor, even now, would it be easy, even for an unbeliever, to find a better translation of the rule of virtue from the abstract into the concrete, than to endeavour so to live that Christ would approve our life.

JEAN S. MILNER   (*1893*-   )

HIS BELIEF IN GOD

His belief in God and His practice in prayer of the Presence of God, made a tremendous difference in Jesus' life. It filled Him with virile power and a glorious radiance. The paintings of medieval artists of a pale, tubercular, pallid Christ present conceptions of Him which are not found in the pages of the New Testament. Few words were more often upon His lips than these: "Be of good cheer." Those words run and ripple and sing all through the Gospels. The Jesus of history was aglow with a radiant gladness. His vigorous, contagious, buoyant and unbounded joy was based not upon wishful thinking, nor empty sentimentality but upon a great faith which rested upon the eternal verities which lie at the heart of Reality.

Jesus was fearless, daring, heroically courageous. There was a reason. One of the greatest things He ever said is recorded in the fourteenth chapter of John. Powerful political and ecclesiastical forces have spread a net about Him and are preparing to draw it, to do Him to death. He knows and His disciples know He is about to die. He is telling them good-by. In telling them not to be afraid He says, "Ye believe in God!" He knew as no one else has ever known that if men really did believe in and *experience* God it would make all the difference in the world in the manner in which they would face life and meet death with courage and heroism in their hearts. He was absolutely fearless because He was one of those very rare souls for whom God is real. In prayer He made His life at one with the Infinite Life.

I have been at night on the Sea of Galilee, under the full moon and stars; the night so quiet, so filled with mystic awe and wonder, the silence broken only by the "drip, drip from a lightly suspended oar." Far off, lining the distant shore were the hills and mountain tops where the Jesus of history knelt in prayer. Sitting quietly in the boat, my eyes drinking in the whole scene, I have caught glimpses of the secret of the grandeur of the soul of Jesus Christ. He prayed and in prayer He knew that God is. God to His mind was no mere speculative intellectual problem. Never once do we find the Jesus of history attempting to prove the existence of God by trying to refute the shallow arguments of the bewildering confusions and contradictions of sophisticated intellectuality.

The existence of God was as real to the mind of Christ as the existence of life. He would no more have undertaken to prove by argument the reality of God than He would have thought of attempting to prove by argument the reality of life. God to the mind of the Jesus of history was Reality. And on that knowledge He staked His all. God, to His mind, was infinitely more than a mere affirmative belief. God, to Him, was the *tremendous experience*. He felt the Life of God living in full and perfect amplitude in His life. No man has ever duplicated the Galilean's at-one-ness with God but He summoned all men to share something of that Divine afflatus with Him.

Believing in God He believed also in the immortality of the soul. He was not afraid of His rendezvous with Death. He told His followers the Dark Angel would not destroy Him. When He told them good-by He said He would see them again. And He did. He did not believe man is doomed to die. He knew, as all thoughtful men know, that we are born with dreams, hopes and hungers in our hearts which nothing here ever can completely satisfy. He refused to commit Himself to that contradiction of life which claims we are born to live, grow, climb and struggle heroically up and up to the zenith of the meaning of it all, which is—zero, oblivion, the eternal quiet of an

eternal nothingness. Jesus did not believe Death is the last word. He
believed in the supremacy of Life because He believed in God.

GEORGE MOORE   (*1852–1933*)

HE TELLS OF JOHN THE BAPTIST

A man travels the world over in search of what he needs and returns home to find it, Jesus answered gently . . . And as if foreseeing
an ardent disciple he began to speak to Joseph (of Arimathea) of
God, his speech moving on with a gentle motion like that of clouds
wreathing and unwreathing, finding new shapes for every period,
and always beautiful shapes. He often stopped speaking and his eyes
became fixed, as if he saw things beyond the things we all see; and
after an interval he would begin to speak again; and Joseph heard
that he had met John among the hills and listened to him, and that
if he accepted baptism from him it was because he wished to follow
John: but John sought to establish the kingdom of God within the
law, and so a dancing-girl asked for his head. It seemed as if Jesus
were on the point of some tremendous avowal, but if so it passed
away like a cloud.

CHRISTOPHER MORLEY   (*1890–   *)

INTENT OF PARABLES CONSIDERED

It would seem fairly obvious that the miracles and parables of the
New Testament, like the various creeds themselves, were intended
as vivid and stunning apologues. To batter them down to the level
of facts seems to degrade them, as it would be degrading to reject

Keats' sonnet because there are no peaks on the isthmus of Darien, and because it wasn't Cortes. The newspaper man prefers to take his stand with Tolstoy, who said, in that thrilling book "A Confession": "I wish to understand in such a way that everything that is inexplicable shall present itself to me as *necessarily* inexplicable." He prefers that when there is an available and mortally recognizable way of understanding things, they should be so understood. Take, for example, the story of the miracle at Cana. To a man trained to observe the delightful way in which testimony arises and is transmitted, how does that story explain itself? Here is a wedding party, at which appears the amazing stranger. He seems a man more fascinating, more charming, more utterly delightful, than any that those country folk have ever encountered. They are all very merry, the toasts go round, the wine runs short. But the ruler of the feast, turning to the stranger, says, prettily enough, I think, "With you here, water is as good as wine." Some one else takes it up, echoing the sentiment, seeking to add to it. "Right!" he cries. "Our friend here makes the water into wine. Here's to you!" and with friendly applause the gathering ratifies the compliment. One of the servants overhears, and carries the incident into the kitchen. How quickly it grows and passes down the village street! "They've got some one in there who's turning water into wine!" Can it be denied that this is the way that human events are reported?

There is one more Biblical passage I should like to refer to, one that has often been considered a knotty saying. It is the parable of the talents and the unprofitable servant. I like to conceive Deity in the guise of that hard master who wanted his own with usury. I can imagine God saying to the newly dead, "What did you think of that world I gave you?" "Not so bad, on the whole," replies the embarrassed soul. "What!" cries God. "Simpleton, do you mean to say you took it as you found it, accepted it, swallowed it down without question? Depart from me, unprofitable servant! You were supposed to remould it nearer to your heart's desire, to create out of my materials a new world of your own."

*　　　*　　　*　　　*

Men talk of "finding God," but no wonder it is difficult; He is hidden in that darkest of hiding-places, your own heart. You yourself are a part of Him. The chief danger is to be too prosaic. : . . The journalist, whatever his sins and stupidities, . . . will not do any great poet, such as Christ, the dishonour of taking him too literally.

LEWIS MUMFORD (*1895-*)

"LIKE A GUIDE TO THE HILL PASSES"

Like a guide to the hill passes, Jesus took short cuts across the untraversable mountains of class pride, intellectual arrogance and professional specialization. In his philosophy, the dialectical wisdom of Aristotle might not lead one as close to the core of life as the innocence of a little child. He devaluated the inflated currency of the intellect. Faith in the realities of life and spirit made the great and the humble stand on the same level. This was a shocking assumption to those who had paid dearly for wealth, knowledge, position: were all their efforts then worthless? Were the poor and the ignorant their equals? . . .

If Moses was the moralist, the hygienist, the organizer, Jesus was the mystic and the psychologist. The first worked on the mind through the body, and on the person through the community. The second reversed this process: the divine in man must be nourished if every other law and duty be pushed aside; and the divine was that which furthered the processes of growth and made it possible for man to slough off his deadselves, as the snake sloughs off its skin. Jesus saw that no wider, stricter observance of law could recover for life the freedom and energy it had lost in the very perfection of human institutions: in his view, goodness could obstruct life no less than wickedness, and without a perpetual challenge would undoubtedly do so. Among modern poets and philosophers, Emerson, Whitman, and Bergson come closest to sharing this philosophy. . . .

Jesus gave love a social mission and a political province. Who was one's neighbor? Anyone who needed one's help. The parable of the Good Samaritan is a condemnation of any form of isolationism.

This was a simple doctrine, backed by simple demonstrations. While the accounts of some of Jesus's miracles are incredible if one judges them by their actual contents, most of them are consistent with his whole vision of life if one judges them by their direction and intention. The restoration of sight to the blind, of speech to the dumb, of the use of their legs to the crippled: the casting out of neurotic "devils" and the return of sanity—always the end of the miracle is normal health, and the ability to go on living. Those whom Jesus converted to his faith did not receive any superhuman powers. . . .

The upshot of Jesus's typical miracles is that the patient becomes whole again; *life goes on*. The return to life was not postponed until the Resurrection Day. The very simplicity of Jesus's performances as a whole carries conviction.

J. MIDDLETON MURRY   (*1889–*   )

"HE WILL STAND OUR SCRUTINY"

The spiritual body of Jesus exists and is immortal. Some make their life-giving contact with it through the Eucharist; for others that contact is impossible. But they, through the effort of making the earthly life of Jesus real to themselves, find their souls possessed by love and veneration for the Prince of men. A fount of living water is unsealed in them.

And it may be that this, and this alone, is the great *Christian* experience, ultimate and eternal, though our ways to it must be our own. Of those ways, we may say this, that if they shall truly bring us to Jesus who is eternal, they must be ways which do not compel us to make sacrifice of aught we truly believe, and know, and are. . . .

He would not have us less than men; and we shall lose nothing by remaining men of our own century and our own country. At the last we shall greatly gain. We shall look like men, on the man Jesus. He will stand our scrutiny. Keep we our heads as high as we can, they shall be bowed at the last.

THOMAS PAINE   (*1737–1809*)

"VIRTUOUS AND AMIABLE"

Nothing that is here said can apply, even with the most distant disrespect, to the real character of Jesus Christ. He was a virtuous and an amiable man. The morality that he preached and practiced was of the most benevolent kind; and though similar systems of morality had been preached by Confucius, and by some of the Greek philosophers, many years before; by the Quakers since; any by many good men in all ages, it has not been exceeded by any.

THEODORE PARKER   (*1810–1860*)

"HE HAD FAITH IN MAN"

When Jesus, the son of Mary, a poor woman, wife of Joseph, the carpenter, in the little town of Nazareth, "began to be about thirty years old," and began also to open his mouth in the synagogues and the highways, nobody thought him a great man at all, as it seems. "Who are you?" said the guardians of public opinion. He found men expecting a great man. This, it seems, was the common opinion that a great man was to arise, and save the Church, and save the State. They looked back to Moses, a divine man of antiquity, whose great life had passed into the world, and to whom men had done honor in various ways; amongst others, by telling all sorts of wonders he wrought, and declaring that none could be so great again; none get so near to God. They looked back also to the prophets, a long line of divine men, so they reckoned, but less than the awful Moses; his stature was far above the nation, who hid themselves in his shadow. Now the well-instructed children of Abraham thought the next great man must be only a copy of the last, repeat his ideas, and work in the old fashion.

*　　*　　*　　*

There were men not counted in the organized sects; men weary of absurdities; thirsting for the truth; sick, they knew not why nor of what, yet none the less sick, and waiting the angel who should heal them, though by troubled waters and remedies unknown. These men had not the prejudices of a straightly organized and narrow sect. . . . They were "unlearned and ignorant men," those early followers of Christ. Nay, Jesus himself had no extraordinary culture—as the world judges of such things. His townsmen wondered, on a famous occasion, how he had learned to read. He knew little of theologies, it would seem. . . . The men of Galilee did not need theology. . . . They did need religion; they did see it as Jesus unfolded its loveliness; they did welcome it when they saw; welcome it in their hearts.

*　　*　　*　　*

Jesus looked to God for his truth, his great doctrines not his own—private, personal, depending on his idiosyncrasies, and therefore only subjectively true,—but God's, universal, everlasting, the Absolute Religion. I do not know that he did not teach some errors also along with it. I care not if he did. It is by his truths that I know him, the Absolute Religion he taught and lived; by his highest sentiments that he is to be appreciated. He had faith in God and obeyed God; hence his inspiration, great, in proportion to the greater endowment, moral and religious, which God gave him, great likewise in proportion to his perfect obedience. He had faith in Man none the less. Whoever yet had faith in God that had none in Man? I know not.

Surely no inspired prophet. As Jesus had faith in Man, so he spoke to men. Never yet, in the wide world, did a prophet arise, appealing with a noble heart to a noble life, to the soul of goodness in man, but that soul answered to the call. It was so most eminently with Jesus.

* * * *

This then was the relation of Jesus to his age; the sectarians cursed him; cursed him by their Gods; rejected him, abused him, persecuted him, sought his life. Yes, they condemned him in the name of God. . . . The Religionists, the sects, the sectarian leaders rejected him, condemned him, slew him at the last, hanging his body on a tree.

* * * *

The character of Jesus has not changed; his doctrines are still the same; but what a change in his relation to the age—nay to the ages. The stone that the builders rejected is indeed become the head of the corner, and its foundation, too. He is worshiped as a God. That is the rank assigned him by all but a fraction of the Christian world. It is no wonder. Good men worship the best thing they know—and call it God. . . . Jesus was the Prince of Peace, the King of Truth, praying for his enemies—"Father forgive them, for they know not what they do!" The Jehovah of the Old Testament—was awful and stern—a man of war, hating the wicked. The sacerdotal conception of God at Rome and Athens was lower yet. No wonder then, that men soon learned to honor Jesus as a God, then as God himself. . . . It is for his Truth and his Life, his Wisdom, Goodness, Piety, that he is honored in my heart—yes, in the world's heart. It is for this that in his name are churches built, and prayers are prayed; for this that the best things we know, we honor with his name.

Francis G. Peabody   (*1847–1936*)

A DOMINANT NOTE OF STRENGTH

What then, was the character of Jesus Christ? What kind of Person is this from whom so rich and persuasive a teaching proceeds? Detaching ourselves, so far as practicable, from the traditions and presuppositions which thrust themselves between the Gospels and their readers; setting ourselves in imagination, if we may, on a hillside in Galilee or in a street in Jerusalem, in the days of Jesus, what, we ask ourselves, is the impression we receive from this new teacher who arrests our attention and compels our obedience?

It would be of extraordinary interest if we might in the first place picture to ourselves the external appearance and physical traits of Jesus. The simple record, however, offers practically no material for the reproduction of his face or form. It is indeed reported, not without great suggestiveness, that the first impression of his teaching was for the moment created not so much by its contents, striking as these were, as by the demeanour and personality of the Teacher. "He taught as one having authority," is the first comment of the narrator. There was a calmness and mastery, a force and restraint, an originality and reverence, which dominated the scene. As Jesus proceeded in his ministry, this effect of His personal bearing is often evident. To a soldier He seemed like a commander who was born to be obeyed; to many a hearer He had but to say, "Follow me," and busy men left all and followed; to minds possessed by devils He had but to speak and they grew self-controlled and calm. . . . Little children, on the other hand, came when He called, and nestled in His arms; women followed Him and ministered unto him gladly. Command and sympathy, power and charm, must have been singularly blended in a person Who drew to himself such varied types of loyalty. Authority and affection, playfulness and gravity, the light of love and the shadow of rebuke, must have touched in quick succession the face of Jesus. . . .

On almost every page of the Gospels there are indications that the new master was neither unlettered nor untrained, but equipped with intellectual as well as spiritual authority. . . . An interesting witness of this untaught wisdom may be found in the attitude of Jesus to the world of nature. It would be misleading to speak of his mind as scientific, for there is in him no trace of the special discipline in which students of science are trained. His attitude towards nature, however, is the prerequisite of the scientific mind. Nature in every phase and form is his instructor, his companion, his consolation, and each incident of nature is observed by him with sympathetic insight and keen delight. He is a poet rather than a naturalist; but with him as with all great interpreters of nature, poetic insight gives significance to the simplest facts. The hen and her chickens, the gnat in the cup, the camel in the narrow street, the fig-tree and its fruit, the fishermen sorting their catch—all these and many others of the slightest incidents which met his observant eye become eloquent with the great message of the Kingdom. . . .

A further and still more striking evidence of this intellectual mastery was a certain lightness of touch which Jesus often employed in controversy, and which sometimes approaches the play of humour, and sometimes the thrust of irony. His enemies attack Him with bludgeons, and he defends himself with a rapier. No test of mastery is more complete than this capacity to make of playfulness a weapon of reasoning. The method of Jesus pierces through the subtlety and obscurity of His opponents with such refinement and dexterity that the assailant hardly knows that he is hit. Inside of a direct reply, the immediate question is parried and turned aside, and the motive which lies behind is laid bare. . . .

There are two ways in which the conduct of Jesus discloses a character whose dominant note is strength, and both of these habits of life increase the pathos and impressiveness of his character. The first is the prodigality of his sympathy; the second is his solitude of soul. . . . He is equally at home with the most varied types. He moves with the same sense of familiarity among rich and poor, learned and ignorant, the happy and the sad. . . . The sympathy of Jesus is the channel through which his power flows, and the abundance of the stream testifies to the reserve of power at the source.

The second mark of the conduct of Jesus is his spiritual solitude. Give himself as he may to others in lavish word and deed, there remains within the circle of these relationships a sphere of isolation and reserve. Eager as he is to communicate his message, there are aspects of it which, he is forced to see, are incommunicable, so that his language has at times a note of helplessness. Men see, but they do not perceive; they hear, but they do not understand. No man knoweth the Son but the Father; neither knoweth any man the Father save the Son. . . .

Here indeed is the pathos of the character of Jesus; yet here also we approach the source of his strength. It was in this detachment of nature, this isolation of the inner life, that Jesus found his communion with the life of God. . . . The tide of the Spirit ebbs from him in the throng, and when he goes apart He is least alone, because the Father is with him. Thus from utterance to silence, from giving to receiving, from society to solitude, the rhythm of his nature moves, and the power which is spent in service is renewed in isolation. . . . He is able to bear the crosses of others because he bears His own.

WILLIAM LYON PHELPS   (*1865–1943*)

FREEDOM IN HIS SERVICE

We cannot emphasize too strongly the fact that Christianity is a personal religion. The gateway to Christianity is not through an intricate labyrinth of dogma, but by a simple belief in the person of Christ. Leave dogma to those who enjoy it; the true Christian is simply a member of Christ's society, of his party, one of his followers. I cannot understand the nature of the Infinite Energy; but I can follow Jesus Christ, because he took the form of a young man, and we have the story of his life, actions, and words. I think he was wiser and better than Abraham Lincoln, George Washington, or Theodore Roosevelt; I find it easier to be a Christian partisan than to be a Republican or Democrat. I have more faith in the practical wisdom and knowledge of Jesus than I have in that of Julius Caesar or of any statesman, soldier or philosopher. He had more common sense than any person I ever saw, heard, or read of; he was the most independent and the most courageous individual of whom we have any record. In his service there is freedom.

In the beginning was the Word, and the Word was made flesh and dwelt among us. God speaks to me not through the thunder and the earthquake, not through the ocean and the stars, but through the Son of Man, and speaks in a language adapted to my imperfect sight and hearing. I want to follow the Best I know, and here it is. If any one can show me anything better, I will follow that.

John Cowper Powys   (*1872–*   )

"A TERRIFYING REALIST"

St. Luke's Jesus is a terrifying realist. He is so much a realist that he refuses, just as his heroic antagonist Nietzsche did, to dodge or cover up with ideal phrases the ultimate contradiction between the will to power in us and the will to sacrifice. Neither of them compromised: for the one said, "Not my will but Thine be done!" and the other said, "Not I, but the Overman!" But we must confess the truth—the truth which as children, learning our "gentle-Jesus" rigmaroles, we longed to cry out!—the truth that St. Luke's Jesus is startlingly, shockingly, violently *arbitrary*. Inconsistency is the life-breath of realism. It is not our instinct, it is our reason that is consistent—"and that way madness lies." Had St. Luke's Jesus displayed the "sweet reasonableness" with which Matthew Arnold credited him humanity would never have been brought to worship him as a

God. Nietzsche has described some of the qualities of his Overman; but a far more interesting problem is "What are the qualities necessary to a Man-God?"

And this great problem has been solved once for all by St. Luke. This great biographer emphasizes in his magical picture of Jesus exactly those qualities that lend themselves most to the desire, to the desperate *determination* of the anonymous generations of humanity that some particular "Son of Man" should be also the "Son of God." And is it necessary to repeat, what our vermicular pilgrim through the library of Theophilus has already discovered, that among these essential qualities in the making of a God is not justice, not morality, not self-control, not stoicism, not reason, not consistency, that supply the necessary chemistry? And this is natural enough; for all these are qualities adapted rather to *disciples* of the "kingdom" than to its "King."

J. B. Priestley (1894–   )

A FIGURE OF SELF-SACRIFICE

Jesus is the great symbolic figure of self-sacrifice. Nearly all the conventional moralists, if they had known him during his last years, would not have hesitated to denounce him as a tremendous egoist, steeped in selfishness. He took leave of his occupation, his home, relatives, friends, encouraged other men to take leave of theirs. He must be held responsible for a wholesale neglect of duty. Yet how could he have realised his own nature, and helped millions of others to realise theirs, if he had followed any other course of conduct? . . . It is clear that unless many men had not led lives that made them seem to countless good folk sheer monsters of selfishness, the world would have lost much of value.

W. S. Rainsford   (1850–1933)

WHERE DIVINENESS LIES

Jesus was realest of the real. He shared the beliefs of His time. He believed in the nearness of the parousia—as did Paul—and was mistaken. He was under *all* the conditions not only of humanity, but of the humanity of His time and place. So much was essential to a true incarnation. Incarnation meant conditions. He did not know any more about philosophy or philology, about history or natural laws, than did any Jew about Him, *except in so far as a pure heart helps knowledge.*

The more convincedly we believe in the *Incarnation,* the more strongly must we hold to the conditions and limitations of it; without them the Incarnation is not real. Where, then, is the Divineness? It is in the perfection of His obedience, and the resulting absoluteness of His moral and spiritual verdicts.

Ernest Renan   (1823–1892)

FOUNDER OF AGELESS PURE WORSHIP

Translated by Charles Edwin Wilbour

On the day when he pronounced these words ["the true worshippers shall worship the Father in spirit and in truth"], he was indeed the Son of God. He for the first time gave utterance to the idea upon which shall rest the edifice of the everlasting religion. He found the pure worship, of no age, of no clime, which shall be that of all lofty souls to the end of time. Not only was his religion, that day, the benign religion of humanity, but it was the absolute religion: and if other planets have inhabitants endowed with reason and morality, their religion cannot be different from that which Jesus proclaimed at Jacob's well. Man has not been able to abide by this worship; we attain the ideal only for a moment. The words of Jesus were a gleam in thick night; it has taken eighteen hundred years for the eyes of humanity (who do I say! of an infinite small portion of humanity) to learn to abide it. But the gleam shall become the full day, and, after passing through all the circles of error, humanity will return to these words, as to the immortal expression of its faith and its hopes.

JOHN RUSKIN   *(1819–1900)*

TRANSFIGURATION A PREPARATION FOR DEATH

We are afraid to harbour in our own hearts, or to utter in the hearing of others, any thought of our Lord, as hungering, tired, sorrowful, having a human soul, a human will, and affected by the events of human life as a finite creature is; and yet one-half of the efficacy of His atonement, and the whole of the efficacy of His example depend on His having been this to the full.

Consider, therefore, the Transfiguration as it relates to the human feelings of our Lord. It was the first definite preparation for His death. He had foretold it to His disciples six days before; then taken with Him the three chosen ones into "an high mountain apart." . . . What other hill could it be than the southward slope of that goodly mountain, Hermon, which is indeed the centre of all the Promised Land, from the entering in of Hamath unto the river of Egypt; the mount of fruitfulness, from which the springs of Jordan descended to the valleys of Israel. Along its mighty forest avenues, until the grass grew fair with the mountain lilies, His feet dashed with the dew of Hermon, He must have gone to pray his first recorded prayer about death; and from the steep of it, before he knelt, could see to the south all the dwelling-place of the people that had sat in darkness, and seen the great light, the land of Zabulon and of Naphtali, Galilee of the Gentiles; could see, even with His human sight, the gleam of that lake by Capernaum and Chorazin, and many a place loved by Him, and vainly ministered to, whose house was now left unto them desolate; and, chief of all, far in the utmost blue, the hills above Nazareth, sloping down to His old home; hills on which the stones yet lay loose, that had been taken up to cast at Him, when He left them forever.

"And as He prayed two men stood by Him." Among the many ways in which we miss the help and hold of Scripture, there is none more subtle than our habit of supposing that, even as man, Christ was free from the Fear of Death. How could He then have been tempted as we are?—since among all the trials of the earth none spring from the dust more terrible than that of Fear. It had to be borne by Him . . . and the presence of it is surely marked for us enough by the rising of those two at His side.

GEORGE WILLIAM RUSSELL (AE) (1867–1935)

INCARNATE IN ALL HUMANITY

Among the many immortals with whom ancient myth peopled the spiritual spheres of humanity are some figures which draw to themselves a more profound tenderness than the rest. Not Aphrodite rising in beauty from the faery foam of the first seas, not Apollo with sweetest singing, laughter, and youth, not the wielder of the lightning could exact the reverence accorded to the lonely Titan chained on the mountain, or to that bowed figure heavy with the burden of the sins of the world; for the brighter divinities had no part in the labour of man, no such intimate relation with the wherefore of his own existence so full of struggle. The more radiant figures are prophecies to him of his destiny, but the Titan and the Christ are a revelation of his more immediate state; their giant sorrows companion his own, and in contemplating them he awakens what is noblest in his own nature; or, in other words, in understanding their divine heroism he understands himself. For this in truth it seems to me to mean: all knowledge is a revelation of the self to self, and our deepest comprehension of the seemingly apart divine is also our farthest inroad to self-knowledge; Prometheus, Christ, are in every heart; the story of one is the story of all; the Titan and the Crucified are humanity. If, then, we consider them as representing the human spirit and disentangle from the myths their meaning, we shall find that whatever reverence is due to that heroic love, which descended from heaven for the redeeming of a lower nature, must be paid to every human being. Christ is incarnate in all humanity. Prometheus is bound for ever within us. They are the same. They are a host, and the divine incarnation was not spoken of one, but of all those who, descending into the lower world, tried to change it into the divine image, and to wrest out of chaos a kingdom for the empire of light. The angels saw below them in chaos a senseless rout blind with elemental passion, for ever warring with discordant cries which broke in upon the world of divine beauty; and that the pain might depart, they grew rebellious in the Master's peace, and descending to earth the angelic lights were crucified in men. They left so radiant worlds, such a light of beauty, for earth's grey twilight filled with tears, that through this elemental life might breathe the starry music brought from Him. If the "Foreseer" be a true name for the Titan, it follows that in the host which he represents was a light which well foreknew all the dark paths of its journey; foreseeing the bitter struggle with a hostile nature, but foreseeing perhaps a gain, a distant glory o'er the hill of sorrow, and that chaos, divine and transformed, with only gentle breathing, lit-up by the Christ-soul of the universe. There is a transforming power in the thought itself: we can no longer condemn the fallen, they who laid aside their thrones of ancient power, their spirit ecstasy and beauty on such a mission. Perhaps those who sank lowest did so to raise a greater burden, and of these most fallen it may in the hour of their resurrection be said, "The last shall be first."

MAURICE SAMUEL   (*1895-*   )

NAMES TOO OVERWHELMING

We shall not understand the maniacal, world-wide seizure of anti-Semitism unless we transpose the terms. It is of Christ that the Nazi-Fascists are afraid; it is in *his* omnipotence that they believe; it is *him* that they are determined madly to obliterate. But the names of Christ and Christianity are too overwhelming, and the habit of submission to them is too deeply ingrained after centuries and centuries of teaching. Therefore they must, I repeat, make their assault on those who were responsible for the birth and spread of Christianity. They must spit on the Jews as the 'Christ-killers' because they long to spit on the Jews as the Christ-givers.

PERCY BYSSHE SHELLEY   (*1792–1822*)

GOD AS HE EXPLAINED HIM

The thoughts which the word "God" suggests to the human mind are susceptible of as many variations as human minds themselves. The Stoic, the Platonist, and the Epicurean, the Polytheist, the Dualist, and the Trinitarian, differ infinitely in their conceptions of its meaning. They agree only in considering it the most awful and most venerable of names, as a common term devised to express all of mystery, or majesty, or power, which the invisible world contains. And not only has every sect distinct conceptions of the application of this name, but scarcely two individuals of the same sect, who exercise in any degree the freedom of their judgment, or yield themselves with any candour of feeling to the influences of the visible world, find perfect coincidence of opinion to exist between them. It is [interesting] to inquire in what acceptation Jesus Christ employed this term.

We may conceive his mind to have been predisposed on this subject to adopt the opinions of his countrymen. . . . Jesus Christ probably [studied] the historians of his country with the ardour of a spirit seeking after truth. They were undoubtedly the companions of his childish years, the food and nutriment and materials of his youthful meditations. The sublime dramatic poem entitled *Job* had familiarized his imagination with the boldest imagery afforded by the human mind and the material world. *Ecclesiastes* had diffused a seriousness and solemnity over the frame of his spirit, glowing with youthful hope. . . .

He had contemplated this name as having been profanely perverted to the sanctioning of the most enormous and abominable crimes. We can distinctly trace, in the tissue of his doctrines, the persuasion that God is some universal Being, differing from man and the mind of man. According to Jesus Christ, God is neither the Jupiter, who sends rain upon the earth; nor the Venus, through whom all living things are produced; nor the Vulcan, who presides over the terrestrial element of fire; nor the Vesta, that preserves the light which is enshrined in the sun and moon and stars. He is neither the Proteus nor the Pan of the material world. But the word God, according to the acceptation of Jesus Christ, unites all the attributes which these denominations contain, and is the [interpoint] and overruling Spirit of all the energy and wisdom included within the circle of existing things. It is important to observe that the author of the Christian system had a conception widely differing from the gross imaginations of the vulgar relative to the ruling Power of the universe. He everywhere represents this Power as something mysteriously and illimitably pervading the frame of things. Nor do his doctrines practically assume any proposition which they theoretically deny. They do not represent God as a limitless and inconceivable mystery; affirming, at the same time, his existence as a Being subject to passion. . . .

Jesus Christ has said no more than the most excellent philosophers have felt and expressed—that virtue is its own reward. It is true that such an expression as he has used was prompted by the energy of genius, and was the overflowing enthusiasm of a poet: but it is not the less literally true [because] clearly repugnant to the mistaken conceptions of the multitude. God, it has been asserted, was contemplated by Jesus Christ as every poet and every philosopher must have contemplated that mysterious principle. He considered that venerable word to express the overruling Spirit of the collective energy of the moral and material world. He affirms, therefore, no more than that a simple, sincere mind is the indispensable requisite of true science and true happiness. He asserts that a being of pure and gentle habits will not fail, in every thought, in every object of every thought, to be aware of benignant visitings from the invisible energies by which he is surrounded.

JOSEPH R. SIZOO   (1884-   )

"HE LIVED WITH GENTLENESS"

Someone has defined life as sensitiveness, a feeling for others. That was supremely true of Jesus. Every man's sorrow was His sorrow; every man's sin was His burden. Many times one reads of Him sentences such as these: "When He saw the multitude He was moved with compassion for them."

*   *   *   *

The most striking characteristic and the most moving quality in the life of Jesus were his capacity for friendship. His abiding good will ran across the frontier of every racial, social, economic and political frontier. He held in the embrace of His love all mankind: The rich and the poor, the old and the young, the moron and the savant. It is true that he had intimate friends. There were those who lived in the inner circles of His comradeship. He loved some more than others. But beyond these intimate friendships Jesus lived with a sense of good will toward all mankind.

*   *   *   *

The glory of Jesus was that He lived with gentleness. He introduced a new virtue into the world, for the most beautiful and arresting thing about Him was that he was gracious. He was never impatient, never unkind: He never spoke an unlovely word nor did an unlovely deed. He met rudeness with respect, pertness with politeness and coldness with courtesy. The inbred calm, the compassionate understanding and the serene magnanimity of Jesus will live to hallow and haunt all those who would live the good life.

*   *   *   *

We all live for something. Some people live for money; some people live for power; but Jesus lived for love. A sense of brotherhood emanated from His life like an advancing summer. So great was His compassion to all, that in the end He faced His accusers and betrayers with the prayer, "Father, forgive them for they know not what they do." Jesus was great, not because He knew more than other men, but because He cared more than other men. He never permitted wrong done to Him to embitter His soul nor to force something of that same attitude in His spirit. The outgoing of His compassion reached to every human need and want.

*   *   *   *

Jesus taught the world to pronounce the name "man" with a new reverence. Because life has such great value He called a man a fool who played with it. Because personality has incredible worth he was willing to go to any extreme to help man find it again. Because man has such great possibilities He sat many hours in long conversation with those who had bruised their souls. It was because of His reverence for personality that He never walked across the threshold of a single person without his consent. He never forced the door into any man's life.

Whatever else men may say or think of Jesus, this at least all ages have confessed that He was One with great compassion. He dragged the Sorrows of ages across His soul. He could not keep Himself out of the world's misery. At midnight it was a Hebrew scholar; at daybreak it was a foundering ship; at noonday it was a fallen woman by the well; in the afternoon it was a company of hungry unemployed. At eventide the shadows of the lame, the halt and the blind fell across the threshold of His home and He healed them.

GOLDWIN SMITH   (1823–1910)

"NO PARALLEL IN HISTORY"

To the personal influence exerted by Jesus nineteen centuries after his death, and the devotion of which he is still the object, there is absolutely no parallel in history; before them the glory of Sakyamouni and of Mahomet pales. This is no doubt to be ascribed to deification. But it is also due in no small measure to spiritual impression. A figure less divine could hardly have been deified, much less have continued to be deified and be the object of adoring love, not only to pious hearts, but to high intellects down even to the present day.

OSWALD SPENGLER   (1880–1936)

AN INCOMPARABLE FIGURE
Translated by Charles Francis Atkinson

The incomparable thing which lifted the infant Christianity out above all religions of this rich Springtime is the figure of Jesus. In all the great creations of those years there is nothing which can be set beside it. Tame and empty all the legends and holy adventures of Mithras, Attis, and Osiris must have seemed to any man reading or listening to the still recent story of Jesus's sufferings—the last journey to Jerusalem, the last anxious supper, the hours of despair in Gethsemane, and the death on the cross.

Here was no matter of philosophy. Jesus's utterances, which stayed in the memory of many of the devoted, even in old age, are those of a child in the midst of an alien, aged, and sick world. They are not sociological observations, problems, debatings. Like a quiet island of bliss was the life of these fishermen and craftsmen by the Lake of Gennesareth in the midst of the age of the great Tiberius, far from all world-history and innocent of all the doings of actuality, while round them glittered the Hellenistic towns with their theatres and temples, their refined Western society, their noisy mob-diversions, their Roman cohorts, their Greek philosophy. When the friends and disciples of the sufferer had grown grey and his brother was president of their group in Jerusalem, they put together, from the sayings and narratives generally current in their small communities, a biography so arresting in its inward appeal that it evolved a presentation-form of its own, of which neither the Classical nor the Arabian Culture has any example—the Gospel. Christianity is the one religion in the history of the world in which the fate of a man of the immediate present has become the emblem and the central point of the whole creation. . . .

There was a moment in his life when an inkling, and then high certainty, came over him—"Thou art thyself It!" It was a secret that he at first hardly admitted to himself, and only later imparted to his nearest friends and companions, who thereafter shared with him, in all stillness, the blessed mission, till finally they dared to reveal the truths before all the world by the momentous journey to Jerusalem. If there is anything at all that clouds the complete purity and honor of his thought, it is that doubt as to whether he has deceived himself which from time to time seizes him, and of which, later, his disciples told quite frankly. He comes to his home. The village crowds to him, recognizes the former carpenter who left his work, is angered. The family—mother and all the brothers and sisters—are ashamed of him and would have arrested him. And with all these familiar eyes upon him he was confused and felt the magic power depart from him (Mark vi). In Gethsemane doubts of his mission mingled themselves in the terrible fear of coming things, and even on the cross men heard the anguished cry that God had forsaken him.

Even in these last hours he lived entirely in the form of his own apocalyptic world, which alone was ever real to him. What to the Roman sentries standing below him was reality was for him an object of helpless wonder, an illusion that might at any moment without warning vanish into nothingness. He possessed the pure and unadulterated soul of the townless land. The life of the cities and their spirit were to him utterly alien. Did he really see the semi-Classical Jerusalem, into which he rode as the Son of Man, and understand its historical nature? This is what thrills us in the last days—and the collision of facts with truths, of two worlds that will never understand one another, and his entire incomprehension of what was happening about him.

So he went, proclaiming his message without reservation, through his country. But this country was Palestine. He was born in the Classical Empire and lived under the eyes of the Judaism of Jerusalem, and when his soul, fresh from the awful revelation of its mission, looked about, it was confronted by the actuality of the Roman State and that of Pharisaism. His repugnance for the stiff and selfish ideal of the latter, which he shared with all Mandaeanism and doubtless with the peasant Jewry of the wide East, is the hall-mark of all his discourses from first to last. It angered him that this wilderness of cold-hearted formulae was reputed to be the only way to salvation. Still, thus far it was only another kind of piety that his conviction was asserting against Rabbinical logic. Thus far it is only the Law versus the Prophets.

But when Jesus was taken before Pilate, then *the world of facts and the world of truths were face to face in immediate and implacable hostility*. It is a scene appallingly distinct and overwhelming in its symbolism, such as the world's history had never before and has never since looked at. The discord that lies at the root of all mobile life from its beginning, in virtue of its very *being,* of its having both existence *and* awareness, took here the highest form that can possibly be conceived of human tragedy. In the famous question of the Roman Procurator: "What is truth?"—the one word that is race-pure in the whole Greek Testament—lies *the entire meaning of history,* the exclusive validity of the deed, the prestige of the State and war and blood, the all-powerfulness of success and the pride of eminent fitness. Not indeed the mouth, but the silent feeling of Jesus answers this question by that other which is decisive in all things of religion— *What is actuality?* For Pilate actuality was all; for him nothing. Were it anything, indeed, pure religiousness could never stand up against history and the powers of history, or sit in judgment on active life; or if it does, it ceases to be religion and is subjected itself to the spirit of history. . . .

There is no bridge between directional Time and timeless Eternity, between the *course* of history and the *existence* of a divine world-order, in the structure of which the word "providence" or "dispensation" denotes the form of causality. *This is the final meaning of the moment in which Jesus and Pilate confronted one another.* In the one world, the historical, the Roman caused the Galilean to be crucified—that was his Destiny. In the other world, Rome was cast for perdition and the Cross became the pledge of Redemption— that was the "will of God." . . .

Jesus never lived one moment in any other world but this. He was no moralizer, and to see in moralizing the final aim of religion is to be ignorant of what religion is. Moralizing is nineteenth-century Enlightenment, humane Philistinism. To ascribe social purposes to Jesus is a blasphemy. His occasional utterances of a social kind, so far as they are authentic and not merely attributed sayings, tend merely to edification. They contain nothing whatever of new doctrine, and they include proverbs of the sort then in general currency. His *teaching* was the proclamation, nothing but the proclamation, of those Last Things with whose images he was constantly filled, the dawn of the New Age, the advent of heavenly envoys, the last judgment, a new heaven and a new earth. Any other conception of religion was never in Jesus, nor in any truly deep-feeling period of history. . . .

"My kingdom is *not* of this world," and only he who can look into the depths that this flash illumines can comprehend the voices that come out of them. It is the Late, city periods that, no longer capable of seeing into depths, have turned the remnants of religiousness upon the external world and replaced religion by humanities, and metaphysic by moralization and social ethics.

In Jesus we have the direct opposite. "Give unto Caesar the things that are Caesar's" means: "Fit yourselves to the powers of the fact-world, be patient, suffer, and ask it not whether they are 'just.'" What alone matters is the salvation of the soul. "Consider the lilies" means: "Give no heed to riches *and poverty,* for both fetter the soul to cares of this world." "Man cannot serve both God and Mammon" —by Mammon is meant the *whole* of actuality. It is shallow, and it is cowardly, to argue away the grand significance of this demand. Between working for the increase of one's own riches, and working for the social ease of everyone, he would have felt no difference whatever.

WILLARD L. SPERRY   (*1882–*   )

LIVED EVER IN TWO WORLDS

The whole life and thought of Jesus and, at the last, his dying were sustained by the dual awareness of heaven and earth. Waldo Frank once said of Lincoln that the peculiar quality of religiousness which we feel in Lincoln's speeches—particularly the Second Inaugural— was due to his conscious attempt to live in two worlds at the same time. Our traditional vocabulary, as in the Prayer, calls these worlds heaven and earth. But they may with perfect propriety be given other names; eternity and time, the substance and the shadow, reality and appearance, the ideal and the actual. In all our more important experiences more than one world is at stake.

Jesus lived constantly in two worlds at the same time. He was not an ascetic, a runaway from history and the society of men, a wholly other-worldly recluse. But neither was he a "worldly" man. He was in the world, but he was not of the world, whatever those words mean and however they are to be realized.

There are moods and moments of life when we get no little inspiration from that last paragraph in Spengler's book about *Technics,* his jeremiad pronounced upon what he believes to be our dying age of industrialism:

We are born into this time and must bravely follow the path to the destined end. There is no other way. Our duty is to hold the lost position, without hope, without rescue, like that Roman soldier whose bones were found in front of a door at Pompeii, who, during the eruption of Vesuvius, died at his post because they forgot to relieve him. That is greatness. That is what it means to be a thoroughbred.

Such a stand, such a sense of duty, and such dying are undoubtedly greatness. But that stand is a transaction at one level and in a single world only. The incident, as Spengler celebrates it, is unlike the story of the death of Jesus, in which some other world than this is felt as very present. Let us grant of this other world that it is the object of our faith and not, as yet, the stuff of our knowledge. Therefore, until religion passes out of the area which must be occupied by faith and its truths achieve something like mathematical verification, we must face the fact that our beliefs may not correspond to reality. Meanwhile, there is no doubt at all as to what Jesus believed; he believed in the two independent, yet interdependent worlds, which the very idea of religion requires. And as the end drew near, the veil between the worlds was rent asunder for him by that faith.

Benedictus de Spinoza   (*1632–1677*)

HIS VOICE THE VOICE OF GOD

Translated by B. H. M. Elwes

We may be able quite to comprehend that God can communicate immediately with man, for without the intervention of bodily means He communicates to our minds His essence; still, a man who can by pure intuition comprehend ideas which are neither contained in nor deducible from the foundations of our natural knowledge, must necessarily possess a mind far superior to those of his fellow men, nor do I believe that any have been so endowed save Christ. To Him the ordinances of God leading men to salvation were revealed directly without words or visions, so that God manifested Himself to the Apostles through the mind of Christ as he formerly did to Moses through the supernatural voice. In this sense the voice of Christ, like the voice which Moses heard, may be called the voice of God, and it may be said that the Wisdom of God (i.e., wisdom more than human) took upon itself in Christ human nature, and that Christ was the way of salvation. I must at this juncture declare that those doctrines which certain churches put forward concerning Christ, I neither affirm nor deny, for I freely confess that I do not understand them. What I have just stated I gather from Scripture, where I never read that God appeared to Christ, or spoke to Christ, but that God was revealed to the Apostles through Christ; that Christ was the Way of Life, and that the old law was given through an angel, and not immediately by God; whence it follows that if Moses spoke with God face to face as a man speaks with his friend (i.e., by means of their two bodies) Christ communed with God mind to mind. . . .

I do not think it necessary for salvation to know Christ according to the flesh: but with regard to the Eternal Son of God, that is the eternal Wisdom of God, which has manifested itself in all things, and especially in the human mind, and above all in Jesus Christ, the case is far otherwise. For without this no one can come to a state of blessedness, inasmuch as it alone teaches, what is true or false, good or evil. And inasmuch as this wisdom was made especially manifest through Jesus Christ, as I have said, His disciples preached it, in so far as it was revealed to them through Him, and thus showed that they could rejoice in that spirit of Christ more than the rest of mankind.

T. DeWitt Talmage   (*1832–1902*)

HIS THE SPIRIT OF WORK

The spirit of Christ was the *spirit of work*. There was not a lazy moment in all His life. Whether he was talking to the fishermen on the beach, or preaching to the sailors on the deck, or addressing the rustics amid the mountains, or spending the summer evenings in the village, He was always busy. Hewing in the carpenter's shop. Helping the lame man to walk without any crutch. Curing the child's fits. Providing rations for a hungry host. Always busy, He was. The hardy men that pulled out the net from Gennesaret, full of floundering treasures; the shepherds who hunted up the grassy plots for their flocks to nibble at; the shipwright thumping away in the dock-yards; the wine-makers of En-gedi dipping up the juice from the vat and pouring it into the goat-skins—none were half so busy as He whose hands and head and heart were all full of the day's work. From the day on which he stepped out from the caravansery of Bethlehem to the day when He set His cross in the socket on the bloody mount, it was work, work, work all the way.

*   *   *   *

The spirit of Jesus was a *spirit of gentleness*. I know that sometimes He made wrathful utterances against the hypocrite and the Pharisee; but for the most part His words and His demeanor were gentle and loving and kind and patient and inoffensive and pleasant. When you consider the fact that He had an omnipotence with which He might have torn to pieces the assailers of His character, it makes his gentleness seem more remarkable. Little children, who always shy off from a rough man, rushed into His presence and clambered on Him, until people had to tell them to stand back. Invalids, so sore with disease that they shuddered to have anyone come near them, asked Him to put His hand on their wounds; it was so very soothing. There was not a mother with so sick and delicate a babe that she was afraid to trust it in the Saviour's arms. His footstep was so gentle it would not wake up the faintest slumberer. Some rough people hustled a bad woman into His presence, and said: "Denounce her now. Blast her. Kill her." Jesus looked at her, and then looked at the assailants, and said: "Let him that is without sin cast the first stone." When a blind man sat by the wayside making a great ado because he had no vision, the people told him to hush up— that he was bothering the Master; but Christ came where he was and said to him, "What wilt thou that I do unto thee?" Gentleness of voice. Gentleness of hand. Gentleness of foot . . . the most impulsive and precipitate nature must be attracted by the gentleness of Christ. The calmness of his look shamed boisterous Gennesaret into placidity.

ALBERT PAYSON TERHUNE   (*1872–1942*)

NOT A STAINED-GLASS FIGURE

It was not until I spent long months in Syria, in my young manhood, that Christ took on a new reality to me. In those days Palestine, for the most part, was much as it had been in our Lord's day. In the back country and in the small hill towns, customs and habits and modes of thought were as primitive as when He lived there. . . .

In that atmosphere and in those surroundings I dwelt; and somehow I grew to feel I was a part of it all.

Through no conscious will of mine it taught me to understand Christ the Man; where once I had but worshiped vaguely Christ the God.

I tramped the cruelly rough trails His tired feet had pressed. I halted in the same hamlets or among their ruins. I studied the farmers or villagers or fisherfolk who lived the same lives and thought the same thoughts as had their prototype ancestors in His time.

Out of it all there came to me a new and wonderful perception of Jesus. . . .

Christ was not physically weak. I believe He was one of the hardiest and most muscular men of His time; and a terrifically formidable adversary to clash with.

Once more, remember, I am taking my facts about Him from the Bible and from the Bible alone. It is from the Bible's own statement that I know Him for a man of mighty bodily strength.

In the first place he was a Nazarene carpenter. Carpenter work, in that day and in that region, was no job for a weakling.

In my own young manhood the Nazareth carpenter shop was not far different from what it had been in our Lord's youth. I used to stand by the hour at the unfronted entrance of the shop and watch the men at work.

They had no modern labor-saving appliances. Tough logs must be hewn by hand with awkward tools. Beams and joists weighing hundreds of pounds often must be handled and swung aloft without pulleys. The day's labor called for more strength than skill.

The Nazareth carpenter and his helpers whom I used to watch were squat fellows. They were bulging of muscle; stalwart in every inch; unbelievably powerful at lifting and chopping and hammering.

The fragile and womanish body of the Christ of the stained-glass windows and of the old Masters' paintings (Honthorst's *"Christ Before Caiaphas"* in the National Gallery, in London, is the only exception I have seen)—how long could such a puny physique have lasted in a job like that? Yet, presumably, from His twelfth until His thirtieth year—"His eighteen silent years"—Christ was toiling constantly at just such labor. None but a strong man could have done that.

Let us see what physical condition these eighteen years of heaving training put Him in.

When he began His ministry he fasted for forty days, in the wilderness. Now and then, during my own lifetime, notoriety-seekers have undertaken forty-day fasts. What was the result? Long before the end of the ordeal they were in a state of collapse. Weeks of recuperation and of careful feeding and of complete rest were needed to build up their hunger-wasted systems before they could begin again the daily routine of life.

What happened to Christ immediately after His forty-day fast?

"And Jesus returned in the power of the Spirit into Galilee. . . . And He taught in their synagogues."

In other words, He went straight to work at His ministry without the need of resting from His frightfully depleting days and nights of starvation. No one but a man of incalculable endurance and strength could have done such a thing.

Barely had He returned to Nazareth from His fasting when His fellow-Nazarenes mobbed Him, crowding murderously around Him "on the brow of the hill whereon their city was built, that they might cast Him down headlong."

A weakling or even a normally strong man who had not yet had time to recover from a forty-day vigil of fasting—could have made pitifully little defense against such a wholesale assault. None but a giant in strength could hope to fight his way through an angry mob.

It would have needed a miracle to save the pallidly meager Christ of the stained-glass windows from the rush of the Nazarene manslayers.

But the real-life Christ—the Christ whose splendidly muscled body had been hardened by eighteen years of grinding heavy carpenter work—was a physical match for the yelling rabble. We read:

"But He, passing through the midst of them, went His way."

St. Luke devotes only those eleven words to the scene of Christ's

successful struggle through the close-packed human wolves. Yet the
eleven words are enough to give us a vivid mind-picture of the giant
strength cleaving its irresistible path through the rabble of less powerful men who sought to oppose its passage.

I think we are led to the notion that Christ was emaciated and
pale and weak, because of the medieval paintings of Him. There were
so-called holy men—hermits and mystics and the like—wandering
through Europe in the Middle Ages. Many of them were living skele-
tons, with matted hair and beards and thin, ethereal faces. Artists
used them as models for their pictures of our Lord, perhaps thinking
that the holier the fanatic's fame represented them, the more they
must resemble Jesus.

These painters forgot that our Lord was the friend and the welcome dinner guest of sinners. They forgot that little children flocked
joyously to Him, drawn by His gentle strength and loveableness.

Children never would have climbed onto the knees of the coldly
bloodless Christ delineated in most of the medieval paintings. Assuredly, sinners would not have sought such an attenuated glum
mystic, as their boon comrade and helper.

I used to try to duplicate some of the daily foot journeys of Christ,
through the Holy Land. I was young and an athlete, and I was well
shod. Jesus had been barefoot, and often wearied by long journeys
on the preceding days and by scarcity of food. Yet I found one or
two of those walking records, across the steep mountains, impossible
for me to equal.

No frail stain-glass Christ could have accomplished such body-
wracking hikes. It called for almost as much strength as for the
fighting of a free path through the Nazarene mob.

Nor would the drones and the greedy money-changers and their
horde of clerks and hangers-on have fled in terror from the Temple;
if a man of mere average strength had attacked them with a weapon
no more formidable than a petty "scourge of small cords."

Francis Thompson *(1859–1907)*

"NO MAN HAD SEEN HIM SMILE"

Of the most beautiful among the sons of men it is recorded that, though many had seen Him weep, no man had seen Him smile. Nor with beauty end her gifts to men. Solomon, who found in knowledge but increase of sorrow, might have found in sorrow increase of knowledge: it is less wisdom that reveals mourning, than mourning that reveals wisdom—as the Hindoo gathers secret things from gazing in the pool of ink. Power is the reward of sadness. It was after the Christ had wept over Jerusalem that He uttered some of His most august words; it was when His soul had been sorrowful even unto death that his enemies fell prostrate before His voice. Who suffers, conquers. The bruised is the breaker.

Hendrik Willem Van Loon *(1882–1944)*

NEEDS NO EXPLAINING

This leads me to still another question which no man of this Western world has been able to escape these last two thousand years: "What think you of the Christ?"

Fortunately, I can give you a completely straightforward answer. I think everything of him. I unqualifiedly accept him as one of the greatest of my gay philosophers. But I have always experienced great difficulties in getting at him because his figure was completely obscured by the dark shadow of that Paul of Tarsus who in his Pharisaic self-righteousness and arrogance had undertaken to explain him to the rest of the world as though he ought to be explained. The simple, lovable carpenter of Nazareth, so beautifully and sublimely unconscious of the practical world around him, so bravely fighting his lonely battle against those forces of malice and evil and greed which turn our lovely planet into a perpetual vale of tears—yes, he is a teacher whom I would most happily follow unto the ends of the earth. But not if Paul the tentmaker has to be one of our companions. For that brash individual would forever be pushing his unwelcome self between us, and instead of letting me listen to the Master, he would volunteer to explain what the Master really intended to say (even before he had said it) until in despair I would either have pushed him aside (in which case he would have called me a dirty Nazi or something equally unpleasant) or I would have been obliged to bid these wanderers farewell and strike out for myself—as indeed, I have been obliged to do.

That (as I am seriously convinced) is exactly what Paul has done to millions of other people. Like myself they very likely would have become Christians if only Paul had let them. Now I am obliged to meet Christ in a sort of clandestine and roundabout way. That, however, has in no way diminished the welcome I receive. I sometimes even fear that he regrets our separation as much as I. But what can he do? For his compassion is so great that he can even understand and forgive Paul. Has he ever really liked him? I don't know, but I doubt it. I doubt it very much.

Marie François Arouet de Voltaire   (1694–1778)

AN INCOMPREHENSIBLE MYSTERY

Translator Anonymous

In those days, prepared by divine providence, it pleased the eternal Father to send His Son upon earth—an adorable and incomprehensible mystery, which we presume not to approach.

We only say, that if Jesus preached a pure morality; if He announced the kingdom of heaven as the reward of the just; if He had disciples attached to His person and His virtues; if those very virtues drew upon Him the persecutions of the priests; if, through calumny,

He was put to a shameful death; His doctrine, constantly preached by His disciples, would necessarily have a great effect in the world. Once more let me repeat it—I speak only after the manner of this world, setting the multitude of miracles and prophecies entirely aside. I maintain it, that Christianity was more likely to proceed by His death, than if He had not been persecuted. You are astonished that His disciples made other disciples. I should have been much more astonished, if they had not brought over a great many to their party. Seventy individuals, convinced of the innocence of their leader, the purity of His manners, and the barbarity of His judges, must influence many a feeling heart.

LEW WALLACE   (1827–1905)

THE FACE OF A SINLESS SOUL

He was moving slowly towards them in a clear space a little to their front, a form slightly above the average in stature, and slender, even delicate. His action was calm and deliberate, like that habitual to men much given to serious thought upon grave subjects; and it well became his costume, which was an under-garment full-sleeved and reaching to the ankles, and an outer robe called the tallith; on his left arm he carried the usual handkerchief for the head, the red fillet swinging loose down his side. Except the fillet and a narrow border of blue at the lower edge of the tallith, his attire was of linen yellowed with dust and road-stains. Possibly the exception should be extended to the tassels, which were blue and white, as prescribed by law for rabbis. His sandals were of the simplest kind. He was without scrip or girdle or staff.

These points of appearance, however, the three beholders observed briefly, and rather as accessories to the head and face of the man, which—especially the latter—were the real sources of the spell they caught in common with all who stood looking at him.

The head was open to the cloudless light, except as it was draped with hair long and slightly waved, and parted in the middle, and auburn in tint, with a tendency to reddish golden where most strongly touched by the sun. Under a broad, low forehead, under well-arched brows, beamed eyes dark blue and large, and softened to exceeding tenderness by lashes of the great length sometimes seen on children, but seldom, if ever, on men. As to the other features, it would have been difficult to decide whether they were Greek or Jewish. The delicacy of the nostrils and mouth was unusual to the latter type; and when it was taken into account with the gentleness of the eyes, the pallor of the complexion, the fine texture of the hair, and the softness of the beard, which fell in waves over his throat to his breast, never a soldier but would have laughed at him in encounter, never a woman who would not have confided in him at sight, never a child that would not, with quick instinct, have given him its hand and whole artless trust; nor might anyone have said he was not beautiful.

The features . . . were ruled by a certain expression which, as the viewer chose, might with equal correctness have been called the effect of intelligence, love, pity, or sorrow; though, in better speech, it was a blending of them all—a look easy to fancy as a mark of a sinless soul doomed to the sight and understanding of the utter sinfulness of those among whom it was passing; yet withal no one could have observed the face with a thought of weakness in the man; so, at least, would not they who know that the qualities mentioned—love, sorrow, pity—are the results of a consciousness of strength to bear suffering oftener than strength to do; such has been the might of martyrs and devotees and the myriads written down in saintly calendars. And such, indeed, was the air of this one.

ALEXANDER WHYTE   (*1837–1921*)

STEEPED IN THE SPIRIT

It must often have struck you with wonder that not one word is said
in the whole of the New Testament about our Lord's intellect; only
always about His heart. The four Gospels say not one syllable about
our Lord's bodily appearance; no nor one syllable about the talents
and the endowments of His mind. Neither the strength of His understanding, nor the tenacity of His memory, nor the brilliancy of
His imagination, nor the eloquence of His speech—not one of all
these things is ever once referred to; only the meekness, and the
lowliness, and the tenderness of His heart. I am not naming them in
the same day with Our Lord. But the moment I go to the Bible and
name you Moses, or Isaiah, or John, or Paul, or go outside the Bible
and name you, say Plato, or Dante, or Shakespeare, or Newton, or
Edwards, you immediately think of the magnificent minds of those
men. The strength, the grasp, the height, the depth, the beauty, the
originality, the attainments, and the performances of those men;
in one word, the amazing minds of those men at once rise up before
you. But after what cast our Lord's mind was made; to what family
of minds His human mind belonged, if it belonged to any of our families of mind; of all that we read not one word. Nor are we ourselves
able, after all our study of our Lord, to say a single word about the peculiar talents or special endowments of His human mind. Not one
word. Only, every page of the four Gospels is full of the meekness
and the lowliness and the love of His heart. Every page, both of the
four Gospels and of all of the Epistles, is overflowing with His amazing humility, His obedience unto death, and His unquenchable and
unconquerable love to God and man. In one word it is the holiness of
our Lord's heart that fills the New Testament full and makes it the
unparalleled and unapproachable Book that it is.

It is never once said that our Lord had mind without measure,
though I must suppose that was so. The one thing that it is ever
said He had without measure was the Spirit of God. Whatever was

the nature and the degree of His mind and His understanding; both His mind and His understanding and His heart, were all filled with the Holy Ghost as full as they could hold. Our Lord's whole human spirit within Him was steeped in the Spirit of God.

OSCAR WILDE　　　　　　　　　　　　　　　(*1856–1900*)

A TRUMPET CALLING TO HEAVEN

I see a far more intimate and immediate connection between the true life of Christ and the true life of the artist; and I take a keen pleasure in the reflection that long before sorrow had made my days her own and bound me to her wheel I had written in *The Soul of Man* that he who would lead a Christ-like life must be entirely and absolutely himself, and had taken as my types not merely the shepherd on the hillside and the prisoner in his cell, but also the painter to whom the world is a pageant and the poet for whom the world is a song. I remember saying once to André Gide, as we sat together in some Paris *café,* that while metaphysics had but little real interest for me, and morality absolutely none, there was nothing that either Plato or Christ had said that could not be transferred immediately into the sphere of Art and there find its complete fulfilment.

Nor is it merely that we can discern in Christ that close union of personality with perfection which forms the real distinction between the classical and romantic movement in life, but the very basis of his nature was the same as that of the nature of the artist—an intense and flamelike imagination. He realised in the entire sphere of human relations that imaginative sympathy which in the sphere of Art is the sole secret of creation. He understood the leprosy of the leper, the darkness of the blind, the fierce misery of those who live for pleasure, the strange poverty of the rich. Some one wrote to me in trouble, "When you are not on your pedestal you are not interesting." How remote was the writer from what Matthew Arnold calls the "the Secret of Jesus." Either would have taught him that whatever happens to another happens to oneself, and if you want an inscription to read at dawn and at night-time, and for pleasure or for pain, write up on the walls of your house in letters for the sun to gild and the moon to silver, "Whatever happens to oneself happens to another."

Christ's place indeed is with the poets. His whole conception of Humanity sprang right out of the imagination and can only be realised by it. What God was to the pantheist, man was to him. He was the first to conceive the divided races as a unity. Before his time there had been gods and men, and, feeling through the mysticism of sympathy that in himself each had been made incarnate, he calls himself the Son of the one or the Son of the other, according to his mood. More than any one else in history he wakes in us that temper of wonder to which romance always appeals. There is still something to me almost incredible in the idea of a young Galilean peasant imagining that he could bear on his own shoulders the burden of the entire world; all that had already been done and suffered, and all that was yet to be done and suffered: the sins of Nero, of Caesar Borgia, of Alexander VI, and of him who was Emperor of Rome and Priest of the Sun: the sufferings of those whose names are legion and whose dwelling is among the tombs: oppressed nationalities, factory children, thieves, people in prison, outcasts, those who are dumb under oppression and whose silence is heard only of God; and not merely imagining this but actually achieving it, so that at the present moment all who come in contact with his personality, even though they may neither bow to his altar nor kneel before his priest, in some way find that the ugliness of their sin is taken away and the beauty of their sorrow revealed to them.

I had said of Christ that he ranks with the poets. That is true. Shelley and Sophocles are of his company. But his entire life also is the most wonderful of poems. For "pity and terror" there is nothing in the entire cycle of Greek tragedy to touch it. The absolute purity of the protagonist raises the entire scheme to a height of romantic art from which the sufferings of Thebes and Pelops' line are by their very horror excluded, and shows how wrong Aristotle was when he said in his treatise on the drama that it would be impossible to bear the spectacle of one blameless in pain. Nor in Aeschylus nor Dante, those stern masters of tenderness, in Shakespeare, the most purely human of all the great artists, in the whole of Celtic myth and legend, where the loveliness of the world is shown through a mist of tears, and the life of a man is no more than the life of a flower, is there anything that for sheer simplicity of pathos wedded and made one with sublimity of tragic effect, can be said to equal or even approach the last act of Christ's passion. The little supper with his companions, one of whom has already sold him for a price; the anguish in the quiet moon-lit garden; the false friend coming close to him so as to betray him with a kiss; the friend who still believed in him, and on whom as on a rock he had hoped to build a house of refuge for Man, denying him as the bird cried to the dawn; his own utter loneliness, his submission, his acceptance of everything; and along with it all such scenes as the high priest of orthodoxy rending his raiment in wrath, and the magistrate of civil justice calling for water in the vain hope of cleansing himself of that stain of innocent blood that makes him the scarlet figure of history; the coronation ceremony of sorrow, one of the most wonderful things in the whole of recorded time; the Crucifixion of the Innocent One before the eyes of his mother and of the disciple whom he loved; the soldiers gambling and throwing dice for his clothes; the terrible death by which he gave the world its most eternal symbol; and his final burial in the tomb of the rich man, his body swathed in Egyptian linen with costly spices and perfumes as though he had been a king's son. When one contemplates all this from the point of view of art alone one cannot but be grateful that the supreme office of the Church should be playing of the tragedy without the shedding of blood: the mystical presentation, by means of dialogue and costume and gesture even, of the Passion of her Lord; and it is always a source of pleasure and awe to me to remember that the ultimate survival of the Greek chorus, lost elsewhere to art, is to be found in the servitor answering the priest at Mass.

Yet the whole life of Christ—so entirely may sorrow and beauty be made one in their meaning and manifestation—is really an idyll, though it ends with the veil of the temple being rent, and the darkness coming over the face of the earth, and the stone rolled to the door of the sepulchre. One always thinks of him as a young bridegroom with his companions, as indeed he somewhere describes himself; as a shepherd straying through a valley with his sheep in search of green meadow or cool stream; as a singer trying to build out of the music the walls of the City of God; or as a lover for whose love the whole world was too small. His miracles seem to me to be as exquisite as the coming of spring, and quite as natural. I see no difficulty at all in believing that such was the charm of his personality that his mere presence could bring peace to souls in anguish, and that those who touched his garments or his hands forgot their pain; or that as he passed by on the highway of life people who had seen nothing of life's mystery saw it clearly, and others who had been deaf to every voice but that of pleasure heard for the first time the voice of love and found it as "musical as Apollo's lute"; or that evil passions fled at his approach, and men whose dull unimaginative lives had been but a mode of death rose as it were from the grave when he called them; or that when he taught on the hillside the multitude forgot their hunger and thirst and the cares of this world, and that to his friends who listened to him as he sat at meat the coarse food seemed delicate, and the water had the taste of good wine, and the whole house became full of the odour and sweetness of nard. . . .

It is tragic how few people ever "possess their souls" before they die. "Nothing is more rare in any man," says Emerson, "than an act of his own." It is quite true. Most people are other people. Their thoughts are someone else's opinions, their lives a mimicry, their passions a quotation. Christ was not merely the supreme individualist, but he was the first individualist in history. People have tried to make him out an ordinary philanthropist, or ranked him as an altruist with the unscientific and sentimental. But he was really neither one nor the other. Pity he has, of course, for the poor, for those who are shut up in prisons, for the lowly, for the wretched; but he has far more pity for the rich, for the hard hedonists, for those who waste their freedom in becoming slaves to things, for those who wear soft raiment and live in king's houses. Riches and pleasures seemed to him to be really greater tragedies than poverty or sorrow. And as for altruism, who knows better than he that it is vocation not volition that determines us, and that one cannot gather grapes of thorns or figs from thistles?

To live for others as a definite self-conscious aim was not his creed. It was not the basis of his creed. When he says, "Forgive your enemies," it is not for the sake of the enemy, but for one's own sake that he says so, and because love is more beautiful than hate. In his own entreaty to the young man, "Sell all thou hast and give to the poor," it is not of the state of the poor he is thinking, but of the soul of the young man, the soul that wealth was marring. In his view of life he is one with the artist who knows that by the inevitable law of self-perfection, the poet must sing, and the sculptor think in bronze, and the painter make the world a mirror for his moods, as surely and as certainly as the hawthorn must blossom in spring, and the corn turn to gold at harvest-time, and the moon in her ordered wanderings change from shield to sickle, and from sickle to shield.

To the artist expression is the only mode under which he can conceive life at all. To him what is dumb is dead. But to Christ it was not so. With a width and wonder of imagination that fills one almost with awe, he took the entire world of the inarticulate, the voiceless world of pain, as his kingdom, and made of himself its external mouthpiece. Those of whom I have spoken, who are dumb under oppression and "whose silence is heard only of God," he chose as his brothers. He sought to become eyes to the blind, ears to the deaf, and a cry in the lips of those whose tongues had been tied. His desire was to be to the myriads who had found no utterance a very trumpet through which they might call to heaven. And feeling, with the artistic nature of one to whom suffering and sorrow were modes through which he could realise his conception of the beautiful, that an idea is of no value till it becomes incarnate and is made an image, he made of himself the image of the Man of Sorrows, and as such has fascinated and dominated art as no Greek god ever succeeded in doing.

GOD

HIS DIVINITY CALLED DEBATABLE

No argument that I have ever heard can satisfy my judgment, that the doctrine of the divinity of Christ is *not countenanced* by the New Testament. As little can I say that it is clearly revealed. It is often obscurely intimated; sometimes directly, and sometimes indirectly, asserted; but left, on the whole, in a debatable state, never to be either demonstrated or refuted until another revelation shall clear it up.

Anonymous *

SENT AS GOD AND MAN

Translated by Rev. L. B. Radford

For this is no earthly discovery, as I said, which was delivered into their charge; it is no mortal idea which they regard themselves bound so diligently to guard; it is no stewardship of merely human mysteries with which they have been entrusted. But God Himself in very truth, the almighty and all-creating and invisible God, Himself from heaven planted among men and established in their hearts the Truth and the Word, the holy, incomprehensible Word, sending to men not a servant, as one might imagine, or an angel or ruler, or one of those who administer earthly things, or one of those who have been entrusted with the ordering of things in heaven, but the very Artificer and Creator of the universe Himself, by whom He made the heavens, by whom He enclosed the sea within the bounds of its own, whose mysteries all the elements faithfully observe, from whom the sun has received the measure of his daily course to keep, whom the moon obeys and He bids her shine at night, whom the stars obey as they

* This is taken from an ancient document called *The Epistle* to Diognetus, of unknown authorship and undetermined date. Some authorities place it in the second century, others as late as the seventh century.

follow the course of the moon, by whom all things have been ordered and defined and placed in subjection, the heavens and things in the heavens, the earth and things in the earth, the sea and things in the sea, fire, air, abyss, things in the heights above, things in the depths beneath, things in the space between—He is was whom God sent to men.

Did he send Him, as a man might think, on a mission of domination and fear and terror? Indeed He did not, but in gentleness and meekness He sent Him, as a king sending his own son who is himself a king; He sent Him as God, He sent Him as man to man, He sent Him with the idea of saving, of persuading, not of forcing; for force is no part of the nature of God. He sent Him as inviting, not as pursuing man; He sent Him in love, not in judgment. For He will send Him in judgment; and who shall stand before His presence? (Dost thou not see them) flung to the wild beasts, to make them deny their Lord, and yet unconquered? Dost thou not see that the more of them are punished the more their numbers increase? These things look not like the achievements of man; they are the power of God; they are the proofs of His presence.

St. Augustine (Bishop of Hippo)   *(354 A.D.–430 A.D.)*

"THE COUNTRY WHITHER WE GO"

Translated by Rev. R. G. Macmullen, M.A.

Ye know brethren, for ye have learnt it as believing in Christ, and continually too do we by our ministry impress it upon you, that the humility of Christ is the medicine of man's swollen pride. For man would not have perished, had he not been swollen up through pride. . . .

He then Who could do so great things, was hungry, and athirst, was wearied, slept, was apprehended, beaten, crucified, slain. This is the way; walk by humility, that thou mayest come to eternity. Christ-God is the Country whither we go. Christ-Man is the Way whereby we go. To Him we go, by Him we go; why fear we lest we go astray? He departed not from the Father; and came to us. He sucked the breasts, and contained the world. He lay in a manger, and He fed the angels. God and man, the same God Who is Man, the same Man Who is God. . . .

Fear Christ above; recognize Him below. Have Christ above bestowing His bounty, recognize Him here in need. Here He is poor, there He is rich. . . . Lo, we have proved Christ poor; that Christ is Rich, who knows not? And even here it was a property of these riches to turn water into wine. If he who has wine is rich, how rich is He who maketh wine? So then Christ is rich and poor; as God rich, as Man, poor.

Henry Ward Beecher *(1813–1887)*

"THE NAME ABOVE EVERY NAME"

If you gather together the witnesses and the martyrs that have lived in every age since the Master lived—the great men and the nobles, of whom the world was not worthy; the men that died in prisons; by the rack, and at the stake; the men that followed their Master through suffering into death—there is not one name of them all that is not dwarfed by the side of the name of Jesus. There is not one of them that has his calmness, his simplicity, his depth, his spiritual fervor and foresightedness, his essential divinity. There is not one that has the compass of being which all of us perceive in him.

If you go from the best specimens of men to philosophers, to poets, to scholars who have developed on the Greek side—on the side of reason, that is—I need not say that whatever admiration is bestowed upon them, no one would dream that their name was to be mentioned by the side of Him of Nazareth and of Calvary. Artists, benefactors, the crowd of great men that have adorned and enriched and blessed the world—multitudes there have been of them; but they are each and all of them unspeakably inferior to Christ in the conception of men. In the very thought and feeling of the race, they are below the name of Jesus. Cite any single name from any department of life, and put the name of Christ by it, and it goes out in a moment, as a star goes out when the sun rises. . . .

Is there anywhere out of Christ such a conception of justice, such imperialness, such sovereignty, as there is in him? Is government anywhere set forth in colors so serene and pure, so august and rightful, as in him? Is there anywhere else, in all those names that signify authority, power and government, such paternity as there is in the name of Jesus Christ? Already his name stands higher for the very qualities which go to make courts illustrious; for the very things that make men glorious in history. Once, a culprit, under the hand of Rome, which reached through the whole earth, he died, despised and rejected of men, and made his grave with the wicked; but now, all through the world, those governments and those potentates that do not acknowledge and worship the Son are feeble and barbarous. The wheel has turned around. Power was with paganism when Christ was upon the earth; power is today with Christianity; and in all the government in all the world where power really inheres, it is true that that name is, ostentatiously often, but whether ostentatiously or not, really placed higher than any other; and he is today King of kings and Lord of lords.

ROBERT HUGH BENSON   (*1871–1914*)

"A GOD THAT HIDEST THYSELF"

We are told that the hidden life is one of wasted powers; that "the man would be much more useful doing some honest work instead of shutting himself up and dreaming"—and all the rest of it. . . .

This hidden life is a marked characteristic of the life of Jesus Christ in the Gospels. If we believe that He was the Eternal Word of God, it appears to us at first sight simply inexplicable that that Word should have been silent for so long. He was to spend thirty-three years upon earth, and of those thirty-three He passed ten in silence, so far as the world was concerned, for every one of His public ministry. Further, even that public ministry itself was continually broken by silences. Again and again we hear of nights in prayer, and of withdrawals from the crowd. And, in the one incident in the Gospels where types of the Active and Contemplative lives, in the presence of Martha and Mary, are strongly contrasted, it is Mary, we are told, the silent worshiper, who has "chosen the better part," and who has "the one thing needful." If it is indeed a fact that Jesus Christ reproduces in His mystical body that Life which He lived in the "days of his flesh," this huge and apparently disproportionate element of hiddenness is exactly what we should expect from a Church in which He really lives. Even after the Incarnation itself there is still truth in the cry of the Old Dispensation, "Verily thou art a God that hidest Thyself."

GEORGES BERNANOS   (*1888–*   )

POVERTY HIS BRIDE

Translated by Pamela Morris

Our Lord took poverty as his bride, and invested the poor man with such dignity that now we'll never get him off his pedestal. He gave him an ancestor—and what an ancestor! A name, and what a name! And now the revolt of the poor man inspires us more than his resignation, he seems to be already part of the Kingdom of God, where the first shall be the last; he is like a spectre at the King's Feast, in his wedding garment. . . . Ah, the poor take some getting rid of! Well, they're still having a last try in Russia. . . .

After all, theirs isn't such a fool's plan. Get rid of the poor—that's always been the idea, since the poor man bears witness of Jesus

Christ, the heir of Jewry, isn't that it?—but instead of making him a beast of burden or wiping him off the face of the earth, they've got the notion of turning him into a small *rentier* or even . . . into a low-grade government official.

*   *   *   *

The poor are an easy audience to gull, when you know how to go about it. Go and talk cures to an incurable, he'll be only too anxious to believe you. Nothing easier, come to think of it, than to make them feel poverty as a shameful illness, unworthy of a civilized country, that we're going to get rid of the filthy thing in no time. But which one of us would dare to speak thus of the poverty of Jesus Christ?

*   *   *   *

"If you really sought our Lord you'd end by finding Him," I used to say. He always answered: "I'm looking for God among the poor, where I've the best chance of ever finding Him." But the trouble was that his "poor" were chaps of his own sort. They weren't really poor at all, they were rebels, masters! I said to him one day: "And suppose Jesus were really waiting for you in the guise of one of these worthy people you despise so? Because apart from sin, He takes on Himself and sanctifies all our wretchedness. A coward may be only some poor creature crushed down by overwhelming social forces like a rat caught under a beam; a miser may be miserably anxious, deeply convinced of his impotence and raked with fear of not 'making good.'" Some people who seem brutally heartless may suffer from a kind of "poverty-phobia"—one often meets it—a terror as difficult to explain as the nervous fear of mice or spiders. "Do you ever look for Christ among people of that kind?" I asked him. "And if you don't, then what are you grousing about? You've missed Christ, yourself." And perhaps, after all, he did miss Him.

ANNIE W. BESANT   (*1847–1933*)

HIS DIVINITY REJECTED

On examining these four biographies of Jesus, we find a remarkable similarity between the three of them, amid many divergences of detail. Some regard them therefore, as the condensation into writing of the oral teaching of the apostles, preserved in the various Churches they severally founded, and so naturally, the same radically although diverse in detail. . . . We gather from them an idea of Jesus which is substantially the same: a figure, calm, noble, simple, generous; pure in life, eager to draw men to that love of the Father and devotion to the Father which were his own distinguishing characteristics; finally, a teacher of a simple and high-toned morality, perfectly un-fettered by dogmatism. The effect produced by the sketch of the fourth Evangelist is totally different. The friend of sinners has dis-appeared (except in the narrative of the woman taken in adultery, which is generally admitted to be an interpolation), for his whole time is occupied in arguing about his own position; "the common people" who followed and "heard him gladly" and his enemies, the Scribes and Pharisees, are all massed together as "the Jews," with whom he is in constant collision; his simple style of preaching—parabolic indeed, as was the custom of the East, but consisting of parables intelligible to a child—is changed for mystical discourses causing perpetual misunderstandings, the true meaning of which is still wrangled about by Christian theologians; his earnest testimony to "your heavenly Father" is replaced by a constant self-assertion; while his command "do this and ye shall live," is exchanged for "believe on me or perish."

*   *   *   *

We have noted the numerous discrepancies between the history of this gospel and that of the three synoptics, we have discovered it to be equally opposed to them in morals as well as in history; in doctrine as in morals. We have seen that, while it degrades God to enthrone

Jesus, it also degrades Jesus, and so lowers his character that it defies recognition. Finally, we have found it stands alone in supporting the Deity of Jesus from his own mouth. . . . I rejected it from beginning to end.

NAPOLEON BONAPARTE   (*1769–1821*)

"JESUS IS NOT A MAN"

Translator Anonymous

The nature of Christ's existence is mysterious, I admit; but this mystery meets the wants of man—reject it, and the world is an inexplicable riddle—believe it, and the history of our race is satisfactorily explained. . . .

Christ never hesitates, never varies in his instructions, and the least of his assertions is stamped with a simplicity and a depth which captivates the ignorant and the learned, if they give it their attention.

Nowhere is to be found such a series of beautiful thoughts, fine moral maxims, following one another like ranks of a celestial army, and producing in the soul the same emotion as is felt in contemplating the infinite extent of the resplendent heavens on a fine summer night. . . .

What a proof it is of the divinity of Christ, that, with so absolute an empire, his single aim is the spiritual melioration of individuals, their purity of conscience, their union to the truth, their holiness of soul.

My last argument is, there is not a God in heaven, if a mere man was able to conceive and execute successfully the gigantic design of making himself the object of supreme worship, by usurping the name of God. Jesus alone dared to do this; he alone said clearly and unfalteringly of himself, *I am God;* which is quite different from saying *I am a god,* or *there are gods.* History mentions no other individual who has appropriated to himself the title of God in the absolute sense. . . .

How then should a Jew, the particulars of whose history are better attested than that of any of his contemporaries,—how should he alone, the son of a carpenter, give out all at once that he was God, the Creator of all things. He arrogates to himself the highest adoration. He constructs his worship with his own hands, not stones but with men. You are amazed at the conquests of Alexander. But here is a conqueror who appropriates to his own advantage, who incorporates with himself not a nation but the human race. Wonderful! The human soul with all its faculties becomes blended with the existence of Christ.

NOTE: Above is from NAPOLEON'S ARGUMENT FOR THE DI-VINITY OF CHRIST AND THE SCRIPTURES in a conversation with General Bertrand, at St. Helena, publ. by The American Tract Society, N.Y., 1844. pp. 1, 2 & 3. This pamphlet states that the above is a "translation from a French Tract printed in Paris, with the title 'Napoleon.' The narrative is confirmed by a letter from the Reverend Dr. D. De Felice, Professor in the Theological Seminary at Montauban, France, in a communication inserted in the New York Observer of April 6, 1842. Professor De Felice closes his communication by translating from a recent French Journal the following conversation related by Count de Montholon the faithful friend of the Emperor." The pamphlet then contains the following: (pp. 7 & 8)

I know man, and I tell you that Jesus is not a man!

The religion of Christ is a mystery which subsists by its own force, and proceeds from a mind which is not a human mind. We find in it a marked individuality, which originated a train of words and maxims unknown before. Jesus borrowed nothing from our knowledge. He exhibited in himself the perfect example of his precepts. Jesus is not a philosopher; for his proofs are miracles, and from the first his disciples adored him. In fact, learning and philosophy are of no use for salvation; and Jesus came into the world to reveal the mysteries of heaven and the laws of the Spirit.

Alexander, Caesar, Charlemagne and myself founded empires; but upon what did we rest the creations of our genius? Upon *force*. Jesus Christ alone founded his empire upon love; and at this hour millions of men would die for him.

WALTER RUSSELL BOWIE   (*1882*–   )

"HE HIMSELF WAS GOD"

Jesus has had an influence which seems super-human because he *was* super-human. He has brought to man the touch of the power of God because he himself was God come down to man. The marching rhythm of the Nicene Creed proclaims him "God of God, light of light, very God of very God, begotten not made, being of one substance with the Father, by whom all things were made."

When the disciples knew Jesus first, they had no theories about him. Simply they were drawn to him, and wanted to follow where he went. They shared his life, and the power of his life touched them. Day by day he widened the horizon of their thinking. In the face of Jesus they saw the fact of God; and looking at him they understood the measure of life—so strong, so joyous, and so unafraid—which belonged to the soul that God had filled. Therefore when they asked themselves what God is like, they did not have to go to the dull definitions of the Scribes; they turned to Jesus, who spoke with authority, and who was authority. Even in all His awful greatness, God must yet be essentially like Jesus; for in Jesus they had found all that they could conceive of as adorable in God.

PHILLIPS BROOKS   (*1835–1893*)

A WONDROUS REVELATION

There have been great creative moments in the history of the world, as all history and science seem to show,—moments when after long, silent preparations, suddenly the old order broke and a new, as if by magic, came into its place. So it has been in physical and social and political history. But in neither was there any magic. The same force which was in the last changing conviction had been in all the preparation. The flower is but the ripening of the same juices that built the stem. So it is with conversion to the very last. The Christ who in Eternity opens the last concealment, and lays His comfort and life close to the deepest needs of the poor, needy, human heart, is the same Christ that first laid hands upon the blind eyes, and made them see the sky and the flowers.

It is a wondrous revelation of the Saviour. He comes to us by showing that He has been always with us. He finds the material of the Christian life in us, and builds it by His touch. Does this seem to lessen and depreciate His work? Does it take from its absolute importance? Do you ask what is the fate of the material if it is not used? That He has answered Himself in the Parable of the Talents.

HEYWOOD BROUN   (*1888-1939*)

GOOD WILL ALL-INCLUSIVE

We were sitting in a high room above the chapel and although it was Christmas Eve my good friend the dominie seemed curiously troubled. And that was strange, for he was a man extremely sensitive to the festivities of his faith.

The joys and sorrows of Jesus were not to him events of a remote past but more current and living happenings than the headlines in the newspapers. At Christmas he seems actually to hear the voice of the herald angels.

My friend is an old man, and I have known him for many years, but this was the first time the Nativity failed to rouse him to an ecstasy. He admitted to me something was wrong. "Tomorrow," he said, "I must go down into that chapel and preach a Christmas sermon. And I must speak of peace and good will toward men. I know you think of me as a man too cloistered to be of any use to my community. And I know that our world is one of war and hate and enmity. And you, my young friend, and others keep insisting that before there can be brotherhood there must be the bashing of heads. You are all for good will to men, but you want to note very many exceptions. And I am still hoping and praying that in the great love of God the final seal of interdiction must not be put on even one. You may laugh at me, but right now I am wondering about how Christmas came to Judas Iscariot."

It is the habit of my friend, when he is troubled by doubts, to reach for the Book, and he did so now. He smiled and said, "Will you assist me in a little experiment? I will close my eyes and you hold out the Bible to me. I will open it at random and run my fingers down a page. You read me the text which I blindly select."

I did as he told me and he happened on the twenty-sixth chapter of St. Matthew and the twenty-fourth verse. I felt sorry for him, for this was no part of the story of the birth of Christ, but instead an account of the great betrayal.

"Read what it says," commanded the dominie. And I read: "Then Judas, which betrayed Him, answered and said, 'Master, is it I?' He said unto him, 'Thou hast said.'"

My friend frowned, but then he looked at me in triumph. "My hand is not as steady as it used to be. You should have taken the lower part of my finger and not the top. Read the twenty-seventh verse. It is not an eighth of an inch away. Read what it says." And I read, "And He took the cup and gave thanks and gave it to them, saying, 'Drink ye all of it.'"

"Mark that," cried the old man exultantly. "Not even to Judas, the betrayer, was the wine of life denied. I can preach my Christmas sermon now, and my text will be 'Drink ye all of it.' Good will toward men means good will to every last son of God. Peace on earth means peace to Pilate, peace to the thieves on the cross, and peace to poor Iscariot."

I was glad, for he had found Christmas and I saw by his face that once more he heard the voice of the herald angels.

SIR THOMAS BROWNE (*1605–1682*)

FAITH THAT NEEDS NO MIRACLES

Some believe the better for seeing CHRIST'S Sepulchre; and, when they have seen the Red Sea, doubt not of the Miracle. Now, contrarily, I bless my-self and am thankful that I lived not in the days of Miracles, that I never saw CHRIST nor His Disciples. I would not have been one of those Israelites that pass'd the Red Sea, nor one of CHRIST'S patients on whom he wrought His wonders; then had my faith been thrust upon me, nor should I enjoy that greater blessing pronounced to all that believe and saw not. 'Tis an easie and necessary belief, to credit what our eye and sense hath examined. I believe He was dead, and buried, and rose again; and desire to see Him in His glory, rather than to contemplate Him in His Cenotaphe or Sepulchre. Nor is this much to believe; as we have reason, we owe this faith unto History; *they* only had the advantage of a bold and noble Faith, who lived before His coming, who upon obscure prophesies and mystical Types could raise a belief, and expect apparent impossibilities.

'Tis true, there is an edge in all firm belief, and with an easie Metaphor we may say, the *Sword* of Faith; but in these obscurities I rather use it in the adjunct the Apostle gives it, a *Buckler;* under which I conceive a wary combatant may lye invulnerable. Since I was of understanding to know we knew nothing, my reason hath been more pliable to the will of Faith; I am now content to understand a mystery without a rigid definition, in an easie and Platonick description.

* * * *

. . . There is but One Who Dyed salvically for us, and able to say unto Death, *Hitherto shalt thou go, and no farther;* only one enlivening Death, which makes Gardens of Graves, and that which was sowed in Corruption to arise and flourish in Glory: when Death it self shall dye, and living shall have no Period, when the damned shall mourn at the funeral of Death, when Life not Death shall be the wages of sin, when the second Death shall prove a miserable Life, and destruction shall be courted.

WILLIAM JENNINGS BRYAN   (*1860–1925*)

HE EXEMPLIFIED FORGIVENESS

The most difficult of all virtues to cultivate is the forgiving spirit. Revenge seems to be natural with man; it is human to want to get even with an enemy. . . . This was not the spirit of Christ. He taught forgiveness and in that incomparable prayer which He left as a model for our petitions, He made our willingness to forgive the measure in which we may claim forgiveness. He not only taught forgiveness but He exemplified His teachings in His life. When those who persecuted Him brought Him to the most disgraceful of all deaths, His spirit of forgiveness rose above His sufferings and He prayed, "Father, forgive them, for they know not what they do."

But love is the foundation of Christ's creed. The world had known love before; parents had loved their children, and children their parents; husbands had loved their wives, and wives their husbands; but Jesus gave a new definition of love. His love was as wide as the sea, its limits were so far-flung that even an enemy could not travel beyond its bounds. Other teachers sought to regulate the lives of their followers by rule and formula, but Christ's plan was to purify the heart and then to leave love to direct the footsteps.

How shall we account for Him? Here is the greatest fact of history; here is One who has with increasing power, for nineteen hundred years, moulded the hearts, the thoughts and the lives of men, and He exerts more influence today than ever before. "What think ye of Christ?" It is easier to believe Him divine than to explain in any other way what He said, did and was.

JOHN BUNYAN   (*1628–1688*)

"WAS LOOKED UPON OF GOD"

For by this Scripture I saw that the man Christ Jesus, as he is distinct from us as touching his bodily presence, so he is our righteousness and sanctification before God. Here, therefore, I lived for some time, very sweetly at peace with God, through Christ. Oh! methought, Christ! Christ! there was nothing but Christ that was before my eyes: I was not now (only) for looking upon this and the other benefit of Christ apart, as of his blood, burial, or resurrection; but considering him as a whole Christ; as he in whom all these and all other his virtues, relations, offices, and operations, met together, and that he sat on the right hand of God in heaven. It was glorious to me to see his exaltation, and the worth and prevalency of all his benefits, and that because now I could look from myself to him, and would reckon that all those graces of God that now were green on me, were yet but like those cracked groats and four-pence-half-pennies, that rich men carry in their purses when their gold is in their trunks at home. Oh, I saw my gold was in my trunk at home! In Christ, my Lord, and Saviour. Now Christ was all: all my righteousness, all my sanctification, and all my redemption. Further, the Lord did also lead me into the mystery of union with the Son of God; that I was joined to him, that I was flesh of his flesh, and bone of his bone; and now was that a sweet word to me in Ephes. v. 30. By this also was my faith in him, as my righteousness, the more confirmed in me; for if he and I were one, then his righteousness was mine, his merits mine, his victory also mine. Now could I see myself in heaven and earth at once; in heaven by my Christ, by my head, by my righteousness and life, though on earth by my body or person. Now I saw Christ Jesus was looked upon of God, and should also be looked upon by us as that common or public person, in whom all the whole body of his elect are always to be considered and reckoned; that we fulfilled the law by him, died by him, rose from the dead by him, got the victory over sin, death, the devil, and hell by him; when he died, we died; and so of his resurrection, "Thy dead men shall live; together with my dead body shall they rise," saith he. And again, "After two days he will revive us: and the third day we shall live in his sight." Which is now fulfilled, by the sitting down of the Son of Man on the right hand of the majesty in the heavens, according to that of the Ephesians, he "hath raised us up together, and made us sit together in heavenly places in Christ Jesus."

FRANCIS CRAWFORD BURKITT   (*1864-1935*)

"MORE ALIVE THAN EVER"

Modern representations of Jesus Christ have tended to portray Him as above all a Teacher, a Wise Sage who saw by unerring instinct what was essential in human life and conduct. But His career was not that of a Sage. Typical teachers of mankind are Socrates and Plato, in modern times Kant and Darwin, in the East Confucius and the Buddha. All these lived long, they trained up a generation to think along the lines of their new ideas, most of them took pains to organize in some way the propagation or preservation of their philosophy. The Founders of religions, again, or of particular modes of life, such as St. Benedict, have drawn up Rules for their followers. If Moses be the legendary founder of the Israelite religion, then the Pentateuch is legitimately called the Law of Moses. Moses and Benedict both lived to a good old age, and they needed it for their work. How different was the career of Jesus, yet how marvellously influ-

ential, notwithstanding apparent failure! Therefore His special characteristic cannot have been that of the Sage, the Teacher, the Founder.
It was something distinct from all these, something so well expressed
by Renan at the end of his *St. Paul,* "The son of God is unique. To
appear for a moment, to flash forth a sympathetic but piercing radiance, to die very young, that is the life of a God. To struggle, to argue,
to convince, that is the life of a Man. . . . Paul is now seeing the end
of his reign, Jesus, on the contrary, is more alive than ever."

This, it seems to me, is more than a piece of fine rhetoric; it expresses a great deal of historical truth. As I once ventured to say
(*Cambridge Biblical Essays, page* 198), it is not as a Philosopher but as
Prometheus, that we worship Christ—the Man who came down from
Heaven to give the Divine Fire. Jesus Himself once described His
mission as that of a man lighting a fire, and whatever course He may
have taken in doing it, it is at least certain that His fire has burned
for nineteen centuries and that it is alight still. The way that the
Fire was lit finds its justification in the history of the Fire.

HORACE BUSHNELL   (*1802-1876*)

"TRUEST OF ALL TRUTHS"

We take up the account of Christ in the New Testament, just as we
would any other ancient writing, or as if it were a manuscript just
brought to light in some ancient library. We open the book, and discover in it four biographies of a certain remarkable character, called
Jesus Christ. He is miraculously born of a Mary, a virgin of Galilee,
and declares himself, without scruple, that he came out from God.
Finding the supposed history made up, in great part, of his mighty
acts, and not being disposed to believe in miracles and marvels, we
should dismiss the book as a tissue of absurdities too extravagant for
belief, were we not struck with the sense of something very peculiar
in the character of this remarkable person. Having our attention ar-

rested thus far by the impression made on our respect, we are out on inquiry, the more we study it, the more wonderful as a character, it appears. And before we have done, it becomes, in fact, the chief wonder of the story; lifting all the other wonders into order and intelligent proportion around it, and making one compact and glorious wonder of the whole picture; a picture shining in its own clear sunlight upon us, as the truest of all truths—Jesus Christ, the Divine Word, coming out from God, to be incarnate with us, and be the vehicle of God and salvation to the race.

On the single question, therefore, of the more than human character of Jesus, we propose, in perfect confidence, to rest a principal argument for Christianity as a supernatural institution; for, if there be in Jesus a character which is not human, then has something broken into the world that is not of it, and the spell of unbelief is unbroken.

*   *   *   *

There is yet one other and more inclusive distinction of the character of Jesus, which must not be omitted, and which sets him off more widely from all the mere men of the race, just because it raises a contrast which is, at once, total and experimental. Human characters are always reduced in their eminence, and the impressions of one they have raised, by a closer and more complete acquaintance. Weakness and blemish are discovered by familiarity; admiration lets in qualifiers; on approach, the halo dims a little. But it was not so with Christ with his disciples, in closest terms of intercourse, for three whole years; their brother, friend, teacher, monitor, guest, fellow-traveler; seen by them under all the conditions of public ministry and private society, where the ambition of show, or the pride of power, or the ill-nature provoked by annoyance, or the vanity drawn out of confidence, would most certainly be reducing him to the criticism even of persons most unsophisticated, he is yet visibly raising their sense of his degree and quality; becoming a greater wonder and holier mystery, and gathering to his person feelings of reverence and awe at once more general and more sacred. Familiarity operates a kind of apotheosis, and the man becomes divinity, in simply being known. . . .

The most conspicuous matter, therefore, in the history of Jesus, is, that what holds true, in all our experience of men, is inverted in him. He grows sacred, peculiar, wonderful, divine, as acquaintance reveals him. At first he is only a man, as the sense reports him to be; knowledge, observation, familiarity, raise him into the God-man. He grows pure and perfect, more than mortal in wisdom, a being enveloped in sacred mystery, a friend to be loved, and a sorrow that contains the element of worship! And exactly this appears in the history, without any token of art, or even apparent consciousness that it does appear —appears because it is true.

EDMUND CAMPION   (1540–1581)

TRIUMPHS GAINED WITH HIM

Translated by Rev. Joseph Rickaby

Christ is rich, who will maintain you: He is a king, who will provide you: He is a sumptuous entertainer, who will feast you; He is beautiful, who will give in abundance all that can make you happy. Enrol yourselves in His service, that with Him you may gain triumphs, and show yourselves men truly most learned, truly most illustrious.

THOMAS CARLYLE   (1795–1881)

A LIGHT SHINING IN DARKNESS

Two men I honour, and no third. First, the toil-worn Craftsman that with earth-made Implement laboriously conquers the Earth, and makes her man's. . . .

A second man I honour, and still more highly: Him who is seen toiling for the spiritually indispensable; not daily bread, but the bread of Life. Is not he too in his duty; endeavouring towards inward Harmony; revealing this, by act or by word, through all his outward endeavours, be they high or low? Highest of all, when his outward and his inward endeavour are one: when we can name him Artist; not earthly Craftsman only, but inspired Thinker, who with heaven-made Implement conquers Heaven for us! If the poor and humble toil that we have Food, must not the high and glorious toil for him in return, that we have Light, have Guidance, Freedom, Immortality? —These two, in all their degrees, I honour: all else is chaff and dust, which let the wind blow whither it listeth.

Unspeakably touching is it, however, when I find both dignities united; and he that must toil outwardly for the lowest of man's wants, is also toiling inwardly for the highest. Sublimer in this world know I nothing than a Peasant Saint, could such now anywhere be met with. Such a one will take thee back to Nazareth itself; thou wilt see the splendour of Heaven spring forth from the humblest depths of Earth, like a light shining in great darkness.

WILLIAM ELLERY CHANNING   *(1780–1842)*

AN EXAMPLE WITHOUT RIVAL

The character of Christ . . . is singularly fitted to call forth the heart, to awaken love, admiration and moral delight. As an example it has no rival. As an evidence of his religion, perhaps it yields to no other proof; perhaps no other has so often conquered unbelief. . . . The character of Christ is a strong confirmation of the truth of his religion.

The more we contemplate Christ's character, as exhibited in the Gospel, the more we shall be impressed with its genuineness and reality. It was plainly drawn from the life. The narratives of the Evangelists . . . set before us the most extraordinary being who ever appeared on earth, and yet they are as artless as the stories of childhood. . . . The Evangelists write with a calm trust in his character, with a feeling that it needed no aid from their hands, and with a deep veneration, as if comment or praise of their own were not worthy to mingle with the recital of such a life. . . .

The character of Christ, taken as a whole, is one which could not have entered the thoughts of man, could not have been imagined or feigned . . . it bears every mark of genuineness and truth . . . it ought therefore to be acknowledged as real and of divine origin. . . .

When I consider him, not only as possessed with the consciousness of an unexampled and unbounded majesty, but as recognising a kindred nature in all human beings, and living and dying to raise them to a participation of his divine glories; and when I see him under these views allying himself to men by the tenderest ties, embracing them with a spirit of humanity, which no insult, injury, or pain could for a moment repel or overpower, I am filled with wonder as well as reverence and love. I feel that this character is not of human invention, that it was not assumed through fraud, or struck out by enthusiasm; for it is infinitely above their reach. When I add this character of Jesus to the other evidences of his religion, it gives to what before seemed so strong, a new and vast accession of strength. . . . The character of Jesus is not a fiction; he was what he claimed to be, and what his followers attested. Nor is this all. Jesus not only *was,* he is still, the Son of God, the Saviour of the world. He exists now; he has entered that Heaven to which he always looked forward on earth. There he lives and reigns.

John Jay Chapman   (1862–1933)

MYSTICISM A MOTIVE POWER

Was the very nature of life in the universe changed through Christ's existence, or by his life? We do not know enough about the nature of life to say: but it is quite probable. All that we know about God is his continuity, backward and forward, up and down and across. The element of time being illusory, like the emptiness of space, it is very likely that the nature of Being is qualified by every event, and of life by every life.

There are many people, who, like Phillips Brooks, not to speak of all the Catholic saints, actually feel Christ in their bosoms. It has of recent years, I mean during the last few decades of scepticism, become a mental habit for people to classify such experiences as illusory. But the reality of continuous power cannot be called an illusion. The most unlike and most invisible things go hand in hand in human history, and some kind of mysticism is always a motive power in human affairs. . . .

I remember thinking Phillips Brooks an absurd figure with his Christ in his bosom, a deceived person who went about exhorting the world and deceiving others. And now I see him as a man through whose bosom passed the axis of an indestructible force, which joined him with all men. This is the true church of Christ. It was Christ that revealed this structure which passes between man and man, and it is his influence that keeps revealing it freshly. I am not offended if you call this river of life—this immortal core of Godhead—the mystical body of Christ, so long as you leave it there nakedly in the universe and do not try to clap a cover on it or claim it for your sect. All men are part of it; nor is there any belief, conduct or experience through which a man can forfeit his membership in it.

VICOMTE DE CHATEAUBRIAND   (*1768–1848*)

PATTERN OF SORROW AND INDIGENCE

Translated by Charles I. White

We have seen, from the earliest ages, kings, heroes and illustrious men, become the gods of nations. But here the reputed son of a car-

penter in an obscure corner of Judea is a pattern of sorrow and in-
digence; he undergoes the ignominy of a public execution; he selects
his disciples from among the lowest of the people; he preaches naught
but sacrifice, naught but the renunciation of earthly pomp, pleasure
and power; he prefers the slave to the master, the poor to the rich,
the leper to the healthy man; all that mourn, all that are afflicted, all
that are forsaken by the world, are his delight; but power, wealth,
and prosperity, are incessantly threatened by him. He overthrows the
prevalent notions of morality, institutes new relations among men, a
new law of nations, a new public faith. Thus does he establish his
divinity, triumph over the religion of the Caesars, seat himself on the
throne, and at length subdue the earth. No! if the whole world were
to raise its voice against Jesus Christ, if all the powers of philosophy
were to combine against its doctrine, never shall we be persuaded
that a religion erected on such a foundation is a religion of human
origin. He who could bring the world to revere a cross,—he who held
up suffering humanity and presented virtue as an object of veneration to mankind,—he, we insist, can be no other than a God.

Jesus Christ appears among men full of grace and truth; the authority and the mildness of his precepts are irresistible. He comes to the
most unhappy of mortals, and all his wonders are wrought for the
wretched. "His miracles," says Bossuet, "have a much stronger character of beneficence than of power." In order to inculcate his doctrines, he chooses the apologue or parable, which is easily impressed
on the minds of the people. While walking in the fields, he gives his
divine lessons. When surveying the flowers that adorn the mead, he
exhorts his disciples to put their trust in Providence, who supports the
feeble plants and feeds the birds of the air; when he beholds the fruits
of the earth, he teaches them to judge of men by their works; an infant is brought to him, and he recommends innocence; being among
shepherds, he gives himself the appellation of *good shepherd,* and
represents himself as bringing back the lost sheep to the fold. In
spring, he takes his seat upon a mountain, and draws from the surrounding objects instruction for the multitude sitting at his feet. From
the very sight of this multitude, composed of the poor and the unfor-

tunate, he deduces his beatitudes:—*Blessed are they that mourn—blessed are they that hunger and thirst,* etc. Such as observe his precepts, and those who slight them, are compared to two men who build houses, the one upon a rock, the other upon sand. According to some commentators, he designed in this comparison to describe a flourishing village upon a hill, and huts at the foot of it destroyed by an inundation. When he asks some water of the Samaritan woman, he expounds to her his heavenly doctrine under the beautiful image of a well of living water.

The bitterest enemies of Jesus Christ never dared to attack his character. . . . There are no philosophers of antiquity but have been reproached with some vices: the very patriarchs had their foibles. Christ alone is without blemish: he is the most brilliant copy of that supreme beauty which is seated upon the throne of heaven. Pure and sanctified as the tabernacle of the Lord, breathing naught but the love of God and men, infinitely superior by the elevation of his soul to the vain glory of the world, he prosecuted, amid sufferings of every kind, the great business of our salvation, constraining men by the ascendency of his virtues to embrace his doctrine and to imitate a life which they were compelled to admire.

G. K. CHESTERTON   (*1874–1936*)

RATIONAL EXPLANATIONS OF HIS LIFE

I maintain . . . that a man reading the New Testament frankly and freshly would *not* get the impression of what is now often meant by a human Christ. The merely human Christ is a made-up figure, a piece of artificial selection, like the merely evolutionary man. Moreover there have been too many of these human Christs found in the same story, just as there have been too many keys to mythology found in the same stories. Three or four separate schools of rationalism have worked over the ground and produced three or four equally rational explanations of his life. The first rational explanation of his life was that he never lived. And this in turn gave an opportunity for three or four different explanations; as that he was a sun-myth or a corn-myth, or any other kind of myth that is also a monomania. Then the idea that he was a divine being who did not exist gave place to the idea that he was a human being who did exist. In my youth it was the fashion to say that he was merely an ethical teacher. . . . Then somebody said he was a madman with a Messianic delusion. Then others said he was indeed an original teacher because he cared about nothing but Socialism; or (as others said) about nothing but Pacifism. Then a more grimly scientific character appeared who said that Jesus would never have been heard of at all except for his prophecies of the end of the world. . . . Among other variants on the same theme was the theory that he was a spiritual healer and nothing else. . . . Now each of these explanations in itself seems to me singularly inadequate; but taken together they do suggest something of the very mystery which they miss. There must surely have been something not only mysterious but many-sided about Christ if so many smaller Christs could be carved out of him.

HENRY SLOANE COFFIN   (*1877-*   )

WHO SEES HIM SEES THE FATHER

Critical scholars who wrote reconstructions of the figure of Jesus taught that He spiritualized the realistic Messianic expectations of contemporary Judaism; that He conceived His Messianic role to be that of the Founder and Teacher of the kingdom of God; and that, when He was misunderstood and rejected, He resolved to die for His cause and thus carry it to victory. Jesus was modernized, and made acceptable to Nineteenth-Century minds. . . .

The historic Jesus, who lived, taught, suffered, and triumphed, and whose impression on the faith of His first followers is preserved for us in the New Testament, is to the Church the authoritative disclosure of the living God, Whoever sees Him with trust and loyalty sees the Father. . . . Where does God make Himself authentically known? Our answer is more nearly the answer of an earlier day than that of our immediate predecessors. We recognize with the New Testament that God has not left Himself anywhere without witness, that He has always been seeking and speaking to men as they were able to hear Him. But for us His complete Self-unveiling is in Christ, and is recorded in the Scriptures which interpret the events leading up to His advent and issuing from it in the founding of the Church. . . .

Christianity is an historic faith. Its God is the God of Abraham, Isaac and Jacob, the God of the prophets, above all the God and Father of the Lord Jesus Christ. He has revealed Himself most significantly for man's redemption and the creation of a new society in certain events of the past, of which the Scriptures, put together and treasured by the Church, are the life-transmitting record. He is revealing Himself today, but not as One other than He showed Himself in Christ. Jesus, therefore, permanently defines God for us, although we are not confined to the disclosure of God in Him. There must be a constant transmission of the heritage in the Christian classic if each new generation is to be possessed by the creative Spirit who wrought in the seers of Israel and in the Son of God. The Christian Church has its normative and authoritative Word of God given in the Bible read in the light of Jesus Christ.

*   *   *   *

The Church declares that her Lord is with His followers always, that His Spirit dwells and works unceasingly in and through the fellowship of believers, that her God is "a very present help." But this does not mean that the current experience of her members supply the main revelation of the Invisible with whom they have to do. That revelation has been given, and given once for all in its fullness, in the life, death and resurrection of Jesus Christ. This revelation is transmitted in the tradition of the Christian Church—in its Canon of Holy Scripture, in its hymns, in its prayers, in its sacraments, in its whole life. The individual Christian is the heir of this tradition, and whether he be aware of it or not, it mediates God to him. His present fellowship with God is through the historic figure of Christ, recorded in the Gospels and vital in the Church.

SAMUEL TAYLOR COLERIDGE   (1772-1834)

THE LIGHT-GIVING LIGHT OF MEN

It is the life of Christ, the co-eternal Son of God, that is the only true life-giving light of men. We are assured, and we believe, that Christ is God: God manifested in the flesh. As God, he must be present entire in every creature;—(for how can God, or indeed any spirit, exist in parts?)—but he is said to dwell in the regenerate, to come to them who receive him by faith in his name, that is, in his power and influence; for this is the meaning of the word "name" in Scripture when applied to God or his Christ. Where true belief exists, Christ is not only present with or among us:—for so he is in every man, even the most wicked: but to us and for us. *That was the true light, which lighteth every man that cometh into the world. He was in the world, and the world was made by him, and the world knew him not. But as many as received him, to them gave he power to become the sons of God, even to those that believe in his name; which were born, not of blood, nor of the will of the flesh, nor of the will of man, but of God. And the Word was made flesh and dwelt among us.* John i. 9-14. Again—*We will come unto him, and make our abode with him.* John xiv. 23. As truly and as really as your soul resides constitutively in your living body, personally and substantially does Christ dwell in every regenerate man.

HERBERT ELLSWORTH CORY   (*1883*-   )

HIS EXISTENCE PROVED

Leaving aside the pre-Christian revelations, for to deal with them
would require a whole separate volume of Biblical exegesis, let us
turn to the supreme Revealer, Jesus Christ. Assuming our Lord to
have existed—and this can be proved by modern methods of scientific history, as we shall see soon—we have to consider His Divinity.
His own protestations, although they have been challenged by some
pettifogulizers whose disagreements among themselves have reached
the point of *opera bouffé,* are unequivocal. We next consider the
possibility that He was insane or that He was mendacious. His super-
lative wisdom belies the charge of insanity. His humility in the
home of Mary and Joseph for thirty years, His sufferings during His
three years of preaching, and His prophecy of His own premature
and most dreadful death are all against the theory that He was an
ambitious liar.

In proof of the historical existence of Jesus there is a veritable library of Apologetics. . . . As a matter of fact the witnesses for the
historical authentification and for the proofs of the Divinity of Jesus,
from the earliest days, are far more comprehensive than the testimonies for the existence of many famous historical characters whose
reality we accept without question.

DOROTHY DAY   (*1899*-   )

SO LITTLE UNDERSTOOD

When He prayed in agony in the garden—when the weight of our
sins descended upon Him, all the sins that had been and that would
be committed throughout the world forever after; when He suffered
all the temptations, all the horror, all the remorse for the rest of the

world—His disciples did not understand that either. He watched and suffered alone in His agony. He had told them that the next day He was to die. And in spite of His miracles they paid so little attention to His words that they slept, as the Friend they loved most in the world struggled against the thought of His death. They left Him alone, they slept, and the next day they fled, so little did they understand His teachings, though they had been with Him for three years. They did not understand even after they had eaten with Him at the Last Supper. They did not understand until the Holy Spirit descended upon them and it was *given* to them to understand.

So how can I understand or try to tell you about it? If they who lived with Him, who could see Him as man, eat with Him, sleep with Him, and wander with Him through the countryside, if they were "offended" and dispersed, how can I try to tell you what is in my heart?

JOHN B. DELAUNAY   (*1886–   *)

A BRINGER OF JOY

An eerie light creeps up the sky, glorifying every blade of grass, weaving its gold thread into the tattered rags of the shepherds, and on the wings of the peaceful night floats an astounding melody. At first the shepherds shielded their eyes against this unwonted glory, but they are soon reassured: "Fear not," sings the angel, "for, behold, I bring you tidings of great joy, that shall be to all the people." No regret is voiced about the filled cubicles of the village inn. No reproach about Israel's unworthiness and Rome's unspeakable degradation. Sackcloth will not be the uniform of Christ's regiment—only tidings of joy, of overflowing gladness. . . .

And from now on the sun of joy warms the chilled earth. The gladness of the Divine Child streams from His Eyes upon the mother, upon the foster-father, upon shepherds, upon silk-clad Magi, and upon Simeon and Anna, and upon the land of Egypt. It is true that the shadow of the Rood has already fallen upon Nazareth's walls and broods over joyful Mary, but, in spite of dark forebodings, the little house is warm with holy joy. Whether at work or at play, or at the meal time or the hour of rest, "the benignity of Christ has appeared upon the earth," and no one needs ever be sad. Always and everywhere, as on the day of the Annunciation, "hearts are magnified."

Lest men, mistaking counterfeit for reality, believe that holiness needs be long-faced and unattractive, there must be nothing forbidding or gloomy in Christ's personal appearance. At a word or look of His, poor fishermen, hard realists of toil, abandon fishing nets and the creature comforts of home life. Labor today has not yet discovered the divine attractiveness of the great Laborer.

Thousands of men, women, and children, even forgot their meals to follow Him unto the mountain, an astounding tribute to the charm of a joyful personality. Too unnoticed has been the unnamed lad whose thoughtful mother had supplied him with a lunch of tasty broiled fish wrapped in fragrant leaves. The evening has fallen. Everyone is faint with hunger. Think of it, even that much pampered boy has forgotten to eat mother's cooking. And it is that happy forgetting that multiplies the loaves and the fishes before the smile of the sympathizing Master. . . .

And when the Divine Eyes gaze upon nature, He does not, like the prophets, select the sublime and awe-inspiring grandeur of landscape and seascape. Rather does He pick the unspectacular and smile-provoking aspects of every day life. . . .

His eye takes in the many-colored fashion-show of field flowers, and, as He walks along the Jordan, His ears catch the rustling of the reed shaken by the wind. Not for a moment, while His feet tread the earth, does He lose sight of the beauty of the earth He has created. . . .

Is it necessary to recall Christ's humaneness and almost womanly thoughtfulness about the bodily needs of man? Had not the Father fitted unto Him a body also? Did He not change water into wine— not ordinary wine, but the delicate bouquet of the desert beverage —in order that the jollity of the wedding feast be not marred by the crimson of embarrassment on the bridegroom's cheek? And think of the lavishly filled baskets after the five thousand have been fed— that too in a land where food is so scant. And did not our joyful Brother pick a well-appointed banquet hall . . . as the background for the broken alabaster vase and the healed sinner's heart, and as the sounding-board of the "go-thou-in-peace" that awakens in Magdalen and in every sin-burdened brother of mine, a joy that was, and is, Paradise indeed.

Finally, behold eleven wearied fishermen. All the long night they have toiled, but have caught nothing. Bodies are broken with fatigue, and eyes ache with watching. Little matters now but rest. Tomorrow will dawn with the care of an unprovided day. "Behold the Lord stands on the shore," but their blurred vision sees Him not. Only the love of John has recognized the Master. Even Peter who had such poignant reasons for recognizing One Who had forgiven him, even Peter must be told that "it is the Lord." . . . And when at last the boats are bright with the silvery scales of the haul, and the fishermen have come to land, too excited to think of the cause of their joy, behold there are "hot coals lying, and a fish laid thereon, and bread."

Pause over Christ's adorable thoughtfulness. In a moment he will entrust the world to His Apostles, an epochal moment of history. Instead of investing this tremendous event with the lightning of Mt. Sinai, He, as it were, harmonizes it with the fragments of well-cooked food. From earliest dawn, the Divine Hands have been busy over coals, like those of a mother preparing food for a child. And ponder his adorable playfulness. The Apostles did not recognize Him in the unexpected catch of fishes, but drawn faces break into a happy smile at the divine tenderness that plies them with a hot breakfast after the hopeless night.

FEODOR DOSTOIEVSKY   (*1821–1881*)

HE LOVED MAN'S GLADNESS

Translated by Constance Garnett

"*And when they wanted wine, the mother of Jesus saith unto him,
They have no wine*" . . . Alyosha heard.

"Ah, yes, I was missing that and I didn't want to miss it, I love that
passage; it's Cana of Galilee, the first miracle. . . . Ah, that miracle!
Ah, that sweet miracle! It was not men's grief, but their joy Christ
visited, He worked His first miracle to help men's gladness. . . .
'He who loves men loves their gladness, too' . . . *He* was always
repeating that, it was one of his leading ideas. . . ."

"*Jesus saith unto her, Woman, what has it to do with thee or me?
Mine hour is not yet come.*

*His mother saith unto the servants, Whatsoever he saith unto you,
do it.*" . . .

"Do it. . . . Gladness, the gladness of some poor, very poor, people. . . . Of course they were poor, since they hadn't wine enough
even at a wedding. . . . The historians write that, in those days, the
people living about the Lake of Gennesareth were the poorest that can
possibly be imagined . . . and another great heart, that other great
being, His Mother, knew that He had come not only to make His
great terrible sacrifice. She knew that His heart was open even to the
simple, artless merrymaking of some obscure and unlearned people,
who had warmly bidden Him to their poor wedding. 'Mine hour is
not yet come,' He said, with a soft smile (He must have smiled
gently to her). And, indeed, was it to make wine abundant at poor
weddings He had come down to earth? And yet He went and did
as she asked Him."

HENRY DRUMMOND (*1851–1897*)

TO GIVE MEN LIFE

The Churches have always held that Christ was the source of Life. No spiritual man ever claims that his spirituality is his own. "I live," he will tell you; "nevertheless it is not I, but Christ liveth in me." Christ our Life has indeed been the only doctrine in the Christian Church from Paul to Augustine, from Calvin to Newman.

*   *   *   *

It ought to be placed in the forefront of all Christian teaching that Christ's mission on earth was to give men Life. "I am come," He said, "that ye might have Life, and that ye might have it more abundantly." And that He meant literal Life, literal spiritual and Eternal Life, is clear from the whole course of His teaching and acting. . . . It is a canon of interpretation, according to Alford, that "a figurative sense of words is never admissible except when required by the context." The context, in most cases, is not only directly unfavourable to a figurative meaning, but in innumerable instances in Christ's teaching Life is broadly contrasted with Death.

*   *   *   *

He Himself assures me, "This is Life Eternal, that they might know Thee, the only true God, and Jesus Christ whom Thou hast sent." Do I not now discern the deeper meaning in *"Jesus Christ whom Thou hast sent"*? Do I not better understand with what vision and rapture the profoundest of the disciples exclaims, "The Son of God is come, and hath given us an understanding that we might know Him that is True"?

*   *   *   *

We do not pretend that Science can define this Life to be Christ. It has no definition to give even of its own life, much less of this. But there are converging lines which point, at least, in the direction that it is Christ. There was One whom history acknowledges to have been the Truth. One of His claims was this, "I am the Life." According to the doctrine of Biogenesis, life can only come from life. It was His additional claim that His function in the world was to give men Life. "I am come that ye might have Life, and that ye might have it more abundantly." This could not refer to the natural life, for men had that already. He that hath the Son hath another Life. "Know ye not your own selves how that Jesus Christ is in you."

*　　*　　*　　*

The Christian life is the only life that will ever be completed. Apart from Christ the life of man is a broken pillar, the race of men an unfinished pyramid. One by one in sight of Eternity all human Ideals fall short, one by one before the open grave all human hopes dissolve. The Laureate sees a moment's light in Nature's jealousy for the Type; but that too vanishes. . . . One Type remains. "Whom He did foreknow He also did predestinate to be conformed to the Image of His Son." And "when Christ who is our life shall appear, then shall ye also appear with Him in glory."

SHERWOOD EDDY   (*1871*-   )

"HUMANITY'S ETERNAL CONTEMPORARY"

This Jesus, strong, pure and loving, stands before us, our very brother-man. We find in him, moreover, a wonderful balance and symmetry of character. Who is this young rabbi-carpenter, who lays aside his tools and goes out to call all men to be his brothers and children of his Father in Heaven?

Someone may say, Are we not all divine? If so, what is the difference between Jesus and ourselves? Yes, I know that God is in me—as a sinner that is being saved. But God was in Jesus as a Saviour of sinners. . . .

Think also of his spiritual finality. Jesus is never out of date. He is humanity's eternal contemporary. If he were merely a good man, a well-meaning carpenter of Galilee, an unlettered peasant, we ought now, after nineteen centuries of progress, to be turning out from Oxford and Cambridge, Yale and Harvard, Paris and Berlin, better men than Jesus. Concerning what other historic character could we transfer his every attribute to God without a sense of blasphemy, and dare to say God was like him? . . . And let us remember that in the question of Jesus's divinity, it is not a mere estimate of a historic person that is at stake, but the character of God himself, our way of construing the universe, our attitude to humanity, the meaning and destiny of life itself. Your casual opinion or estimate of Socrates or Buddha, of Bacon or Shakespeare matters little; but what you think of and do with Jesus becomes for you the test of life and the touch-stone of destiny. For he is the moral ideal realized.

JONATHAN EDWARDS (*1703–1758*)

EMANATIONS OF BEAUTY

We have shown that the Son of God created the world for this very end, to communicate Himself in an image of His own excellency. He communicates Himself properly only to spirits, and they only are capable of being proper images of His excellency, for they only are properly 'beings', as we have shown. Yet He communicates a sort of shadow or glimpse of His excellencies to bodies which, as we have shown, are but the shadows of beings and not real beings. He who, by His immediate influence, gives being every moment, and by His spirit actuates the world, because He inclines to communicate Himself and His excellencies, doth doubtless communicate His excellency to bodies, as far as there is any consent or analogy. And the beauty of face and sweet airs in men are not always the effect of the corresponding excellencies of mind; yet the beauties of nature are really emanations or shadows of the excellency of the Son of God.

So that, when we are delighted with flowery meadows and gentle breezes of wind, we may consider that we see only the emanations the sweet benevolence of Jesus Christ. When we behold the fragrant rose and lily, we see His love and purity. So the green trees and fields, and singing of birds, are the emanations of His infinite joy and benignity. The easiness and naturalness of trees and vines are shadows of His beauty and loveliness. The crystal rivers and murmuring streams are the footsteps of His favor, grace, and beauty. When we behold the light and brightness of the sun, the golden edges of an evening cloud, or the beauteous bow, we behold the adumbrations of His glory and goodness; and in the blue sky, of His mildness and gentleness. There are also many things wherein we may behold His awful majesty: in the sun in His strength, in comets, in thunder, in the hovering thunder-clouds, in ragged rocks and the brows of mountains. That beauteous light with which the world is filled in a clear day is a lively shadow of His spotless holiness, and happiness and delight in communicating Himself. And doubtless this is a reason that Christ is compared so often to those things, and called by their names, as the Sun of Righteousness, the morning-star, the rose of Sharon, and lily of the valley, the appletree among trees of the wood, a bundle of myrrh, a roe, or a young hart. By this we may discover the beauty of many of those metaphors and similes which to an unphilosophical person do seem so uncouth.

In like manner, when we behold the beauty of man's body in its perfection, we still see like emanations of Christ's divine perfections, although they do not always flow from the mental excellencies of the person that has them. But we see the most proper image of the beauty of Christ when we see beauty in the human soul.

FREDERICK WILLIAM FABER   (*1814-1863*)

THE FIRST WORD EVER SPOKEN

Bethlehem was not His first home. The dark cave within, and the moonlit slope without, are not like the scenery of His everlasting home. He is the Eternal Word. He is the first Word ever spoken, and He was spoken by God, and He is in all things equal to Him by whom He was spoken. He was uttered from Eternity, and the Father who uttered Him, or rather who is forever uttering Him, is not prior to the word He utters. His home has no scenery, no walls, no shape, no form, no color, no spot that can be loved with a local love. It is in the Bosom of the Father. It is amid the unlocalized fires of the Godhead. There in the white light, inaccessible through the brilliance of its whiteness, we confusedly discern the magnificence of a Divine Person. He is unbegotten. He is not a word whom any one could utter, for there is no one to utter Him, and He is besides adorably unutterable. He is not a breath breathed forth of divine love; for there were none whose mutual love could breathe Him forth, and He is besides adorably unproceeding. The Word expresses Him, not because He utters Him, but because He is uttered by Him. The Holy spirit is His fiery breath, the Breath of the Father and the Son, coequal with them both, but with no procession from His blessed self. This Divine Person whom we confusedly discern, is like a Fountain, a fountain of golden light flowing with uncreated waters. Yet the Fountain is not a fountain without its waters, and the waters are coequal with the Fountain. Out of Him flows the Son; from Him and from His Word proceeds the Holy Ghost, all coequal, coeternal, consubstantial. Yet He is the First Person, and gloriously without superiority or precedence. He is the sole Fountain of Godhead, yet it is the very glory of the Fountain that its double streams are coequal with itself. He in His adorable sublimity is the unsent inseparable Companion of the Two Divine Persons who are sent, and who send themselves. Him, without images, we discern in the breathlessness of our far-seeing faith. Him, without light, we behold in the darkness of His blinding majesty. Him, in His outstretched immensity, we compass in the fondness of our adoring love. Him, in His name less incomprehensibility, we sweetly understand in the knowledge that We are His sons.

PETER FINLAY, S.J.   (*1851–*   )

"NOBLEST PRODUCT OF OUR RACE"

"Whom do men say that I am?" Christ asked of the Apostles; . . . Whom do the New Testament writings prove Christ to have been?

That he was a man, in all essentials like other men, is beyond controversy. . . . If anything is clear from New Testament history, it is that there was a man, Christ, born of a human mother into the world of Palestine some nineteen hundred years ago; that he lived among His fellows, a man like themselves, with human feelings, thoughts and wishes; that He suffered, and shrank from suffering; that He loved, and was gladdened by others' love; that He was put to death, and died upon a cross. No fact in all history, profane or sacred, is more certain than the existence and the reality of the human nature of Jesus Christ.

But was He more than man? I do not mean in the sense that He had a Divine mission, a God-given message to communicate, a God-given authority to make laws and to enforce them. He might be a mere man and yet have both; as Moses and others of the Prophets had. But was He Himself Divine? Had He the very nature of God? Were His words the words of God? Are His promises the promises of God? . . .

Christ Himself claims persistently and in the clearest manner to be God. Therefore I conclude he was God. I do not usually admit a man's claim merely because he puts it forward; but I do in the case of Christ. . . .

The world, whatever its religious opinion, is agreed that, if the

Gospel story be a true one, Christ was an absolutely perfect man. There is no other human character in all authentic history, there is no creation of poet or philosopher, which we would think for a moment of comparing with Him. We feel, indeed, that He must have lived and taught and acted as the Evangelists describe Him; that their story must be true; they could never have invented it. He stands apart from all who went before, and have followed after, not more in arresting the attention of mankind, and challenging their judgment of Him, than in the singular unanimity with which He has been proclaimed the highest type and expression of our humanity. "Whom do men say that I, the Son of Man, am?" He asks at Cesarea Philippi; and the answer of mankind, of orthodox, of heretic, and of infidel alike, has only grown in distinctness and in emphasis through the centuries since then. As they realize more fully how much the world owes Him, they reply more clearly: "If the Christ of the Gospel be as He is depicted there, then He is the noblest product of our race."

ANATOLE FRANCE   (*1844–1924*)

MARY DESCRIBES THE MASTER

Translated by Frederic Chapman

Mary, with arms outstretched, barred her way.

"Beware, lady," she cried, "of worshipping vain idols. Do not demand of images of stone words of hope and life. There is only one God, and with my hair I have wiped His feet."

At these words the flashing of her eyes, dark as the sky in a storm, mingled with tears, and Laeta Acilia said to herself:

"I am pious, and I faithfully perform the ceremonies religion demands, but in this woman there is a strange feeling of a love divine."

Mary Magdalen continued in ecstasy. "He was the God of Heaven and earth, and He uttered His parables seated on the bench by the threshold, under the shade of the old fig-tree. He was young and beautiful. He would have been glad to be loved. When He came to supper in my sister's house I sat at His feet, and the words flowed from His lips like the waters of a torrent. And when my sister complained of my sloth, saying: 'Master, tell her it is but right that she should aid me to prepare the supper,' He smiled and made excuse for me, and permitted me to remain seated at His feet, and said that I had chosen the good part.

"One would have thought to see Him that He was but a young shepherd from the mountains, and yet His eyes flashed flames like those that issued from the brow of Moses. His gentleness was like the peace of night and His anger more terrible than a thunderbolt. He loved the humble and the little ones. Along the roadside the children ran towards Him and clung to His garments. He was the God of Abraham and Jacob, and with the same hands that had created the sun and the stars, He caressed the cheeks of the newly born whom their happy mothers held out to Him from the thresholds of their cottages. He was himself as simple as a child, and He raised the dead to life. Here among my companions you see my brother whom He raised from the dead. Behold, lady! Lazarus bears on his face the pallor of death, and in his eyes is the horror of one who has seen hell."

St. Francis of Assisi   (*1182–1226*)

LADY POVERTY HIS SPOUSE

Translated by Constance, Countess de la Warr

Behold, LORD JESUS, Poverty is the queen of virtues, for her Thou didst leave the throne of the angels and camest down to this earth; in Thine eternal love Thou hast espoused her in order to have, by her, in her and of her perfect sons. . . .

When Thou camest forth from the Virgin's womb, she received

Thee in the holy manger, in a stable, and during Thy sojourn in the world she deprived Thee of all things in such a manner that Thou hadst not where to lay thy head. Inseparable companion, when Thou didst begin the battle of our redemption, she followed Thee faithfully; in the height of Thy Passion, she alone stood beside Thee like a squire. Thy disciples forsook Thee and denied Thee; she did not go away, but faithfully at that time supplied Thee with the whole escort of her sisters. Even Thy Mother, who alone remained steadfastly attached to Thee and shared Thy Passion with so much anguish, Thy Mother because of the height of the cross could not reach Thee. But Lady Poverty, with all her privations, like a gentle maiden embraced Thee more chastely than ever, she was more intimately united with Thee in Thy crucifixion. She took no trouble, as is usual, to polish and arrange Thy Cross. She did not furnish—will it be believed?—nails enough to pierce Thee; they were neither sharp nor polished; she prepared but three, and they were rough, big and blunt to make Thee suffer more. And while Thou wert dying of thirst, this faithful spouse took care that Thou shouldst be denied even a little water, and that impious soldiers should offer Thee a draught so bitter that far from drinking it scarcely wouldst Thou taste it. Thou didst give up Thy soul in the close embrace of this spouse. But, faithful spouse, she did not leave Thee at the scene of Thy burial; sepulchre, spices, linen, she only allowed you what was borrowed. Neither was this most holy spouse absent from Thy resurrection; she rejoiced in Thy kisses when Thou didst rise gloriously from the tomb, leaving there what had been given or lent. Thou didst take her with Thee to the skies, leaving to the world all that is of the world. And then to Lady Poverty Thou hast given the seal of the kingdom of heaven wherewith to mark those beings who desire to walk in the way of perfection.

BENJAMIN FRANKLIN (*1706–1790*)

A DEIST VIEW OF HIM

As to Jesus of Nazareth, my opinion of whom you particularly desire, I think the system of morals and his religion, as he left them to us, the best the world ever saw or is likely to see; . . . I have . . . some doubts as to his divinity; though it is a question I do not dogmatize upon, having never studied it, and think it needless to busy myself with it now, when I expect soon an opportunity of knowing the truth with less trouble. I see no harm, however, in its being believed, if that belief has the good consequence, as probably it has, of making his doctrines more respected and better observed; especially as I do not perceive that the Supreme Being takes it amiss, by distinguishing the unbelievers in His government of the world with any peculiar marks of His displeasure.

JAMES ANTHONY FROUDE (*1818–1894*)

FAITH OR EVIDENCE THE CHOICE

It has been said recently by "A Layman" . . . that the resurrection of our Lord is as well authenticated as the death of Julius Caesar. It is far better authenticated, unless we are mistaken in supposing the Bible inspired; or if we admit as evidence that inward assurance of the Christian, which would make him rather die than disbelieve a truth so dear to him. But if the layman meant that there was as much proof of it, in the sense in which proof is understood in a court of justice, he could scarcely have considered what he was saying. Julius Caesar was killed in a public place, in the presence of friend and foe, in a remarkable but still perfectly natural manner. The circumstances were minutely known to all the world, and were never denied or doubted by any one. Our Lord, on the other hand, seems purposely to have withheld such public proof of His resurrection as would have left no room for unbelief. He showed Himself, "not to all the people"—not to His enemies, whom His appearance would have overwhelmed—but "to witnesses chosen before"; to the circle of His own friends. There is no evidence that a jury could admit that He was ever actually dead. So unusual was it for persons crucified to die so soon, that Pilate, we are told, "marveled". The subsequent appearances were strange, and scarcely intelligible. Those who saw Him did not recognize Him till He was made known to them in the breaking of bread. He was visible and invisible. He was mistaken by those who were most intimate with Him for another person; nor do the accounts agree which are given by the different Evangelists. Of the investigation in the modern sense (except in the one instance of St. Thomas, and St. Thomas was rather rebuked than praised) there was none and could be none. The evidence offered was different in kind, and the blessing was not to those who satisfied themselves of the truth of the fact by a searching inquiry, but who gave their assent with the unhesitating confidence of love.

*   *   *   *

Of evidence for the resurrection, in the common sense of the word, there may be enough to show that something extraordinary occurred; but not enough, unless we assume the fact to be true on far other grounds, to produce any absolute and unhesitating conviction; and in as much as the resurrection is the key-stone of Christianity, the belief in it must be something far different from that suspended judgment in which history alone would leave us.

JAMES M. GILLIS   (*1876–*   )

MORE THAN MERELY MAN

Of old when Jesus Christ walked the earth . . . men began to ask, "Who is He? What is He." And to-day, nineteen hundred years since these questions were first asked, we hear them again, and we are compelled to determine again what can be the answer to them. . . .

It is a strange fact, and a sad fact, that many to-day do not know the answer to this question. Jesus is, is by admission of all, whether believers or unbelievers, the Founder of Christianity, and the Author of a new civilization. He is the most important figure in history, yet there are those, even among the learned, who admit . . . that they have no definite conviction concerning the ultimate cause of His greatness. . . .

Fling out into the world to-day the question He himself flung back upon the Jews in His day: *"What think you of Christ, whose Son is He?"* and you will be astounded at the number and variety and the uncertainty of the answers that will come ringing about your ears. He is "the wise man of Judea, the Jewish Socrates, a Prophet sent by God." He is the "ideally perfect character." He is the "paragon of humanity." He is the "supreme exemplification of the union of humanity and divinity." "Yes, but whose Son is He?" "Son of Mary, Son of David, Son of Abraham." "Yes, yes, but is He not the Son of God?" "Son of God? we are all sons and children of God." "But is He not the Son of God in a sense in which we are not, and cannot be? We are sons by adoption. Is He not Son of God by nature? Is He not the same as God, equal to God, is He not a Divine Person?" And these agnostic Christians reply, "We do not know. We cannot tell. Speak not to us of nature and person in God. We know not what you mean. We cannot concern ourselves with the intricacies of metaphysics, and with difficult theological questions."

*   *   *   *

We all know that Jesus was a genuine man, possessed of a human heart, a human mind and soul, and a human body; a complete human nature like our own. The waves and billows of every human emotion passed over His soul. He wept and rejoiced, He brooded and worried, and grieved and pitied; He was elated and dejected in turn. He was warmed by love and friendship and sympathy; He was chilled by hatred and indifference and ingratitude; He was frequently disappointed and saddened and shamed. He was not even immune to temptation, for he was as thoroughly human as any child of Adam.

Even those who reject the traditional and orthodox view of Him, none the less glory in the perfection of His humanity. . . .

Now these testimonials to the beauty of the character of Jesus are pleasant to quote, but we must not let them obscure the point at issue. The principal and only problem concerning the Nature of Christ is this: Can we study His mind, His sayings, His deeds, His life and His death, and above all, the enormous and eternal consequences of His life and death, and conclude that He is adequately explained by being named "human"? Granting that He is superior in genius and sanctity and practical achievement to any other man, are we to be-believe that He was, after all, essentially the same in nature with the master philosophers and poets and prophets of our race; that His nature surpasses theirs in degree only, and not in kind? In other words, is Jesus merely a man, or is He more than man? Is He only human, or is He also divine? . . .

When we ask the question, "Is Christ divine?" we mean, "Is He God?" We do not ask, Is He a man who enjoyed a particularly close union with God, or a man in whom the Godhead dwelt more intimately than in any other man? but, Has He the right to say, "I am God", just as truly as you and I have the right to say, "I am a man." . . . Not only had Jesus Christ the right to say, "I am God," but He did say it, and since He said it, it is true. The argument is from Christ's own consciousness, witnessed by Christ's own testimony. For this argument we require two preliminary concessions.

But the concessions are so easily made, that no reasonable person could refuse to make them.

First—We ask men to admit that Christ was not a liar.

Secondly—We ask men to admit that Christ was not a lunatic.

Truly this is a trifling concession, but when it is granted, the divinity of Jesus is a foregone conclusion. If He was sane, He could not so wildly and so outrageously mistake His own nature as to *imagine* Himself God. If He was truthful He could not claim to be God, knowing Himself to be only man.

*   *   *   *

The conclusion is obvious. He that made these claims is no mere man. And the Christian world has made no mistake in maintaining that none but a God could either decently make the claims, or have them effectually recognized by an unending series of generations of believers. Jesus assumed and exercised the prerogatives of God. If He be not God indeed, we are thrown on the other horn of the dilemma—He is not even a good man. *"Why callest thou Me good?"* said Jesus. *"There is none good, save God."* There is profound meaning in the sentence. Why dost thou call Jesus good? Thou canst not call Him good unless thou callest Him God. Say He is not God, and you must say that His enormous pretensions are only blasphemy. If He be a blasphemer, why dost thou call Him *"a good man?"*

Bonaventure Griffiths

MAN BUT ALSO GOD

Christ was indeed a man. Being man He was in all things like to us, sin excepted. He came into the world by being born as a man. He hungered and thirsted. He sorrowed and rejoiced. He had compassion on the afflicted. He loved good and hated evil. He suffered for

His fellow men even to the point of laying down His life for them. And being man death took final possession of His body.

But Christ was also God. During His life on earth He had spoken in symbol of the great place the tomb would have in relation to man. It was characteristic of Christ, Whose Kingdom was not of this world, to make the grim finality of the sepulcher, which marks the end of all things earthly, the starting point of eternal life. From the darkness of that tomb the Light of the World was to burst forth in renewed splendor, ageless and undying, the eternal hope of all the living. The lifeless human body of Christ had been sealed in the grave. The glorified Christ, the Man God, was to come forth. Death was to be swallowed up in victory.

* * * *

Christ, the great Nazarene, suffered and died and was buried. To many of His own day, as in all ages after, He was a great man but likewise a "stumbling block," and His doctrine "foolishness." Yet to those who believed, He was "the power of God and the wisdom of God."

F. P. G. GUIZOT   (*1787–1874*)

THE TYPE OF SELF-DEVOTION

Translator Anonymous

And in truth, Jesus Christ, the Master of St. Paul, is strong in his sufferings, and imparts his strength to his disciples; from his cross he accomplishes what erewhile, in Asia and Europe, princes and philosophers, the powerful of the earth, and sages, attempted without success; he changes the moral state and the social state of the world; he pours into the souls of men new enlightenment and new powers; for all classes, for all human conditions, he prepares destinies be-

fore his advent unknown; he liberates them at the same time that
he lays down rules for their guidance; he quickens them and stills
them; he places the divine law and human liberty face to face, and
yet still in harmony; he offers an effectual remedy for the evil which
weighs upon humanity; to sin he opens the path of salvation, to un-
happiness the door of hope.

Whence comes this power? What are its source and its nature?
How did those who were its witnesses and instruments think and
speak of it at the moment when it was manifested?

They all, unanimously, saw in Jesus Christ, God; most of them,
from the first moment, suddenly moved and enlightened by his
presence and his words; some with rather more surprise and hesitation, but some penetrated and convinced in their turn.

*   *   *   *

Jesus Christ, God and man, has characteristics which appertain to
him alone. These have founded his power and occasioned the success of his works, a power and a success which belong to him alone.
It is not a human reformer, but God himself, who, through Jesus
Christ, has accomplished what no human reformer has ever accomplished, or even conceived, the reform of the moral and social condition of the world, the regeneration of the human soul, and the
solution of the problems of human destiny. It is by these signs, by
these results, that the divinity of Jesus Christ is manifested. How was
the Divine incarnation accomplished in man? Here, as in the union
of the soul and the body, as in the creation, arises the mystery; but
if we cannot fathom the reason of it, the fact not the less exists. When
this fact has taken the form of dogma, theology has sought to explain
it. In my opinion this was a mistake; theology has obscured the
fact in developing and commenting upon it. It is the fact itself of the
incarnation which constitutes the Christian faith, and which rises
above all definitions and all theological controversies. To disregard
this fact, to deny the divinity of Jesus Christ, is to deny, to overthrow
the Christian religion, which would never have been what it is, and
would never have accomplished what it has, but that the Divine in-

carnation was its principle, and Jesus Christ, God and man, its author.

God has done more than manifest himself in Jesus Christ. He has done more than place upon the earth and before men his own living image, the type of sanctity and the model of life. The Creator has accomplished, through Jesus Christ, toward man, his creature, an act of his beneficence and at the same time of his sovereign power. Jesus Christ is not only God made man to spread the divine light upon men; he is God made man to conquer and efface in man moral evil, the fruit of the sin of man. He brings not only light and law, but pardon and salvation. And it is at the price of his own suffering, of his own sacrifice, that he brings these to them. He is the type of self-devotion at the same time as of sanctity. He has submitted to be a victim in order to be a saviour. The incarnation leads to the cross, and the cross to the redemption.

L. P. JACKS   (1860–   )

"THE DONOR OF IMMORTALITY"

The central theme of the New Testament, as it emerged before me in the course of this reading, is *Immortality*—not the immortality of anybody and everybody, but of *the believer in Christ as risen from the dead*. This theme I found everywhere present, both in Epistles and Gospels, either on the surface or beneath it; sometimes in the foreground with the light full on it (as in I Corinthians 15), sometimes in the middle distance, sometimes in the background; but its presence, whether in one position or another, always the unifying element, holding the parts together and making of the New Testament a unitary whole. . . .

This central theme I found presented in forms both explicit and implicit. The explicit form is presented in the Pauline Epistles, all of which bear more or less directly on the gift of immortality, the passage from death to life, bestowed on the believer and on him alone, by Christ, declared the Son of God, not (as many have said) by the beauty of his life, nor the grandeur of his teaching, nor, even, by his death on the Cross but *by the resurrection of the dead* (Rom. I, 3). The *whole* of the New Testament seemed to me covered, explained and held together by the saying "If Christ be not risen from the dead, then is our preaching vain."

Christ the vanquisher of death, the donor of immortality in virtue of his resurrection, and proved the Son of God by *that,* and by nothing short of that, is the first form in which the Central Figure appears in the New Testament, chronologically earlier than that in the Gospels, not one of which was in existence when the Epistles, which show no knowledge of the Gospel story, were written.

The figure of Jesus as presented in the Gospels seems, at first sight, widely different from the Christ of the Epistles both Pauline and Johannine. Whereas in the Epistles the figure is spiritual and in the heavens, in the Gospels it is of flesh and blood on the earth. But, reading the Gospels as wholes and continuously, instead of selectively and piecemeal, it was strongly borne in on me that the figure is intended to be the same in both. In the Gospel of Mark, for instance, the first verse introduces Jesus as the "Son of God" and thence proceeds through successive stages to the crowning moment at the end, when Jesus is finally *proved* the Son of God by rising from the dead—the culminating act which makes the whole, not a biography of Jesus, which it was never intended to be, but the *Gospel,* the good news, which it professes to be—the Gospel of the saving Christ, the risen Son of God. The same with the other Gospels, and even more plainly. The figure they present is the figure of Him who, when he had done what else became him to do, *rose from the dead,* the common *terminus ad quem* of them all, and who, by rising from the dead, crowned all and revealed himself as the Son of God, the donor of immortality to all who were his. Eliminate the Resurrection from the Dead and you deprive the Gospels, one and all, of their *motif,* and unifying purpose. They would then cease to be *Gospels* and become collections of more or less edifying matter for which it would be hard to find a specific name. Lofty ethics? Deeds of beneficence? Noble words and gestures? Yes, of course. But the ethics, deeds, words and gestures of an Immortal. What else would you expect from one who rose from the dead? All is in keeping.

RUFUS M. JONES   (*1863–*)

HIGHEST AND COMPLETEST PERSON

Another truth which I endeavored to interpret, with vividness and reality, was the perfect union of the divine and human nature of Christ. When I began my work there were two well-known tendencies in evidence. On the one hand the divinity of Christ was emphasized to such an extent that His humanity was quite lost. He was thought of as a Being from another world, of another order, supernatural, mysterious, unlike us at every point. He was an unearthly visitor, a celestial being, not one of us in any sense. On the other hand there was the tendency to deny His uniqueness, to insist on a humanity for Him like ours, and to grant to Him nothing more. He belonged to our sphere, our order, our type. He was a highly endowed, prophetically gifted, man.

Here once more the real trouble lay in a misreading of the full truth of both the divine and the human. They were thought of as set over against each other, separated by a chasm. God over there yonder, and undivine man down here, so that if Christ belonged wholly to God He did not partake of this world, or if He belonged to our nature then He was "mere man" and could not properly be called divine. For me that "chasm" was unreal. God is and always was *here*. We have intimate commerce with one another. We could not be persons in any real sense without partaking of God, nor could He be really God and not share with us in grace and love and fellowship. He needs us and in a deeper sense we need Him. The Vine must have branches to be a Vine. The terms human and divine are correlative, just as finite and infinite are. God's true nature and character as love and grace can be revealed to us only in the terms

which fit our life sphere. We can discover power everywhere in nature. We can find beauty in sunsets and flowers and faces. But we
can know what love and unselfish goodness are only through persons. Christ is the highest and completest person through whom these
aspects of character have broken into manifestation in our world. He
is as completely divine as He is completely human. He belongs as
truly to us as He truly belongs to God. In Him we see what God is
like and in Him we know at last what it means to be a completely
normal human person.

Jean Baptiste Henri-Dominique Lacordaire   (*1802–1861*)

THE TRUE SON OF GOD

Translator Anonymous

Jesus Christ then presented himself to his disciples as the Son
of God—not as the Son of God in the sense in which we are all sons
of God, but as the Son of God in its true and proper sense: had it
been otherwise, he would not in so marked a manner have manifested
to his apostle the joy he felt at his confession. Moreover, on other occasions he spake, if possible, more clearly to them. Philip said to him:
Lord, show us the Father, and it is enough for us. Jesus Christ grew
indignant at his demand, and said to him: *So long a time I have been
with you, and you have not known me? Philip, he that seeth me,
seeth the Father also. How sayest thou show us the Father? Believe
you not that I am in the Father, and the Father in me?* And, at another time, manifesting his divine filiation yet more clearly, he said
to one of his disciples who still wavered: *God so loved the world as to
give his only-begotten Son . . . He that believeth in him is not
judged; but he that doth not believe is already judged, because he
believeth not in the name of the only-begotten Son of God.* Jesus
Christ stood forth then as the Son of God without equal or rival,

and in so strict a sense, that he was in his Father and his Father in him, and that to see him was to see his Father.

So much for friends and disciples. But, besides friends and disciples, there is another tribunal before which every new doctrine must appear, namely, the tribunal of the people. After having spoken in secret to the chosen ones, it becomes needful to quit the chamber, to appear in public, to speak to mankind of all ages and conditions, to those who have not leaned upon the bosom of the Master, who have not received the education of friendship, who know not what is required of them, who oppose to the word of doctrine a host of passions blended with as many prejudices. Jesus Christ did this; he heard the murmurs of the crowd around him, and was undaunted before the account which he had to give them of himself. *How long,* cried they to him, *dost thou hold us in suspense? If thou be the Christ, tell us plainly.* Jesus Christ answered them: *I speak to you, and you believe not; the works that I do in the name of my Father, they give testimony of me. I and the Father are one.*

JEAN BAPTISTE HENRI-DOMINIQUE LACORDAIRE   *(1802–1861)*

HIS TRUTH AFFIRMS HIS DIVINITY

Translator Anonymous

Assuredly there remain many questions to solve, even when it is admitted that Jesus Christ lived, that his history is authentic, that publicity sheds the clearest light upon the origins of Christianity and Christendom. . . . Either Jesus Christ and his apostles were sincere, or they were impostors; to say they were sincere is in the main to admit the divinity of their work; for, the reality of the life of Christ being established on the one hand, and the sincerity of their work being admitted on the other, we cannot, before the nature and the course of events which form its tissue, avoid this conclusion: Jesus

Christ is God. If, on the contrary, it is affirmed that Jesus Christ and
his apostles were impostors, the position is one which the mind will
hardly accept. Because all that belongs to Jesus Christ, all the
apostles, all the martyrs, manifest the sincerity of man in its highest
degree; because God has placed in the person of Jesus Christ, in the
life of his apostles, in the death of his martyrs, a character of truthfulness which leaves no room for the supposition that all that beautiful history, for three whole centuries, is nothing but a mass of
imposture steeped in blood.

Frank Glenn Lankard   (*1892–*)

PERSONIFIED THOUGHT OF GOD

Serious-minded people now agree that twenty centuries ago there lived
a man by the name of Jesus who became the driving power of a religion that in the space of three centuries became the recognized religion of imperial Rome. The Christ-myth contention of a few years
back has died for the want of a second. Christianity did not start
with a book, or a law, but with a Person. The corner stone of the
new cathedral was a life. The creator of the new radiance was a
Personality.

When Simon Peter declared, "Thou art the Christ," he had made
a confession which was not the result of a process of reasoning but
the inevitable climax of a deepening fellowship. Peter had left the
fishing boats of Galilee and with a devotion characteristic of his
nature had given himself up with adventurous abandon to the Man
who commanded his affections and his will. It was the revelation of
fellowship, the discovery in experience that well up in the words,
"Thou art the Christ." The conviction which Peter voiced the others
came to share.

The early followers of the Nazarene took Jesus as their Lord and
in that conviction set out to tell the Good News about one who

for them had become the Way, the Truth, and the Life. It was natural and quite inevitable that the earliest of the Christians should seek to establish the claim that their Master was none other but the Son of God. Jesus, only a short time before, had been a resident of Palestine. All this was common knowledge. Indeed, many of the listeners to Peter, John, and Paul had seen and heard Jesus. These people did not need to be reminded that Jesus of Nazareth was a real character, but they needed to catch the meaning and the significance of the experience that the disciples had had with Jesus. Those earliest followers had seen in that face a light not seen before on land or sea. They could only interpret that strange light in terms of divinity. They felt in Jesus a warmth and radiance that to their minds could only come from the Divine. When they remembered the words and deeds of their Master, it seemed to them that heaven had bended very low and that the greatness and goodness of God had overshadowed them. How natural, then, that the earliest disciples should call attention to his divineness and have little or nothing to say of his humanity! . . .

If we should say that the early disciples found only humanity in Jesus and failed to grasp the hand-clasp of earth and heaven, it would be unfair to the facts. . . . They were aware that they had been living with an eating, breathing man but there was something there not of this world. That something caught and held and commanded them. Their leader was possessed by something that man alone does not give. When the disciples thought of Jesus they realized that he personified their deepest thought of God. The disciples could not think of God apart from Jesus or Jesus apart from God. In their thinking, God and Jesus belonged together. For them, in the person of Jesus, "the consciousness of God shone most brightly and the fires of the Divine love burned most warmly." . . .

The disciples didn't begin with a doctrine about the person of Jesus. They didn't begin to follow Jesus with any theory of divinity at all with reference to him. They began with the Teacher of Nazareth and ended with God.

C. S. LEWIS   (1898–   )

A FRIGHTENING ALTERNATIVE

Among these Jews there suddenly turns up a man who goes about
talking as if He was God. He claims to forgive sins. He says He has
always existed. He says He is coming to judge the world at the end
of time. Now let us get this clear. Among Pantheists, like the Indians,
anyone might say that he was part of God, or one with God: there'd
be nothing very odd about it. But this man, since He was a Jew,
couldn't mean that kind of God. God, in their language, meant the
Being outside the world Who made it and was infinitely different
from anything else. And when you've grasped that, you will see that
what this man said was, quite simply, the most shocking thing that
has ever been uttered by human lips.

I'm trying here to prevent anyone from saying the really silly
thing that people often say about Him: "I'm ready to accept Jesus
as a great moral teacher, but I don't accept His claim to be God."
That's the one thing we mustn't say. A man who was merely man and
said the sort of things Jesus said wouldn't be a great moral teacher.
He'd either be a lunatic—on a level with the man who says he's a
poached egg—or else he'd be the Devil of Hell. You must make your
choice. Either this man was, and is, the Son of God: or else a madman or something worse. You can shut Him up for a fool, you can
spit at and kill him as a demon; or you can fall at His feet and call
Him Lord and God. But don't let us come with any patronising
nonsense about His being a great human teacher. He hasn't left that
open to us. He didn't intend to. We are faced, then, with a frighten-
ing alternative. This man . . . either was (and is) just what He said
or else a lunatic, or something worse. Now it seems obvious that He
wasn't either a lunatic or a fiend: and consequently, however strange
or terrifying or unlikely it may seem, I have to accept the view that
He was and is God. God has landed on this enemy-occupied world
in human form.

And now, what was the purpose of it all? What did He come to do? Well, to teach, of course; but as soon as you look into the New Testament or any other Christian writing you'll find they're constantly talking about something different—about His death and His coming to life again. It's obvious that Christians think the whole point of the story lies there. They think the main thing He came to earth to do was to suffer and be killed. . . .

The central Christian theory is that Christ's death has somehow put us right with God and given us a fresh start. Theories as to *how* it did this are another matter. A good many different theories have been held as to how it works; what all Christians are agreed on is that it does work.

Sir Oliver Lodge   (*1851–1940*)

THE CHRISTIAN IDEA OF GOD

Undoubtedly the Christian idea of God is the simple one. Overpoweringly and appallingly simple is the notion presented to us by the orthodox Christian Churches:—

A babe born of poor parents, born in a stable among cattle because there was no room for them in the village inn—no room for them in the inn—what a master touch! Revealed to shepherds. Religious people inattentive. Royalty ignorant, or bent on massacre. A glimmering perception, according to one noble legend, attained in the Far East —where also similar occurrences have been narrated. Then the child growing into a peasant youth, brought up to a trade. At length a few years of itinerant preaching; flashes of miraculous power and insight. And then a swift end: set upon by the religious people; his followers over-awed and scattered, himself tried as a blasphemer, flogged, and finally tortured to death.

Simplicity most thorough and most strange! In itself it is not unique; such occurrences seem inevitable to highest humanity in an unregenerate world; but who, without inspiration, would see in them a revelation of the nature of God? The life of Buddha, the life of Joan of Arc, are not thus regarded. Yet the Christian revelation is clear enough and true enough if our eyes are open, and if we care to read and accept the simple record which, whatever its historical value, is all that has been handed down to us.

MARTIN LUTHER   (*1483-1546*)

CONQUERS SIN AND DEATH

Translated by William Hazlitt

All the wisdom of the world is childish foolishness in comparison with the acknowledgment of Christ. For what is more wonderful than the unspeakable mystery, that the Son of God, the image of the eternal Father, took upon him the nature of man. Doubtless, he helped his supposed father, Joseph, to build houses; for Joseph was a carpenter. What will they of Nazareth think at the day of judgment when they shall see Christ sitting in his divine majesty; surely they will be astonished, and say: Lord, thou helpest build my house, how comest thou now to this high honour?

When Jesus was born, doubtless, he cried and wept like other children, and his mother tended him as other mothers tend their children. As he grew up, he was submissive to his parents, and waited on them, and carried his supposed father's dinner to him, and when he came back, Mary, no doubt, often said: "My dear little Jesus, where hast thou been?" He that takes not offense at the simple, lowly, and mean course of the life of Christ, is endued with high divine art and wisdom; Yea, has a special gift of God in the Holy Ghost. . . .

Christ had neither money, nor riches, nor earthly kingdom, for he gave the same to princes and kings. But he reserved one thing peculiarly to himself, which no human creature or angel could do— namely, to conquer sin and death, the devil and hell, and in the midst of death to deliver and save those that through his word believe in him. . . .

When Jesus Christ utters a word, he opens his mouth so wide that it embraces all heaven and earth, even though that word be but a whisper. The word of the emperor is powerful, but that of Jesus Christ governs the whole universe.

A. J. MAAS   (*1858–1927*)

HE SPOKE IN HIS OWN NAME

The divinity of Jesus is proved by some writers by an appeal to prophecy and miracle. But though Jesus fulfilled the prophecies of the Old Testament to the letter, He Himself appears to appeal to them mainly in proof of His Divine mission; He shows the Jews that he fulfils in His Person and His work all that had been foretold of the Messias. The prophecies uttered by Jesus Himself differ from the prophecies of the Old Testament in that Jesus does not speak in the name of the Lord, but in His own name. If it could be strictly proved that they were made in virtue of His own knowledge of the future and of His own power to dispose of the current of events, the prophecies would prove His Divinity; as it is they prove at least that Jesus is a messenger of God, a friend of God, inspired by God. This is not the place to discuss the historical and philosophical truth of the miracles of Jesus, but we know that Jesus appeals to His works as bearing witness to the general truth of His mission (John, x, 25, 33, 38), and also for the verity of some particular claims (Matt., ix, 6; Mark, ii, 10, 11, etc.). They show, therefore, at least that Jesus is a Divine legate and that His teaching is infallibly true.

JOHN A. MACKAY   (*1889*-   )

SOLE KEY TO THE SCRIPTURES

The loftiest description that can be given of God is that He is the God of Jesus Christ. In the man Christ Jesus, God and His will became fully known. The apprehension of this ushered a new day-spring into the gloom of the Roman world. God was in Him; God is like Him; He is God's chief gift to the world; in Him, as the "Word become flesh," God's grace and truth flow to mankind. The living God revealed Himself in this person so that Pascal and a host besides him, beholding the divine glory in Christ, were constrained to say, "Thy God shall be my God." By so doing they fulfilled the essential character of Biblical truth in a personal relationship with the Almighty. But to make this declaration in truth is to experience redemption.

*   *   *   *

God meets man in Jesus Christ. "How can we know the way to the Father?" said Philip. Jesus answered him, "I am the way." In Christianity everything that has to do with the "way" is concentrated in a Person. The way to God is not primarily a psychological process. It is not a geographical route; nor a religious hierarchy; nor a holy shrine; nor esoteric knowledge. The Christian way to God is a person who becomes the object of that belief and commitment which is called faith. In Jesus Christ God and man meet. On the one hand, Christ is the embodiment of all that the Bible means by the word "grace," that is the gracious approach of God to man for his redemption, in which all the resources of deity are made available for man. On the other hand, He is the object of commitment in thought and in life which we call faith. . . . In this way Jesus Christ is doubly the Truth. He is the personal, absolute Truth, in Whom is summed up all that God is and all that man is. He is the Truth in as much as faith in Him is the gateway to a knowledge of the ultimate meaning of life. . . . No one can understand the Scriptures who does not unlock their treasures with the true and only Key which is Christ.

At the centre of Christianity is no mere idea, no matter how luminous or comprehensive, but a person. In a very real sense . . . "Christianity is Christ."

Bishop William Thomas Manning (*1866*–)

A WONDER AND GLORY

His life did not begin in Bethlehem. Only His human life began there. Through all eternity He was with the Father. "All things were made by him." "In the beginning was the Word, and the Word was with God, and the Word was God." For us men and for our salvation He "came down from heaven." This is the wonder and glory of the Gospel. God so loves us that He came Himself, and still comes to us, in Christ. "The Word became flesh and dwelt among us." We cannot fathom this great truth. But we know that in Jesus God comes to us Himself. We know that Jesus is "God of God, Light of Light, Very God of Very God." We know that Jesus is our Friend, our Master, our Savior, our Lord and our God. Our faith in Him, our help from Him, or love for Him, depend upon our realizing and knowing *Who He is*.

The work of Jesus here on earth did not end at His Ascension. His work for the whole world *began* then. To His Church He gave His promise: "Lo, I am with you alway." And this promise He fulfills. His influence is felt everywhere, but the Church is the pledged sphere of His ministry to us.

Don Marquis   *(1878–1937)*

JUDAS IN TORMENT

CAIAPHAS

Galilean, this is the night.

JUDAS *(dully)*

Aye. This is the night.

CAIAPHAS

Thou art resolved?

JUDAS *(as before, dully)*

Yea. I am resolved.

CAIAPHAS

Thou knowest we could have taken this man at anytime without thy help, but that he has friends among the rabble, and if we took him openly there would be brawling in the streets that would bring down the Roman legions on the City.

JUDAS *(moody and brooding, thinking of something other than the immediate dialogue)*

I have guessed thy reasons and why thou makest use of me.

CAIAPHAS

Thou knowest where he goes of nights?

JUDAS

To a certain garden on the Mount of Olives . . . an old walled garden beyond the brook Kedron.

CAIAPHAS

Thou canst lead my servants there tonight?

JUDAS

Aye. Thou goest too?

CAIAPHAS

Nay. It is necessary that I summon the Sanhedrin against his taking. For we shall put the man on trial this very night.

JUDAS

Do thy servants know him?

CAIAPHAS

Thou must give them some sign.

JUDAS

Aye. I will give thy servants a sign. (*moodily, half to himself*)
It was not an hour since that he gave a sign to me.

CAIAPHAS

What dost thou mutter?

JUDAS

An hour since, I was at supper with him. And he said to one
of our company that he would dip a sop of bread and give it to
the one who should prove a traitor. And he dipped the sop and
gave it to me.

CAIAPHAS

How could he know?

JUDAS

He knows what men think ere they begin to think it. (*A brief
pause. When Judas continues he speaks as if under the spell of
some influence he cannot resist. He broods over this influence,
somewhat as if he were wondering at himself, at times, and the
part he plays.*) Priest, he can plunge his eyes into the secret
chambers of thy soul and see the thoughts that thou hast hidden
there . . . He knows what shape thy deeds will take before
thou hast dreamed them. (*There is a kind of hopelessness and
helplessness in the manner of Judas; from time to time, as the
scene progresses, broken up by sudden flares of emotion and
passion. He alternates between this helplessness in the hands of
fate, for which he holds Jesus responsible, and sudden fierce fits
of rebellion against it and hatred of Jesus, the cause of it. He
feels himself, literally, "possessed".*)

CAIAPHAS

The man is a magician. He has bewitched thee!

JUDAS

Thou sayest. He did, in a manner, bewitch me from the very
first.

CAIAPHAS

Galilean, why didst thou yield thy soul to him?

JUDAS

Master, I . . . I cannot tell thee. But when I looked upon him first I knew . . .

(*Pauses*)

CAIAPHAS

Thou didst know . . . what?

JUDAS

That here was one I must follow. (*Pauses*) Nay, I cannot tell thee! Unless thou, too, hadst fallen under the spell of him, thou couldst not understand. (*Pauses; seems to fall visibly under the spell of Jesus again; speaks stammeringly out of great bewilderment*) When he first . . . when he first . . . looked at me . . . and I looked at him . . . there was a moment . . . I do not know how to tell you . . . but the world was different . . . somehow . . . different . . . and I . . . I was different from myself . . .

(*Sinks down on a stone bench*)

CAIAPHAS

Dost thou not know that Beelzebub is very cunning in his snares?

JUDAS (*in a sudden acute agony of suffering and mental confusion*) Beelzebub . . . Beelzebub . . . How can one know what comes from Beelzebub and what from Jehovah? . . . Beelzebub . . . Jehovah . . . Satan . . . Jesus . . . Beelzebub . . . Angels . . . devils . . . Spirits that come from God and spirits that come from hell, how can I tell which is which? (*Rises and tears at his breast*) They are all in me, I tell you, priest. They walk through my heart as if it were a street . . . they rush through me like a crowd and make a turmoil in my soul . . . How can I know what is from God and what is from Satan? I am a city full of spirits, and they riot in the streets. (*Sinks again, exhausted, on the stone bench, and says, with intensity, in a low voice tinged with hatred*) It is Jesus of Nazareth who has done this thing to me!

CAIAPHAS

He is a potent wizard, and he must not be suffered to walk the earth.

JUDAS (*bewildered again, speaking as if out of a dream; striving to understand himself*)

And yet . . . at first . . . there was a time, at first . . . when I loved the man.

CAIAPHAS

Now, may Jehovah have mercy on thee for that!

JUDAS

I loved him . . . I loved him . . . (*Still in his trance. Brief pause.*) I loved him till the man betrayed me.

CAIAPHAS

He—betrayed—*thee*?

JUDAS (*as much to himself as to Caiaphas*)

Aye! He betrayed me! What else! These many weeks, Yea, these months past, he has persecuted me and driven me! He has persecuted me with his knowledge of my dreams and speculations; he has taken from me my power to be myself . . . When he spoke his words have carried a meaning to my ears that others have not guessed . . . I am not able to control my thoughts, and he has heard my thoughts as if I had spoken them aloud . . . I have seen it in his eyes and in his manner that he knew . . . (*A brief pause*) Even when I withdrew myself from him I knew there was no recess so hidden nor so far but that my mind was open to him. . . . And so it was that I grew to fear him and to wish that I might escape . . . (*Rises again, and speaks wildly, obsessed by fear and hatred*) But there is no escape from him! There is no escape! On every side I am beleaguered. His eyes are a thousand cohorts, and I am encompassed about!

CAIAPHAS

Peace. Thou art beside thyself.

JUDAS (*beginning in his more brooding manner*)

When he began to say that there was one of his followers who would betray him the thought came to me . . . the fear came to me . . . that perhaps it might be I . . . I said to myself, "Can it be I that he means? Has he seen that in me and I did not know was there myself?" (*Brief pause; he progressively works himself up again during remainder of speech*) And that thought . . . it would not let me rest! It gnawed at me till my heart was ragged! It has been a hound upon my track, and a dog that followed my footsteps. And he has known it, for he knows everything I think! It has driven me to the doing of it. (*Brief pause, and then, intensely, for it is the excuse he makes to himself for being a traitor*) And if I betray him it is because he has betrayed me first! (*Brief pause, then he works himself up into excitement again as he continues*) Yea, he betrayed me! It was at the time of Feast of the Tabernacles that he said to Peter, "Have I not chosen you twelve, and one of you is a devil?" . . . And when he said it, he looked at me . . . he looked at me . . . Am I a devil? If so, it is he that hath wrought me a devil and made me a devil and shown me a devil to myself! (*Well-nigh exhausted again, dully*) Yea, there are devils in me! There are devils in me!

CAIAPHAS

Thou dost well to hate him!

JUDAS

Wouldst thou not hate the man whose words pierced thee ever through and through? (*Pauses; then a return to his groping bewilderment*) But . . . I do not know how it is . . . even yet . . . even now . . . as I hate, at times I also love. (*Helplessly, bewildered, and a little wild*) Tell me, how can that be, Master? That I hate him, and yet at times I love him still?

CAIAPHAS

It is because thou art bewitched.

JUDAS

Yea, I am bewitched . . . I am a town that is full of ghosts . . . angels and demons . . . demons and angels . . . I know not which is which nor whence they came . . . but they struggle within me . . . they are at war . . . angels and demons . . . they rage and riot through my veins.

CAIAPHAS

Judas, this is a deed for which thou wilt be remembered through the ages.

JUDAS (*dull, stupid, brooding again, unheeding*)

The ages . . . the ages . . . I shall be remembered through the ages?

CAIAPHAS

Thou dost well, in the sight of Jehovah, to deliver this man to the Sanhedrin.

JUDAS (*sinking on to bench, exhausted, dull*)

I care naught for the Sanhedrin.

CAIAPHAS

What dost thou care for, Galilean?

JUDAS (*feverishly, flaring up*)

I care for naught but what I am to do, and I burn to do it, to get it done!

CAIAPHAS

When it is done, and this wizard no longer walks the earth, thou shalt have peace.

JUDAS (*brooding*)

Peace? Shall I have peace, indeed? Or will he continue to look on me from beyond the grave?

DON MARQUIS   (*1878-1937*)

DIED FOR HIS BELIEF

I believe there is a contemporary school of thought which holds that when Jesus spoke of his Father he meant that God is the Father of all of us—the Father of Jesus, and of you, and of me, and of everybody else, in much the same way. And I rather inclined, myself, to the opinion that such was the meaning of Jesus. But the careful and repeated examination of the Bible necessary for this play has convinced me that it was *not* his meaning. I cannot escape the conviction that he intended to convey that he was the Son of God in a sense special and unique; that he differed from other men who might call God their Father not merely in the degree of his spirituality, but also in the character of his relationship to his Father. You may or you may not believe this, I may or may not believe it—but I cannot evade the belief that Jesus himself believed it. He seems to have been as explicit as possible in this claim; either the four Gospels have not reported him correctly, or he meant just that: at least, I can make nothing else out of it, and I began an examination of the Bible with a contrary view. It was for this assertion, that he was the Son of God, that the Sanhedrin condemned him, for the Sanhedrin considered it blasphemy; if he had meant anything else or anything less he would have answered otherwise when the question was discharged at him point-blank by Caiaphas, and his life or death hung upon the answer; he died for that belief because it *was* his belief. To think of him as lying for some belief he did not really hold seems to me to be merely idiocy. You or I may hold what opinion we will, but I do not see how, if we accept his reported utterances as evidence, we can have any doubt as to the opinion of Jesus himself.

THOMAS L. MASSON   (*1866–1934*)

RECALLING HIS RECORDED WORDS

The only way we can come to understand the real Christ is by interior recollection, by sitting still, unhampered by text or tradition and seeking Him in this way. This must be our first approach to Him, as it gives Him His first approach to us. We might have to sit still for 38 years as did the cripple in the fifth chapter of John. Some people who are very keen on the doctrine of Grace, think that Christ must come to us and that many are called but few chosen. But how indeed, is anybody to know what is happening to anyone else? All

I know is that you have to want something in your life very intensely, having tried a good many other things and having had them fail you. And that a sudden awareness, a kind of revelation or conversion . . . gets you and you understand that life is really worth living, after all.

And then, reading these recorded words of Christ in a new spirit, you see them differently. For example, what does *bread* mean? Read up on that and you will see that there is a mystery here which cannot be solved in a baker's shop. I suggest, just for practice, that if you are in the habit even of saying the Lord's prayer, you use the present tense, and say "He gives us this day our daily bread." Also, if you will read all the other things that Christ said, you will see that when He stated that our Heavenly Father knows before hand what we need, He was conveying this interior idea.

DMITRI MEREJKOWSKI   (*1865-1941*)

WHEN HE SPOKE TO CHILDREN

Translated by H. Chrouschoff Metheson

Sometimes he wept, but he never laughed, *aliquando flevit sed nunquam risit,* is the correct surmise or memory of Lentulus. That convulsion of the face which may not be human or even animal, but purely devilish, laughter, never distorted this unique, this perfect human face.

He never laughed, but He surely often smiled. How frequently is that living smile on living lips contained in the parables. Could one imagine His face without a smile at the moment when He is speaking to the children? "He was always joyous, gay"—*hilaris*—again surmises or remembers Lentulus.

Very little children also weep but do not laugh, and when they do begin to laugh, they do it clumsily, as though it was not natural, and immediately afterwards they become solemn, almost stern. They seem to have retained a glimmer of other-worldly majesty.

Jesus was nearer to children than to adults.

"I was with you among the children, and ye knew me not."

Unless we change and become as children, we shall not enter His kingdom, we shall not see his face:—

He who looks for me will find me among seven-year children, for I, who am concealed in the Fourteenth Aeon (the deepest antiquity) reveal myself to children.

And they brought young children to him, that he should touch them: And he took them up in his arms and put his hands upon them, and blessed them (Mark X, 13, 16).

In our coarse world, perhaps the coarsest of all worlds, this is surely the tenderest thing that ever happened. It is like a luminous cloud, the stuff of another world. It may be that only those who saw Him in that bright cloud of children's faces could realize the divine beauty of His face. Grown-up people are "amazed" or they are "afraid," but children rejoice, as though when looking in His eyes they recognize something, remember that which grown-up people have already forgotten—the heavenly peace of the sky, heavenly light of the sun.

ALICE MEYNELL   (*1849–1922*)

THE HIDDEN BOYHOOD LIFE

The meditations of the many centuries of Christian devotion have poured upon those vacant spaces of the Biblical history where Mary of Nazareth stands, or rather is hidden, as the mother of a Child, of a Boy, of a young Man living at home in a village. Mother, foster-father, and Child are shown to us in Scripture for a few days or hours out of many years; at the Nativity; at the Epiphany; in Egypt; then twelve years after the Nativity, some score of years before the Mission, in Jerusalem. Here at last Christ speaks. Joseph and Mary had retraced anxious steps in search of Him, meeting their kinsfolk group by group, returning whence they came, to the spring and source of the stream, the fountain of the national life, to the mysterious Temple that was the symbol of the Body of their Son. The few words spoken within the group of three, so often called the earthly Trinity—man, woman, and child—the question and answer, are set down, and no more. These are preserved for us of all the questions and answers of the life in the narrow house. We may suppose that the publicity of this manifestation of the growing Boy—the first manifestation since the Epiphany—suggested the public record of the Gospel, the daily words and daily actions remaining a confidence, or even a secret, of the house. Or we may suppose the daily conversation, never less than holy, to have been always less than prophetic, and the words in the Temple to have been kept in Mary's heart as a great exception, a surprise, an omen, a menace, and a promise.

However this may be, in that maternal heart lay the Gospel of the youth of Christ. Before the pens of the four greatest writers of the world had been set to their task, the New Testament lurked in one woman's memory and in her watchfulness. It was her work to choose and reject what should be said. . . .

The whole world would not contain the books that might be written of the mere three years of our Saviour's work on earth, says His Beloved Disciple, speaking with the sudden hyperbole that surprise us at the end of his Gospel of contained and mastered emotion. It is because he is the one Evangelist who does comment, and explain, who turns the leaf back and adds an after-thought; who undertook to answer for the two most mystical of the miracles—the Transsubstantiation at Cana and the Raising of Lazarus—who, moreover, took upon himself the record of the words of Christ in the upper chamber and of the singing of the hymn, and in whose recital we are aware of the breaking heart of the friend of Christ; it is because we know him so spiritual, and so exalted, that the extravagant and enthusiastic phrase startles and delights us.

Why then did he who knew so much that his knowledge caused him to write thus fantastically, set down so little? But for that scantiness his posterity and the posterity of all Evangelists and all Apostles have sought to make amends. The world of books has hardly been able to contain what has been written about the Gospels; the before and after of the Gospels; the systems, the speculation, the teaching, the followings, the revolts. . . .

NICHOLAS OF CUSA   (*1401–1464*)

STUPENDOUS AND MARVELLOUS SIGHT

Translated by Emma Gurney Salter

The mind's eye cannot be sated in beholding thee, Jesu, because thou art the fulfilment of all beauty the mind can picture, and in this icon I conjecture Thy right marvellous and astounding sight, Jesu blessed above all. For thou, Jesu, whilst Thou didst walk this world of sense, didst use eyes of flesh like unto ours. With them Thou didst see, even as we men do, one object and another, for there was in Thine eyes a certain spirit which informed the organ, like the sensitive mind in an animal's body. In that spirit there was a noble power of discernment whereby Thou, Lord, didst see and distinguish an object of one colour and another of another. And, yet more, from the aspect of the face and eyes of the men whom Thou seest Thou didst judge truly of the passions of the soul—anger, joy, sorrow. And more subtly still Thou didst comprehend from few tokens what was hidden in a man's mind (for nothing is conceived in the mind that is not in some way shown in the face, which is the heart's herald, and especially in the eyes). By all these tokens thou didst much more truly reach the inmost places of the soul than an created spirit can. From any one sign, albeit of the slightest, Thou didst perceive the man's whole thought, even as understanding men grasp from a few words an idea that requireth a whole long discourse to set it forth, and even as the learned, from running their eye hastily over a book, can narrate the writer's whole intent as though they had read it through.

Thou, Jesu, didst excel in this manner of vision all the perfection, swiftness, and keenness of all men past, present and to come, and yet this sight was human because it was not perfected without the eye of flesh. Howbeit, it was stupendous and marvellous. For if there be men who, after prolonged and subtle examining, can read the mind of a writer, under characters and signs newly devised at the time, and unseen before, Thou, Jesu, didst perceive all things under every sign and figure.

If, as we read, there was once a man who, by certain tokens in the eye, knew the thoughts of an interrogator, even the verses that he might be repeating to himself, Thou, Jesu, hadst more skill than all in grasping all the mind's thought from each glance of the eye. I myself have seen a deaf woman who reads everything from the movement of her daughter's lips and understood it as if she had heard it. If such a thing is possible by long practice among deaf and dumb persons, and Religious who converse by signs, Thou, Jesu, who, as a Master of masters, actually knewst all that is to be known, didst more perfectly form a true judgment of the heart and its thoughts from the slightest glances and signs invisible to us.

But unto this Thy human sight, most perfect albeit finite and limited unto an organ, there was united an absolute and infinite sight—the sight whereby Thou, as God, didst see alike all things and each, absent as well as present, past as well as future. Thus, Jesu, with Thy human eye Thou sawest such accidentals as are visible, but, within Thy divine, absolute sight, the substance of things. None save Thee, Jesu, ever in the flesh beheld the substance or essence of things. Thou alone sawest most truly the soul and spirit and whatsoever there was in man.

BEVERLEY NICHOLS   (*1899–*   )

A TREMENDOUS QUESTION

In his brillant preface to *Androcles and the Lion* Shaw adopts towards the personality of Jesus exactly the same attitude as most men adopt towards the personality of Shakespeare, saying, 'We don't care whether he was Bacon or anybody else you like to mention. We've got the plays, and that's all that matters.' . . .

Now it is most important that we expose this fallacy of Shaw's, once and for all, because it is a fallacy which she shares with millions of other loose-thinking persons. We are constantly meeting people who say, gaily, 'Of course, nobody believes in hell nowadays' (in itself a highly inaccurate observation), and we are constantly reading articles in the popular papers in which emphasis is laid on the 'beauty' of Christianity, or its 'practicability' or its 'modernity', while all the time the flaming fact of its *truth,* or the hideous fact of its falsehood, is calmly ignored.

Do the people who live in this Christian no-man's-land, the people who think that Jesus was 'a most exceptional man, my dear, really *too* remarkable, greater than Shakespeare even, or Beethoven . . .' do these people who set Jesus on an earthly pedestal, forgetting that by their action they are dragging him from the heavens, do they realize the absolutely terrifying implication of their attitude?

Mind you, I am not saying they are wrong. I am only asking them if they realize what they are implying.

They are implying that for nearly two thousand years the world has been in the thrall of a Jewish lunatic. They are implying that the most exquisite creations of art, the most sublime examples of heroism, the whole fabric of decent government in the Western world, has been executed at the command of a crazy Oriental who could no more rise from the dead than he could get out of a strait-jacket, and could no more feed five thousand than he could buy a herring if he hadn't the cash on him.

These, gentle readers, are the alternatives. And I want you to realize the sort of problem that this intellectual honesty will force us to face.

It means, for example, that when we talk about the resurrection we must not imply a merely 'spiritual' resurrection, nor a mere survival of the dead man's ideas, nor a pious legend derived from a hotchpotch of Greek manuscripts. We must imply that on a certain hour between night and day, in an Eastern tomb, there was a strange stirring, while immense and incalculable forces poured back life into the body of a dead man, so that he was able to rise up and walk out into the moonlight. We must imply this and nothing less. We must believe the thing happened; it must be so real to us we must be able to hear, in our hearts, the faint sigh in the tomb as the life spirit flooded back into the tortured body, must be able to smell, in our own nostrils, the medley of strange scents which floated back to him, the scent of spices, and dust, and stale blood.

Can we pursuade ourselves, beyond any shadow of doubt, that these things happened, merely by a cold-blooded examination of the evidence?

That is the tremendous question we have to ask ourselves. It is certainly the greatest question with which we shall ever be faced in this earthly life.

ALFRED NOYES   (1880-   )

A NEW BOND PROCLAIMED

The great simple phrase—*"et homo factus est"*—contains all the long process of evolution, as Eternity contains all the sequence of Time. It contains all the wonder of the first birth of the spirit. One seems to be aware of a universe hushed in awe over the first helpless man-child in whom it could be said that the transition from the sub-human was accomplished; a child laid in the wild manger of the brute creation, aeons before the discovery that the inns of the world had no room; aeons before the building of the first inn; while from all the starry heights to which his innocent face was upturned there shone the quiet annunciation and prophecy of the new bond between heaven and earth: *"Unto us a child is born; unto us a son is given."*

The man child had emerged from the brute creation; a new and higher order of values had been evolved; but the process did not end there. It pointed beyond itself. The advent of man was a prophecy of the greater event and still higher order towards which he was moving as his final cause and true origin. The full sacramental significance of the process was not apparent to him until he was met on the upward way by the Power descending, and the central Figure of religious history, in whom the long prophesied meeting was accomplished, became the child of His own children and called himself "The Son of Man". . . . This title . . . hinted, or rather took for granted a deeper origin. The same hint was unconsciously implicit in the dramatic irony with which the Supreme Representative of the genus homo was announced by the Roman pro-consul to a mocking world. The agnostic, Pilate, was quite innocent of any irony in his classification of Jesus Christ; but the "grand sequence of events" had its own significance. There was a wider and deeper consciousness behind it than his own; and when he was caught up in the orderly movement of the universal drama, as a musician is caught up by the surrounding orchestra and forced to play his part, the most poignantly ironic annunciation of all Time was made in the single dark phrase, *Ecce Homo*.

W. E. Orchard   (*1877-*   )

HIS A UNIQUE PLACE

It is true that the craving for an Incarnation of God seems to lie at the heart of all religious systems. The way in which this craving is manifested takes many forms. . . . The only thing which approaches the Christian idea at all is the attempt to deify the founders of religion or regard them as incarnations of the Divine.

Now to deny that Christ was the incarnation of God is to say that this incurable tendency of religion has not been fulfilled, that the craving it is designed to answer is an impossible one. It means that religion is man's prayer, but a prayer which has never been answered. And that condemns all religion as equally false. In the face of this it seems an easy way out to admit that the idea of Incarnation is right, but that it must be universalised, and every individual regarded as an incarnation of God, or the great sages and prophets of mankind regarded as successive incarnations of Christ: for so in the new phraseology it is proposed to use the term Christ. But this equally fails to satisfy. If God is incarnate in all men, we have simply no revelation whatever of what the character of God is like: and if Christ is successively incarnate in Zoroaster, Buddha, Jesus, Mohammed, we are left with extraordinary contradictions in character and teachings as a result. . . . To place Jesus among the sages of mankind and the founders of religions is not only to forget his peculiar consciousness, but it is to make those among whom He is placed of immensely less value. Only if Jesus is the Word which was immanent in all the prophets, can we understand, with Him as interpreter, what they were stammering to say, and value it at its highest. . . .

Therefore if religion is to have any value at all, and if the great religious teachers are to be given a high place, it is essential to give Jesus Christ a unique place, the place which Christianity itself gives to Him. To dispute that uniqueness is to deny the hope of all religion, and to put Him among the great teachers is not fair to them. Without Christ it is impossible to maintain our reverence for religion as such, or to believe that it is inspired: and if we are forced to that conclusion there is nothing else about man which is left to share a better fate. Therefore it is imperative to show that Christ is unique and that what dwelt in others as an informing spirit was in Him His very self.

BLAISE PASCAL   (*1623–1662*)

HIS SUBLIME ORDER OF HOLINESS

Translator Anonymous

Jesus Christ, without riches, without any external display of science, stands in his own order, that of holiness. He neither published inventions, nor reigned over kingdoms; but He was humble, patient, pure before God, terrible to devils, and altogether without sin. Oh! with what illustrious pomp, with what transcendent magnificence did He come to such as see with the eyes of the heart, and are the discerners of true wisdom! . . .

It had been useless for our Lord Jesus Christ to have come as an earthly king, in order that he might shine in His kingdom of holiness. But how consistently did he come with the character of His proper order!

It is ridiculous to be scandalised at the mean condition of Jesus Christ, as if that meanness stood in the same order with the greatness which He came to display. Let us contemplate this greatness in His life, in His sufferings, in His obscurity, in His death, in the choice of His attendants, in their forsaking Him, in His secret resurrection, and in all the other parts of His history; we shall see it is to be so great as to leave no ground for being offended at his meanness, for there was no meanness in Him.

JEAN JACQUES ROUSSEAU   (*1712–1778*)

HIS LIFE AND DEATH THOSE OF A GOD

Translator Anonymous

I will confess to you further that the majesty of the Scriptures strikes me with admiration, as the purity of the gospel hath its influence on my heart. Peruse the words of our philosophers with all their pomp of diction; how mean, how contemptible are they, compared with the Scriptures! Is it possible that a book at once so simple and so sublime should be merely the work of man? Is it possible that the Sacred Personage, whose history it contains, should be himself a mere man? Do we find that he assumed the tone of an enthusiast or ambitious sectary? What sweetness, what purity in his manner! What an affecting gracefulness in his delivery! What sublimity in his maxims! What profound wisdom in his discourses! What presence of mind, what subtlety, what truth in his replies! How great the command over his passions! Where is the man, where the philosopher who could so live and so die, without weakness and without ostentation? When Plato describes his imaginary good man loaded with all the shame of guilt, yet meriting the highest reward of virtue, he describes exactly the character of Jesus Christ: the resemblance was so striking that all the fathers perceived it.

What prepossession, what blindness must it be to compare the son of Sophroniscus to the son of Mary? What an infinite disproportion there is between them! Socrates, dying without pain or ignominy, easily, supported his character to the last, and if his death, however easy, had not crowned his life, it might have been doubted whether Socrates, with all his wisdom, was anything more than a vain sophist. He invented, it is said, the theory of morals. Others, however, had before put them into practice; he had only to say what they had done, and reduce their examples to precepts. Aristides had been just, before Socrates defined justice; Leonidas gave up his life for his country before Socrates declared patriotism to be a duty; the Spartans were a sober people before Socrates recommended sobriety: before he had even defined virtue, Greece abounded in virtuous men. But where could Jesus learn, among his compatriots, that pure and sublime morality of which he only hath given us both precept and example? The greatest wisdom was made known amidst the most bigoted fanaticism, and the simplicity of the most heroic virtues did honour to the vilest people on earth. The death of Socrates, peacefully philosophising with his friends, appears the most agreeable

that could be wished for; that of Jesus, expiring in the midst of agonis-
ing pains, abused, insulted, cursed by a whole nation, is the most
horrible that could be feared. Socrates, in receiving the cup of poison,
blessed the weeping executioner who administered it; but JESUS,
in the midst of excruciating tortures, prayed for his merciless tormentors.

Yes, if the life and death of Socrates were those of a sage, the life
and death of JESUS are those of a God.

John Ruskin   (*1819-1900*)

TRUE TO ALL, AS TO PETER

I suppose there is no event in the whole life of Christ to which, in
hours of doubt or fear, men turn with more anxious thirst to know
the close facts of it, or with more earnest and passionate dwelling
upon every syllable of its recorded narrative, than Christ's showing
Himself to His disciples at the Lake of Galilee. There is something
preeminently open, natural, full fronting our disbelief in this manifestation. The others, recorded after the resurrection, were sudden,
phantom-like, occurring to men in profound sorrow and wearied
agitation of heart; not, it might seem, safe judges of what they saw.
But the agitation was now over. They had gone back to their daily
work, thinking still their business lay netwards, unmeshed from the
literal rope and drag. "Simon Peter saith unto them, 'I go a-fishing.'
They say unto him, 'We also go with thee.'" True words enough,
and having far echo beyond those Galilean hills. That night they
caught nothing; but when the morning came, in the clear light of it,
behold, a figure stood on the shore. They were not thinking of anything but their fruitless hauls. They had no guess who it was. It
asked them simply if they had caught anything. They said no. And
it tells them to cast yet again. And John shades his eyes from the
morning sun with his hand, to look who it is; and though the glint-

ing of the sea, too, dazzles him, he makes out who it is, at last; and
poor Simon, not to be outrun this time, tightens his fisher's coat about
him, and dashes in, over the nets. One would have liked to see him
swim those hundreds yards, and stagger to his knees upon the beach.

Well, the others get to the beach, too, in time, in such slow way as
men in general do get, in this world, to its true shore, much impeded
by that wonderful "dragging the net with fishes"; but they get there
—seven of them in all; first the Denier, and then the slowest believer, and then the quickest believer and then the two throne-seekers,
and two more, we know not who.

They sit down on the shore, face to face with Him, and eat their
broiled fish as He bids. And then, to Peter, all dripping still, shivering, and amazed, staring at Christ in the sun, on the other side of
the coal-fire,—thinking a little, perhaps, of what happened by another coal-fire, when it was colder, and having had no word once
changed with him by His Master since that look of His,—to him,
so amazed, comes the question, "Simon, lovest thou Me?" Try to
feel that a little; and think of it till it is true to you.

GEORGE SANTAYANA   (*1863–   )

THE EXEMPLAR OF PURE SPIRIT

Christ in the Gospels continually tells us that he is subject to the
"Father," who has "sent" him into this world. Liberation, as a Christian should desire it, cannot be liberation from fortune or domination over it. Spirit is *sent* into this world: it does not command this
world, much less create it. It may work miracles here, when it feels
the silent consent or monition of the Father prompting it to in-
voke them; but they are secondary, and the fuss the world makes
about them is disheartening. The "Father" represents the realm of
matter, where the sun shines on the just and the unjust, where to
him that hath shall be given, where the lilies of the field flourish and

the sparrows fall, where the house built on a rock will stand (for a season), where the poor are always with us, and where there shall be weeping and gnashing of teeth. Miracles belong to that natural sphere, and manifest the hidden sympathies and harmonies between its parts. The spirit notes them, but does not dwell upon them, or value them except as evidences of the unfathomable fatherly power on which spirit itself depends.

Jewish tradition unhesitatingly identified this universal power with Jehovah, conceived at once as a national patron and as the divine vindicator prophetically invoked by an aggressive conscience; but these strains are separable and not spiritual. The "Father" we hear of in the Gospels bears a more intimate and a more universal relation to the spirit. He generates and inspires it, and at the same time subjects it to the chances and cruelties of an impartial natural economy. To this economy the spirit submits painfully yet gladly; because the beauty and terror of that impartiality liberate the spirit itself from its accidental bonds. Family, race, religion, human conceit, human hypocrisy are transfixed by the clear spirit in Christ with a terrible detachment; but where love is refused, this is not because it does not exist; it exists overpoweringly for everything that the Father has created, that is simple, that is young, that suffers and is mangled in the hideous madhouse of this world.

Thus we see by the example of Christ that spirit, even when conceived to have been originally disembodied and voluntarily incarnate, is neither contaminated by its descent nor made proud by its intrinsic elevation. In Christ spirit did not need to be saved, it was free initially; yet it was inspired to love and willing to suffer; neither tempted, like the gods of Greece, to become an accomplice to human passions, nor like Lucifer to shut itself up in solitary pride. It was humble towards universal power, wisely respectful towards the realm of matter. Salvation could not consist in pretending to be independent, that is, in becoming mad. It could not consist in correcting the divine economy, and becoming creative, that is, in becoming guilty. Humility, piety, is a prerequisite to spirituality. It is much more than a prudential virtue, good for those who wish to prosper in the world. It enables spirit to recognize the truth and to be inwardly steady, clear, fearless, and without reproach.

* * * *

For us to wish to become divine persons like Christ would be chimerical and, for the pious Christian, blasphemous; but Christ may come and dwell within us, transfusing our human nature with divine light, so that our natural functions, while continuing to be performed, and performed perhaps more healthily and beautifully than before, will now be performed with detachment and humility and an eye seeing what lies beyond.

JEROME SAVONAROLA (1452–1498)

IF NOT GOD, A BLASPHEMER

Translated by O'Dell Travers Hill

Whoever you may be, I put this question. If a mortal promised to do everything—if he had conceived such an idea, and began with you first, what would you say? Would you not suspect such a person to be foolish? Would you not simply laugh at such follies? If, then, Jesus of Nazareth is not God, how is it that, without any help, this sacrilegious Seducer has prevailed against the laws of his country, against princes, against wise men, against the whole universe in opposition to him, against the powers of heaven and hell, in fine, against God Himself, even so far as to make himself equal to God, to receive honours due only to the Divinity, and to fulfil with an infinite success, in spite of difficulties, and the contradictions generated by long centuries, all the prophecies? Why then, O Jews, did your God, who governs and rules the world, permit such a great and impious crime? And you, Gentiles, I summon you as a testimony— Why did your God not extinguish this rival? How was it that this despised man, who was nailed to an infamous cross, died and was buried, left after him a force, a virtue, capable of generating so many and so great prodigies? Whoever, I will not say among men, but among those who have passed for Gods, can be compared with him? The anger, the sacrileges, the incestuous loves of the gods of paganism—are not they crimes even in the eyes of their worshippers?

PAUL SCHANZ   (*1841–1905*)

WHEN HE ROSE AGAIN

Is it not strange, it will be asked, that the disciples failed to recognize Christ when He appeared? Mary saw but knew Him not, and mistook His voice for the gardener's. The disciples going to Emmaus thought they were walking and conversing with a stranger. At the Lake of Genesareth none recognized Him. Is not this strange? and how shall we explain it? In truth we cannot offer a better explanation than that given by St. Luke: "but their eyes were held that they should not know Him" (Luke xxiv. 16). And this explanation is quite sufficient. The risen Saviour had it in His power to appear or not, to make Himself known or not, as it pleased Him. This effect he might bring about by objective or subjective means, that is, either by appearing in "another shape" (Mark xvi. 12), or by working on the minds of the Apostles, or, most probably, by combining both methods. Mary recognized her beloved master by the endearing name "Miriam," and the disciples in Emmaus by the breaking of bread; the recognition in both cases being effected by a familiar act which brought back to their minds their former life and conversation with Him.

It is singular, no doubt, that, in the apparition on the lake, the disciple whom Jesus loved, should first recognize Him. But is it not also very natural? Would not the fire that glowed in the pure heart of the virgin Apostle, burst into flame, as He who had come to cast fire on earth (Luke xii. 41), drew nigh? We should certainly infer so from the words of the disciples at Emmaus: "Was not our heart burning within us, whilst He spoke in the way and opened to us the Scriptures?" (Luke xxiv. 32).

In other apparitions they recognized Him at once. The fact that at one time, they thought they saw a spirit (Luke xxiv. 37), presents no difficulty. On the contrary, it harmonizes with the natural feelings of men (Matt. xiv. 26) as well as with the disturbed state of mind in which the disciples must have been since the terrible night of the passion. It was so difficult for them, as it would be for every one, to realize that He who had died on the cross, was now living. For this reason He convinced them by every token of reality; He ate and drank with them, though as St. Augustine thinks, He did so after the manner of angels.

MONSIGNOR FULTON J. SHEEN   (1895-   )

OUR CONTEMPORARY, BECAUSE ETERNAL

There are really three phases to the complete life of Christ, or the Whole-Christ: His Earthly Life, His Glorified Life, His Mystical Life.

His Earthly Life covered a space of about thirty-three years, extending from His Birth at Nazareth through His Public Life, Crucifixion, and Resurrection, to His Ascension into heaven, from whence He came. In His Glorified Life in Heaven, He sits at the right hand of the Father, not only enjoying the Eternal Repose merited by His glorious triumphs, but also continuing to exercise the power given to Him by His Father to teach, govern, and sanctify men. His Mystical Life in the Church began on the day of Pentecost when He sent His Spirit upon the Apostles, in order that He might not be external to His Church as an example to be copied, but *internal* with it as a life to be lived.

The complete life of Christ must include these three phases, and without any one of them we know not Christ. Those who consider only the earthly life of Christ develop either a sentimental spirituality or else end by regarding Him only as a good man and a teacher of humanitarian ethics; those who consider Him only in His Heavenly Life of Glory regard Him as an absentee landlord disregarding both His promise to send His Spirit and His abiding interest in the souls whom He came to save.

The Whole-Christ embraces not only the Earthly Life in which He redeemed, but also the Glorified and Mystical Life by which He pours out the fruits of Redemption upon the world. For the present it suffices us to know that He is not only our Truth because of His Teaching, not only our Way because of His Example, but also our Life because our Saviour and our Redeemer. His Life is not something gone from us, but living amongst us, making our lives livable, hopeful, and glad. Our eyes need not look back to Bethlehem, for the Wise Men and the simple shepherds are still at the feet of Christ. There is nothing past in Him Who is Eternal. There are no memories of Him Who is the "same yesterday, today, and tomorrow." There are no distances from here to Galilee, for He Who is Divine has pitched His tent in the very center of our hearts and civilization. Why, *Christ is our contemporary*—because He is Eternal Life.

Henry K. Sienkiewicz   (*1846–1916*)

"QUO VADIS, DOMINE?"

Translated by S. A. Binion and S. Malevsky

At dawn . . . two dark figures were stealing along the Appian Way towards the valley of the Campania. One of them was Nazarius, the other the Apostle, Peter, who was leaving Rome and his distracted brethren. In the East the sky was already assuming a slight tinge of green, which changed gradually into a saffron color. From out the shadows appeared trees with silvery foliage, white marble villas and the arches of aqueducts stretching along the plain towards the city. The green tinge of the sky was becoming shot with gold. Soon the rays began to redden and illuminate the Alban Hills, which appeared as if wrapped in a violet frame. The dawn was mirrored in drops of dew trembling on the leaves of trees. The haze grew thinner and unveiled a wider view of the plain, the houses that dotted it, the cemeteries, towns and groups of trees, among which gleamed the white columns of temples.

The road was deserted. The peasants who brought vegetables to the city had evidently not yet harnessed their horses. The blocks of stone with which the road was paved as far as the mountains echoed from the wooden-soled shoes of the wayfarers.

The sun rose over the hills, and then a wonderful vision burst upon the Apostle. It seemed to him that the golden disc, instead of rising higher in the sky, came gliding down from the heights and moved along the road. Then Peter stopped and said:

"Dost thou see the brightness approaching us?"

"I see nothing," replied Nazarius.

Peter, shading his eyes with his hands, continued:

"Some figure is approaching us in the gleam of the sun."

But no sound of footsteps reached their ears. Nazarius saw only that the trees in the distance were trembling as if shaken, and that the light was spreading more widely over the valley. With amazement in his eyes he looked at the Apostle.

"Rabbi, what troubles thee!" he cried in alarm.

Peter dropped his staff; his eyes looked straight ahead, his mouth was open, his face expressed wonder, delight, ecstasy.

Suddenly he fell upon his knees, with his hands stretched out, and cried:

"O Christ! O Christ!" and he pressed his face towards the earth, as though kissing some one's feet. Then the voice of the old man was heard, choked with tears.

"Quo Vadis, Domine?" ("Whither goest Thou, O Lord?")

Nazarius did not catch the answer, but to Peter's ears came a sad, sweet voice, which said: "As thou art deserting my people, I go to Rome to be crucified a second time."

The Apostle lay on the ground, his face in the dust, motionless and silent. It seemed to Nazarius that he had fainted, or perhaps even that he was dead. But suddenly he arose, and, without a word, turned back towards the City of the Seven Hills.

The lad, seeing this, repeated like an echo:

"Quo Vadis, Domine?"

"To Rome," replied the Apostle.

And he returned.

IGOR I. SIKORSKY   (*1889–*   )

THE LESSONS OF THE CROSS

When Christ was dying, His mother, His beloved disciple and a few distressed followers were standing near the Cross. They most certainly had faith in their loyal courageous hearts, but outwardly they were helpless, and the whole immense tragedy was also the symbol of the Kingdom of God as it is on the earth. The dark forces that incited a misguided mob to shout for the death of Christ are today just as evil, active and aggressive as they were two thousand years ago. Under the unreliable and powerless outer polish of civilization, there is the same vicious beast with lust for power and readiness to spill streams of innocent tears and blood in order to conquer or retain domination over gold and over men.

*   *   *   *

Not only men, but even Christ, with His superhuman power, was overburdened in the Garden of Gethsemane and later on the Cross when He exclaimed, "O, My God, why hast thou forsaken me?" Christ and the greatest among His followers remained loyal and faithful to God, Who appeared outwardly to have "forsaken them," to have left them defenseless in the hands of triumphant wickedness. But this inner act of supreme spiritual heroism may be beyond the power of a weaker human being in spite of his faith and idealism. The apparent indifference of the divine power with respect to the triumphant wickedness may cause heart-break and rebellion even against heaven itself. This is probably the extreme in human revolt and despair.

* * * *

Calvary and the tragic events that immediately preceded it must be considered as the greatest possible mental and physical agony which any human being could be called to suffer in this life. Yet Christ voluntarily accepted them. Whatever verbal argument can be presented to deny or explain the meaning of the suffering of the innocent, Christ confirmed the existence of such meaning by wilfully accepting the greatest possible suffering. He would have been able to avoid the cross not only by His miraculous power but even by natural means. But instead of that He went to Jerusalem on the last visit against the advices of His followers, knowing what would happen; and He actually instigated the tragedy by telling Judas, "That thou doest, do quickly" (John 13: 27). The chain of events that were started by Calvary brought the supreme glory of resurrection, which in turn caused the greatest spiritual and even intellectual rebirth that ever happened on earth. Yet even these immense visible results must be considered as incidental, because the true objectives of the ministry of Christ are mostly in the higher, eternal plan of life and not in the present temporary one.

CHARLES LEWIS SLATTERY   (*1867–1930*)

HIS AUTHORITY IN HIMSELF

Jesus Christ recognised Himself always as one sent from God; yet He neither looked forward to one higher than Himself, nor did He

utter His truth in any Name outside Himself. The vague anticipations of the Messianic idea reached their climax in Him and were
lost,—lost because the highest anticipations were so totally inadequate
for the Person He showed Himself to be. Further, when He taught
He did not even pause to say, "Thus saith the Father"; it was always,
"Ye have heard that it was said by them of old time . . . ; but *I*
say unto you . . . ."; or, "Verily, verily, I say unto you . . . ." He implied that His own word was absolute. He was not a prophet. He
was whose authority was in Himself.

Who then was Christ? Just at this point it is necessary to go the
length of divine claim: for it will be wiser, for the sake of clearness,
to go slowly. He knew Himself sent from God, and His mission
was to display to men the Character of God. It was not so much a
matter of teaching as of living: He must live out in His own character the character of the Father. . . .

He was sent from God: He pointed to Himself: in Himself He
had displayed the Character of the Father. Now what characteristic
of God did He make it His deliberate purpose to manifest? There
can be but one answer. By His own Life he demonstrated God to be,
first of all and above all, a Father—a Father of Love. . . . He had
one absorbing purpose—to show men who God really is. Not by
words, but by His own Life, He was to make clear God's character
once for all. He showed God beautiful and happy, as the Greeks had
discovered. He demonstrated that the Romans were right when they
said that He was the Embodiment of Law. By His Life, too, He
showed that in saying God is the Noble, the Righteous One, His
own nation had won the highest truth given hitherto to the world.
Every day He was to prove that God's chief prerogative is to love
men, to sympathise with them. . . .

As he pitied and helped the poor, the sick, the bad, so He taught
men that God pitied and helped and loved these same desolate souls.
We know that the temptation to depart from this one fixed purpose
came to Him time and again. In His nature he had locked other
attributes of the Father. He once said plainly that He had it in His
power to pray to the Father, and thereby to receive more than twelve

legions of angels. He laid aside whatever power was His that He might cling to that demonstration of the Father's character whose aspect is supreme. In a world as hard and self-complacent as the world of Christ's day a complete Love could meet no other reception. And the Cross was the summit of the demonstration. It was, for some, ridiculous; for others, blasphemous. The whole world cried out that it was impossible for the Great God of the universe to be sorry for the distress of men—men so small, weak and unholy. So Christ died on the Cross, not by accident, not because He became involved in one chance fray with the authorities after another; but because He freely chose to do it, because He accepted all the consequences which His deliberate purpose demanded.

IGNATIUS SMITH   (*1886–*   )

PETER'S ANSWER RE-ECHOED TODAY

The character and the teachings of Jesus have been subjected to a searching scrutiny that is unique. Before His birth there was a divinely aroused curiosity about His personality; Herod sought an investigation of Him as a Babe; the pitiless light of investigation was centered on Him during the three years of His public life; every century of the last nineteen hundred years has competed with its predecessor in analyzing the character of the Messiah. Friend and foe, animated by love and hatred have laid bare every word, deed and motive of the Master. But the more He has been attacked, the better He has been known. The more pitilessly His teachings have been carded the greater became the power of Jesus among the teeming millions of this world. . . .

One year before He died Jesus is alone with the Apostles at the foot of the mountain near Caesarea Philippi. The populace that usually followed Him from place to place is left behind and Christ and His associates kneel in common prayer. Arising, Jesus addresses to them this question: "Whom do *men* say that the Son of man is?" The Apostles answer: "Some John the Baptist, and others some Elias, and others Jeremias, or one of the prophets." Jesus said to them: "But whom do *you* say that I am?" Simon Peter answered and said: "Thou art Christ, the son of the living God." . . .

Some men say that Christ is the greatest humanitarian this world has ever seen. He loved the poor and downtrodden. He fed the hungry. His heart went out to the unfortunate. He defended the outcast and gave consolation and encouragement to the afflicted.

Others say that Christ is the greatest teacher and preacher the world has ever heard. His teachings are adaptable to all men of all time. They are simple and easily understood and yet they reach down into the very soul of every great problem of life. They gripped by the magnetism of His personality, the audiences that listened to Him; they leap over the barrier of the ages to hypnotize with equal power the peoples who read them today.

Others say that Christ is the greatest statesman the world has ever produced. He wrote the platform on which all constructive civilization rests. He formulated the program which enduring nations have followed. He outlined the policies the departure from which has spelled ruin for governments and disastrous misery for peoples for almost twenty centuries.

Others say that Christ is the greatest reformer and uplifter the race has ever produced. He battered down the class distinctions of wealth, power, social prestige and learning, and built a common democracy based on the equality of all men before God. He scathingly rebuked the deceivers of the people.

Others say that Christ was the noblest man on all the great stages of human history. He was strong, courageous, pure, sociable, religious, patient in suffering, independent in persecution, sincere, determined and merciful.

These and many other laudatory answers are given . . . by persons of every religious persuasion to the question that Christ once proposed and would propose again today: "Whom do *men* say that I am?" The answers are true but unfortunately they are only partly true. And if Christ were with us today He would turn to believers, as He once turned to Peter, and ask: "Whom do *you* say that I am?" And down through the corridors of time, from hundreds of millions of throats, picking up volume at the turn of each century, picking up harmony and resonance from the sanctuaries of every nation, energized by the voices of the seven hundreds of millions of Christians in the world today, raised on high by the religious voices of America, from the temple, from the home, from the workshop, from the market place, and from the office comes the symphony of living faith: "Thou art Christ, the Son of the living God."

ROBERT E. SPEER   (*1867-*   )

"HE KNEW THE FATHER LOVE"

Jesus had been a child. He is the only founder of a religion whose religion concerns itself with its founder's childhood. So far as we know, He Himself never referred to His birth and boyhood, though two of the Gospels preserve the story of it (Matt. 1, 2; Luke 1, 2). But He was a child all His days, and His religion is the exaltation of the spirit of the child.

How much he thought of children is indicated in this very fact. Men must return to their childhood to become members of His kingdom (Matt. 18: 3; Mark 10: 15). The spirit of His kingdom was the spirit of the child (Matt. 18: 4).

He dearly loved little children, and they drew near to Him with instinctive confidence. And their mothers trustfully brought them to Him (Matt. 18: 2; 19: 13). When His disciples discouraged this, He rebuked them (Mark 10: 13, 14). Men appealed to Him without fear for their children (Mark 5: 23), and mothers knew His rebuffs were meant to be borne down when they pleaded for children they loved (Mark 7: 24-30).

He constantly thought of the children. He knew the father love that could not withhold good gifts from the child (Matt. 7: 11). One of the horrors of the cruelty of unbelief would be this, He said, that it would lead the father to deliver up his child to death, and children to rise up against parents and put them to death (Matt. 10: 21; Mark 13: 12). One of the supremest tests of faith would be the willingness to put Christ above child (Matt. 19: 29). And one of its supremest rewards would be a joyous increase of children's love and gladness (Mark 10: 30). Children came into His Parables (Luke 7: 32; 11: 7). And when the Jews accepted the responsibility of His blood for themselves and their children (Matt. 27: 25), Jesus answered them by bidding those who wept for Him to weep rather for themselves and for their children (Luke 23: 28). The awfulness of the day of judgment fast coming down on Jerusalem would lie in the dreadful suffering it would bring on the little child and those who loved Him (Luke 23: 29; 19: 44).

In His doctrine of His kingdom He identified Himself with little children. He met a dispute for preeminence among His disciples by taking a little child in His arms, and saying, "Whosoever shall receive one of such little children in My name receiveth Me" (Mark 9: 33-37; Matt. 18: 5). An offense against a "little one", child or disciple, was intolerable (Matt. 18: 6, 10, 14; Luke 17: 2).

He regarded his disciples as children (Matt. 18: 1-14). He had the sweet faculty of merging companionship into the noble and simple confidence of children's friendship. He addressed His disciples as "children" (Mark 10: 24), and "little flock" (Luke 12: 32), and "boys" (John 21: 5). And He longed to make Jerusalem's children His own, and shelter them cozily as a hen gathers her little ones under her wings (Matt. 23: 37; Luke 13: 34). On His last evening with His disciples, before His betrayal, after Judas had gone out, and when the time for the final words of tender counsel and love had come, He began, "Little children," a word so tender it occurs elsewhere in the New Testament only in one of the most entreating and passionate appeals of Paul (Gal. 4: 19), and in the First Epistle of John, where it seems like an echo of the last evening when the Lord's lips spoke, "My dear little children," (I John 2: 1, 12, 28; 3: 7, 18;

4: 4; 5: 21). On this same evening He told them that He could not go and leave them orphans. He would come back to them (John 14: 18).

There has always been, and will always be, under heathen religions real parental love, but only Christianity makes a place for the child, and that place the chief place. Jesus, as Dr. Stalker says, "lifted childhood up, and set it in the midst. If the patter of little feet on the stairs and the sound of little voices in the house are music to us, and if the pressure of little fingers and the touches of little lips can make us thrill with gratitude and prayer, we owe this sunshine of life to Jesus Christ."

ARCHBISHOP FRANCIS J. SPELLMAN   (*1889–*   )

THE CONCEPT OF BROTHERHOOD

The concept of universal brotherhood preached by Jesus Christ . . . is a brotherhood inspired by a common faith in the Fatherhood of God, the potential universality of man's redemption and the ceaseless mission of the Spirit of God striving to unite all classes of people in the bonds of a true fraternity of a common Faith, Hope and Charity.

*   *   *   *

Among the titles given to Our Blessed Lord by the prophets of the Old Testament was "Prince of Peace." No title was more appropriate. When He became man it was a time of universal peace. On the night of His birth angels sang His praises of glory to God in the highest and on earth peace to men of good-will. St. Paul beautifully told the effect of His coming when he wrote: "He is our Peace. . . . And coming He preached peace to you that were afar off: and Peace to them that were nigh."

This blessing of peace was constantly in the mind and on the lips of Our Blessed Lord Himself. To His disciples He said: "Peace I leave to you: My peace I give unto you." Peace was the object of His teaching. "These things I have spoken to you, that in men you may have peace." Over the City of Jerusalem He wept, because that unhappy, though privileged city, would not know the things that were for her peace. On the very evening of His glorious resurrection He appeared to His apostles and said: "Peace be to thee." From His words and His works, therefore, no title given to Christ by the prophets who foretold His coming was more fitting than that of the "Prince of Peace."

CHARLES H. SPURGEON   (1834–1892)

AN INCOMPARABLE BEING

Jesus is "curtained from the sight of the gross world" by the wilful unbelief of mankind, or else the sight of him would have begotten veneration for him. Men know not the gold which lies in the mine of Christ Jesus, or surely they would dig in it night and day. They have not yet discovered the pearl of great price, or they would have sold their all to buy the field wherein it lies. The person of Christ strikes eloquence dumb when it would describe him; it palsies the artist's arm wherewith fair colours he would portray him; it would o'ermatch the sculptor to carve his image even were it possible to chisel it in the massive block of diamond. There is nought in nature comparable to him. Before his radiance the brilliance of the sun is dimmed; yea, nothing can compare with him, and heaven itself blushes at its own plainness of countenance when his "altogether lovely" person is beheld. Ah, ye who pass him by without regard, it is well said by Rutherford, "Oh, if ye knew him, and saw his beauty, your love, your heart, your desires, would close with him and cleave to him. Love by nature, when it seeth, cannot but cast out its spirit and strength upon amiable objects, and good things, and things love-worthy; and what fairer thing is there than Jesus Christ?" The Jewish world crucified him because they knew not their King; and we rejected him because we had not seen his adaptation to our wants, and believed not the love he bore to our souls.

JEREMY TAYLOR   (*1613–1677*)

LOWLINESS AND POVERTY HIS CHOICE

Jesus was pleased to be born of a poor mother, in a poor place, in a cold winter's night, far from home, amongst strangers, with all the circumstances of humility and poverty. And no man shall have cause to complain of his coarse robe, if he remembers the swaddling clothes of this Holy Child; nor to be disquieted at his hard bed, when he considers Jesus laid in a manger; nor to be discontented at his thin table, when he calls to mind the King of heaven and earth was fed with a little breast-milk. But since the eternal wisdom of the Father, "who knew to choose the good and refuse the evil," did choose a life of poverty, it gives us demonstration, that riches and honours, those idols of the world's esteem, are so far from creating true felicities, that they are not of themselves eligible in the number of good things; however, no man is to be ashamed of innocent poverty, of which many wise men make vows, and of which the Holy Jesus made election, and his apostles after him public profession. . . .

He that cried in the manger, that sucked the paps of a woman, that hath exposed himself to poverty and a world of inconveniences, is the Son of the living God, of the same substance with his Father, begotten before all ages, before the morning-stars; he is God eternal.

WILLIAM TEMPLE, Archbishop of Canterbury   (*1881*–   )

JEWISH IDEA OF THE MESSIAH

The first disciples inevitably began by thinking of their Master as a man; yet from the first there was in Him something mysterious which was the starting-point for a fuller apprehension. There were strange sayings uttered by John the Baptist which had attributed to Him such powers as a man could hardly exercise. His teachings had both a graciousness and an authority that seemed hard to reconcile with his supposed origin. His wonderful works exceeded what was known of contemporaries or recorded of any in past times except the greatest. After a period of specially close intercourse with Him they were ready to follow St. Peter in acknowledging Him as the promised Messiah. But this is still far short of a confession of His Deity. In our day many people identify the terms super-human and divine. They think that if in our Lord besides humanity there was something more than humanity, that something must be divinity. But this is quite a baseless assumption, and the Jews did not make it. What from the scene at Caesarea Philippi onwards the Apostles certainly believed is that their Master was more than human in the sense in which we are human. The Messiah was at that date conceived as a superhuman and celestial Being, who might properly be spoken of as in a peculiar sense the Son of God; but he was not conceived as divine in such a fashion as would lead to His being spoken of as God the Son.

*   *   *   *

Our faith in the Godhead of Jesus Christ does not rest chiefly on any single text or group of texts; it is a faith to which men found themselves irresistibly impelled by their growing spiritual experience as in the fellowship of the Holy Ghost they more and deeply apprehended the grace of our Lord Jesus Christ and the love of God.

*   *   *   *

Now functions, that is, actions and reactions, are all we know. If Jesus Christ performs the acts of God, then Jesus Christ is God in the only sense in which any name can justifiably be attributed to any object. The method by which in the New Testament the supreme affirmation is reached is the only method by which any such affirmation could be scientifically justified.

The belief in the Godhead of Jesus Christ is not the mere identification of Jesus with Jehovah as known to the writers of the Old Testament. Rather it is the enlargement and enrichment of the thought of God by the necessity of making room within it for what men had learned concerning God through the teaching, and still more through the Life, Death and Resurrection of Jesus Christ.

COUNT LYOF N. TOLSTOI   (*1828–1910*)

TITLE OF GOD RIGHTLY HIS

Translator Anonymous

To me now the chief matter is, not whether Jesus Christ was God, or from whom descended the Holy Ghost, or when and by whom was a certain Gospel written, or if it may not even be attributed to Christ; but the light itself is of importance to me, that it still shines upon me after eighteen hundred years with undimmed brightness; but how to call it, or of what it consists, or who gave it existence, is immaterial to me.

*   *   *   *

If Christ were not God, a great man only, then still less can his teaching engender sects; for a great man is only great so far as he expresses clearly what others have rendered incomprehensible. His words may be dark, but never misty, and there will, and must be, many ways into the darkness, but all will tend towards elucidation. All clear, deep insight into his obscurity, at one with the spirit of his teaching, uncontradicted by the plainer facts of it, and bringing the whole into conformity, will be accepted eagerly by all, and cannot of itself form sects, or rouse animosity.

* * * *

Up to the present time, some, conceiving Christ to be the second person of the Trinity, accept his teaching only as it accords with that pseudo-revelation of the Holy Ghost which they find in the Old Testament, the Epistles, the Edicts of the Councils, and the Patristic writings, and preach a strange creed founded thereon which they assert to be the faith of Christ. Others, who do not believe Christ to be God, understand his teaching by the interpretation of Paul and others; believing him to have been a man, they would, however, deprive him of the right every man may claim, of being only answerable for his own words, and in trying to explain his teaching credit him with what he would never have dreamed of saying. This school of critics, well represented by Renan, without giving themselves the trouble of extricating in the teaching of Jesus what he taught himself from what is ascribed to him, without endeavoring to obtain from it any deep meaning, explain his appearance and the propagation of his faith by incidents in his life, and from the circumstances of his time. The problem, however, which they have failed to explain is, that eighteen hundred years ago there appeared a poor man who taught, was beaten and executed; and though since his time many others have in like manner perished for their belief, this one man is still thought by thousands to be—God. . . .

The modern school of criticism to which I have referred was so pleased with its own assertion of the non-divinity of Christ, that it has since directed all its efforts to complete the proof of his humanity, forgetting that the more successful be the process, the more difficult will the final solution be as to the reason of his influence. . . .

It is not a contradiction of the divinity of Christ that is required, but an exposition of his teaching in all its purity, so lofty and so simple as to obtain for its founder the title of God.

Sigrid Undset (*1882–*)

IN THE GARDEN OF GETHSEMANE

Translated by E. P. Romsden

In the very blackest darkness lies a man on His face praying, and His sweat falls like drops of blood on the earth. And the Man is both God and man. The immeasurable space around Him is filled with hovering suns and spheres—His stars, which He has placed in the eternal ring-dance of the worlds. And on this tiny earth where He has chosen to sojourn His moon shines clearly over waste oceans and over waving tree-tops, wild and sturdy forests where no person has yet pushed his way to spoil them with the ferocity and paltriness of humanity. All is His. And this little sphere alone is unutterably full of beautiful things. When God wishes to become Man, how strange that He did not choose to taste of the best of all the good things with which He had filled the earth: hunting in the moonlit woods, feasting with the wisest and the most beautiful of the creatures He had created. He might have allowed them to vie with one another to win the favour of the God-man—by showing their wisdom, their wit and their strength. He might have permitted them to lay at His feet the very best they could produce from the raw materials that He had given into their hands: weapons, ornaments, woven wool and coloured silks, noble wines in earthen vessels, and extracts of the scents of flowers in beautifully formed crocks of alabaster. But what type of people did He choose to Himself as friends and disciples? Rather stupid, slow peasant men if easily moved. And tonight, though they were very deeply stirred when He instituted the sacrifice of the new covenant and talked with them, they have not understood enough of what is passing in the Master's mind to prevent them from falling asleep. And yet He has asked them to watch with Him. A stone's throw away they now lie and sleep. Up in the town His enemies are busying themselves with their plans. At last they will get hold of this Jesus of Nazareth. The Roman who tomorrow is to be His judge lies lightly sleeping, and Pilate's slaves, in the room where he has eaten, gather the withered roses up from the floor and clear the tables after the evening meal.

*　　*　　*　　*

From immemorial ages men had dreamt of God and the gods and of their meeting with divinity; imagined very clearly exactly what a god should be like. They had thought them exactly like themselves, had built them altars and temples, and had offered to them all that was most beautiful, all that was most costly, all that they loved most. Rulers and seers traced their origin to the gods. And now that God has become man, justifying humanity's dream of blood-relationship, and has become the son of a woman—now is the time to give Him those gifts which they have prepared for him. A place between thieves and robbers, a cross of naked planks on the place of execution, nails through hands and feet, a crown of thorns without any roses.

Jesus Christ, God and man, lies on His face in the Garden of Gethsemane and sees before Him the cross which His friends prepare for Him. They will do it also tomorrow, the days after tomorrow, all days until the end of the world. Until the end of the world humanity will answer to his words, "Learn of me for I am meek and lowly in heart"—"No, God, learn from *us.*"

HAROLD BLAKE WALKER   (*1904–*   )

THE PORTRAIT OF GOD

Throughout the centuries Christendom has looked to the Jesus of history for its most authentic insights into the nature and character of God. When the fourth Gospel reported Jesus as saying, "He that believeth on me, believeth not on me, but on him that sent me," there was summed up in a unique way the experience of early Christians with their Master. His life inescapably pointed to a power behind him, suggested a reference beyond him, revealed a reality within him. His spirit, so rich in "grace and truth," gave birth to the conviction that "God was in Christ." "Love so amazing, so divine," as to claim "my life, my all" inspired the persistent question, "What manner of man is this?" and the answer "the only begotten of the Father."

* * * *

The doctrine of the Divinity of Jesus is concerned not so much to glorify the Master as it is to say something about God. . . . By way of Jesus, the Everlasting put on a new face. He became for men not the detached mind, sitting silently behind the canopy of heaven, but a Living Spirit, closer than breathing, nearer than hands and feet. He escaped the confining fetters of inexorable law and indifferent force, and assumed the stature of a friend that "sticketh closer than a brother." "God cares!" Such is the good news Jesus brought to a baffled humanity. . . .

The portrait of God painted in the words and ways of Jesus is one of spiritual beauty and tenderness. Lost though we may be in sin and evil, he would forever "seek and save that which is lost." He "seeth in secret"; "knoweth your heart"; reacheth out in love to the leper and the outcast, to the hurt and the wounded, to the sick and the imprisoned. His "grace is sufficient" to sustain the exile and the refugee, the hungry and the despised. Even the "lilies of the field" are the concern of the Father, who likewise knows the birds as they nest. God cares for them; how much more will he care for you. "Ye are of more value than many sparrows." Here is pictured for us all the spirit of a Compassionate Goodness at the heart of reality.

GERALD GROVELAND WALSH, S.J.   (*1892–   *)

"A LUMINOUS EXAMPLE"

Jesus Christ is, at once, true God and true man. He represents an ideal of human nature that (as Professor Latourette points out in *Anno Domini*) has unfailingly won the hearts of men in every crisis in the history of Western culture. But the special aspect of that mystery that seems to me peculiarly important today is that Jesus Christ was perfectly human, precisely because his human nature was in unfailing communion with the Divine Nature. He was not less a man, but most a man, because He was also God. This is important to remember because, so it seems to me, the truth that is written largest across the pages of modern history, philosophy, literature, and art is the fact that men cannot be trusted to continue for long to be normal and human once they lose contact with God. . . .

What, therefore, loyalty to the ideal of human living, as revealed in the luminous example of Jesus Christ, can do for our day is to keep alive the conception of Christian Humanism; and this conception, in turn, seems to me the only adequate reply to the masses of our contemporaries who have been misled by the dangerous illusion of national demigods.

In this connection I should like to recall one short phrase from the Gospel of St. Luke (II, 52) which seems to me particularly worthy of meditation by every man and woman of today who is preoccupied by the problem of integrating human life in terms of both natural and supernatural values. Everyone has been moved by William Hunt's famous picture, "Christ Among the Doctors." It is not so often recalled that when the Child Jesus had astonished the wisest of the rabbis in the temple, He returned to His home in Nazareth and, being subject to the authority of Mary and Joseph, grew in wisdom and age and in grace with God and man. In that short phrase it seems possible to find the reconciliation of the three pairs of contrasts that have done so much to disintegrate modern living: subjection to authority and growth of individuality, wisdom (or unchanging values) and age (or the lessons of actual experience), supernatural grace and human charm. . . .

Is there, we ask, any intelligible meaning in suffering, any satisfying motive for sacrifice, with both of which the world today is filled? Is Fatalism or Stoicism the only source of comfort in days like these? Or is it possible that faith can give us both intellectual light and spiritual strength? The answer to this last question, that is to say, the answer of faith, has never been given more splendidly than in the words of Saint Paul:

That I may live in God, with Christ I am nailed to the cross. And I live, now not I, but Christ liveth in me. . . . I live in the faith of the Son of God, Who loved me and delivered Himself for me (Galatians II, 19, 20).

That answer has given meaning to suffering and a motive for sacrifice to every generation of Christian saints and martyrs. It is, of course, the answer of love. In a purely logical or legal view of life pain and loss will always seem other names for wickedness and waste.

In this connection Catholic meditation is never tired of calling to memory the story in the Gospel of the girl who poured out over the feet of Christ the vase filled with perfume "of great price" (John XII, 3). To Judas Iscariot, "he that was about to betray" Jesus, the action seemed one of wanton waste. "Why was not this ointment sold for three hundred pence and given to the poor?" As a Pragmatist he was just plain puzzled. (As to his parade of humanitarianism, this, we are told by the Evangelist, was pure pretense: "Now he said this, not because he cared for the poor; but because he was a thief, and having the purse carried the things that were put therein.") But Our Lord linked the action with His death and burial. "Let her alone," He said. He read in the symbol the irrepressible language of the heart, the language of love. And His best comment on such "waste" has, perhaps, been conveyed to us in His sublime paradoxes:

Amen, amen, I say to you, unless the grain of wheat falling into the ground die, itself remaineth alone. But if it die it bringeth forth much fruit. He that loveth his life shall lose it, and he that hateth his life in this world keepeth it unto life eternal (Ibid., 24, 25).

Then there is His other comment: "Greater love than this no man hath, that a man lay down his life for his friends" (John XV, 13). Before this Mystery of the Cross there is nothing one can say but: "He that hath ears to hear let him hear." The mystery is bound to be to some a stumbling block, to others foolishness:

But unto them that are called, both Jews and Greeks, Christ the power of God and the wisdom of God. For the foolishness of God is wiser than men; and the weakness of God is stronger than men (I Cor., I, 24, 25).

At any rate, . . . faced with the fearful phenomenon of hate which has been associated with the crooked cross, the swastika, the language of love that speaks in the Mystery of the Cross is heard with an accent that is sweeter and softer than ever before. So that, even today, in all suffering and in every sacrifice we can lift our eyes and see "the shade of His hand outstretched caressingly."

WOODROW WILSON   (1856–1924)

"HE IS OUR REVELATION"

And so we have seen Scripture become mere plain philosophy, the words of Christ the words of a teacher who has seen the ultimate realities and speaks them very simply, with the simplicity of utter authority. . . .

If life be thus personal, if it be of law, if the law of highest compulsion be the law of our own spirits, how shall we dispense with the knowledge of him who is the Father of Spirits; and yet how can we know Him whom we have not seen,—how can we know him except in the person of Christ, the express image of the Father, the Word that became flesh and "dwelt among us, full of grace and truth?" . . .

And so the type and symbol is magnified,—Christ, the embodiment of great motive, of divine sympathy, of that perfect justice which sees into the hearts of men, and that sweet grade of love which takes the sting out of every judgment. "We look not at the things which are seen, but at the things which are not seen": we do not, we cannot, see Christ, but there he stands, the most indubitable fact of history, with a sway over the hearts and lives of men which has not been broken or interrupted these nineteen hundred years. No man can ever think of him as dead, unreal, a thing of books, a creature of theology. "The things which are seen are temporal," but He, He is the embodiment of those things which, not seen, are eternal,—the eternal force and grace and majesty, not of character, but of that which lies back of character, obedience to the informing will of the Father of our spirits.

The force and beauty of Christ seem not to have been his own, as if original. He spoke always of his father, and of himself only as doing his father's will and speaking his father's words. There dwelt in him a spirit, great and universal, as that of the round world itself, compact of law and truth, a spirit greater than the world, conveying life and vision from the source from which all worlds and existence itself must have taken origin. He is our revelation. In him is our life explained and our knowledge made comprehensible. He is the perfect elder brother of our spirits. In him we are made known to ourselves,—in him because he is God, and God is the end of our philosophy; the revelation of the thought which, if we will but obey it, shall make us free, lifting us to the planes where duty shall seem happiness, obedience liberty, life the fulfillment of the law. Science is our intimation; literature is the imperfect voice of our fellow-men, seeking, like ourselves, an exit for their hopes; philosophy is what we would fain convince ourselves of but cannot see: in all of these the things which are unseen and real lurk, but elude us. In Christ, in the God whom he reveals, the veil is torn away. Look! Look there and have your fill of what you have sought most. You must ever seek in vain until you raise your eyes to the Christ where he is lifted up. "As Moses lifted up the serpent in the wilder-

ness, even so must the Son of Man be lifted up: that whosoever believeth in him should not perish but have eternal life,"—that life
which subsisteth upon the things which are not seen.

FRANCIS YEATS-BROWN   (*1886–*   )

DOCTRINES THAT DISTURB

I believe that Christ was very man made Very God, the Incarnation
of man's potential Divinity. Unfortunately, this is not Christianity
as taught in any Church, but a neomonophysite (The monophysites
believed that Our Lord has one nature, the divine and the human
being combined in Him as soul is with body) heresy. Heresy or not,
I hold, in all humility and confidence, that this is what Christ meant
when He said "I [am] in them, and thou in me, that they may be
made perfect in One." I shall not argue this conviction. The whole
tenor of Christ's life tells me, beyond possibility of personal doubt,
that the Divinity that descended on Him other men may also attain.

*   *   *   *

"Swami-ji," I said, "I have realized recently that though I call
myself a Christian, there are irreconcilable differences between what
I believe, and what any of our Churches teach. There are Sayings and
Actions of Christ which would lead to the whole world's redemption: deeds and words of the most perfect beauty; but the doctrine
. . . the doctrine disturbs me."

"Why do you have to belong to a Church? In Hinduism we are
more catholic."

"I needn't, but I believe in authority. I believe in being in touch
with the thought and experience of wise men down the centuries.
Yet I cannot accept what they say."

"I have been in the same difficulty myself. I sought many years
for a guru."

"And you found him eventually?"

"Yes. . . . You believe in miracles?"

"Of course I do! They happen every day. But I don't understand why the fig-tree should have been cursed, for instance, or why an evil spirit should possess the swine."

"What does it matter? If you read the New Testament in the light of the Vedanata, Christ's words are clear."

"How? That God is a Spirit, and that that is the great reality?"

"Roughly, yes. Beside the Immanent Divine, the sense world is illusion."

"I am prepared to accept that. It can be reconciled with the general direction of human knowledge. But . . . well, take the Virgin Birth. It seems so unnecessary, and there have been so many others. And the Appearances after the Crucifixion: even the most devout scholars are puzzled by the contradictory accounts in the Gospels."

"I couldn't explain them, but then I wouldn't try. Surely they are details? You have no responsibility in the matter. Your responsibility is not to this or that evidence concerning the Resurrection, but to your own resurrection."

BRIGHAM YOUNG   (*1801–1877*)

OUR CAPTAIN AND LEADER

Our Lord Jesus Christ—the Savior, who has redeemed the world and all things pertaining to it, is the Only Begotten of the Father pertaining to the flesh. He is our Elder Brother, and the Heir of the family, and as such we worship Him. He has tasted death for every man, and has paid the debt contracted by our first parents.

Jesus is our Captain and leader: Jesus, the Savior of the world— the Christ that we believe in.

Our faith is concentrated in the Son of God and through Him to the Father; and the Holy Ghost is Their minister to bring truths to our remembrance, to reveal new truths to us and teach, guide and direct the course of every mind until we become perfected and prepared to go home, where we can see and converse with our Father in Heaven.

The Latter-day Saints believe in Jesus Christ, the only begotten Son of the Father, Who came in the meridian of time, performed his work, suffered the penalty and paid the debt of man's original sin by offering Himself up, was resurrected from the dead and ascended to His Father; and as Jesus descended below all things so he will ascend above all things. We believe that Jesus Christ will come again, as it is written of Him: "And while they looked steadfastly toward heaven as He went up, behold two men stood by them in white apparel; which also said, 'Ye men of Galilee, why stand ye gazing up into heaven? This same Jesus which is taken from you into heaven shall so come in like manner as ye have seen Him go into heaven.'"

We believe that Jesus Christ will descend from heaven to earth again even as he ascended into heaven. "Behold, He cometh with clouds, and every eye shall see Him, and they also which pierced Him: and all kindreds of the earth shall wail because of Him." He will come to receive His own, and rule and reign King of nations as he does King of Saints; "For he must reign till He hath put all enemies under His feet. The last enemy that shall be destroyed is death." He will banish sin from the earth and·its dreadful consequences, tears shall be wiped from every eye and there shall be nothing to hurt or destroy in all God's holy mountain.

Jesus Christ will draw all men unto Him, except those who contend against the power of God and against His Kingdom until they have sealed their own damnation.

TEACHER

Karl Adam   (1876-   )

HIS DOCTRINE FROM HIMSELF

Translated by Dom Justin McCann, O.S.B.

When we read St. Matthew's Gospel it immediately becomes plain
to us that Jesus regarded His preaching as a substantial part of His
redemptive work and looked upon Himself as eminently a teacher.
In His first sermon in the synagogue at Nazareth, He preached from
a passage in the prophet Isaias which emphasized this teaching office
of the redeemer: "the spirit of the Lord is upon me, wherefore he
hath anointed me, to preach the gospel to the poor." He laid express
claim to the honourable title of Master: "You call me Master and
Lord, and you say well, for so I am." He claimed the title in an exclusive fashion: "Neither be ye called masters; for one is your Master,
Christ."

Humanly speaking we may say that the quality above all others
which gave His preaching its power was its originality; He had not
got His doctrine from another; He had not, like St. Paul, sat at the
feet of any Gamaliel. He had been brought up as a carpenter, in what
we should call working-class conditions, nor had the means of human
culture been accessible to him. We hear nothing of any teacher of
His, and His own towns-folk were amazed at His preaching: "How
came this man by this wisdom? Is not this the carpenter's son?" What
He gave the people was His own, and not learnt from another: "I
speak that which I have seen with my Father." The sole book that
He constantly cites is the Holy Scriptures, the written word of His
Father. Jesus lived and moves in the language, imagery and thought
of the Old Testament; but He uses the Old Testament, not as the
devout scholar or humble disciple, but as the Lord and Master who
has come to fulfil its every word. . . . The Old Testament has for
Him no supreme and final authority, for He Himself, the Incarnate
God, is that authority. Hence His independent judgments and His
setting aside the authority even of Moses. Even when He is ex-
pounding sacred Scripture, He is independent of it, remaining wholly

227

Himself in mind and will. . . . The people were quickly alive to the difference: "They were astonished at his doctrine, for he was teaching them as one having power, and not as the Scribes." A greater than they, and a greater than Moses had now come, one who had not to make laborious search for truth, but already possessed it in Himself, in His own immediate experience. He had but to dip into the rich treasure of His own mind in order, as He expresses it, to bring forth new things and old.

His preaching is so exceedingly simple, yet at the same time so forcible, just because it is based on this immediate and personal knowledge. It is characteristic of Him that He says the most striking and arresting things in so simple and natural a way that they seem inevitable.

Felix Adler   (*1851–1933*)

NOT JUST A MAN

I was particularly struck with the originality of Jesus' teachings, a quality in them which to my amazement I had found disputed not only by Jews, but by representative Christians. . . . Christian teachers likewise—I remember particularly a recent sermon to that effect —have taken the ground that Jesus added nothing new to the ethical insight of mankind. . . . Thus, to mention only a single capital instance, it has been asserted that the Golden Rule as taught by Jesus is not original, but substantially the same rule that had been laid down by Confucius 500 years before the time of Jesus. But on closer scrutiny it will be seen that the two Golden Rules are by no means the same. As propounded by the Chinese sage the rule appears to mean: Keep the balance true between thyself and thy neighbor; illustrate in thy conduct the principle of equilibrium. As impressed upon his disciples by Jesus it means: Look upon thy neighbor as thy other self; act towards him as if thou wert he. . . .

The mythological idealization of Jesus, indeed, I put aside as a thing that did not concern me. On the other hand, to say with certain modern liberals that he was just a man, an infinitely gracious personality, one who exemplified in his life the virtues of forgiveness and self-sacrifice, did not satisfy me either. Buddha too had taught forgiveness. . . . It could not then be the bare precept of forgiveness that lets light on the secret of Jesus. . . .

I came to conclude that the ethical originality of Jesus consists in a new way of dealing with the problem of evil, that is, of evil in the guise of oppression. . . . Jesus said, Resist not evil in the guise of oppression, it is irresistible. . . . Shall then evil triumph? Is the victim helplessly at the mercy of the injurer? . . . Quite a different meaning is implied. And here the teaching of Jesus takes its novel turn. There is a way, he says to the victim, in which you can spiritually triumph over the evil-doer, and make your peace with irresistible oppression. Use it as a means of self-purification; pause to consider what the inner motives are that lead your enemy, and others like him, to do such acts as they are guilty of, and to so violate your personality and that of others. The motives *in them* are lust, greed, anger, wilfulness, pride. Now turn your gaze inward, look into your own heart and learn, perhaps to your amazement, that the same evil streams trickle through you; that you, too, are subject, even if it be only subconsciously and incipiently, to the same appetites, passions, and pride, that animate your injurers. Therefore let the sufferings you endure at the hands of those who allow these bad impulses free rein in their treatment of you lead you to expel the same bad impulses that stir potentially in your breast; let this experience fill you with a deeper horror of the evil, and prove the incentive to secure your own emancipation from its control. In this way you will achieve a real triumph over your enemy, and will be able to make your peace with oppression. There are other intolerable evils in the world besides oppression which nevertheless must be tolerated. The method of Jesus can be applied to these also. This method I regard as a permanent contribution to the ethical progress of humanity.

BRONSON ALCOTT   (*1799–1888*)

IF HIS DIARY EXISTED

I should like to read a Diary of the Prophet of Nazareth, written
by his own hand, and detailing his hindrances, hopes, purposes—a
faithful portrait of his own heart. Such a document, now brought to
light, would reveal as nothing else the injustice of time concerning
this noble man. Christendom would read it with dismay. Church and
State would be riven asunder by it. Few, if any, of our institutions
would stand in the light of its sublime ethics. Something like the
finding of such a record is needful to a republication of his doctrines.

POPE BENEDICT XV   (*1854–1922*)

HALL MARK OF CHRISTIANS

Indeed, as you well know and as We have often called to mind, nothing was so often and so insistently taught by the divine Master to
His disciples as this precept of fraternal charity as the one which includes all the others in itself; and Our Lord called that precept new
and His own, desiring that it should be as the hall mark of the
Christians by which they might easily be distinguished from all
others.

No other, indeed, was the testament that He left to His followers
when He died, praying them to love one another, and loving one another try to imitate the ineffable unity that exists between the Persons of the Holy Trinity: "That they may be one as we also are one
that they may be made perfect in one."

And the Apostles, following the order of the Divine Master and
taught by His very voice, were unceasing in their exhortation to the
faithful: "But before all things have a constant mutual charity among

yourselves"; "And above all these things have charity which is the bond of perfection"; "Dearly beloved, let us love one another for charity is of God." . . .

What has already been said to teach the precept of charity holds good for the pardoning of offenses, no less solemnly commanded by the Lord: "But I say to you, love your enemies; do good to them that hate you, and pray for them that persecute and calumniate you, that you may be the children of your Father who is in Heaven, who maketh His sun to rise upon the good and bad." Hence that terribly severe warning of the Apostle St. John: "Whosoever hateth his brother is a murderer and you know that no murderer hath eternal life abiding in himself."

Finally, Jesus Christ taught us to pray the Lord so that we ask for forgiveness on condition of forgiving others: "And forgive us our debts as we also forgive our debtors." And if sometimes the observance of this law seems too severe and difficult, the Redeemer of the human race Himself assists us not only with the Divine Grace but also by His admirable example, for as He hung on the cross He prayed pardon of His Father for those who so unjustly and wickedly tortured Him: "Father, forgive them, for they know not what they do." . . .

Christian charity in fact is not confined to not hating our enemies and loving them as brothers; it desires also that we do good to them, following the rule of the Divine Master who "went about doing good and healing all that were oppressed by the Devil," and ran the course of His mortal life giving it all up to doing untold good to men, even shedding His blood for them. . . .

To the mind of anyone who sees this picture of misery by which the human race is oppressed there must come back at once the story of the Gospel traveler who was journeying from Jerusalem to Jericho and fell among thieves who robbed him and covered him with wounds and left him half dead by the wayside. The two cases are very much alike; as to the traveler there came the good Samaritan, full of compassion, who bandaged his wounds, pouring oil and wine over them, took him to the inn and undertook all care of him, and so, to cure the wounds of the human race the hand of Jesus Christ is needed, of whom the Samaritan was figure and image.

EDWARD INCREASE BOSWORTH   (*1861–1927*)

LEARNED OBEDIENCE THROUGH SUFFERING

Jesus lived almost all of his life as a private citizen. Only for a little while near the end did he become a public character. When he appeared as a public teacher he had a mature character and a well established viewpoint, which must have been developed during the years of his private life. He must have passed through a profound religious experience during this period and thought deeply on the subjects he discussed in his public teaching. This does not mean that the great crises through which Jesus so rapidly passed in the course of his brief public career contributed nothing to the deepening of his religious experience and the further development of his character. It was the conviction of the early Christian leaders that Jesus "learned obedience through the things that he suffered" and that only in this way did he become "unto all them that obey him the author of eternal salvation."

We know very little about the details of Jesus' life before he became a public character. . . . Jesus' life had been so commonplace and even poor in its material circumstances that the portrayal of it would have hindered rather than helped in the presentation of him to the Greco-Roman world as the majestic Messiah of God, the Lord of heaven and earth soon to return to the earth in heavenly power.

*   *   *   *

It is not impossible to picture the character making process that went on in Jesus; for we have learned from his teaching the elements of enduring character and the process by which they come into being. But when it is all done we seem not to have accounted for that which appeared later in his public life. There seem to be certain original dimensions of personality which we do not measure, a certain something coming up in him with overflowing fulness from the underlying life of God which we do not understand. Evidence of this we find later in the period when his kindling sense of mission was upon him.

CHARLES REYNOLDS BROWN   (*1862–*   )

THE CONVERSION OF ZACCHEUS

How many of the Master's personal contacts were altogether casual! There was nothing cut and dried about them. No one had made an appointment with him in advance. They just came along in the day's work.

He was passing through a crowded street, when a suffering woman brushed against him, believing that if she could only touch the hem of his garment, she would be healed. He recognized the appeal of faith and the woman was healed. He was passing through the outskirts of another city, when a blind man shouted after him, hoping that he might receive his sight—and we are told that he did. He stopped at a public well and asked a Samaritan woman for the loan of her cup—"Give me a drink"—and it led to a conversation which changed that woman's whole life. Casual contacts they were, all of them, yet each one meant the upward movement of a human soul.

He "entered and passed through Jericho." He had no speaking engagements there apparently—he was just passing through on his way perhaps from Galilee to Jerusalem by way of the Jordan valley. He found the streets lined with people—it was like the Fourth of July or Labor Day in one of our cities. The people were eager to see this teacher, this healer, this leader in a movement which might mean a new quality of life for their whole nation. There was such a crowd that unless one were strong enough to elbow his way to the front, or tall enough to see over the heads of others, he had not a dog's chance to see anything.

There was one man on the street that day who "sought to see Jesus but could not for the crowd." "He was little of stature," yet he was the richest man in Jericho. He was the Collector of Internal Revenue for that district. The tax collector in any community is not likely to be as popular as Santa Claus, but there in Palestine where the taxes were farmed out at that time, the people hated him as they hated the devil. Some man would pay the Roman Government a fixed sum for the right to collect taxes in a given area, and then take all he could get. One sees instantly how this opened the way for no end of graft and extortion. The people called the tax collectors "publicans and sinners." They stood socially about where the bootleggers stand with us. They could not even go to church without hearing some Pharisee say, "Thank God, I am not unjust, an extortioner, an adulterer, or even as this publican"—this tax collector. Zaccheus that day was simply an undersized, unpopular man in a crowd, which robbed him of any sense of significance. His own personal interests were menaced by the mob.

He had to get out of the crowd in order to see the Lord. He found himself nothing but a helpless atom in a mass of humanity. Had he been instructed in our modern phraseology, which seems so precious and diverting to some people, he too might have suffered from "an inferiority complex." He might have called himself "a parasite infesting the epidermis of a midge among the planets." He was "in the jam"—it was like the rush hour in the subway or like the crowd in some huge stadium on the day of a great football game. Hated as he was, people would not allow him to elbow his way to the front. No tall person would stand aside to allow Zaccheus to see—there was no "after you, please" for tax collectors. He was cut off from any chance of seeing the Master, as completely as if he had been walled up in a stone prison. Unless he got out of the crowd, there was no vision for him. . . .

There was that rich a man in Jericho—he had money to burn, but he wanted to see the Lord. He was tremendously in earnest about it. He too had heard of this man of Nazareth, who spake as never man spake, who forgave men's iniquities and healed their diseases, who redeemed their lives from defeat and satisfied their needs with good things, so that their strength was renewed. He could not see the Master "because of the crowd"—he therefore ran on ahead "and climbed up into a sycamore tree to see him, for he was to pass that way." Imagine the Mayor of a city, or the Collector of Internal Revenue, or the richest man in town, climbing a tree in order to see a teacher of religion! But there he was, peering out through the branches that day when the Master came along.

When Jesus saw him he called him at once into a closer relation to Himself. "Zaccheus," he said to the man in the tree—that was the man's name, but no one in Jericho ever called him that. The people there called him "wolf," "dog," "swine," because he was a tax collector. It meant everything to hear his name spoken in his own home-town in tones of respect—it was like a cup of cold water on a hot day. It put the man at once into a better frame of mind. "Zaccheus, make haste and come down, for to-day I must abide at thy house." Zaccheus had a good home, plenty to eat, all the necessary materials for hospitality, but no respectable person in Jericho would accept his invitations. "Eat with a tax collector!" That was why Jesus had to invite himself.

"Zaccheus made haste and came down and received him joyfully." The two men walked down street together as friends. Zaccheus walked that day as one who dreamed. He had meat to eat which the thoughtless knew not of. He might almost have been singing to himself, "O Master, let me walk with thee."

"When the people saw it, they all murmured." Gone to be the guest of a man who is a sinner! Screw loose somewhere! A man is known by the company he keeps! If this man were a prophet, he would not have come to Jericho and passed by all the leading church members in order to take dinner with a tax collector. They were horrified, as some people were horrified when a certain President of the United States, Theodore Roosevelt, invited Booker T. Washington, a Negro, to break bread with him at the White House. The kingdom of heaven had not fully come at that time in the city of Jericho, just as it has not fully come as yet in the city of Washington.

Jesus heard them sneer, and he went straight ahead, side by side with the publican, as serenely as if he had been walking with the angels through the streets of the New Jerusalem. The menace of the crowd was not taken seriously by him. He stood high enough to see over their heads—his eyes rested upon a broader, finer prospect.

He was ready always to pay the full price of doing good in his own way. Bigotry and race prejudice had no place in his plan of action. He was willing to face the ridicule and suspicion of the mob in order to put himself in open alliance with the best he saw in the natures of those he would help. His enemies called him "the friend of publicans and sinners." He accepted the title and gloried in it, as if they had conferred upon him some honorary degree. He was "just that," he said. "They that are whole have no need of a physician, but they that are sick." He was "the Great Physician" and his business was with the sick. "I come not to call the righteous"—people who think they are good enough already just as they are—"but sinners to repentance"—that is to try again and do better. There was never an hour when the Master was not being wounded for their transgressions and bruised for their iniquities that by his stripes, they might be healed. . . .

What an hour it was for that dishonest little man to be taken out of the crowd and brought face to face with the Lord of life at his own table! Here within speaking distance, within arm's length was the Son of Man revealing this man to himself and helping him to realize his own true self. Zaccheus, a publican and a sinner, a grafter and a miser, hated and despised by all his fellow townsmen—aye, he was all that! But Zaccheus also, potentially, a son of Abraham, a child of the covenant, a man capable of having his part in that kingdom of God on earth in which all nations are to be blessed.

The man within the man, the higher capacity of the man in waiting, the better nature of the man now overborne by his own evildoing but destined to come into its own! It was that which Jesus saw that day. It was that with which he desired to have fellowship. When Zaccheus got out of the crowd that he might see the Lord, turning his back upon the presence of the mob, he was brought at once into close, personal fellowship with the Highest and Holiest Being who ever walked this earth. When the meal was over, the Master could say, "Today, salvation has come to this house. Zaccheus also is a son of Abraham, for the Son of Man is come to seek and to save that which is lost." He had restored to that man's life something which had been lost out of it.

Then, without an hour's delay, the Master sent him back into the crowd again to shew what the Lord had done for him. There at the table they talked about religion. It was a religion which was not all up in the air, made up mainly of rhapsodies and high-sounding phrases. The Master made religion as real as life itself. When the meal was over, this stingy, little grafter was saying, "Lord, if I have taken anything from any man wrongfully" (for he knew that he had, many a time—that was one of the ways in which he had become the richest man in Jericho) "I restore him fourfold." Four for one! That was restitution, "good measure, shaken down, pressed together, and running over." When any man is ready to sing his song of penitence in that key—four sharps, as it were—we know that he has the real thing in his heart. "I will restore fourfold to every man I have wronged."

He had been dishonest, and he had also been stingy. He gets up at the very place where he had fallen down. "I restore, I give! Half of my goods, I give to the poor." Give was a new word for Zaccheus. Buy and sell, get and gain, hold and invest—all these words he could pronounce and spell and live. But the word "give"—he could scarcely get it out at first—it almost stuck in his throat like Macbeth's "Amen," when he had most need of blessing. It was like Sanscrit to Zaccheus, yet in that hour when salvation came to his house, he bravely uttered it. "The half of my goods, I give to the poor."

That took him at once back into the crowd. The men he had wronged, to whom he was to restore fourfold, were not there in his own house—they were out there in the crowd. The needy people he was to help with the half of all his goods were not there at his own table—they were scattered about in the poorer parts of the city. It was out there in the street that Zaccheus began to let his light shine, that men might see his good work and glorify the Father.

How "realistic" it all is! It might well satisfy these extreme modernists who are half-crazy over what they call "realism." Tears can easily be shed, and often they have no more significance than so much rainwater. Remorse is cheap—it may be nothing more than the discomfort which some bad man feels upon being found out. But repentance which shows itself in restoring fourfold, and giving away half of all it has to help the needy, is more precious than rubies. It means an about-face, a change of front, the cutting out of evil, the forward, upward movement of a human soul. Back into the crowd, this changed man went to do just that.

Divine help can be gained at the mountaintop (as we see in that story of the Transfiguration) but the new life has to be lived where the people are massed together. The Master prayed at the mountaintop, in white raiment with his face shining like the sun, and then straightway, he came down to the foot of the mountain to heal a sick boy. . . .

It is natural to cherish a certain dread of the mob spirit, the mob psychology, and to shun those ways of life which are characteristic of the crowd. But to tell the whole truth at last, it has to be borne in mind, that the Master loved the crowd. The people knew it— "the common people heard him gladly," because they felt that he cared. He spoke their language and entered sympathetically into their struggles. He had been tried at all points as they were being tried. He bore their griefs and carried their sorrows. He waited upon the Father for the renewal of his strength, yet he never got too far away from the crowd to reach out a hand of help, warm, friendly, ungloved. And when he breaks bread with his followers today, either in his own house and at his table, or in their homes and at their tables (as he broke bread that day in the home of Zaccheus), he bid them "go and do likewise." For he that dwelleth in the spirit and practice of good will toward his fellow beings, dwelleth in God and God in him, for God is good will.

GEORGE A. BUTTRICK   (*1892*–   )

LOVE, NOT FEAR, HIS WEAPON

It will be admitted that He "spoke with authority." But He did not covet the title of best-informed man in His community. He was not an artist, or sculptor, or statesman, or the head of a family. He disowned omniscience: "But of that day and that hour knoweth no one, not even the angels in heaven, neither the Son. . . ." He apparently accepted many current concepts. He "was meek and lowly in heart." Yet He spoke with authority.

Again, the primary appeal of Jesus was not to fear. That appeal is valid within limits. . . . Jesus used the appeal sparingly, within valid limits; but He did not exploit the external threat. He made his plea to a higher kind of fear. . . . Jesus used love, not fear, as His best weapon. Yet He spake with authority.

Nor did Jesus build on the literal infallibility of a Book. The Sermon on the Mount goes beyond the ethic of the Mosaic Law. Jesus loved the Book. Only a mind saturated in it and reverencing it could have quoted it as He quoted it. But He did not deal in proof texts. He did not use the Old Testament as a thesis in anthropology, or even as an excursion into theology. He found in it the verities of life; yea, He found in it the verities of God. He found, not an impossible certainty of literal fact, but the vital certitude of regnant and compassionate Spirit. He made no false appeal to the Bible. Yet He spake with authority.

What was His authority? The shepherd went back to his hills and the fisherman to his lake, saying: "Whence hath this Man this wis-

dom? So gentle He; yet His words are a command." It was the
authority of a Life! . . . Jesus was authority because in Him pierc-
ingly and persuasively Light broke upon our world.

SIR HALL CAINE   *(1853–1931)*

THE LAW OF LOVE TAUGHT

Jesus taught the coming of the kingdom of God, but this included
also a new national morality for the kingdom of this world also.
He condensed the law into two sentences: "Love God" and "Love
your neighbour." He denounced the spirit of conceit in the words:
"Hypocrite, cast out first the beam out of thine own eye, and then
shalt thou see clearly to pull out the mote that is in thy brother's
eye." His preaching was convincing. His sermons, including the
composite Sermon on the Mount, give a vivid picture of Jesus preaching. We hear him clearly. We can almost distinguish his voice. It is a
persuasive voice, but it is also an imperative one. He speaks with
authority.

G. K. CHESTERTON   *(1874–1936)*

THE WANDERING TEACHER OF NAZARETH

We often hear of Jesus of Nazareth as a wandering teacher; and there
is a vital truth in that view in so far as it emphasises an attitude
towards luxury and convention which most respectable people
would still regard as that of a vagabond. It is expressed in his own
great saying about the holes of the foxes and the nests of the birds,
and, like many of his great sayings, it is felt as less powerful than it is,
through lack of appreciation of that great paradox by which he
spoke of his own humanity as in some way collectively and repre-

sentatively human; calling himself simply the Son of Man; that is, in effect, calling himself simply Man. It is fitting that the New Man or the Second Adam should repeat in so ringing a voice and with so arresting a gesture the great fact which came first in the original story; that man differs from the brutes by everything, even by deficiency; that he is in a sense less normal and even less native; a stranger upon the earth. It is well to speak of his wanderings in this sense and in the sense that he shared the drifting life of the most homeless and hopeless of the poor. It is assuredly well to remember that he would quite certainly have been moved on by the police and almost certainly arrested by the police, for having no visible means of subsistence. For our law has in it a turn of humour or touch of fancy which Nero and Herod never happened to think of; that of actually punishing homeless people for not sleeping at home.

THOMAS CHUBB   (*1679-1746*)

WORTHY OF IMITATION

That the gospel might come the better recommended to the world Christ was in his own person an example of strict conformity to it, by conforming his affections and actions to that unalterable rule of action which is founded in the reason of things. Christ preached his own life if I may so speak, and lived his own doctrine, and thereby he was at once a standing monument of the practicableness of virtue, and of the present peace and happiness that flows from it. In him we may see what it is to live a godly, a righteous, a sober, and a benevolent life; and that what he requires from us as the ground of God's favour is neither unreasonable, nor impracticable. In him we have an example of a quiet and peaceful spirit, of a becoming modesty and sobriety, just and honest, upright and sincere, and above all of a most gracious and benevolent temper and behaviour. One who did no wrong, no injury to any man, in whose mouth was no guile, who went about doing good, not only by his preaching and ministry, but also in curing all manner of diseases among the people. His life was a beautiful picture of human nature, when in its native purity and simplicity, and shewed at once what excellent creatures men would be, when under the influence and power of that gospel which he preached unto them.

And as his holy life and doctrine drew on him the unreasonable resentment of the clergy among the Jews, who stirred up the rest of the people against him: so this gave an occasion for his sealing his testimony with his blood, and of giving an instance of the greatest benevolence toward mankind. And as his life was an excellent pattern and example of every good word and work, and therefore very fit and proper for his disciples and followers to copy after: so his death was not less exemplary. For he not only laid down his life to promote the greatest, and the most general good to mankind; but he did it in such a manner (by exercising such patience and resignation under the severest trials and most painful afflictions and persecutions), as rendered him highly worthy of our imitation. He was very sensible that the great thing which he had undertaken to prosecute was the saving of men's souls; and as it disposed him to do, and suffer whatever was necessary or expedient to forward this great and gracious design: for it induced him to overlook the cruelty and unreasonable resentment of his persecutors, by pitying and praying for them, whilst he was suffering the most intense pain from them, and even dying by their hands. And thus his life and death were made subservient to his ministry, and served to recommend his gospel to the world.

Paul Claudel   (*1868–*   )

NOT A POLITICAL MOVEMENT

Translated by Rev. John O'Connor

Looking to the picture given by the Gospels as only for the simplest representation, not contested by any—What is Jesus Christ? A Jewish Illuminate, who has left us nothing written, preaching for a few years and finally crucified by the Romans on the initiative and on the condemnation of the Jewish doctrinal authorities. To this obscure personality is attached the greatest religious movement which ever wrought upon mankind.

Let us start and go on from these data alone.

The first thing to notice is that the powerful intellectual and moral agitation of which Jesus was the origin did not in his lifetime eventuate in a material and political movement. There is no trace of a rising, of a rebellion, as later on that of Judas the Gaulonite or Bar Koceba.

The fact underlying the condemnation of Jesus has therefore had a purely doctrinal cause, and this cause must have been extremely grave, seeing the gravity of the condemnation and its execution by the Romans on the eve of the greatest festival of the year, and although public order was never compromised.

Another proof of that gravity is the hatred vowed by the Jews to the memory of Jesus (see Talmud). Just as the virtue, or, if you like, the virulence of His teaching was confirmed by the conversion a year after Calvary of Saint Paul, a Pharisee of the Pharisees. As it never was translated into any political movement, we must needs conclude that the teaching of Christ was related solely to the world of ideas, of conscience. It was something sundered from the temporal. It made a radical distinction between the world of material fact and the moral world.

On the other hand, it never posed as the destruction of the old religion, but as its explanation and development. Christ preaches everywhere in the synagogues from the official pulpits. Still the preaching of Jesus causes a fearful scandal among the authorities officially responsible for the interpretation and administration of religion. They thought themselves threatened both in their belief and in their official position, shaken to the foundations. One feels that the Pharisees are fighting for their lives: so not on the side of Jesus is there mere moral preaching like that of John the Baptist, but doctrine: doctrine pointed out by Him as the sequence and development of the ancient revelation, and yet scandalously new in the eyes of the detainers of the Law. Jesus must have said something frightful.

There is nothing more frightful than blasphemy. But precisely, we see that the deed laid to the charge of Christ is blasphemy, that is to say, an attack on the Godhead Itself. The attribution to the Divinity of a character degrading to His Majesty. What was that blasphemy? On this point we have the contemporary witness of Saint Paul. So long as there is an historic trace of a Christian, from the first conversion authentically ascertained, we see that that Christian believed Christ to be the Son of God, and, if he believed that Jesus was the Son of God, it is because Jesus had told him so Himself (against Renan). This affirmation was, in Jewish eyes, an unheard-of scandal, to them who at that period no longer durst pronounce the "Incommunicable Name."

In all the history of mankind, never has a religious revolutionary dared to proclaim himself the Son of God (God in the fullness and the meaning which the Jews gave Him), and that for very simple reasons: because he too clearly lacked both the moral perfection and the material power to bear out so great a title. Such an affirmation in the midst of the Jewish world was something unheard of, frightful!

So it was absolutely necessary that Jesus should justify this claim, that He should give striking marks at once of His wisdom and of His power; He had to bear witness of Himself, both by holiness and by miracles. This necessity was the greater, that whilst enlisting His disciples into a new way which set them against the whole official authority of Judaism, he promised them nevertheless no material advantage, but on the contrary persecution.

Now the Man who alone of all created beings has ever dared to call Himself the Son of God, we see perish in the basest, cruelest, most humiliating conditions in the most complete abandonment. Is it not manifest that His doctrine could not remain under the stigma of such a painful defeat of its Author, of so complete a denial of His affirmations? For, different from other religions, it consisted less in a body of affirmations impressive in themselves than in the person of the Man who came to make them. Therefore there had to be a revenge. There had to be some sort of proof that this Man, who called Himself the Son of God, had not been overcome. As a matter of fact we do not see that the death of Christ was followed by any depression among His disciples. There was no interpretative explanation dragged in by the neck, no sophisticated taking of comfort. There were none of those bickerings, conflicts, schisms, which would have been the inevitable consequences of an untruth. On the contrary, the death of Christ appears forthwith as a dazzling and triumphant confirmation of His teaching. There reigns among His disciples a wholly new spirit, absolute unanimity of exhilaration, of overflowing joy, of unquenchable confidence, of enterprise in all directions. What was this new deed, this revenge which followed immediately on the catastrophe of Calvary? Saint Paul tells us that it was the Resurrection, the formidable miracle on which all Christianity hangs.

Havelock Ellis   (1859–1939)

DID HE TEACH EUGENICS?

When we survey the history of Man we are constantly reminded of the profound truth which often lay beneath the parables of Jesus, and they might well form the motto for any treatise on eugenics. Jesus was constantly seeking to suggest the necessity of that process of sifting in which all human evolution consists; he was ever quick to point out how few could be, as it was then phrased, "saved," how extremely narrow is the path to the Kingdom of Heaven, or, as many might now call it, the Kingdom of Man. He proclaimed symbolically a doctrine of heredity which is only to-day beginning to be directly formulated: "Every tree that bringeth not forth good fruit is hewn down and cast into the fire." There was no compunction at all in his promulgation of this racial yet necessary doctrine for the destruction of unfit stocks. Even the best stocks Jesus was in favour of destroying ruthlessly as soon as they had ceased to be the best: "Ye are the salt of the earth: but if the salt have lost his savour, . . . it is thenceforth good for nothing, but to be cast out, and to be trodden under the foot of men." Jesus has been reproached by Nietzsche for founding a religion for slaves and plebeians, and so in the result it may have become. But we see that, in the words of the Teacher as they have been handed down, the religion of Jesus was the most aristocratic of religions. Its doctrine embodied not even the permission to live for those human stocks which fall short of its aristocratic ideal. It need not surprise us to find that Jesus had already said two thousand years ago what Galton, in a more modern and—some would add—more humane way, was saying yesterday. If there had not been a core of vital truth beneath the surface of the first Christian's teaching, it could hardly have survived so long. We are told that it is now dead, but that should it ever be revived we may well believe that this is the aspect by which it will be commended. It is a significant fact that at the two spiritual sources of our world, Jesus and Plato, we find the assertion of the principle of eugenics, in one implicitly, in the other explicitly.

RALPH WALDO EMERSON   *(1803–1882)*

THE SOUL'S IMMORTALITY

Jesus astonishes and overpowers sensual people. They cannot unite him to history, or reconcile him with themselves. As they come to revere their intuitions and aspire to live holily, their own piety explains every fact, every word. . . .

Men ask concerning the immortality of the soul, the employments of heaven, the state of the sinner, and so forth. They even dream that Jesus has left replies to precisely these interrogatories. Never for a moment did that sublime spirit speak in their *patois*. To truth, justice, love, the attributes of the soul, the idea of immutableness is essentially associated. Jesus, living in these moral sentiments, heedless of sensual fortunes, heeding only the manifestations of these, never made the separation of the idea of duration from the essence of these attributes, nor uttered a syllable concerning the duration of the soul. It was left to his disciples to sever duration from the moral elements, and to teach the immortality of the soul as a doctrine, and maintain it by evidences. The moment the doctrine of the immortality is separately taught, man is already fallen. In the flowing of love, in the adoration of humility, there is no question of continuance. No inspired man ever asks this question or condescends to these evidences. For the soul is true to herself, and the man in whom it is shed abroad cannot wander from the present, which is infinite, to a future which would be finite.

H. G. ENELOW   *(1877–1934)*

THE TRUE IDEALIST

Translated by Maurice Samuel

What conclusion may we draw as to the attitude of the modern Jews to Jesus? Perhaps it is well, first of all, to dispose of the question asked most often and most instinctively by Christians, namely, whether the modern Jew accepts Jesus as the Messiah. . . . It is commonly understood that the acceptance of Jesus as Divinity is quite out of the question for the Jew. But do the Jews of to-day, or any part of them, find it possible to accept Jesus as the Messiah?

The answer is that they do not find it possible to do so. And for the reason that the ideas associated in the Jewish mind with the Messiah were not only left unrealized by Jesus, but have remained unfulfilled to this day. . . .

On the other hand, the modern Jew realizes the ethical power and spiritual beauty of Jesus. In this regard Jesus takes his place among the noble teachers of morality and heroes of faith Israel has produced. It matters not that Jesus dwelt on certain aspects of the spiritual and the ethical life that other Jewish teachers had failed to treat with the same stress or the same charm. That constituted the originality of Jesus. . . . It does not mean that Jesus was any less in harmony with Judaism because he accented in his teaching the element of love, of kindness, of brotherliness, of indifference to the material world with its cares and rewards. He thus taught a phase of religion that was part of Judaism. . . . Nor is it profitable to debate whether those several teachings of Jesus were duplicated or anticipated by other Jewish teachers. The fact is that in him they found their most harmonious and most complete expression, and that his whole personality, as well as the story of his life, served to impress them most memorably on the mind of the world. . . .

Of course the modern Jew deplores the tragic death of Jesus. Yet, if it was not inevitable—which perhaps it was—it certainly is irrevocable. Some say it was inevitable, as part of a universal scheme of salvation. Others believe that in so far as it was inevitable, it was due to the calamitous conditions of the age . . . and also, in no small measure, to Jesus' own character, which made him choose rather to die than to disentangle the web of circumstance in which he was caught. Yet, Jesus died as the true idealist is ever ready to die, with his ideals untouched, uncomprehended but uncowed, with a faith in that Spirit of which he had ever felt himself a child and a part, . . .

and in whose keeping he felt safe. And who knows whether it was not by this very death that Jesus gained his immortality, that he won his ascendency over human hearts, and an imperishable place in the affections of mankind?

CANON FREDERIC W. FARRAR   (*1831–1903*)

HIS MISSION TO TEACH

Christ came not to revolutionise, but to ennoble and sanctify. He came to reveal that the Eternal was not the *Future,* but only the *Unseen:* that Eternity was no ocean whither men were being swept by the river of Time, but was around them now, and that their lives were only real in so far as they felt its reality and its presence. He came to teach that God was no dim abstraction, infinitely separated from them in the far-off blue, but that He was the Father in whom they lived, and moved, and had their being; and that the service which He loved was not ritual and sacrifice, not pompous scrupulosity and censorious orthodoxy, but mercy and justice, humility and love. He came, not to hush the natural music of men's lives, nor to fill it with storm and agitation, but to re-tune every silver chord in that "harp of a thousand strings," and to make it echo with the harmonies of heaven.

FRANÇOIS DE SALIGNAC DE LA MOTHE FÉNELON   (*1651–1715*)

THE LESSON OF MEEKNESS AND HUMILITY

Translator Anonymous

"Learn of me, for I am meek and lowly in heart." Matt. XI. 29. If any other than Jesus had taught this lesson, the imperfection of the teacher would have furnished us with objections to the doctrine. He therefore taught it himself, and that too by his own example, which is such as should silence all objections; such as should make us adore, be confounded and imitate. What! the Son of God descends from heaven to earth, takes a corruptible body, and dies upon the cross, to shame us of our pride! He who is All, annihilated himself; and I, who am nothing, would be, at least would have others think me, quite other than what I am! What an impudent vanity, and diabolical presumption, is this! Our Lord saith not, be ye meek and lowly; but he saith, "I am meek and lowly in heart"; it is enough to know that he is humble, to conclude that we ought to be so. His example is such an authority as none may find a dispensation for, much less the sinner, who may well choose humility when he has deserved damnation.

Our Lord joins meekness with humility, because humility is the source of true meekness. Pride is ever haughty, impatient, and captious; but he who despises himself is content to be despised. He who thinks nothing due to him, will not think himself neglected. . . .

To meekness our Lord adds lowliness of heart; it is no speculative conviction he requires, but the real bent and inclination of the heart; it is a lowliness to which the will consents, and which it loves for the glory of God.

Dorothy Canfield Fisher   (*1879–*)

MYSTICAL BUT FACTUALLY TRUE

One thing we are all apt to forget is that not only German babies are "natural-born Nazis"—all babies are, ours as much as those in any nation. Any women in charge of a nursery-school will tell you that the natural instinctive reaction of the two-and-a-half-year-old, or three-year-old, when for the first time he sees a group of children his own age playing with things he'd like to have, is the true Nazi or fascist impulse to grab. And having grabbed, to hold for his own if necessary by kicking and biting.

It seems so simple to the child—there are the things he wants; the only obstacle to his having them for his own is that they don't belong to him. But if he can overpower those now in possession of them, he could have all the toys for himself. And how nice that would be! So it seems to the inexperienced, childish brain inside a three-year-old's head.

What a country in the clutch of Nazi rulers does is to try to halt the development of human character at this three-year-old Nazi plane of grab, bite and scratch. The gray matter of the brain may be allowed a purely technical training as the years go by to make the grabbing more successful. But no growth, development or training is to be given the character.

What a country aspiring to a Christian civilization does, is to try steadily from the earliest years on to develop the maturing personality along the lines of Christ's teachings—mystical, yes, but as factually true as a mathematical proportion—that if you share fairly with others, it means in the long run that everyone—you yourself included—has more inner happiness, more outer security, than if you yield to the short-cut impulse to snatch what you want, without regard to the welfare of your fellow-men.

When a young person gets his first glimpse—it is at first no more than an astonished glimpse—at the literal truth of Christ's paradoxical axiom, "He who loses his soul shall find it,"—he has taken the first step away from the dark prison of his heathen self into a Christian realization of his oneness with his fellow-man.

Abbé Constant Fouard (1837-1904)

LAW OF GRACE ANNOUNCED

Translated by George F. X. Griffiths

Christian orators have always delighted in contrasting Moses upon cloud-capped Sinai with Jesus promulgating the New Law upon the

Mount of the Beatitudes. On the one hand we see Jehovah wrapped
in dazzling mists, that flash and thunder before His awful Presence;
and on the other, in the quiet of early morning, we hear a Voice
whose beloved accents thrill the people's heart. . . . In a word, yonder was the Law of death, delivered to a disobedient and awe-struck
nation; here the law of grace is announced to the believing and joyous throngs.

Of all the words that fell from His lips on that day none were more
strange and surprising in their tenor than the Beatitudes proclaimed
by the Saviour; for every prejudice of Israel was overthrown by them.
In truth, Moses, by making use of material images to move this
worldly minded people, had thought to reach their hearts by setting
before their eyes the earthly rewards of righteousness, and had promised Israel that its glory or its shame would finally depend upon its
faithfulness to Jehovah. The Jews had concluded from this that
prosperity always attends upon the godly man: that wealth being a
mark of God's favor, sorrow and trouble are sure tokens of His
wrath. Hence arose, despite the spirit of charity which breathes
throughout the Law, that scorn of poverty and their harsh usage of
the unfortunate and sick, whom they regarded as sinners meeting
with a just punishment; hence too they imbibed their mistaken ideas
as to the Messiah, who was to raise up their nation to a pinnacle of
glory and riches.

Few were the words which Jesus used to dispel such dreams as
these. Instead of wealth He set before these Jews the happiness of
the poor; to the passionate spirits whose visions are all of great vic-
tories He speaks of meekness: tells the hearts in love with pleasure
that there is joy in the gift of tears; to the hungry and thirsty He
says that righteousness shall sustain them: preaches mercy to the
pitiless natures, the loveliness of purity to the sensual man: teaches
the blessedness of the peaceful and long-suffering to a people writh-
ing beneath their yoke. What a disenchantment for the mighty ones
of this world! But for the poor and lowly of earth were there ever
revelation so unhoped for? Only consider for a moment how dread-

ful their destitution was, even here in Israel; think of the oppressions endured by the weak and gentle; imagine the despair of those whom misfortune had overcome, who had no one to wipe away their tears: and remembering this we can understand the joy of wretched and weary souls when they heard Christ speaking these words to them. . . .

Seeing the Master destroy so many of their illusions, the Jews might well believe he wished to revolutionize all Israel: and indeed this is why He was so careful to add that His Mission was not to abolish the Law, but to elevate it to the point of perfection.

MAHATMA MOHANDAS K. GANDHI   (*1869–*   )

AMONG THE MIGHTY TEACHERS

For many years I have regarded Jesus of Nazareth as one among the mighty teachers that the world has had, and I say this in all humility. I claim humility for this expression because this is exactly what I feel. Of course, Christians claim a higher place for Jesus of Nazareth than I, as a non-Christian and a Hindu, am able to feel. I purposely use the word "feel" instead of "give" because I consider that neither I nor anybody else can possibly arrogate to himself the claim of *giving* a place to a great man.

For the great teachers of mankind have not had their places *given* to them. That place has belonged to them as a matter of right, as a matter of service; but it is the privilege of the lowest and the humblest among us to *feel* certain things about them. The relation between ourselves and the great teachers is somewhat after the style of the relation between wife and husband. It would be a terrible thing, a tragic thing, if I were to argue out intellectually for myself what place I was to give the wife of my heart. It is not, indeed, a matter of my *giving* at all. She takes the place that belongs to her as a matter of right in my heart. It is a matter purely of feeling. Thus I can say that Jesus occupies in my heart the place of one of the great teachers who have made a considerable influence in my life.

Henry George   (*1839–1897*)

"AN OBVIOUS MEANING"

"The poor ye have always with you." If ever a scripture has been wrested to the devil's service, this is the scripture. How often have these words been distorted from their obvious meaning to soothe conscience into acquiescence in human misery and degradation—to bolster that blasphemy, the very negation and denial of Christ's teachings, that the All-Wise and Most Merciful, the Infinite Father, has decreed that so many of His creatures must be poor in order that others of His creatures to whom He wills the good things of life should enjoy the pleasure and virtue of doling out alms! "The poor ye have always with you," said Christ; but all His teachings supply the limitation, "until the coming of the Kingdom." In that kingdom of God *on earth,* that kingdom of justice and love for which He taught His followers to strive and pray, there will be no poor. But though the faith and the hope and the striving for this kingdom are of the very essence of Christ's teaching, the staunchest disbelievers and revilers of its possibility are found among those who call themselves Christians.

James Gordon Gilkey   (*1889–   *)

THREE EPOCH-MAKING IDEAS

If Jesus is to be interpreted as a teacher what were the truths he taught? Anyone who studies our all-too-fragmentary records of Jesus' teaching will soon make several significant discoveries. One is that there are many subjects which Jesus never discussed at all, and on which we have no slightest inkling of his opinion. Again, at many points in his teaching Jesus repeated—as all of us do—the ideas current in his day and in his locality. Some of these ideas now prove to be true, while others prove to be false. It is the presence in Jesus' teaching of these inaccurate elements and these distressing gaps which make the familiar attempt to follow Jesus blindly so disastrous. . . . Yet in the Gospel records, incomplete and inaccurate though they are, we find the clear expression of three epoch-making ideas. These ideas, entering the stream of human thought and life in the first century and modifying human beliefs and attitudes ever since, are Jesus' gift to the world.

The first of Jesus' great ideas is that every human being is of infinite value. . . . From this idea, transmitted first to the Western world and now to all the nations by Jesus' followers, has come a momentous readjustment and transformation of human beliefs, attitudes, and institutions. In the final analysis democratic government, universal education, and socially beneficial legislation find one of their most significant sources in Jesus' teaching that every human being is of infinite value. . . .

Jesus' second idea was a logical conclusion from the first. Because every human being is of infinite value all of us owe active kindness to everyone we meet. . . . Simply because he is a human being and needs our help we must do our best for him. This is the idea which found classic expression in the parable of the Good Samaritan, and which appears clearly in the concluding verses in the imaginary account of the Last Judgment. . . .

The third of Jesus' great ideas parallels the first two. Just as we value and help each other so there is in our world, Jesus insists, an Unseen but Loving God who values and helps us all. This is the idea underlying many of the passages in the Sermon on the Mount, particularly the great saying, "Ask and ye shall receive, seek and ye shall find, knock and it shall be opened unto you." Is this third element in Jesus' teaching as true as the other two? Some of us are convinced it is. We believe the facts and situations we observe in Nature and history offer ample grounds for belief in the reality of the God Jesus described.

T. R. GLOVER   (*1869–*   )

GOD THE CENTER OF HIS TEACHING

Jesus then was obviously a teacher and I am inclined to think that few can realize . . . how great was his achievement as a teacher. . . .

In all these arts of the teacher Jesus is incomparable. He roused attention and very wide attention, but he did better than that. To keep attention the teacher has to wake affection, and it is plain that the warmest affection bound his disciples to Jesus and opened their minds to him. He had the gift of saying things that people could not forget. We are lightly told that the use of parable is an ordinary Oriental habit; perhaps it is—Abraham Lincoln had it however, and the Orientals about Jesus complained that they could not understand him, and even his friends had to ask him to explain himself. . . . He told a story amazingly well, cutting away all but the essential and giving that much absolutely alive. . . .

The methods of such a teacher show his mind. Style is thought; a man's style is an index to his thinking. It was so that Jesus thought and we do not. We forget God—Jesus did not; and for him God is alive, always near with a question or a blessing or both. The story lives because Jesus had his eyes on the living God, an actor in every man's drama. You cannot forget a story that Jesus tells. . . .

Jesus was a young man, when he was crucified; and his Gospel is new and young, fresh and freshening, full of ardour and energy. "I am come that they might have vitality and overflow with it." "Because I live, you shall live also." We lose sight of the immense life and vitality that made Jesus. His freshness and some of his charm are lost for us in old acquaintance; we take him for granted. That was the curse of the ancient world; it had exhausted all experiences; it took things for granted, and put up with them; it was dull and all dulness leads to compromise. Jesus *dephlegmatized* his followers, fired them with his own originality, and inspired them with so independent a spirit, with so moving a sense of a living God beside them and before them, that, over the head of their own traditions of God, they accepted the hint of Jesus to re-think God; and the next thing was that they were quickly ready for Paul's interpretation of Jesus. . . . The originality, the force of Jesus emancipated his followers, and gave them a new instinct to expect of God exceeding abundantly more than they had ever asked or thought.

In the centre of all Jesus' teaching is God. . . . Can you take your own conception of God, and, by hard thinking and perhaps as hard reading, eliminate from it everything that is not directly the teaching of Jesus? . . . without some such process of self-examination and fresh study, without some effort of effectual thinking, it is impossible to realize how Jesus conceived of God, and how fresh, how alive and original his conception was or what an impulse it gave to mankind. For in our own effective conception of God, all that really lives comes from Jesus. . . . One may after such a process of examination realize anew the re-invigoration and the vitalization that came from contact with one so entirely alive and with his conception of a God, Who was at once seen to be essentially like himself, and Who, in accord with the old instinct to re-interpret God out of our experience, was more and more conceived in the character of Jesus.

In Christ a new life came to the world; and, as that life stirred within it, the world turned to God, as it found Him in Christ.

JOHANN WOLFGANG VON GOETHE   (*1749–1832*)

APPEARS AS A TRUE PHILOSOPHER

Translated by Thomas Carlyle

The life of that divine Man, . . . stands in no connection with the general history of the world in his time. It was a private life, his teaching was a teaching for individuals. What has publicly befallen vast masses of people, and the minor parts which compose them, belongs to the general history of the world, to the general religion of the world; the religion we have named the First. What inwardly befalls individuals belongs to the Second religion, the philosophical: such a religion was it that Christ taught and practiced, so long as he went about on earth. . . .

In life, he appears as a true Philosopher,—let not the expression stagger you,—as a wise Man in the highest sense. He stands firm to his point; he goes on his way inflexibly, and while he exalts the lower to himself, while he makes the ignorant, the poor, the sick, partakers of his wisdom, of his riches, of his strength, he, on the other hand, in no wise conceals his divine origin; he dares to equal himself with God, nay, to declare that he himself is God. In this manner he is wont, from youth upwards, to astound his familiar friends; of these he gains a part of his own cause, irritates the rest against him, and shows to all men, who are aiming at certain elevation in doctrine and life, what they have to look for from the world. And thus, for the noble portion of mankind, his walk and conversation are even more instructive and profitable than his death; for to those trials every one is called, to this trial but a few. Now, omitting all that results from this consideration, do but look at the touching scene of the Last Supper. Here the wise man, as it ever is, leaves those that are his own utterly orphaned behind him; and, while he is careful for the good, he feeds along with them a traitor, by whom he and the better are to be destroyed.

ARTHUR C. HEADLAM, C.H., D.D.   (*1862*–   )

IN ACCORD WITH HIS TIMES

Three things may be learnt from this analysis of our Lord's words.
It teaches us first something of the Galilean country life. The picture is that of a well-to-do rural community. There are no great signs
of poverty. There is much comfortable wealth. There is much vigour
and enterprise in trade. There is good agriculture. There are rich
flocks and herds. The life is a prosperous and happy one. Nature is
fertile and its aspect is pleasing. The picture is one which harmonizes
with what we may learn from other sources, and forbids us to think
of Nazareth as a poor and mean city.

   Then, next, it helps to assure us that the words of Jesus correspond to and are the natural outcome of the circumstances in which
he lived. They are not such as could have come from a dweller in
Jerusalem; they are very unlike anything which an educated Jew
of that city would have spoken; they are not for the most part such
as would come from the circumstances of the infant Church. This, of
course, cannot be applied to all the words of Jesus; it does not take
away the possibility that the diction and style of our Lord might be
imitated by the Christian Church. But if a tradition was created
there must have been someone to create that tradition, and it will
remain true that the words of our Lord are just such as might be
spoken in the circumstances which the Gospel narrative itself describes—that they are, in fact, the natural words of Jesus of Nazareth.

   And, lastly, it tells us much of our Lord's human characteristics. It
suggests a power of keen observation of human life and of the world
of Nature, of deep sympathy with Nature as with man, a power to
see behind the veil of material things. It implies the experience of
one who has grown up and lived in a household of modest means,
in a rich and fertile country district, who loves natural things, whose
outlook on the greater world is from outside. He had lived among the
townspeople and the landlords and the shepherds; He had seen the
merchants and the rich traveller, the soldiers and the courtiers as

they passed along the roads on either side of His home. The Gospels reflect the characteristics of Galilee. . . .

Our Lord's language is completely in accordance with the religious and scientific ideas of His contemporaries. He acts recognizing fully what both the onlookers and those whom He cured would think. It is obvious that nothing else would have been possible on His part. Let us ask of those who feel troubled by this, what particular theory our Lord should have substituted for that currrent in His time. Do they think that He ought to have talked in the scientific and medical language of the present day? It is obvious that to have done so would have conveyed no meaning to anyone who heard Him, deprived Him of power and influence, made His actions vain and ineffectual. The one condition of being able to exercise His ministry as a man teaching men was that He should do it in accordance with the thought and ideas of the day. What theological theory is implied by this fact is a matter of future enquiry. We are not concerned at the present time with that problem. What is necessary to point out is that a religious teacher who in the first century of the Christian era adopted the scientific language and ideas of the present day would have talked in a language utterly incomprehensible to the people.

JULIA WARD HOWE   (*1819-1910*)

HE TAUGHT LIFE ETERNAL

The promise of a future life is held to have such prominence in Christ's teaching as to lead Paul to say that the Master "brought life and immortality to light." How did He do this? By filling the life of today with the consciousness of eternal things, of truths and principles which would not change if the whole visible universe were to pass away.

No one today, I think, will maintain that Christ created the hope which He aroused to an activity before undreamed of. The majority of the Jews believed in a life after death, as is shown by the segregation of the Sadducees from the orthodox of the synagogue. The new teaching vindicated the spiritual rights and interest of men. From the depths of his own heart was evolved the consciousness of a good that could not die. Man, the creature of a day, has a vested interest in things eternal.

ALDOUS HUXLEY   (*1894–*   )

HIS TEACHINGS ON WAR

For the teaching of Christ in regard to war and the overcoming of evil the chief authorities are the several elements which are contained in the Synoptic Gospels, the relevant passages in St. Paul's Epistles, and such evidence as can be found elsewhere in the New Testament. His teaching has been too frequently sought only in isolated sayings divorced from their setting and interpreted as legislative enactments. But for Christians who believe that His intention was never legislation, that His character is a consistent whole, and that His authority depends upon the quality of His person and the spirit of His actions rather than upon isolated and edited utterance, it is more important to consider the significance of His crucifixion than to debate particular points, such as the alleged use of a whip in the Temple-market (John ii, 15), or the cryptic and despairing "It is enough!" (Luke xxii, 38), or the parable of the strong man armed —who is obviously the devil! (Luke xi, 21).

In any case it is not easy, as the whole record of the Church's attempts to justify war proves (the *Summa Theologiae* falls back upon a quotation from John the Baptist), to quote any authority from Christ. If we appeal to isolated sayings, such words as "Do not offer violence in opposing evil" (Matt. v, 39) which St. Paul explains by adding, "But overcome evil with good" (Rom. xii, 21), or "They that take the sword shall perish by the sword" (Matt. xxvi, 52), are at once more explicit and more representative: and the principle that the more unconventional the sayings are the less likely are they to be later, or edited, is a sound one. . . .

In considering the general meaning of Christ the following points are surely indisputable: (1) He regarded God as always and everywhere the Father whose dealings with His creatures are motivated only by love: to assert that God uses alternative methods—love and justice—and that love is not always applicable is to deny that God is what Jesus taught or that He is in any real sense God. (2) In consequence men are persons, not pawns or slaves, and their freedom to reject must never be overborne by force whether of violence or of bribery or of the supernatural. At His temptation (Matt. iv, 1-11, Luke iv, 1-13) Jesus repudiated these three ways of coercing men. The method of His whole ministry is consistent with this repudiation; He rejected the nationalist policy of the Zealots, the cheapening and materializing of His own demands, the use of psychic or miraculous powers to enforce assent. (3) In presenting His call to His people He refused to admit either by resistance or by flight that the last word lay with armed force: indeed, by accepting the Cross He challenged the common assumption and disproved it. Non-resistance, seeming at first to fail, actually and signally triumphed. His crucifixion transformed His disciples and changed the course of history. The Cross, the symbol of non-resistance, has been, however, inappropriately, the Church's sacred emblem ever since.

The new way of life thus initiated was accepted and proclaimed by the earliest disciples. Love, joy, peace, fortitude were acknowledged as the fruit of Christ's spirit: martyrdom was the Christian answer to militarism: warfare was with the powers of evil—of the spirit not of the flesh. The only book in the New Testament that shows evidence of another way, the Revelation, is a product rather of Jewish apocalyptic than of Christian patience, and was in fact regarded as non-canonical by the best minds of the early Church. For them military service was a thing impossible: violence was condemned: and war was an outrage against God.

Contrary to the widely-held and oft-repeated view that Jesus himself gave no verdict on the rightness or wrongness of war, it is clear

on several grounds that He was convinced of its wrongness, and that
He taught, acted, and suffered accordingly. Several conditions, however, impeded the clear grasp of this verdict on the part of His early
followers; for example, the remoteness of the whole question (as a
practical issue) from the lives of most of them, their consequent ab-
sorption in many more immediate spiritual and moral questions, the
war-stories in Scripture, the difficulty of seeing how the Emperor
(regarded by all as God-ordained) could get on without an army,
and the tendency of simple-minded Christians to take the line of least
resistance in face of a complex problem. Hence during the first three
centuries, we see two processes going on side by side: (1) the ex-
pansion of the Church leading first to the conversion of soldiers
who remained soldiers, and then to the enforced or even voluntary
enlistment of Christians in the army: and (2) the Christian ethic of
love making it increasingly clear that the profession of Christianity
was incompatible with a military life.

Saint Ignatius de Loyola   (1491–1556)

PRECEPTS HE TAUGHT MEN

Translator Anonymous

Now, having considered the example that Christ our Lord has given
us for the first state, which consists in the keeping of the commandments, He being obedient to His parents; and likewise for the second,
which is of evangelical perfection, when He remained in the Temple,
leaving His adopted father and His natural mother in order to devote Himself to the exclusive service of His Eternal Father; we
shall begin at the same time that we are contemplating His life, to
investigate and to ask in what life or estate His Divine Majesty
wishes to make use of us. And thus . . . we shall see the intention
of Christ our Lord, and on the contrary that of the enemy of human

nature, and how we ought to dispose of ourselves so as to attain to perfection in whatever state or life God our Lord may give us to choose. . . .

Consider how Christ our Lord places himself in a great camp in that region of Jerusalem in a lowly place, beautiful and gracious. . . . Consider how the Lord of all the world elects so many persons, apostles, disciples, *etc.,* and sends them throughout all the world, disseminating His sacred teaching among all states and conditions of persons. . . . Consider the address which Christ our Lord makes to all His servants and friends whom He sends on such a journey, recommending to them that they should wish to help all men by drawing them, first to extreme spiritual poverty, and if His Divine Majesty should be pleased, and should wish to elect them, no less to actual poverty; secondly, to a desire of affronts and contempts, for from these two things follows humility; in such sort that there may be three steps: the first, poverty against riches; the second, affront or contempt against worldly honour; the third, humility against pride; and from these three steps they may lead men on to all the other virtues.

WILL IRWIN   (*1873–*   )

THE KINGDOM FOR ALL

There arose among the children of Israel a man of genius named Moses. Whether by direct revelation or by process almost as miraculous, through which genius leaps from star to star, he laid down for his people a code of action so all-embracing and yet so practical that the Ten Commandments with changing interpretations to fit changing times, have remained for thirty centuries the moral guide of the Judean-born religions. Jesus came to express them all and to widen their scope in his final Commandment—"that ye love one another."

Jesus did more. After all, the Hebrew God was a tribal conception. Salvation through oneness with His infinite goodness, belonged to the Children of Israel alone. Dimly here and there in the Old Testament we glimpse a mind groping through the mists of its own time for a wider interpretation. But the Jew, if he thought much about the future at all, still found himself bound by the tribal habit of the troglodyte. . . . But Jesus proclaimed the gospel "to all men." The Kingdom of Heaven was no longer tribal.

E. STANLEY JONES   (*1884-*   )

HE TAUGHT BY ACTION

Jesus the mystic was amazingly concrete and practical. Into an atmosphere filled with speculation and wordy disputation where "men are often drunk with the wine of their own wordiness" He brings the refreshing sense of practical reality. He taught, but He did not speculate.

He did not discourse on the sacredness of motherhood— He suckled as a babe at His mother's breast, and that scene has forever consecrated motherhood.

He did not argue that life was a growth and character an attainment— He "grew in wisdom and stature, and in favor with God and men."

He did not speculate on why temptation should be in this world— He met it, and after forty days' struggle with it in the wilderness He conquered, and "returned in the power of the Spirit to Galilee."

He did not discourse on the dignity of labor— He worked at a carpenter's bench and His hands were hard with the toil of making yokes and plows, and this forever makes the toil of the hands honorable.

We do do not find Him discoursing on the necessity of letting one's light shine at home among kinsmen and friends— He announced His program of uplift and redemption at Nazareth, His own home, and those who heard "wondered at the words of grace which proceeded out of his mouth."

As He came among men He did not try to prove the existence of God— He brought Him. He lived in God, and men looking upon His face could not find it within themselves to doubt God.

He did not argue, as Socrates, the immortality of the soul— He raised the dead.

He did not speculate on how God was a Trinity— He said, "If I by the Spirit of God cast out devils, the kingdom of God is come nigh unto you." Here the Trinity—"I", "Spirit of God", "God"— was not something to be speculated about, but was a working force for redemption—the casting out of devils and the bringing in of the Kingdom.

He did not teach in a didactic way about the worth of children— He put His hands upon them and blessed them, and setting one in their midst tersely said, "Of such is the kingdom of God," and He raised them from the dead.

He did not argue that God answers prayer— He prayed, sometimes all night, and in the morning "the power of the Lord was present to heal."

He did not paint in glowing colors the beauties of friendship and the need for human sympathy— He wept at the grave of His friend.

He did not argue the worth of womanhood and the necessity for giving them equal rights— He treated them with infinite respect, gave to them His most sublime teaching, and when He rose from the dead He appeared first to a woman.

He did not teach in the schoolroom manner the necessity of humility— He girded Himself with a towel and kneeled down and washed His disciples' feet.

He did not discuss the question of the worth of personality as we do today— He loved and served persons.

He did not prove how pain and sorrow in the universe could be compatible with the love of God— He took on Himself at the cross everything that spoke against the love of God, and through that pain and tragedy and sin showed the very love of God.

He did not discourse on how the weakest human material can be transformed and made to contribute to the welfare of the world— He called to Him a set of weak men, as the Galilean fishermen, transformed them and sent them out to begin the mightiest movement for uplift and redemption the world has ever seen.

He wrote no books—only once are we told that He wrote and that was in the sand—but He wrote upon the hearts and consciences of people about Him and it has become the world's most precious writing.

He did not paint a Utopia, far off and unrealizable— He announced that the Kingdom of Heaven is within us, and is "at hand" and can be realized here and now.

He did not discourse on the beauty of love— He loved.

We do not find him arguing that the spiritual life should conquer matter— He walked on the water.

He greatly felt the pressing necessity of the physical needs of the people around Him, but He did not merely speak in their behalf— He fed five thousand people with five loaves and two fishes. . . .

He told us that the human soul was worth more than the whole material universe, and when He had crossed a storm-tossed lake to find a storm-tossed soul, ridden with devils, He did not hesitate to sacrifice the two thousand swine to save this one lost man.

He did not argue the possibility of sinlessness— He presented Himself and said, "Which of you convinceth me of sin?"

He did not merely ask men to turn the other cheek when smitten on the one, to go the second mile when compelled to go one, to give the cloak also when sued at the law and the coat was taken away, to love our enemies and to bless them— He himself did these very things. The servants struck him on one cheek, He turned the other and the soldiers struck Him on that; they compelled Him to go with them one mile—from Gethsemane to the judgment hall— He went with them two—even to Calvary. They took away His coat at the judgment hall and He gave them His seamless robe at the cross; and in the agony of the cruel torture of the cross He prayed for His enemies, "Father, forgive them, for they know not what they do."

He did not merely tell us that death need have no terror for us—
He rose from the dead, and lo, the tomb now glows with light.

Many teachers of the world have tried to explain everything—they
have changed little or nothing. Jesus explained little and changed
everything.

Many teachers have tried to diagnose the diseases of humanity—
Jesus cures it.

Many teachers have told us why the patient is suffering and that
he should bear it with fortitude— Jesus tells him to take up his bed
and walk.

Many philosophers speculate on how evil entered the world— Jesus
presents Himself as the way by which it shall leave.

He did not go into long discussions about the way of God and the
possibility of finding Him— He quietly said to men, "I am the Way."

Many speculate with Pilate and ask, "What is truth?" Jesus shows
Himself and says, "I am the Truth."

Spencer defines physical life as correspondence with environment—
Jesus defines life itself, by presenting Himself and saying, "I am the
Life." Anyone who truly looks upon Him knows in the inmost
depths of his soul that he is looking on Life itself.

RUFUS M. JONES   *(1863-   )*

PREACHING THE "SECOND MILE"

There is no terminus, no finite stopping place, where one can halt and
read his pedometer, and say: "Now I have arrived." Jesus, with infinite wisdom said: "Blessed are they who hunger and thirst for goodness"—not blessed are they who are already good, righteous or
perfect. It is the attitude of spirit, the high resolve, the passion, the in-
satiable hunger and thirst for it that count, not the attainment. The
perfection which He calls for is nothing less than that of being "perfect as our Father in Heaven is perfect." . . .

The Roman soldier could always compel any man whom he met on the road to carry his military "kit" for an even mile, but for no more than that measured mile. Jesus must often have seen an event like that happen on the great Roman road that ran near Nazareth, and he may in his carpenter days have himself carried a soldier's burden to the next milestone. He seized upon this Roman custom as a vivid parable of a great spiritual ideal of the way of life. Everywhere he turned he saw religion and the moral life reduced to calculation and spoiled by the fact that they were thought of as compulsions laid upon men's souls as burdens which they *had* to carry. Religion was "cluttered" with commandments, with customs, with weary performances which had to be gone through whether one liked them or not, what St. Paul called a "yoke too heavy to be borne." There was a great temptation to wear the pedometer, to measure the mile of compulsion, and to stop short when the "must-limit" was reached. Jesus looking on and watching this religion of the compelled mile said once: "When you have done all these things that are required of you, count yourselves unprofitable servants"—you have already begun yet to find the real path of life. . . .

You can find these "second mile" persons beautifully portrayed in the "parable of the great surprise": *"When* was it that we saw thee hungry and thirsty and naked and sick and in prison and we ministered unto Thee?" The Good Samaritan, the woman with the alabaster box, Nicodemus who left all caution behind and came with his hundred pounds of spices for the burial of the one he loved—these are "second mile" persons who know of no outside compulsion, but who have an inward spring of life which thrusts them forth on their uncounted mile.

IMMANUEL KANT   (*1724-1804*)

"AN AMBASSADOR FROM HEAVEN"

Translated by Theodore M. Greene and Hoyt H. Hudson

The Teacher of the Gospel announced himself to be an ambassador from heaven. As one worthy of such a mission, he declared that servile belief (taking the form of confessions and practices on days of divine worship) is essentially vain and that moral faith, which alone renders men holy "as their Father in Heaven is holy" and which proves its genuineness by a good course of life, is the only saving faith. After he had given, in his own person, through preaching and suffering even to unmerited yet meritorious death, an example conforming to the archetype of a humanity alone pleasing to God, he is represented as returning to heaven, whence he came. He left behind him, by word of mouth, his last will (as in a testament); and, trusting in the power of the memory of his merit, teaching, and example, he was able to say that "he (the ideal of humanity well-pleasing to God) would still be with his disciples, even to the end of the world." Were it a question of *historical belief* concerning the derivation and the rank, possibly supermundane, of his person, this doctrine would indeed stand in need of verification through miracles; although, as merely belonging to moral soul-improving faith, it can dispense with all such proofs of its truth.

COUNT HERMAN A. VON KEYSERLING   (*1880-   *)

MORE PROFOUNDLY UNDERSTOOD NOW

Translated by J. Holroyd Reece

There is no doubt that the sayings of Jesus are understood more profoundly to-day than they were heretofore. But this does not mean that we recognise better what Jesus meant, but that we are understanding more profoundly the true, that is to say the objectively correct, meaning of His wisdom, whether Jesus was aware of it Himself or not. Probably He was not aware of it; His immediate disciples certainly were not, and misunderstanding has governed for a long period most Christian manifestations. But this misunderstanding has prepared the road for recognition; without Catholicism, Reformation and counter-Reformation, without dogmatic conflicts and text-criticism, we would never have got to the point from which we can behold the pure meaning of Christianity.

BASIL KING (*1859–1928*)

THE PROMISE OF TRUTH

True, it must not be forgotten that no sect bases its teaching on what it has worked out for itself, but on the revelation made to it in Jesus Christ. Every sect would admit that its own view of truth might have been partial were it not for the fact that in Jesus Christ it has everything. Where the theories of men might be inadequate His immense knowledge comes in as supplementary.

This might be so had He Himself undertaken to give more than a partial view of truth. But He says expressly that He does not. He gives what His hearers might be assumed to be able to assimilate; but that is all. "I have much more to say to you, you are unable at present to bear the burden of it." It being an axiom in teaching to give the pupil only what he can receive, this is the utmost that our Lord attempts.

He goes on, however, to add these words, which are significant: "But when He has come—the Spirit of Truth—He will guide you into all the truth." No doubt that process is even now going on, and will continue to go on in proportion as our race develops.

Joseph Klausner   (*1874-*   )

A MAN OF THE PEOPLE

Translated by Herbert Danby

Looked upon from one side, Jesus is "one of the people." His parables have a most popular appeal. They are, almost every one of them,
drawn from life in the village or small town. As a rule he conducted
himself as an ordinary, simple man, a Galilaean artisan. His attraction
was his simplicity, his very ordinariness, his homeliness in whatever
he did or said. He loved the wild flowers with their multiplicity of
colouring, and the birds which could be sold two for a farthing; he
liked little children to be brought to him, "for theirs is the kingdom
of heaven;" the cock-crow, the hen with her chickens, the flush of the
skies at evening and their overcast look in the morning—all these find
place in his sayings and parables.

But looked at from another side, he is by no means an illiterate,
an *"am ha-aretz"*: he is as expert in the Scriptures as the best of the
Pharisees, and he is quite at home with the Pharisee's expository
devices. He is saturated with the great ideas of the Prophets and the
Psalms; he can employ them for his own spiritual needs, he can
expound them and adapt them and supplement them. He knows
also the "tradition of the elders," the rulings of the Pharisees, and
the "words of the Scribes."

And this, too, had its effect on his followers. In the eyes of the
simple Galilaeans, . . . his women admirers, the fishermen, the peasants and the petty officials, he appeared to be a great teacher of the
Law—a "Rab." The Pharisees themselves could not ignore his teaching. He could dispute with them and confute them, no matter whether
the arguments turned on Scriptural proofs or post-Scriptural traditions.

Without doubt this aroused enthusiasm among his disciples, for
among them were also to be found students of the Law—otherwise
they could never have preserved his arguments and parables and say-

ings, which, at times, were of a depth which the ordinary person could not have fathomed.

Again, on the one hand, Jesus is a teacher, a "Rab." of the Pharisaic school—not a "Ba'al-Halakha" (one concerned only in the more legalistic interpretations of Scripture) but a "Ba'al-Haggada" (one whose interest lay rather in the popular, edifying application of Scripture). He called around him the afflicted and the downtrodden, and he tells them how "his yoke is easy and his burden light"; he takes compassion on the simpler folk who were "like sheep without a shepherd"; and he stood aside from the three parties of his day—the Sadducees, the Pharisees and Essenes.

On the other hand, he demands that a man forsake all for his sake, family, home and possessions, and even his very self ("let him hate even his own soul"); for such a one only can be his disciple and enter the kingdom of heaven and be accounted worthy of the "Days of the Messiah." Gentleness and charm on the one side, the extremest moral demands on the other . . . nothing can more influence and attract people to something new, no matter whether that something be of the smallest or the gravest importance.

Yet again, one time we see Jesus indulgent and forgiving and easily appeased; he pardons his disciples when they commit light or grave offences; he does not play the pedant with the sinner; he knows that "the spirit is willing but the flesh is weak." But another time we find him utterly unbending, pedantic and passionate, protesting and reproving in the severest terms. To his most favoured disciple, Simon Peter—whom but a little while ago he had named an enduring "rock" —he calls out, "Get thee behind me, Satan!" . . . He applies the harshest possible terms of rebuke to the Pharisees, terms which, in their general application, are by no means justified. He is capable even of acts of violence, of expelling the money-changers and dove-dealers from the Temple.

These two extremes, extreme kindliness of heart and the most violent passion, show in him a character akin to that of the Prophet— save only that he had not the wide political perspective of the Prophets nor their gift of divine consolation to the nation. However this may be, these two contradictory attributes are the sign of the great man. Only such a man, mighty in forgiveness and equally mighty in reproof, could exert so ineffaceable an influence on all who came in contact with him.

Finally, Jesus is, on the one hand, "a man of the world." To a great extent he has a sense of realities. His parables and sayings prove amply that he knew life and the world as they really are. He can avoid his enemies and persecutors when such action is necessary; he can be evasive in his answers (*e.g.*, the payment of tribute to Caesar, or the authority he claimed for his action in the Temple); and sometimes he parries in argument with a delicate though crushing sarcasm, unequalled in acuteness and pungency.

JOHN LaFARGE, S.J.   (*1880–*   )

MADE ALL THINGS ONE

Christ spoke not only as the Son of God, not only as the Great Teacher, but also as the supreme representative of the human race itself, who in His own person made all things one, as our Leader, in the practical *work* of achieving these relationships.

The teachings of Christ proclaimed the moral unity of the human race, based upon men's natural unity as children by creation, of a common Father and as sharing a common physical origin. This moral unity was immortally symbolized by Christ in the expression "neighbor," as applied to all men, regardless of supposed racial or national limitations. The opening words of the Lord's Prayer, "Our Father," reminded men of that natural unity upon which all human neighborliness was based.

From this moral unity of all mankind the Saviour drew positive lessons of human relationships of justice, mercy, patience, forgiveness, charity, respect for the young and the weak, etc., which had escaped the attention of moralists whether theistic or pagan.

Christ preached moreover a unity based not on man's natural life alone but upon the prerogatives of the supernatural life conferred upon mankind by the Redemption, and the prerogatives formed by the personal relationships of all individual sharing in that supernatural life with His Own Divine Person. Through the institution of His Church as a universal, perpetual, supra-national Society, all mankind was offered participation in a unity infinitely higher than that which the mere fact of common creation and common anthropological origin afforded. This highest unity is symbolized in the figure of the Mystical Body of Christ.

GOTTFRIED WILHELM LEIBNITZ   (*1646–1716*)

GOD REVEALED TO MAN

Translated by Dr. George R. Montgomery

Jesus Christ has revealed to man the mystery and the admirable laws of the kingdom of heaven, and the greatness of the supreme happiness which God has prepared for those who love him.

The ancient philosophers knew very little of these important truths. Jesus Christ alone has expressed them divinely well, and in a way so clear and simple that the dullest minds have understood them. His gospel has entirely changed the face of human affairs. It has brought us to know the kingdom of heaven, or that perfect republic of spirits which deserves to be called the city of God.

He it is who has discovered to us its wonderful laws. He alone has made us see how much God loves us and with what care everything that concerns us has been provided for; how God, inasmuch as he cares for the sparrows, will not neglect reasoning beings, who are infinitely more dear to him; how the hairs of our head are numbered; how heaven and earth may pass away but the word of God will not pass away; how God has more regard for the least one among intelligent souls than for the whole machinery of the world; how we ought not to fear those who are able to destroy the body but are unable destroy the soul, since God alone can render the soul happy or unhappy; and how the souls of the righteous are protected by his hand against all the upheavals of the universe, since God alone is able to act upon them; how none of our acts are forgotten; how everything is to be accounted for; even careless words and a spoonful of water which is well used; in fact how everything must result in the greatest welfare of the good, for then shall the righteous become like suns and neither our sense nor our minds have ever tasted of anything approaching the joys which God has laid up for those that love him.

GOTTHOLD EPHRAIM LESSING   (*1729-1781*)

"FIRST TRUSTWORTHY TEACHER"

Translated by W. B. Ronnfeldt

That section of the human race, which it had been God's purpose to include in *one* system of Education,—and it had been His purpose to include in *one* system only that section which was already united in itself by ties of language, action, government, and other natural and political relations,—was now ripe for the second great step in Education. . . .

The better part of that portion of the human race had long been accustomed to be ruled by a *shadow* of such nobler incentives. The Greek and Roman did everything in their power to continue to live, after this life, in the memory of their fellow-citizens.

It was time that men's actions should be influenced by another and a *true* life, to be attained after the present.

And thus Christ became the first *trustworthy,* practical teacher of the immortality of the soul.

He was the first *trustworthy* teacher. Trustworthy on account of the prophecies which seemed to be fulfilled in Him; trustworthy on account of the miracles which He wrought; trustworthy on account of His own resurrection after a death by which He had set a seal to His doctrine. Whether we can today still prove this resurrection and these miracles, I forbear to say. I must likewise leave aside the question of the personality of Christ. All this may at that time have been of importance for the *acceptance* of His teaching; today it no longer affects our recognition of the truth of it to the same extent.

He was the first *practical* teacher. For to suspect, to wish, to believe, the immortality of the soul to be a philosophical speculation is one thing; to shape one's inward and outward conduct in accordance therewith, is another.

This, at any rate, Christ first taught us. For although among some nations it was already before His time an accepted belief that evil actions would be punished in the life to come, yet this applied only to such actions as were injurious to the civil community, and which consequently were already punished by that community. It was reserved for Him alone to enjoin an inner purity of heart in view of a future life.

WALTER LIPPMANN   (*1889–*   )

BUDDHA, PLATO, JESUS

No teacher has ever appeared in the world who was wise enough to know how to teach his wisdom to all mankind. In fact, the great teachers have attempted nothing so utopian. They were quite well aware how difficult for most men is wisdom, and they have confessed frankly that the perfect life was for a select few. It is arguable, in fact, that the very idea of teaching the highest wisdom to all men is the recent notion of a humanitarian and romantically democratic age, and that it is quite foreign to the thought of the greatest teachers. Gautama Buddha, for example, abolished caste within the religious order which he founded, and declared that the path to Nirvana was open to the lowest outcast as well as to the proudest Brahman. But it was necessary to enter the order and submit to its stringent discipline. It is obvious that Buddha never believed that very many could or would do that. Jesus, whom we are accustomed to think of as wholly catholic in his sympathies, spoke the bitter words: "Give not what is holy to the dogs and cast not your pearls before swine." In Mohammedanism that which is mystical is esoteric: "all those emotions are meant only for a small number of chosen ones . . . even some of the noblest minds in Islam restrict true religious life to an aristocracy, and accept the ignorance of the multitude as an irremediable evil."

There is an aristocratic principle in all the religions which have obtained wide acceptance. It is significant that Jesus was content to leave the governance of the mass of men to Caesar, and that he created no organization during his lifetime beyond the appointment of the Apostles. It is significant, because it shows how much more he was concerned with the few who could be saved than with arranging the affairs of the mass of mankind. Plato, who was a more systematic teacher than either Jesus or Buddha, did work out an elaborate social order which took account not only of the philosophers, but of all the citizens of the state. But in that very attempt he rested upon the premise that most men will not attain the good life, and that for them it is necessary to institute the laws. . . .

Perhaps because they looked upon the attempts as hopeless, perhaps because they did not know how to go about it, perhaps because they were so wise, the greatest teachers have never offered their full wisdom to the multitude.

HALFORD E. LUCCOCK   (*1885-*   )

IMAGE BREAKER, IMAGE MAKER

To look at the universe through the eyes of Jesus reveals deeper distances, it shows man a new dimension in himself. A primary service of the Christian faith is to the imagination, is to give men a new picture of themselves, a positive, not a negative image. That was one great thing which Jesus did for men, as the record of his meetings with men is preserved in the Gospels. He was an image breaker and an image maker. He broke negative images and replaced them with positive ones—"Thou shalt be Peter." He gave men a new rating of themselves. It is that rating which brings the release from tension in the presence of a vast bewildering universe.

EUGENE WILLIAM LYMAN   (*1872–*   )

DISCOVERED HUMAN VALUES

Jesus himself embodies ethical religion uniquely and supremely. That which made him spiritually possible—without which he could not have transcended the legalism and apocalypticism of his day—was the ethical religion of the Old Testament prophets. Though he "came not to destroy," he did destroy much of the religion of his day. If he had not, he would not have been put to death; for it was the religious leaders of his people who demanded his death—the Pharisees because he rejected the ceremonialism of the synagogue teaching, and the Sadducees because he condemned the prevailing temple worship. . . . It was the prophetic ethical religion which Jesus *fulfilled*—making it a new ferment destined to break the old religious forms. The Old Testament prophets had placed human values foremost in the service of God, and drawing his inspiration from them, Jesus created a universal religion by effecting a complete interpenetration of love for God and love for man. The psychology of the prophet always involves a measure of mysticism, and Jesus is no exception in this respect—witness the "Johannine passage" in Matthew (11: 25–27). And that integrated view of the world in ethical monotheism which the Old Testament prophets achieved was carried further by Jesus through a fresh penetration into its meaning and through its thoroughgoing application to every aspect of life. But Jesus' supreme creative work was in his profound discovery of human values, in his embodiment of those values in life and deed, and in his interpretation of God in light of them.

*   *   *   *

Another connotation of the term faith as it appears in ethical religion is *trust*. This aspect of faith is particularly evident in the teaching of Jesus as given in the Synoptic Gospels. The opposite of faith as Jesus means it is not so much doubt or unfaithfulness as fear. He sought to deliver his fellowmen from the fear of demons, and from whatever held them in spiritual bondage, by wakening in them faith—a trust that they were always in the hands of the Heavenly Father. The childlike spirit, to which he said the kingdom of heaven belonged, is a spirit of teachableness, of fresh openness of mind, of trustfulness. The filial spirit, which summed up life for Jesus, includes confidence in a living bond between God and man.

*   *   *   *

We see the ethical fruitage of Jesus' communion with God when we read that, beholding the multitudes "he was moved with compassion for them, because they were distressed and scattered as sheep not having a shepherd"; and when we find him facing the crisis of his mission with the words, "The Son of Man also came not to be ministered unto, but to minister, and to give his life a ransom for many." And we see how communion with God nourished his moral passion when we find him explaining his mission at the outset from the passage in Second Isaiah: "The spirit of the Lord is upon me, because he anointed me to preach good tidings to the poor." Thus the ethical religion of the Hebrew prophets, as it was deepened and universalized by the spirit of Jesus, became a powerful leaven in human history in that it brought into vital unity communion with Divine Reality and the creation and conservation of the values of life.

ARTHUR CUSHMAN McGIFFERT   (*1861–1933*)

INSISTENCE ON FORGIVENESS

Jesus was a devout and loyal Jew, and the God whom he worshipped was the God of his people Israel—the God of Abraham, Isaac, and Jacob. He was not a theologian or philosopher, and he indulged in no speculations touching the nature and character of God. So far as we can judge from the Synoptic Gospels and from his attitude reflected there, he did not regard it as his mission to promulgate a new God or to teach new ideas about God, but rather to summon his fellows to live as God—his God and theirs—would have them live. . . .

In spite of his sternness and severity, the God of Jesus, as of the Jews in general, is good and gracious and merciful. It is not his will that any should perish; he goes out seeking that which is lost and rejoices over it when it is found. His goodness extends even to the wicked and unthankful, and it is just in this unmerited kindness that his perfectness consists, a perfectness men ought to make their own. His providential care is also emphasized, a care that makes all anxiety unnecessary on the part of the disciples. . . .

Jesus did insist with emphasis upon the duty of forgiving one's fellows, but when he spoke of divine forgiveness he seems as a rule to have been interested not so much to assure his followers that God forgives sins as to warn them against presuming upon forgiveness. Thus he says: "Verily I say unto you all sins shall be forgiven to the sons of men and the blasphemies wherewith they shall blaspheme; but whosoever shall blaspheme against the Holy Spirit hath never forgiveness, but shall be guilty of an eternal sin." "Forgive us our debts as we also have forgiven our debtors. . . . For if ye forgive men their trespasses, your heavenly Father will also forgive you; but if ye forgive men not, neither will your Father forgive your trespasses." "And his lord was wroth and delivered him to the tormentors until he should pay all that he owed. So likewise shall my heavenly Father do unto you, if ye from your hearts forgive not every one his brother." . . .

Jesus' attitude in the matter of forgiveness is the more remarkable because as a rule the Jews made much of forgiveness and were accustomed to insist that there was no sin so grievous it might not be pardoned if repented for, repentance being emphasized ordinarily as the one indispensable and sufficient condition of forgiveness. . . .

His concern was not so much with divine forgiveness as with human, and that he was interested chiefly to impress upon his disciples the duty of forgiving their fellows. It was not enough simply to repent, as was commonly thought; they must forgive if they would be forgiven. . . .

As a matter of fact, the gospel of Jesus was not the gospel of divine forgiveness—that needed no special emphasis. The burden of his preaching, like that of John the Baptist, was the kingdom of God; that is, the sovereignty or rule of God, the very heart of Jewish religion and the supreme hope of pious Israelites. And as is abundantly shown, not only by the passages referred to above, but also by his sharpening of the law in the Sermon on the Mount, he demanded more than was generally demanded rather than less; he set up a higher ethical standard and insisted upon a more perfect conformity to it. Like Amos, he emphasized life rather than ritual and required justice and mercy rather than sacrifice; and like him, too, he judged his generation severely and believed that it needed a thoroughgoing moral reformation. With a view thereto he was concerned less to offer men pardon than to summon them to righteousness; less to comfort than to convict of sin. . . .

Summing it all up, we may say that Jesus' idea of God was wholly Jewish. At no point, so far as we can judge from the Synoptic Gospels, did he go beyond his peoples' thought about God. His uniqueness, so far as his teaching goes, lay not in the novelty of it, but in the insight and unerring instinct with which he made his own the best in the thought of his countrymen. His piety seems to have been nourished particularly on Deuteronomy, the Psalms, and Isaiah, and it is the idea of God found in those writings that are chiefly reflected in his words. So far as the God of the Christians is different from the God of the Jews, it is due not to Jesus' teaching about God, but to the teaching of Paul and those that came after, or still more to the personality of Jesus and the interpretation his followers put upon it.

JOHN MACMURRAY (*1891–*)

UNDERSTANDING, NOT ETHICS

To call any doctrine "ethical" is to assert that it consists of statements about value and not about fact; that it is concerned not with what is, but with what ought to be. If we call the teaching of Jesus an ethic we imply that Jesus was a moralist, concerned to determine the nature of the good life—which is not the life that men actually live—and to determine the rules by which men ought to act. We imply that his effort was to construct an "ideal" of life, by which actual life is condemned, and which perhaps, others might use as a pattern; which they should try to "live up to." Anyone who thinks like this ought to read the Gospels, and attend to the form of Jesus' teaching, for it is certainly not the form that moralists employ. Jesus speaks usually in the indicative mood, not in the imperative. The term "ought" and its equivalents scarcely occur in his teaching. We can, of course, substitute for such a statement as "He that saveth his life shall lose it," the statement "Self-sacrifice is a virtue," or "One ought not to try to save one's life," and imagine that we are saying the same thing in other words. In fact, by giving the assertion an ethical form, we have changed its reference and turned it into its contradictory. What Jesus said was that the intention of saving one's life is self-frustrating and therefore stupid. It is an attempt to achieve the impossible. So far from implying that it is good to lose your life, he implies the precise opposite. He assumes, as axiomatic, that to lose one's life is sheer waste, and offers that as a pragmatic reason for not trying to save it. It is a fuller and richer version of what all students of ethics know as "the paradox of Hedonism"—that the way to get happiness is to forget it and aim at something else.

But it is not merely the absence of the ethical form, with its characteristic words and phrases, that is noteworthy in Jesus' teaching. There is evidence of a deliberate avoidance of it. There are occasions recorded upon which Jesus was invited to enunciate ethical principles, and we find that he does not respond. What an opportunity for an ethical teacher is given by the urgent question of the rich young ruler, or the lawyer; "What must I do to inherit eternal life?" Yet Jesus, on both occasions, refuses to take it. In both cases he turns the question back on the inquirer by referring him to the law. And when that turns out to be unsatisfactory, he says in the one case "Sell all thou hast, and give to the poor, and come and follow me," while in the other he tells the story of the Good Samaritan and invites the lawyer to pass his own judgment on it. When invited to settle an issue involving a moral question between two brothers, he replies angrily, "Who made me a judge or a divider?" When asked to discuss the moral problem of the relation of sin and suffering—"Who did sin, this man or his parents, that he was born blind?"—his reply carries an undertone of exasperation at the stupidity the question betrays. Indeed, one of his rare categorical imperatives is directed against the habit of which all ethical teaching, in our sense, is the elaboration. "Judge not, that ye be not judged." It is the blindness and foolishness of men, rather than their wickedness, which surprises him. The Pharisees are "blind guides of the blind." They can read the signs of the sky but not the signs of the times. "Art thou a master of Israel," he says to Nicodemus, "and knowest not these things?" To his disciples he says, "How is that ye do not understand?" To the crowds who listen to his parables, "He that hath ears to hear, let him hear." His own crucifixion is for himself not a crowning example of immorality, but of ignorance. "Father, forgive them," he says, "for they know not what they do."

It is an integral understanding of life that Jesus wishes, then, to impart; not an ethic which is an understanding of what life is not but ought to be. His disciples rightly described it as a "gospel"—as good news about the coming of the kingdom—"glad tidings of great joy which shall be to all people." An ethic, whatever it may be, whether law to be obeyed or ideal to be followed, is certainly not news, nor is it about what shall be. Paul, for all his occasional lapses into the vein of the moralist (they are far less frequent than is generally supposed), is quite clear that the gospel stands in strong contrast to the law,—that is to say the *moral* law,—because it does away with the principle of judgment by a standard of goodness, which must result in condemnation and punishment. That is why for Paul Jesus is the beginning of a new order of things, a new creation. "If any man be in Christ he is a new creature; old things are passed away; behold! all things are become new." And the old order is—the world of the moral law.

Edward S. Martin   (*1856–1939*)

LOVED OF THE MULTITUDE

Christ walked about in Galilee with very little regard for the rules made by the Pharisees, diffusing wisdom, creating an atmosphere. He wasn't a Dry; he left most of the details of life to be governed by competition, the less important things yielding to those that were more important to the spirit. That men should love one another was important. That they should love God was important, though what God is was left very considerably to their powers of conjecture. The organized-church people are apt to want to put clamps on people to keep them from doing something that the said organized Christians think is wrong. . . . But you may do all they would have you do, and still miss out. St. Paul understood perfectly well what that came to. He was concerned about the details of life but he said you might get them all right and still miss the great point and the great power of the Christian religion. "Sounding brass and tinkling cymbals"—he understood about those things. What the times need is not so much a great drive to put over the religion of the churches on an increased number of members as a better and fuller understanding of the mind of Christ. . . . Christ drew people unto him; he was marvellously attractive. The Jewish authorities did not like him but the multitude did. Great revivalists seem to have had that power. When it comes it does its work. That is what we should hope to get in increased volume out of religion—more love in the world, more love of our neighbor, which is the main way by which we express love of God.

JAMES MOFFATT   (1870–1944)

MORE THAN A PROPHET

Jesus taught men by what he was and what he did as well as by what he said. But he gave himself explicitly to the task of instructing people about God, as we have already seen. We might say of his words what Aeschines, the Greek orator, said about Demosthenes: his words are not words but wonders. Sometimes they were terse proverbs and pithy sayings. Sometimes they were parables. Sometimes they were short addresses elicited by some incident or situation of the day. He would ask questions and answer questions. Indoors or outdoors he mixed naturally in the common life of the people, watching how they lived, and finding the text for his words in anything that happened within his circle or came to his notice. Three specimens of his table-talk have been preserved, for unlike John the Baptist he was no austere ascetic, but would dine with Pharisees upon occasion, even though their friendliness was tinged by a certain patronage. Such meals in the ancient East were consecrated by blessings, and naturally led to a flow of soul upon the deeper things of life.

His teaching we have already watched—

> The mountain-sermon and the ruthful gaze,
> The cheerful credence gathered from his face,
> His voice in village-groups at eve or prime.

But here we collect some scattered fragments. On prayer, to begin with, for Jesus prayed and taught men how to pray. It is note-

worthy that the two main difficulties which he detected about ordinary prayer were lack of faith and the unforgiving temper. The
connexion between our sense of God's pardon and our pardon of
others is a new advance in religion. Again the counsel to pray in
secret may sound obvious, "but in contrast to the publicity of Oriental religious life, it marks a great advance in the direction of making
religion an inward thing." And the only sort of prayer he recognized
was the prayer of men and women in close contact with the actual
needs of their fellow-creatures. The counsels on money are also significant. It has been said that, next to his treatment of women, a
man's treatment of money is the most decisive test of his character—
how he makes it and how he spends it. Jesus viewed money with
some suspicion. The love of it represented to him one of the supreme
forms of worldliness, inducing the heartlessness and inhumanity
which he regarded as damning sins. Once he even bade a man give
up his wealth and property as being dangerous to his soul's welfare.
And always he warned the rich, or would-be rich, against undue
reliance upon their wealth, for it not only interfered with the brotherliness which sought to give everyone full scope for his powers, but
came between the soul and God.

What impresses us most in the teaching is its sheer simplicity. His
words fall from him with a natural power; they are pointed and
trenchant, sometimes pathetic, but never sentimental or far-fetched.
Paradox abounds, so do humour and irony. But Pascal was right in
singling out their divine simplicity as the mark of genius. "Jesus
Christ a dit les choses grandes si simplement, qu'il semble qu'il ne les
a pas pensées; et si nettement, qu'on voit bien ce qu'il en pensait.
Cette clarté, jointe à cette naïveté, est admirable."

To us it is a matter of course that he should have taught. In reality
it was a surprising novelty for anyone who claimed to be messiah.
No Jew ever expected his messiah to teach. It was assumed that he
would legislate wisely and vindicate the authority of the Law, but
never that he would give teaching in this quiet, homely fashion. And
Jesus taught, not to instruct people how to live during the interval
till God intervened to set up a new order of things; he taught the

permanent laws of the kingdom, that is, of the new order of things in which God the Father would be supreme over his people, his will accepted as the rule by which they lived. This Sovereignty of God, his realm or reign, was the centre of the teaching, the new interpretation and revelation of that time-honoured phrase to which such different hopes clung throughout the nation. Jesus revealed it, not by any definition, but by the revelation of his own personality as the leader of the kingdom under God. The instructions he gave were not casual flashes of spiritual intuition, but related organically to this divine order of forgiveness and fellowship whose consummation he eagerly expected. He was inspired by God to introduce this new constitution of religion, and had authority to set aside any regulations or traditions which conflicted with its principles. This was recognized by Jews to be the prerogative of their messiah; but it was one thing to admit it in theory, another thing to admit it as carried out by Jesus.

Even the emphasis he laid upon teaching his disciples was a new thing. Jesus was more than a prophet, but to his contemporaries he seemed often like one of the older prophets of the nation, as he spoke and acted with an inspired vigour which rebuked both the hierarchy and the masses in the name of God. He taught moral responsibility, inwardness of life, and single-mindedness as vital to the service of the Father. But which of the prophets had ever lavished such care on the training and teaching of disciples? Jesus gave far more than any prophet had given to intercourse with his followers. The importance he attached to teaching is one of the characteristic features of his originality as a man of God.

PAUL ELMER MORE (*1864–1937*)

"NEVER MAN SPAKE LIKE THIS MAN"

So far as there is originality in the ethics of Jesus it must be sought rather in the form than in the substance of his doctrine. His genius, though he wrote nothing, was that of a great literary artist: if it were not for the sound of the thing, one might say that he was the master rhetorician of religion. And this literary, or rhetorical, gift might be more narrowly defined as a unique power of condensation and pithy utterance. We do not know the character of his longer discourses, how he held the multitude spellbound for hours until they fainted with hunger; we think we would give the bulk of many libraries to have the record of what is lost forever. Time has deprived us of much, yet it has saved for us what, after all, must have been the strength of his appeal,—those memorable sentences which he tore out of the very heart of truth, bringing together what was dispersed, giving a new turn to what was ineffective, packing into a maxim what had been left more or less to inference. It was such a flash of insight that gave a positive turn to the Golden Rule, and that combined a saying in Deuteronomy with another in Leviticus to form the Great Commandment. It was genius of a like sort that collected petitions scattered through Hebrew literature into the incomparable prayer which expressed the immediate longings of the disciples for the visible kingdom of God, yet could satisfy the deepest spirit of worship through all ages. It was as a poet of words that he summed up the love of natural beauty in one perfect image: "Consider the lilies of the field, how they grow; they toil not, neither do they spin: and yet I say unto you, that even Solomon in all his glory was not arrayed like one of these." Further than that the seeing eye has not gone. And so of his use of parables, his revelation of human sympathy in dealing with the woman of Samaria or with the woman taken in adultery, his resource of defensive epigram in replying to questions about tribute to Caesar and his own authority,

—there is nothing comparable to these in the memoirs of Socrates or in the sacred books of Buddhism; "never man spake like this man."

J. MIDDLETON MURRY   (*1889*–   )

MORE THAN A MAN OF GENIUS

Jesus was above all else a man of genius. . . . I do at least sincerely believe that Jesus of Nazareth was the wisest and the bravest, therefore the greatest man who has lived upon this earth. . . .

Jesus was, of course, more, much more, than a man of genius. To the creative imagination of the great man of genius was added in him the power to live and die for his vision of things to come. Therefore the concept of the man of genius cannot be wholly adequate to his reality; but it is at least relevant to the author of sayings and parables that have haunted the souls of men for nineteen hundred years; and it absolves us from accepting those adamantine and unreal dilemmas with which the more ruthless critics delight to demonstrate their prowess. . . .

Jesus is more than a teacher of an ultimate wisdom. . . . Jesus was a teacher who died to save men who would not listen to his teaching. No other teacher has done that, and that sets him above and apart from all other teachers. It does not mean, as some may hold, that he added to the wisdom of the teacher the blindness of a fanatic. The combination is unthinkable and impossible. It means that to the wisdom of the perfect teacher in him was added the love of the perfect brother. There have perhaps been others as wise as Jesus, but none have had his love. Therefore there have been none so wise. To be wise and love—this is beyond all wisdom.

No one can understand Jesus who does not understand his teaching; but no one can understand his teaching who does not understand his life and death. The teaching without the life, the life without the teaching—these are incomprehensible. Because Jesus

taught Life itself—not how to live—but Life. In the words of the
man who was in spirit, but not in fact, his beloved disciple, who
understood once and for all time the eternal significance of his Master, Jesus "came that we might have life and have it more abundantly." The old ways of approach to that life-giving stream are
closed to many modern men. For these I write. We have to know
him after the flesh. There is for us no other way. But to know him
after the flesh is to know him after the spirit: for we shall find that
he was, in very truth, the ineffable Word made Flesh.

FRIEDRICH W. NIETZSCHE   (1844-1900)

BEQUEATHED A WAY OF LIFE

Translated by H. L. Mencken

I set myself against all efforts to intrude the fanatic into the figure of
the Saviour. What the "glad tidings" tell us is simply that there are
no more contradictions; the kingdom of heaven belongs to *children;* the faith that is voiced here is no more an embattled faith—
it is at hand, it has been from the beginning, it is a sort of recrudes-
cent childishness of the spirit. . . . A faith of this sort is not furious,
it does not denounce, it does not defend itself: it does not come with
"the *sword*"—it does not realize how it will one day set man against
man. It does not manifest itself either by miracles, or by rewards
and promises, or by "scriptures": it is itself, first and last, its own
miracle, its own reward, its own promise, its own "kingdom of
God." . . .

This "bearer of glad tidings" died as he lived and *taught—not*
to "save mankind," but to show mankind how to live. It was a
way of life that he bequeathed to man: his demeanour before the
judges, before the officers, before his accusers—his demeanour on the
cross. He does not resist; he does not defend his rights; he makes no

effort to ward off the most extreme penalty—more, *he invites it.* . . .
And he prays, suffers and loves *with* those, *in* those, who do him evil.
. . . *Not* to defend one's self, *not* to show anger, *not* to lay blames.
. . . On the contrary, to submit even to the Evil One—to *love* him.

ALBERT JAY NOCK   (*1865?-*   )

HIS TEACHING PURELY INDIVIDUALISTIC

I do not find any evidence that Jesus laid down any basic doctrine
beyond that of a universal loving God and a universal brotherhood
of man. There is no report of His having discussed the nature of
God or laying stress on any other of God's attributes, or that He
ever said anything about them. He also exhibited a way of life to
be pursued purely for its own sake, with no hope of any reward but
the joy of pursuing it; a way of entire self-renunciation, giving up
one's habits, ambitions, desires and personal advantages. The doing
of this would establish what He called the Kingdom of Heaven, a
term which, as far as any one knows, He never saw fit to explain or
define. His teaching appears to have been purely individualistic. In a
word, it came to this: that if every *one* would reform *one* (that is to
say, oneself) and keep *one* steadfastly following the way of life
which He recommended, the Kingdom of Heaven would be coex-
tensive with human society. The teaching of Jesus, simple as it was,
was brand-new to those who listened to it. Conduct, "morality
touched by emotion," put forth as the whole sum of religion, was
something they had never heard of.

Simple as the teaching of Jesus may have been, it was also very difficult. Following the way of life which He prescribed is an extremely arduous business, and my opinion is that those who can do
it are, and have always been, relatively few; even those able to understand the terms of its prescriptions would seem to be few. If the
record be authentic, Jesus appears to have been clearly aware that

this would be so. Yet there is abundant evidence that Jesus was not merely offering an impracticable counsel of perfection, for the thing has been done and is being done; mainly, as is natural, in an inconspicuous way by inconspicuous persons, yet also by some like St. Francis and others among the great names one meets in the history of Christian mysticism, whom circumstances rendered more or less conspicuous.

* * * *

The only apologetic for Jesus' teaching that I find in any way reasonable is the one which Jesus Himself propounded—experience. His way of life is not to be followed because He recommended it, or because He was virgin-born, or was a part of the Godhead, or could work miracles, or for any other reason than that experience will prove that it is a good way, none better, if one have but the understanding and tenacity of purpose to cleave to it.

BISHOP EDWIN V. O'HARA   (*1881-*   )

NO OTHER LIFE LIKE HIS

The life of Christ is of infinite significance to every human being. There is none other like it. His teaching is the supreme treasury of wisdom, and His life is the perfect illustration of His doctrine. His example is the highest incentive to virtue; the story of His sufferings and death the most moving revelation of Divine justice and the most effectual deterrent from sin. His whole life is a commentary on the love of God, Who "so loved the world as to give his only-begotten Son; that whosoever believeth in Him may not perish, but may have life everlasting" (John 3: 16).

GIOVANNI PAPINI (*1881-*)

THE MASTER AS A POET

Translated by Dorothy Canfield Fisher

Jesus never wrote—once only He wrote on the sand, and the wind destroyed forever His handwriting—but in the midst of a people of powerful imagination, of the people who wrote the Psalter, the story of Ruth, the book of Job, the Song of Songs, He would have been one of the greatest poets of all times. His victorious youthfulness of spirit, the racy, popular language of the country where He grew up, the books He had read, few but among the richest of all poetry— His loving communion with the life of the fields and of animals and above all His divine and passionate yearning to give light to those who suffer in the dark, to save those who are being lost forever, to carry supreme happiness to the most unhappy (because true poetry dost not catch its fire from the light of the lantern but at the light of the stars and of the sun, and is not found in the writings left behind by great-grandfathers, but in love, in sorrow in the deeply moved soul); these things combined made of Jesus a poet.

POPE PIUS XI (*1857-1939*)

MARRIAGE RAISED TO SACRAMENT

Translator Anonymous

How great is the dignity of chaste wedlock, Venerable Brethren, may be judged best from this that Christ our Lord, Son of the Eternal Father, having assumed the nature of fallen man, not only, with His loving desire of compassing the redemption of our race, ordained it in an especial manner as the principle and foundation of domestic society and therefore of all human intercourse, but also raised it to the rank of a truly and great sacrament of the New Law, restored it to the original purity of its divine institution. . . .

In order, however, that amongst men of every nation and every age the desired fruits may be obtained from this renewal of matrimony, it is necessary, first of all, that men's minds be illuminated with the true doctrine of Christ regarding it; and secondly, that Christian spouses, the weakness of their wills strengthened by the internal grace of God, shape all their ways of thinking and of acting in conformity with that pure law of Christ so as to obtain true peace and happiness for themselves and their families. . . .

In the first place Christ Himself lays stress on the indissolubility and firmness of the marriage bond when He says: "What God hath joined together let no man put asunder," and: "Everyone that putteth away his wife and marrieth another committeth adultery, and he that marrieth her that is put away from her husband committeth adultery." . . .

And this inviolable stability, although not in the same perfect measure in every case, belongs to every true marriage, for the words of the Lord: "What God hath joined together let no man put asunder," must of necessity include all true marriages without exception, since it was spoken of the marriage of our first parents, the prototype of every future marriage. Therefore, although before Christ, the sublimeness and the severity of the primeval law was so tempered that Moses permitted to the chosen people of God on account of the hardness of their hearts that a bill of divorce might be given in certain circumstances, nevertheless, Christ, by virtue of his supreme legislative power, recalled this concession of greater liberty and restored the primeval law in its integrity by those words which must never be forgotten, "What God hath joined together let no man put asunder."

John Cowper Powys   (*1872-*   )

MORE THAN HUMAN LOVE

Suppose that one saw written upon the notice-board of an important modern church the following inscription: "The Power of Jesus does not lie in any magical or cosmic authority, but in His natural human Love." How would a mind, cultured in the exacting and precise sense we are concerned with here, react to such an announcement?

Surely it would deny this statement! Surely it would feel that in spite of a certain sentimental and rhetorical atmosphere about these words the whole stress is wrongly laid. No one would have heard of this human love if it had not been the love of a Person regarded by the mass of men as super-human. Nor would this love—the love of Jesus—be able to exercise the spell over us that it does unless it were regarded as the love of Christ; that is to say as something different from any other man's love not only in degree but in kind; unless, to put it plainly, it were regarded as the love of a Being associated in some special and mysterious way with the dominant secret of the universe.

And if this is true with regard to the value of the love of Christ, it is true also with regard to those ancient poetic dogmas which the world has associated so long with the idea of the Incarnation; such as, for example, the Virgin Birth. All these conceptions hang together; not so much in a theological system—that is a comparatively unimportant aspect of them—as in the psychic, emotional, and poetic body of feeling with which we react to the whole pressure of life.

*   *   *   *

Finally it would seem that since our pilgrim of culture, living here in Europe or America, finds himself surrounded by the psychic influences of Christianity, he would be thick-skinned and insensitive if he did not yield himself up to the profoundest of all the great Christian dogmas, that dogma which more than any other we owe directly to Christ. This is the startling doctrine of the immeasurable and equal value of every living human soul.

Certain very great men—Rembrandt, Dickens, Dostoievsky, Walt Whitman—had the genius to snatch this strange, disturbing, desperate doctrine out of the magnetic vibrations originated by Christ, and use it freely in their art. Here indeed can the lonely culture of a proud spirit bathe itself in the cleansing flood of a real, and authentic humility. The Middle Ages with their "sweet Fools in Christ" have not passed away in vain if the ecstasy of a conscious equality of all souls can still melt the barriers between man and man.

JAMES HARVEY ROBINSON   (*1863–1936*)

A SON OF HIS TIME

It is assumed by most Christians, ignorant of history, that the teachings of Jesus were highly novel and that the prevailing of Christianity was so startling an event as alone to prove its divine character. Neither of these beliefs can be held by one familiar with scholarly books on these matters. There is a gap between the latest books contained in the Old Testament and the earliest writings in the New. This "period of silence" has been narrowed down to somewhat less than two centuries, by the recognition that Daniel, for instance, and certain of the Psalms were written in the second century before Christ. "But recent research," according to one of the chief scholars in this field, R. H. Charles, "has shown that no such period of silence ever existed. In fact, we are now in a position to prove that these two centuries were in many respects centuries of greater spiritual progress than any two that had preceded them in Israel." A number of the religious works of this intermediate period still survive, "written probably for the most part in Galilee, the home of the religious seer and mystic. Not only was the development of a religious but also of an ethical character. In both these respects the way was prepared by this literature for the advent of Christianity, while a study of the New Testament makes it clear that its writers had been brought up in the atmosphere created by these books and were themselves directly acquainted with many of them." Jesus it seems was a son of his time so far as his views and admonitions are reported to us. Many of them can be readily duplicated or paralleled in the contemporaneous literature of Judea. The fatherhood of God and the kingdom not of this world had been already proclaimed. This discovery, be it observed, *in no way diminishes the value or importance* of the gospels; it merely serves to reduce the miraculous and revelationary element in their origin, hitherto claimed for them.

As for the spread of Christianity it was gradual, and turbid with the controversies between innumerable sects, calling themselves the only true followers of Christ. Harnack, one of the greatest certainly of contemporaneous church historians, shows how the revised beliefs spread to Jewish communities scattered over the Roman Empire. It will be remembered that Jesus addressed a terrible rebuke to the clergy of his time, reported in the twenty-third chapter of Matthew. Among his many accusations was that "Ye compass sea and land to make one proselyte; and when he is become so, ye make him twofold more a son of hell than yourselves." This prejudice was shared by gentiles throughout the Roman Empire. The Jews had far more missionary ardor than used to be supposed. If, as it would now appear, the teachings of Jesus were in accord with the advanced religious and ethical ideals of his people, his disciples, who accepted him as the long-expected Messiah, could find ready converts among many Jewish communities throughout the Roman Empire.

JOSIAH ROYCE   (*1855–1916*)

LIGHT ON PARABLES NEEDED

The religion of the Master, as he is said to have taught it, involves many counsels, addressed to the individual man, regarding the art of life and regarding the way of entering what the Master called the Kingdom of Heaven. But these counsels, this preaching of the Kingdom of Heaven,—they appeared, in tradition, as stated in brief outlines and often as expressed in parables. It appears that, at least for the multitudes who listened, often for the disciples themselves, the parables needed interpretation, and that the sayings must be understood in the light of an insight which, at the time these words were first uttered, was seldom or never in the possession even of those who were nearest to the Master.

This further insight, according to the same tradition, was something that, as was held, would come whenever the Master's spirit was still more fully revealed to his disciples. Often when they heard their Teacher speaking most plainly, the disciples, as we are told, did not yet quite understand what he meant. And now, as a fact, the reported sayings and parables of the founder possess, side by side with their so well-known directness and simplicity, certain equally well known but highly problematic traits which, in all the ages which have since elapsed, have led to repeated questions as to what the Master meant by some of the most central doctrines that he taught. For instance, precisely what he taught about the office and work of love, and about self-sacrifice, and about casting off all care for the morrow—such things have often seemed mysterious.

And precisely these more problematic features of the original teachings of the Master are the ones to which the later Christian community gave interpretations that it believed to be due to the guidance of the Master's spirit, and that it therefore inevitably connected with its doctrine regarding his own person and his mission.

*　　*　　*　　*

Jesus unquestionably taught, in the best-attested, and in the best-known, of his sayings, love for all individual human beings. But he taught this as an organic part of his doctrine of the Kingdom of Heaven. The individual whom you are bidden to love as your brother and your neighbor is, even while Jesus depicts him, transformed before your eyes. For, first, he is no longer the separate organism with a separate mind and a detached being and destiny, whom you ordinarily loathe if he is your enemy, and resist if he endangers or oppresses you. No,—when he asks your aid,—though he be "the least of these my brethren"—he speaks with the voice of the judge of all men, with the voice that you hope to hear saying: "Come ye blessed of my Father, for I was hungered and ye gave me meat." In other words, the real man, whom your eyes only seem to see, but whom on the level of ordinary human intercourse you simply ignore, actually belongs to another level of spiritual existence, above the level of our present life of divisions. The mystery of this man is open only to the divine Love.

The Kingdom of Heaven is obviously a community. But this community is itself a mystery,—soon to be revealed,—but so far in the visible world, of which Jesus speaks, not yet to be discovered. This Kingdom is a treasure hid in a field. Its Master has gone into a far country. Watch and be ready. The Lord will soon return. The doctrine of Christian love, as thus taught by Jesus, so far as the records guide us, implies loyalty to the Kingdom; but expresses itself in forms which demand further interpretation, and which the Master intended to have further interpreted.

ERNEST F. SCOTT   (_1868-_   )

NOT MYSTICAL, BUT PRACTICAL

In the Synoptic Gospels Jesus comes before us as above all else a teacher of righteousness. It might almost appear from many of his utterances as if he protested against the value that was commonly attached to religion. He denounces the Pharisees, with their long prayers and scrupulous ceremonial. He declares that kindness to one's neighbor is more important than sacrifice. He takes constant occasion to show sympathy with Samaritans, pagans, publicans and sinners, who were reckoned outside of the religious pale. It was his insistence on the moral as against the religious obligations which excited the hostility of the scribes and priests and led them to compass his death.

It is maintained that Jesus was primarily a moral teacher, and that his message was obscured and perverted by the later theological creeds. To be sure he set out from certain religious beliefs, but this must be regarded as little more than an historical accident. The world was still at the stage when religion was made the basis of everything, and morality could not exist apart from religious sanctions. Jesus, like others, was compelled to adopt them, but he resolved them into a matter of form. When his ethic is separated from its religious framework it only becomes more consistent and intelligible.

After the death of Jesus, and especially when his gospel had taken root in the Gentile world, it was associated with beliefs and practices which had no place in his own mind. The divine nature was supposed to be different in kind from the nature of man, and through Jesus men sought to undergo a change of being. He was the Son of God, who possessed in himself the higher life, and imparted it to those who were united with him by faith and sacrament. This reading of the gospel, which was embodied in the creeds and was hardly questioned until modern times, was undoubtedly foreign to Jesus. His teaching, as we have now come to see, was not mystical but practical. He knew of nothing that could be placed higher than the moral demands. This does not mean, however, that he taught a morality which had no vital connection with religion, and which could ultimately be severed from it altogether.

Indeed, the more we examine his thought the more we become aware that the moral and the religious elements can at no point be separated. This is just as true of the Synoptic teaching, where the religious ideas often seem to be quite absent, as of the Johannine, where they are made supreme.

In the first place, the assumptions on which he rests his ethic are purely religious. He does not argue, like the philosophical moralists, from the constitution of man's nature and the obligations laid on him as a social being, but stakes everything on postulates of faith. When he seeks, for instance, to determine our duty to our fellow-men he sets out from the conviction that every soul has a value in the sight of God. . . .

Again, his demand is not for obedience to certain moral laws but for a new will . . . the Sermon on the Mount, when it is rightly understood, is much more than a series of moral precepts. It turns throughout on the idea that morality is inward,—that right action is worthless unless it proceeds from the regenerated will. This is always the primary conviction of Jesus. . . . For Jesus the one thing necessary was a right relation to God,—a complete harmony of our will with the divine will. . . .

Once more, Jesus conceived of fellowship with God as consisting in moral obedience; and it is here that we find the vital relation of his religion to his ethic. . . . There is nothing in the teaching of Jesus that can properly be called *mystical*. No trace can be found of the fundamental mystical idea that since God is immanent in all things He dwells in ourselves, so that at the center of our being we can meet with God. Jesus accepts the Hebrew belief as it appears in the Old Testament that God is the Sovereign who is enthroned in heaven. Our attitude to Him must be one of obedience and reverence, and there can be no thought of a union with God, such as was contemplated by the later mystics. None the less, the whole teaching of Jesus is grounded in what may be termed an ethical mysticism. He is possessed with the thought of love and goodness as so inherent in the divine nature that by attaining to them we apprehend God. In every act of justice and compassion we become for that moment one with God, and by constant obedience to His will we live the divine life.

PERCY BYSSHE SHELLEY (*1792–1822*)

THE HEAVEN THE MASTER PICTURED

God is represented by Jesus Christ as the Power from which, and through which, the streams of all that is excellent and delightful flow; the Power which models, as they pass, all the elements of this mixed universe to the purest and most perfect shape which it belongs to their nature to assume. Jesus Christ attributes to this Power the faculty of Will. How far such a doctrine, in its ordinary sense, may be philosophically true, or how far Jesus Christ intentionally availed himself of a metaphor easily understood, is foreign to the subject to consider. This much is certain, that Jesus Christ represents God as the fountain of all goodness, the eternal enemy of pain and evil, the uniform and unchanging motive of the salutary operations of the material world. The supposition that this cause is excited to action by some principle analogous to the human will, adds weight to the persuasion that it is foreign to its benevolent nature to inflict the slightest pain. According to Jesus Christ, and according to the indisputable facts of the case, some evil spirit has dominion in this imperfect world. But there will come a time when the human mind shall be visited exclusively by the influences of this benignant Power. Men shall die, and their bodies shall rot under the ground; all the organs through which their knowledge and their feelings have flowed, or in which they have originated, shall assume other forms, and become ministrant to purposes the most foreign from their former tendencies. There is a time when we shall neither be heard or be seen by the multitude of beings like ourselves by whom we have been so long surrounded. They shall go to graves; where then?

It appears that we moulder to a heap of senseless dust; to a few worms, that arise and perish, like ourselves. Jesus Christ asserts that these appearances are fallacious, and that a gloomy and cold imagination alone suggests the conception that thought can cease to be. Another and a more extensive state of being, rather than the complete extinction of being, will follow from that mysterious change which we call Death. There shall be no misery, no pain, no fear. The empire of evil spirits extends not beyond the boundaries of the grave. . . .

This is Heaven, when pain and evil cease, and when the Benignant Principle, untrammelled and uncontrolled, visits in the fullness of its power the universal frame of things. . . .

We die, says Jesus Christ; and, when we awaken from the languor of disease, the glories and the happiness of Paradise are around us. All evil and pain have ceased forever. Our happiness also corresponds with, and is adapted to, the nature of what is most excellent in our being. We see God, and we see that he is good.

IGNATIUS SMITH   (*1886–*   )

HE SET AN IDEAL OF HOME

The most arresting fact in the life of the Divine Christ is that He selected an humble home in which to live. By His divine power he might have commandeered one of the palaces of the Caesars, flung in magnificent array along the Mediterranean. He might have taken up residence in one of the mountain recesses of Palestine or among the hermits in the desert. But He chose to live in a home at Nazareth and there to pass His babyhood, His boyhood and the toiling days of His manhood. To know that Christ selected the home on which to place divine sanction and eternal approval is of inestimable consolation to those who spend even the smallest human effort to make and keep together a home. A warning it is to those who are tinkering with home peace and domestic happiness to know that they are undermining a pillar of society that was ornamented by the living presence of the Son of God.

Picture a little square house of brick or stone covered with sun dried clay and whitewashed. A long courtyard in front. A bake oven in the corner and all surrounded by a wall of loose stones. Close by is the carpenter shop where Joseph worked and where Jesus learned His trade. Step inside the house. Just a few rooms. A scarcity of furniture. A table; a few stools; rugs; mats and cushions. A little oil lamp burns in the corner and the hearth is in the center of the room. There is a closet for the linen and a mortar for the grain. The house is overcrowded, for, besides Jesus, Mary and Joseph, you find there the widowed sister Mary, with her children, the cousins of Jesus, sometimes called the brothers and sisters of the Lord. There are no comforts, no luxuries; there is deep concern about daily bread. This worry is written on the face of Joseph through whose labor the family is supported. Such is the home Jesus chose to live in and to make happy.

This devotion of Jesus to His home and to His parents has written into the ideals of the race an imperishable standard inspiring mankind for nineteen hundred years to imitate Him in devotion to their homes and in their mutual efforts to make every home successful and happy. Christ at home has revolutionized society in the past; if made at home in our homes today will revolutionize them again.

RALPH W. SOCKMAN   (1889-   )

HIS PRACTICAL WISDOM

When churchmen look at Jesus they see one who had an overwhelming sense of mission and yet one who did not go rushing through Palestine refusing the pleasant interludes between the acts of his vocation. The coveted guest at wedding suppers and social dinners did not appear narrow in his interests nor did he give the impression of using every event as an instrument of furthering his one single mission. His disinterestedness was one of the secrets of his charm.

*   *   *   *

Jesus did not advocate pain for the sake of pain. He did not invite conflict and persecution. He never encouraged meaningless asceticism. The follower of the Jesus way of life must see not merely the crown of thorns but the palm branches of jubilation, not only the spear thrust in his side but the locked arms of eager happy comradeship, not merely the Last Supper with its shadows and betrayal but the wedding feast with its unclouded radiance.

* * * *

He not only kindled the exploring spirit with his presence but he openly counseled it with his words. He released the human spring of investigation with such commands as "Seek and ye shall find, Knock and it shall be opened." His counsel was just the opposite of the modern English writer who says: "One-fourth of life is intelligible, the other three-fourths are unintelligible; and our earliest duty is to cultivate the habit of not looking around the corner." Jesus set men looking around the corners of life.

* * * *

If Christianity will study the methods of its Founder it will discover that Jesus counseled his disciples to make their demonstrations of distinctive virtue as deftly as possible so as to avoid arousing unnecessary antagonism. He said: "I send you forth as sheep in the midst of wolves; be ye therefore wise as serpents, and harmless as doves." To be a sheep in the midst of wolves is a role which at best is beset with some difficulties, but Jesus would not have his followers make it any harder than necessity demanded. He did not wish them to invite opposition merely for the sake of opposition or to judge their perfection by the persecution they incurred. He desired them to avoid those stupid tactics which have so often made moralists and reformers irritating rather than irresistible.

Archbishop J. L. Spalding   (*1840–1916*)

REVEALER OF HIDDEN SOURCES

Now the great revealer of the hidden sources of the best human life,
which is also the divine, is Christ; not so much because he was the
first to point out their existence, as because he alone has possessed
the secret and power to make men understand and feel their inestimable worth and charm. Before he taught, the prophets of Israel,
and a few minds of exceptional insight elsewhere, had seen the
vanity of all that is sensuous and transitory, and had recognized the
soul and its need of the Eternal. The prophets had given expression
to their visions in words which are all aglow with the light and
warmth of inspiration: the philosophers had clothed their institutions in language so high and chaste that their words remain forever clear and beautiful and appeal at once to the intellect and the
imagination. But the voice of the prophets died away in the midst
of the desert, and the wisdom of the philosophers was narrowed and
warped until it became the talisman of an inner circle, while the
world moved on heedless of mocking.

To Christ alone has it been given so to deliver the truths of the
divine life, as to thrill the hearts of his hearers, as to make them not
his enthusiastic disciples and lovers alone, but the lovers of all men
and the doers of good. His presence draws and soothes and chastens
the soul. He comes not like the prophets denouncing woe; he comes
not like the philosophers arguing and defining; but he comes as
from the central depths of the Unseen, calm and gentle, wise and
loving. In the sunlight, on the waters, amid the corn and the flowers,
in the face of strife and treachery, in the agony of death itself he is undisturbed and serene, like one who in life's fretful dream rests on the
bosom of the Eternal. The tranquil beauty of immortal things lies
on him and breathes in his words. God is revealed when he appears;
and when he speaks, the truth and love by which souls live are made
known. He is a permanent personal influence, an ideal character to
whom men turn and are conscious they are with the Highest. He is

the model of pure and holy living. He is also an enduring impulse to the practice of whatever is true or right or kind or helpful. By the contemplation of his life mankind have been exalted and purified more than by the disquisitions of all the philosophers and the exhortations of all the moralists. He is so human that the poor and the ignorant and the little are at home with him. He is so divine that the highest and the greatest minds who have lived since he was born have looked to him as to an unapproachable ideal.

With him can be compared no other being who has appeared on earth, whether we consider his character or his teaching or the results which have sprung from both: and this is seen to be so not by those alone who believe in him and love him, but by all who contemplate his life with clear-seeing eyes. . . . He alone of men has claimed to be sinless, and he is the only great historic character in whose presence envy and calumny are silent, though he has done what the human heart is least willing to tolerate. He has asserted in the plainest words his own absolute worth. Socrates effaces himself in the presence of the truth he seeks; but Christ affirms his superiority to all men, his oneness with the Father, and demands the complete self-surrender, which manifests itself in unquestioning obedience and perfect love. He delivers not merely a doctrine and a method. He gives his life, and demands in return that they who believe in him be reborn, that through love of him they may be drawn away from themselves toward God and toward whatsoever things are true, are right, are pure, are fair.

LINCOLN STEFFENS   (*1866–1936*)

HE HAD A CURE FOR EVILS

My drift toward Christianity has been slower than your approach was. I came at mine from a study of the New Testament. When I found that my readers were going to demand of me a remedy I went systematically to read up on remedies. I had none, of course. So I studied socialism, anarchism, the single tax, and, finally (from time to time), the Bible. And I was amazed at the teachings of Jesus. They seemed to me to be new. They certainly were new to me. And this was not alone because for so many years I had paid no attention to religion. I think their freshness was due in part to the irreverent way in which I read the New Testament, but also to the fact that Christianity is seldom taught in the Christian churches. However that may be, I find that Jesus saw what we see; he understood, as his disciples don't, the evils, their causes; and he had a cure. I don't say "the" cure: I don't want to draw conclusions yet. But his remedy is so effective that I now am making a systematic study of what the scholars have found out in their search of the sources of New Testament books. They don't know much yet; they raise more questions than they furnish answers for, but they are separating the authentic from some of the bogus stuff in the Book and enabling one to get a clear, liver, more human sense of the Son of Man. And he comes out gradually with more unity than I had expected.

ROBERT LOUIS STEVENSON (*1850–1894*)

TRUTH EASY TO RECEIVE

Take a few of Christ's sayings and compare them with our current doctrines.

"*Ye cannot*", he says, "*serve God and Mammon.*" Cannot? And our whole system is to teach us how we can! . . .

"*Take no thought for the morrow.*" Ask the Successful Merchant; interrogate your own heart; and you will have to admit that this is not only a silly but an immoral position. All we believe, all we hope, all we honour in ourselves or our contemporaries, stands condemned in this one sentence, or, if you take the other view, condemn the sentence as unwise and inhumane. We are not then of the "same

mind that was in Christ". We disagree with Christ. Either Christ
meant nothing, or else he or we must be in the wrong. Well says
Thoreau, speaking of some texts from the New Testament, and finding a strange echo of another style which the reader may recognise:
"Let but one of these sentences be rightly read from any pulpit in
the land, and there would not be left one stone of the meeting-
house upon another."

It may be objected that these are what are called "hard sayings",
and that a man, or an education, may be very sufficiently Christian
although it leave some of these sayings upon one side. But this is a
very gross delusion. Although truth is difficult to state, it is both
easy and agreeable to receive, and the mind runs out to meet it ere
the phrase be done. The universe, in relation to what any man can
say of it, is plain, patent, and startlingly comprehensible. In itself, it
is a great and travailing ocean, unsounded, unvoyageable, an eternal
mystery to man; or, let us say, it is a monstrous and impassable mountain, one side of which, and a few near slopes and foot-hills, we can
dimly study with these mortal eyes. But what any man can say of
it, even in his highest utterance, must have relation to this little and
plain corner, which is no less visible to us than to him. We are looking on the same map; it will go hard if we cannot follow the demonstration. The longest and most abstruse flight of a philosopher
becomes clear and shallow, in the flash of a moment, when we suddenly perceive the aspect and drift of his intention. The longest
argument is but a finger pointed: once we get our own finger rightly
parallel, and we see what the man meant, whether it be a new star
or an old street-lamp. And briefly, if a saying is hard to understand,
it is because we are thinking of something else.

*   *   *   *

Now, every now and then, and indeed surprisingly often, Christ
finds a word that transcends all commonplace morality; every now
and then he quits the beaten track to pioneer the unexpressed, and
throws out a pregnant and magnanimous hyperbole: for it is only
by some bold poetry of thought that men can be strung up above

the level of every-day conceptions to take a broader look upon experience or accept some higher principle of conduct. To a man who
is of the same mind that was in Christ, who stands at some centre
not too far from his, and looks at the world and conduct from some
not dissimilar or, at least, not opposing attitude—or, shortly, to a
man who is of Christ's philosophy—every such saying should come
home with a thrill of joy and corroboration: he should feel each
one below his feet as another sure foundation in the flux of time and
chance; each should be another proof that in the torrent of the years
and generations, where doctrines and great armaments and empires are swept away and swallowed, he stands immovable, holding by
the eternal stars. But alas! at this juncture of the ages it is not so with
us; on each and every such occasion our whole fellowship of Christians falls back in disapproving wonder and implicitly denies the
saying. Christians! the farce is impudently broad. Let us stand up in
the sight of heaven and confess.

Burnett H. Streeter   (*1874-*)

THE ESTHETIC QUALITY IN HIM

If asked what precisely is the distinctive feature in the ethics of
Christ, I should be inclined to answer, "The fact that it is not ethics at
all." Moses has a law; Confucius has a system; the Stoics have a
philosophy. Christ, instead of a code, gives an ideal; instead of rules,
a life; instead of a philosophy, an art. By this I do not merely mean
that the embodiment of His teaching in life and example is that
which gives it its power; I mean that in His actual teaching Christ
speaks as if He conceived conduct as "the art of life"—an art of
solid building, yet with something of the dancer's gaiety. There is a
kind of aesthetic quality about His approach to moral questions; one
is always left with the feeling that His teaching is, as it were, "beyond
morality." The word "morality" suggests rules, system, law, theo-

retical principles; but in the teaching of Christ there is always a sense of creation and adventure, a suggestion of buoyancy, paradox, *abandon*. For example, that conflict of duties which arises whenever the claims of family and those of some larger group seem incompatible, is one of the difficult ethical problems which have to be solved differently by each individual in each particular case. But Christ does not suggest a scientific approach to it. He flings down the paradox, "He that hateth not his father or his mother cannot be my disciple." In the same spirit He cries, "Love your enemies," "Turn the other cheek."

The gesture of extravagance in sayings like these logically results from an essentially novel conception of God. Christ, if I may venture so to put it, takes God seriously, but not solemnly. To Him God is not the potter, autocrat of the clay He moulds. From a living God there comes forth life, and life means liberty; the creator of personality is the begetter of the free. To Christ, God is not the supernatural lawgiver, the grave administrator of the Eternal Justice; He is like the father of the Prodigal Son, or the shepherd in the tale of the Lost Sheep, for joy shall be in Heaven over one sinner that repenteth more than over ninety and nine just persons which need no repentance; He is One who sends His rain on the just and on the unjust; therefore men who would become God's children must imitate His generosity. . . .

The aesthetic, non-legalistic quality in the ethical teaching of Christ is all-important when the question is raised of the validity of His teaching for other ages than His own. If Christ had legislated, inevitably any legislation that was suitable for life in Palestine in the first century A.D. would have been obsolete in fifty years. Mahomet did legislate; and for his own people in his own age, he legislated well—and just because his laws were so well adapted to his own time they are obsolete today. Again, if Christ had propounded a philosophic theory of ethical principle, as the Stoics did, His teaching would undoubtedly have been one of the milestones in human progress, but would it have been much more? But it is the quality of great art to be eternal. Phidias and Shakespeare do not go out of date. And just because the life and teaching of Christ have this quality of great art they can be an inspiration for all time.

HARRY F. WARD   (*1873*–   )

"IS LIFE AS WELL AS TRUTH"

Additional evidence of where the vitality of the religion of Jesus originates can be seen in the response he gets from two opposite quarters—the poor and the well-to-do. There is an important fact behind the overworked claim that when the revolting proletariat rejects the church it also shouts for Jesus. . . . But what truth is in it means more than the fact that the oppressed find in him a champion of their rights, that his name historically stands for the release of those who are bound and sight to those who sit in darkness. It means that in him the universal righteousness and justice and goodwill has got itself embodied in continuing fashion. When his name sounds, a bigger and more imperious fellowship than clan or creed or class flashes across our vision, a goal that can never be reached by any imperialism no matter how benevolent, by any dictatorship no matter how well meaning. . . .

Jesus emphasized the obligation to serve by sharing. This calls democracy to fulfill itself in the distribution of economic power and the universalizing of cultural opportunity.

*   *   *   *

It is the Golden Rule and the Sermon on the Mount that express Jesus to the common people. Those who come to the gospel untrammeled by any of the doctrinal interpretations of ecclesiastical religion are inevitably impressed by their moral challenge. . . . Scholars tell us that the closer we get to the actual words of the Galilean the clearer it is that his religion is essentially ethical, that this is the characteristic of the doubly attested sayings which are the most authentic part of the record. . . .

Taking the record as it now stands, with whatever has been added by its editors, one cannot read it and classify its religion as either theological, ceremonial, or institutional. It is still predominantly ethical. Jesus avoids discussing subtleties of doctrine with the Scribes; he puts human duties before the call to worship and makes its efficacy depend upon their fulfillment; he utterly condemns the mechanical devices of institutional religion. . . . In failing to accept and proclaim this essential characteristic of his religion official Christianity is in the position that Jesus ascribed to the Scribes and Pharisees. It refuses to enter the Kingdom of Heaven itself and at the same time keeps out those who want to go in.

* * * *

To say that the religion of Jesus is essentially ethical is not to say that he was merely an ethical teacher. It is conceded that he did not leave a theological system or a church organization or a social-economic program. Neither did he leave a set of ethical maxims. He left principles rather than precepts, teaching rather than teachings. . . .

Then it appears that Jesus is life as well as truth. To treat him merely as an ethical teacher, to put him in the same category as the Sophists or the Stoics is to miss the significance of his life and death, and to fail to receive the power of them. It matters not whether this is done by radicals or reactionaries—the result is the same—Jesus is lost. If men want only ethical teaching, they had better take Aristotle—he makes less trouble. But if they try Jesus, whose teaching is not apprehended until it becomes power for living, they will discover how to change the world and thereby how truly to enjoy it.

John W. Wayland   (*1872*–   )

"A TEACHER COME FROM GOD"

One night in old Jerusalem, two great teachers met. Each made a careful estimate of the other. For days, perhaps, they had been studying each other. . . . We shall notice only what the lesser master said of the greater. He said: "We know that thou art a teacher come from God."

That was the estimate that Nicodemus put upon Jesus.

It was a high estimate, by a high authority. No other teacher since that time has ever been quite worthy of the same estimate, applied in the same way. Yet it was a true estimate, truly stated. Nicodemus was seeking the truth. He found the truth in the Great Teacher.

The students of the ages may well sit with Nicodemus at the feet of Jesus. Young Saul of Tarsus at the feet of Gamaliel was less fortunate. All may be pupils and hear his words; those who are teachers will study his methods; those who are prophets will seek his aims; and every apostle will share his power.

That Christ did his work so largely by teaching rather than by some other process is highly significant. If others could have chosen for him his story would be different. Many of the Jews expected him to be a great conqueror, like David; but he chose to be a teacher. The peasants and the fishermen of Galilee wanted to erect a throne and make him a king, but he chose to be a teacher. He could have been rich, and could have done much good work with money, but he chose to be a teacher. The Jews, most of them, challenged him to show signs and wonders, but he chose to be a teacher. The inquisitive, restless, faithless Greeks hoped that he would put forth curious new philosophies, but he chose to be a teacher. He had power to drive men, to kill men, to crush men, to blind men, to compel men, but he chose to be a teacher. And from his great choice, from his great example, the world is gradually learning great lessons: To make a new world we must make new men; to make men anew we must change their minds and hearts. In the realm of spirit Caesar has always failed—Christ has always conquered. Christ is might; Christ is light. . . .

The Great Teacher was simple in speech, making the truth plain. . . . For two thousand years the plain, simple words of Jesus of Nazareth have been models for the world—for the truth-seeking and the truth-telling world. Of all men, the teacher is the truth-seeker and the truth-teller. . . .

The Great Teacher's method was direct. It was direct in several senses. It was direct in that he would say, as Nathan said when he looked David in the eye, "Thou art the man." He did not turn away or soften his words when error needed rebuke; neither did he disguise his pleasure when faith and courage needed approval.

Again, his method was direct in that he did not hesitate or delay when once the moment for speech or action came. More than once he waited because the time was not ripe, but he knew the signs of the times, and directly upon the stroke of occasion his word of wisdom came. . . .

The Great Teacher used many illustrations . . . what we call parables. . . . But the parables that Christ employed with the multitude were not merely illustrations—skylights to truth: they had a special value, a value in pedagogical equity. . . . The Great Teacher's method was progressive. This means simply that he began with the easier things and gradually led up to those that were more difficult.

DANIEL WEBSTER   (*1782–1852*)

A PERPETUAL OBLIGATION

When little children were brought into the presence of the Son of God, his disciples proposed to send them away; but he said, "Suffer little children to come unto me." Unto *me;* he did not send them first for lessons in morals to the schools of the Pharisees or to the unbelieving Sadducees, nor to read the precepts and lessons *phylacteried* on the garments of the Jewish priesthood, he said nothing of differing creeds or clashing doctrines; but he opened at once to the youthful mind the everlasting fountain of living waters, the only source of eternal truths. "Suffer little children to come *unto me*." And that injunction is of perpetual obligation.

LUTHER ALLAN WEIGLE   (*1880–*   )

HIS TEACHING METHOD EXPLAINED

The point of view which regards Jesus as a teacher is not new, but old. Jesus *was* a teacher. The Gospels say so. In that respect the modern appraisals of his teaching method have a clearer basis in the record than the portrayals of him as a business man, an economist, a political rebel, or a protagonist of social reform.

Jesus was a teacher. The four Gospels agree in so representing him. His contemporaries thus spoke of him, and thus addressed him. . . .

Even Bultmann, who calls Jesus a rabbi and holds that he was trained as a scribe, recognizes how different he was from the established teachers of his day. Their authority was external and second-hand; his authority was intrinsic, fresh, and free. The scribes were tied to their books and bound by tradition. And they had multiplied deductions, applications, and exceptions until they were entangled in a thicket of legal technicalities and lost vision and perspective. From all of this Jesus was free. He saw and thought for himself; and he spoke the truth as he saw it simply and directly, without need or fear of precedent.

He spoke with authority, he did not quote authorities. Guignebert, whose *Jesus* is the coldest and most detached of recent scholarly books about him, thus explains the astonishment of the people at his teaching "as one having authority": "The meaning seems to be that he broke away—for good reason—from the form of teaching established in the schools; that he did not necessarily base his preaching upon a text of the Scriptures, to be interpreted and commented upon; and that he did not cite the evidence of famous rabbis; but that his own inspiration was all that he had need of, even when he appealed to the Book, and the freedom, the homeliness and the spontaneity of his words were hampered by nothing, not even the attempt to organize them, because they were inspired and justified by an irresistible force."

Jesus' teaching was rooted in actual situations and directed to human need. He was engaged, not in the mere imparting of subjects, but in teaching people. And his method of teaching people was to give himself to them in unstinted friendship, to live with them day by day, and in speech and action to make his resources available to their need. He went about the work of teaching, not as though he had a certain body of material which he must transmit in a proper, logical, predetermined order to his pupils, but, rather, with a clear recognition that here were living, active, needy persons whom he might help to meet wisely the actual circumstances and situations with which they had to do. . . .

But the most important thing is yet to be said. Jesus' spontaneity, his vitality, his friendliness, would have been of little avail had he lacked insight and understanding. His teaching was with authority because it seemed to his hearers to be true. If we read the Gospels attentively, we are impressed with the reasonableness as well as the directness of Jesus' appeal to those who heard him. His tone was not that of a lawgiver, who commands; nor that of a despot, who threatens punishment or cajoles with promises of reward. Jesus spoke as one who discerns the truth, and sets it before others in order that they too may see it and in its light decide the issues which impend. He challenged his hearers to think for themselves, in the light of the relevant facts. He was no propagandist, capturing the minds of people by appeals to prejudice or passion. It was not his way, says Henry Latham, "to inflame the feelings and blind the eyes of men by kindling speech." His language was restrained, sensible, fair; his

appeal was to intelligence, conscience, will, rather than to emotion or
to the psychology of the crowd.

Oscar Wilde   (1856–1900)

"BE THYSELF," MESSAGE TO MAN

"Know Thyself" was written over the portal of the antique world.
Over the portal of the new world, "Be Thyself," shall be written.
And the message of Christ to man was simply, "Be Thyself." That
is the secret of Christ.

*When Jesus talks about the poor he simply means personalities,
just as when he talks about the rich he simply means people who
have not developed their personalities.* Jesus moved in a community
that allowed the accumulation of private property just as ours does,
and the gospel that he preached was not that in such a community
it is an advantage for a man to live on scanty, unwholesome food,
to wear ragged, unwholesome clothes, to sleep in horrid, unwholesome dwellings, and a disadvantage for a man to live under healthy,
pleasant and decent conditions. Such a view would have been wrong
there and then, and would of course be still more wrong now and
in England. . . . What Jesus meant was this. He said to man, "You
have a wonderful personality. Develop it. Be yourself. Don't imagine
that your perfection lies in accumulating or possessing external
things. Your perfection is inside of you. If only you could realise
that, you would not want to be rich. Ordinary riches can be stolen
from a man. Real riches cannot. In the treasury-house of your soul,
there are infinitely precious things, that may not be taken from you.
And so, try so to shape your life that external things will not harm
you. And try also to get rid of personal property. It involves sordid
preoccupation, endless industry, continual wrong. Personal property
hinders Individualism at every step." It is to be noted that Jesus

never says that impoverished people are necessarily good, or wealthy people necessarily bad. That would not have been true. . . . What Jesus does say is that man reaches his perfection, not through what he has, not even through what he does, but entirely through what he is. And so the wealthy young man who comes to Jesus is represented as a thoroughly good citizen, who has broken none of the laws of his state, none of the commandments of his religion. He is quite respectable in the ordinary sense of that extraordinary word. Jesus says to him, "You should give up private property. It hinders you from realising your perfection. It is a drag upon you. It is a burden. Your personality does not need it. It is within you, and not outside of you, that you will find what you really are, and what you really want." To his own friends he says the same thing. He tells them to be themselves, and not to be always worrying about other things. What do other things matter? Man is complete in himself. When they go into the world, the world will disagree with them. That is inevitable. The world hates Individualism. But this is not to trouble them. They are to be calm and self-centred. If a man takes their cloak, they are to give him their coat, just to show that material things are of no importance. If people abuse them, they are not to answer back. What does it signify? The things people say of a man do not alter a man. He is what he is. . . . After all, even in prison, a man can be quite free. His soul can be free. . . .

And so he who would lead a Christlike life is he who is perfectly and absolutely himself. He may be a great poet, or a great man of science; or a young student at a University, or one who watches sheep upon a moor; or a maker of dramas, like Shakespeare, or a thinker about God, like Spinoza; or a child who plays in a garden, or a fisherman who throws his nets into the sea. It does not matter what he is, as long as he realises the perfection of the soul that is within him.

Sir Francis Younghusband   (*1863–*   )

JOYOUSNESS OF THE SAVIOUR

In summing up His message Jesus said: "These things have I spoken
unto you that my joy might remain in you and that your joy might
be full." This text, though it contains the whole essence of Christianity, has been greatly neglected. Too long have we been taught
to regard Christ as a Man of Sorrow. Too long have we had an instrument of torture held before our eyes as a symbol of our religion.
Christ had His sorrows and, being of an exceptionally sensitive
nature, must have felt them with exceptionally acute severity. And
knowing the bitterness of His opponents He must have had exceptional courage deliberately to face them. But men of other religions
have also had their sorrows. Men of other religions have also deliberately faced death for their convictions. It was neither His grief
nor His heroism that produced the mighty impress His mission made
on mankind. It was His joy. This it was that He wished to remain
in our hearts that our own joy might be complete. Glad tidings of
great joy He brought into the world. And it was these glad tidings,
not the Crucifixion, that made the indelible impression. The Crucifixion only accentuated the value of the tidings. We may admire and
profit by His courage. But if we would profit most by His life and
do what would evidently please Him we would think of Him as He
surely wanted to be thought of—as a Man of Joy; and draw from
His life and teaching all the joy that is in them.

REDEEMER

A SURFACE CONTRADICTION

Translated by Dom Justin McCann, O.S.B.

If we reflect upon our Lord's attitude towards man and His redemption, we may on a superficial view run up against a contradiction. For, on the one hand, our Lord certainly regarded man as in a bad moral state, and on the other, He as certainly expected from him the most sublime virtue; "Be ye perfect, even as your heavenly Father is perfect." On the surface there is a contradiction here, a conflict between a pessimistic and an optimistic view of mankind. . . .

In taking a pessimistic view of our moral condition our Lord was in agreement with the devout folk of His time, who indulged in such views to the point of despair. At an earlier period the prophets had painted the sinfulness both of Jew and Gentile in the most dismal colours. Penance and conversion were the two main topics of their preaching; but they did not expect a conclusive conversion until the Messianic period.

*   *   *   *

Jesus was not blind to the meanness and misery of our poor humanity. He told His hearers to their faces that they were "evil," a "generation of vipers," an "evil and adulterous generation." Therefore the first thing that he had to say to mankind was "Do penance." And His first act was to accept the baptism of John, and so do vicarious penance for the sins of men. . . . For the sake of this "justice" He would enter into the sins of the people and take them upon Himself. . . .

His subsequent preaching also is dominated by the thought that all men are under sin. "Then began he to upbraid the cities, wherein were done the most of his miracles, for that they had not done penance. Woe to thee, Corozain; woe to thee, Bethsaida."

*   *   *   *

So Jesus was no exponent of a cheerful optimism in regard to the moral condition of men. His insight was too clear and Himself personally too pure, for Him not to realize the general wickedness and depravity of the world.

And yet the same Jesus expects from this depraved humanity the most sublime virtue. "Unless your justice abound more than that of the Scribes and Pharisees, you shall not enter into the kingdom of heaven." Nor is the new justice to be better merely in comparison with the justice of the Scribes and Pharisees; it is to be perfect justice conforming to an absolute standard. . . . The new justice excludes not only evil actions, but also bad thoughts and angry feelings. It requires us to love our enemies, not merely as a counsel of perfection, but as a moral duty. Worldly solicitude and the attempt to serve both God and mammon are condemned as heathen conduct. The whole inward man must belong to God and His will. . . .

How is our Lord able to make these severe demands upon us and to promise eternal happiness to those who fulfil them, if all men are "evil," if we are "an evil and adulterous generation"? . . .

We can solve this apparent contradiction only if we take account of our Lord's twofold nature and of the consciousness which was His in virtue of his twofold nature. When He speaks in such severe terms of the sinfulness of men, He is looking at the world around Him and painting it in its actual colours. When He bids us be perfect even as His heavenly Father is perfect, He is looking within at His own inner world and contemplating His own intimate union with God. And entering thus into Himself and realizing the marvellous actuality of that union, He turns to all those who wish to be His disciples and demands the like of them. So that His demands, which to the natural man seem extravagant, are seen to be not so much demands as promises and luminous ideals for all those who receive Him, who believe in Him, who become one flesh and blood with Him.

HENRI FRÉDERIC AMIEL   (*1821–1881*)

"A RAY OF HEAVENLY LIGHT"

Translated by Mrs. Humphry Ward

October 1, 1849—Yesterday, Sunday, I read through and made extracts from the Gospel of St. John. It confirmed me in my belief that about Jesus we must believe no one but Himself, and that what we have to do is to discover the true image of the Founder behind all the prismatic reactions through which it comes to us, and which alter it more or less. A ray of heavenly light traversing human life, the message of Christ has been broken into a thousand rainbow colors, and carried in a thousand directions. It is the historical task of Christianity to assume with every succeeding age a fresh metamorphosis, and to be forever spiritualizing more and more her understanding of the Christ and of salvation.

Christianity, if it is to triumph over pantheism, must absorb it. To our pusillanimous eyes Jesus would have borne the marks of a hateful pantheism, for he confirmed the Biblical phrase "ye are Gods," and so would St. Paul, who tells us we are of "the race of God." Our century wants a new theology—that is to say, a more profound explanation of the nature of Christ and of the light which it flashes upon heaven and upon humanity.

ANONYMOUS

"WHEN A YOUNG MAN DIES"

All the loveliness of life and all the charm of creation were never cherished by anyone quite as much as they were by a young man who surrendered them all and laid down His life one day in spring these many centuries ago. He was more in love with the world's loveliness than any other. For He had made it all. And He Himself was the perfect man, more sensitive than any other to the beauty and the possibilities of having a life to be lived. And so much of life lay before Him!

The hands he stretched on the cross were the fine, capable hands of a craftsman. The body that was hung from iron nails was the fine, clean body of a young man in the vigor of life's new prime. The head that was wreathed with thorns was the head of a poet, a philosopher, a lover of God and men, that knew no peer. Yet He chose to die, to give up all. He closed His eyes in death on all that might have been in the years ahead. His was a sacrifice beyond the capabilities of any merely human sacrifice. For He was God, and He did it that no human sacrifice need ever be in vain.

There never was a silence like that silence when the Word of God was still, never a darkness like the darkness that fell when the Light of the World went out. Yet never has death known less victory. For death, the penalty of sin, is no longer the destroyer of dreams and hopes and love unfulfilled. Because of the sacrifice of the young man Christ, death is swallowed up in victory, the victory of life eternal.

SAINT AUGUSTINE (BISHOP OF HIPPO)   (*354 A.D.–430 A.D.*)

GOD'S MIGHTY MEDICINE

Translated by E. B. Pusey

But I thought otherwise; conceiving only of my Lord Christ, as of a man of excellent wisdom, whom no one could be equalled unto; especially, for that being wonderfully born of a Virgin, He seemed, in conformity therewith, through the Divine care for us, to have attained that great eminence of authority, for an ensample of despising things temporal for the obtaining of immortality. But what mystery there lay in, *"The Word was made flesh,"* I could not even imagine.

Only I had learnt out of what is delivered to us in writing of Him, that He did eat, and drink, sleep, walk, rejoiced in spirit, was sorrowful, discoursed; that, flesh did not cleave by itself unto Thy Word, but with the human soul and mind. All know this, who know the unchangeableness of Thy Word, which I now knew, as far as I could, nor did I at all doubt thereof. For, now to move the limbs of the body by will, now not, now to be moved by some affection, now not, now to deliver wise sayings through human signs, now to keep silence, belong to soul and mind subject to variation. And should these things be falsely written of Him, all the rest also would risk the charge, nor would there remain in those books any saving faith for mankind. Since then they were written truly, I acknowledged a perfect man to be in Christ; not the body of a man only, nor, with the body, a sensitive soul without a rational, but very man; whom, not only as being a form of Truth, but for a certain great excellency of human nature and a more perfect participation of wisdom, I judged to be preferred before others. . . .

But the true Mediator, Whom in Thy secret mercy Thou hast shewed to the humble, and sentest, that by His example also they might learn that same humility, that *Mediator between God and man, the Man Christ Jesus,* appeared betwixt mortal sinners and the immortal Just One; mortal with men, just with God: that because the wages of righteousness is life and peace, He might by a righteousness conjoined with God, make void that death of sinners, now made righteous, which He willed to have in common with them. Hence He was shewed forth to holy men of old; that so they, through faith in His Passion to come, as we through faith of it passed, might be saved. For as Man, He was a Mediator; but as the Word, not in the middle between God and man, because equal to God, and God with God, and together one God.

How hast Thou loved us, good Father, who *sparedst not Thine only Son, but deliveredst Him up for us ungodly!* How hast Thou loved us, for whom, *He that thought it no robbery to be equal with Thee, was made subject even to the death of the cross,* He alone *free among the dead, having power to lay down His life, and power to take it again:* for us to Thee both Victor and Victim, and therefore Victor, because the Victim; for us to Thee Priest and Sacrifice, and therefore Priest because the Sacrifice; making us to Thee, of servants, sons, by being born of Thee, and serving us. Well then is my hope strong in Him, that Thou *wilt heal all my infirmities,* by Him Who *sitteth at Thy right hand and maketh intercession for us;* else should I despair. For many and great are my infirmities, many they are, and great; but Thy medicine is mightier. We might imagine that Thy Word was far from any union with man, and despair of ourselves, unless He had been made flesh and dwelt among us.

Karl Barth (*1886–*)

NOTHING HUMAN FOREIGN TO HIM

Translated by E. G. Homrighausen and Karl J. Ernest

But whatever may be our judgment of the demands of the hour, this is the meaning, content and dynamic of the revelation which met the biblical prophets and apostles: God Himself is here in the fact that Jesus Christ and the Holy Spirit are here. He is with us *as we are.* Yes, He is Himself what we are. He has assumed our nature; He has made our sin His own and He has made our death His. To Him who is endowed with the fulness of the divine majesty, nothing that is human is foreign. He took upon Himself our fate, our godlessness, yea, the torture of our hell. Our deepest misery is His misery also. Yes, exactly in the depths of our misery He intercedes for us, and substitutes Himself for us, warding off the wages justly due us and suffering and making restitution what we could not suffer and where we could not make restitution. He Himself, Jesus Christ, who has suffered the death of a sinner and sits at the right hand of the Father, is our advocate. He Himself, the Holy Spirit, who with groaning that cannot be uttered, makes intercession for us who do not know what we should pray. This is what revelation means, this is its content and dynamic: Reconciliation has been made and accomplished.

ROBERT HUGH BENSON   (*1871–1914*)

DIVINELY A FAILURE

Again and again there came moments when the success of Jesus Christ seemed almost assured. There were moments when the whole world went after Him who seemed so perfectly to meet its ideals; when the world itself would come and take Him by force and make Him a King; when the kingdoms of the world seemed laid at His feet; and yet, somehow or another, it all came to nothing. His whole life on earth was a kind of crescendo of popularity, up to the last moment; and then, in an instant, it all crumbled down again to nothing. Palm Sunday immediately preceded Good Friday. The procession of one was almost a replica of the other. There were a few details different; the spear-shaped palm leaves became palm-shaped spears; but the crowd was the same, the cries were the same, acclaiming the King of the Jews: the central Figure was the same. But the triumph turned to failure so soon as His central claim was made. He was welcomed and honored as a mere earthly King; He was rejected and condemned as a Heavenly King. Humanly considered He was something of a success; Divinely considered He was a failure. As a demagogue he would have triumphed; as a God He was crucified.

WILLIAM BLAKE   (*1757–1827*)

THE MORAL VIRTUE INCULCATED

There is not one Moral Virtue that Jesus Inculcated but Plato and
Cicero did Inculcate before him; what then did Christ Inculcate?
Forgiveness of Sins. This alone is the Gospel, & this is the Life &
Immortality brought to light by Jesus, Even the Covenant of Jehovah,
which is This: If you forgive one another your Trespasses, so shall
Jehovah forgive you, That he may dwell among you; but if you
Avenge, you Murder the Divine Image, & he cannot dwell among
you; because you Murder him he arises again; & you deny he is
arisen, & are blind to Spirit.

JOHN ELOF BOODIN   (*1869–*   )

FOR GOD'S LOST CHILDREN

There came indeed out of Israel a saviour who taught that God is
love, that his grace falls freely like rain and sunshine upon the
just and the unjust, to quicken and give life if they will receive it.
Jesus turned his back upon the religion of sack-cloth and ashes and
proclaimed the good tidings of joy. He turned his back upon the
desert with its self-negation and introversion to find the joy of life
in working for humanity—God's lost children. He showed that it is
not necessary to wait for a national salvation in the far-off future
in order to be happy, for we can even now create a kingdom of
heaven in a sordid world if we tap the resources of love within us.
Love is the secret of the happy life, and where love is there is no
need of expiation, for love is above forgiveness. It requires only the
willing heart. The repentant prodigal goes through no ceremony of
expiation. He is given a banquet. Forgive your brother seven times?
Nay, seventy times seven. Love does not count offences. Love is above

pity in the vulgar sense. The priest and the Levite pity the unfortunate man—and walk on the other side. The good Samaritan forgets all about pity and in love heals his wounds. The test of forgiveness is in the expression of love. To her that loves much, much is forgiven.

PHILLIPS BROOKS   (*1835–1895*)

"IN HIM ALL BROKEN LINES UNITE"

It is so hard for us to believe in the Mystery of Man. "Behold man is this," we say, shutting down some near gate which falls only just beyond, quite in sight of, what human nature already has attained. If man would go beyond that he must be something else than man. And just then something breaks the gate away, and lo, far out beyond where we can see stretches the Mystery of Man. The beautiful, the awful Mystery of Man! To him, to man, all lowest lines have climbed, and having come to him, have found a field where evolution may go on forever.

The Mystery of Man! How Christ believed in that! . . . He who does not believe in that cannot enter into the full glory of the Incarnation, cannot really believe in Christ. Where the mysterious reach of mankind touches the divine, there Christ appears. No mere development of human nature outgoing any other reach that it has made, yet still not incapable of being matched, perhaps of being overcome; not that, not that,—unique and separate forever,—but possible, because of this same mystery of man in which the least of us has share. To him who knows the hither edges of that mystery in his own life, the story of how in, on, at its depths it should be able to receive and contain divinity cannot seem incredible; may I not say, cannot seem strange?

Men talk about the Christhood, and say, "How strange it is! Strange that Christ should have been,—strange that Christ should have suffered for mankind." I cannot see that so we must magnify

Him or bring Him nearest to us. Once feel the Mystery of Man and is it strange? Once think it possible that God should fill a humanity with Himself, once see humanity capable of being filled with God, and can you conceive of His not doing it? Must there not be an Incarnation? Do you not instantly begin to search earth for the holy steps? Once think it possible that Christ can, and are you not sure that Christ must give Himself for our Redemption? So only, when it seems inevitable and natural, does the Christhood become our pattern. Then only does it shine on the mountain-top up toward which we can feel the low lines of our low life aspiring. The Son of God is also the Son of Man. Then in us, the sons of men, there is the key to the secret of His being and His work. Know Christ that you may know yourself. But, oh, also know yourself that you may know Christ! . . .

That Christ should be and should be Christ appears the one reasonable, natural, certain thing in all the universe. In Him all broken lines unite; in Him all scattered sounds are gathered into harmony; and out of the consummate certainty of Him, the soul comes back to find the certainty of common things which the lower faith holds, which advancing faith loses, and then finds again in Christ.

ORESTES A. BROWNSON   (1803–1876)

THE MEDIATOR FROM GOD

There is a tendency in some minds among us, to rank Jesus in the category of ordinary men. . . . Jesus was a man of greater natural endowments, and of more devout piety, truer and deeper philanthropy than other men. He has exerted a great and beneficial influence on the world, will perhaps continue to exert a beneficial influence for some time to come; but he is divine, it is said, in no sense in which all men are not divine, in no sense in which nature is not divine. He had a larger nature, and was truer to it, than other men, and this is all wherein he was distinguished from other men, or had any special divinity.

Persons who entertain this view . . . do not look upon him as having been, in the plain, ordinary sense of the terms, sent from God to be the redeemer and saviour of the world. They gave a very loose explanation of the text, "God so loved the world that he gave his only begotten Son to die, that whoever should believe on him might not perish, but have everlasting life." Jesus was the "Son of God" as all men are sons of God, and in no other sense, and "was given" as all men are given, and not otherwise. . . .

We must regard Jesus, not as *coming* but as *sent,* not as raising himself up to be the Mediator, but as having been raised up by the Father in heaven. He is from God, who commends his love to us by him. It is God's grace, not human effort or human genius, that provides the Mediator. It is impossible then to press Jesus into the category of ordinary men. He stands out alone, distinct, peculiar. This much, I must be permitted to assume in regard to Jesus, if I am to concern myself with Christianity at all. In answer then to the question, Whence comes the Mediator? I reply from God, "who so loved the world that he gave his only begotten Son to die, that whosoever should believe on him might not perish but have everlasting life."

But assuming that God sent the Mediator, what did he send him to do? What was the work to be done for human redemption and sanctification? In other words, what is the condition in which the Gospel assumes the human race to be *without* Christ, and from which God, through the mediation of Christ, is represented as saving it? . . . What is the work to be done? It is to redeem human nature from its inherent depravity, communicate to it a new and divine life, through which individuals may be saved from actual transgression, and raised to fellowship with the Father, by which they really shall become sons of God, and joint-heirs of a heavenly inheritance. . . .

But the human race lives . . . *in solido,* all are members of one and the same body, and members one of another. There is a oneness of life which runs through them all, making them so strictly one, that the whole must feel whatever affects anyone. . . . Consequently, the very moment that this new life of Jesus was communicated to the disciples, it was communicated virtually to the race. . . . By the fact that one generation overlaps another, and thus becomes the objective life, the generation in which Christ appeared must necessarily transmit it to its successor, and that successor to *its* successor, and this generation carry it on to generation, so long as the succession of generations should last.

JOHN BURROUGHS   *(1837–1921)*

GREAT TEACHER AND PROPHET

Science knows God, too, as law, or as the force and vitality which pervade and uphold all things; it knows Jesus as a great teacher and prophet, and as the Saviour of men. How? By virtue of the contract made in the Council of the Trinity as set forth in the creed of Calvinism? No; but by his unique and tremendous announcement of the law of love and the daily illustration of it in his life. Salvation by Jesus is salvation by self-renunciation, and by gentleness, mercy, charity, purity, and by all the divine qualities he illustrated. He saves us when we are like him,—as tender, as charitable, as unworldly, as devoted to principle, as self-sacrificing. His life and death do inspire in mankind these things; fill them with this noble ideal. He was a soul impressed, as perhaps no other soul ever had been, with the oneness of man with God, and that the kingdom of heaven is not a *place,* but a state of mind. Hence, coming to Jesus is coming to our truer, better selves and conforming our lives to the highest ideal. Was not Paul a Saviour of mankind also? Without Paul it is probable that Christianity would have cut but an insignificant figure in this world. He was its thunderbolt; his words still tingle in our ears.

I by no means say that this is the only view that can be taken of Jesus as the Saviour of mankind; I say it is the only view science or reason can take—the only view which is in harmony with the rest of our knowledge of the world.

*　　*　　*　　*

It may be noted that Jesus turned away from or rebuked the more exact, skeptical mind that asked for a sign, that wanted proof of everything, and that his appeal was to the more simple, credulous and enthusiastic. He chose his disciples from among this class, men of faith and emotion, not too much given to reasoning about things. In keeping with this course of action, nearly all his teachings were by parables. In fact, Jesus was the highest type of the mystical, parable-loving Oriental mind, as distinguished from the exact, science-loving Occidental mind.

*　　*　　*　　*

Nothing could be more natural, nothing more in harmony with universal experience, than his coming, and his life as we may read it in the Synoptic Gospels. There was no prodigy, no miracle, no sudden apparition of a superhuman being, clothed in majesty and power, as the popular expectation indicated there would be, but the Messiah came in the natural way as a helpless infant, born of human parents. Instead of a throne, there was a humble cradle in a manger.

It really enhances our notion of his merit, or if you prefer of his divinity, that he could have been rejected by his race and people, that he should have come from a town of proverbial disrepute, that he should have been meek and lowly through life, a man of sorrows, the friend of the humble and the despised, that his kingdom should not have been of this world; in fact, that he should in every way have disappointed expectation.

All this seems in harmony with the course of nature and of human life. It agrees with the truest experience. There is a sort of poetic verisimilitude about it. Indeed, if a God were to appear this is probably the way he would come. All greatest things have an humble beginning. The divine is nearer and more common than we are apt to think. The earth itself is a star in the sky, little as we may suspect it.

V. F. CALVERTON   (*1900–1940*)

HIS MEANING TO THE NEGRO

It was as an expression of this consecrated other-worldly ardor that the Negro spirituals came into being and grew into form. There is more, far more than the ordinary Christian zeal embodied in them. These spirituals are not mere religious hymns written or recited to sweeten the service or improve the ritual. They are the aching, poignant cry of an entire people. Jesus to the Negro is no simple religious savior, worshipped on Sundays and forgotten during the week. He is the incarnation of the suffering soul of a race.

THOMAS CARLYLE   (*1795–1881*)

THE GROWTH FROM ONE SEEDGRAIN

Look eighteen hundred years ago, in the stable at Bethlehem: an infant laid in a manger! Look, thou ass, and behold it; it is a fact,— the most indubitable of facts: thou wilt thereby learn innumerable things. Jesus of Nazareth and the life he led, and the death he died, does it teach thee nothing? Through this, as through a miraculous window, the heaven of Martyr Heroism, the "divine depths of Sorrow", of noble Labour, and the unspeakable silent expanses of Eternity, first in man's history declare themselves. The admiration of all nobleness, divine *worship* of Godlike nobleness, how universal it is in the history of man!

But mankind, that singular entity mankind, is like the fertilest, fluidest, most wondrous element, an element in which the strangest things crystallise themselves, and spread out in the most astounding growths. The event at Bethlehem was of the Year One: but all years since that, eighteen hundred of them now, have been contributing new growth to it,—and see, there it stands: the Church! Touching the earth with one small point: springing out of one small seedgrain, rising out therefrom, ever higher, ever broader, high as the Heaven itself, broad till it overshadow the whole visible Heaven and Earth, and no star can be seen but through *it*. From such a seedgrain so has it grown; planted in the reverences and sacred opulences of the soul of mankind; fed continually by all the nobleness of some forty generations of men. The world-tree of the Nations for so long!

IGNATIUS W. COX, S.J.   (*1883–*)

THE SECOND ADAM AND REDEEMER

When it would seem that man could sink no lower in the scale of degradation, when the fullness of time was come, God made ready to lift man up through a second Adam in the fulfillment of His purpose "to restore all things in Christ." Man had rejected the adopted sonship of God, the participation in the Divine nature by sanctifying grace; man in his sin had desired to be like unto God. The Son of God would take upon Himself human nature, would unite human nature to the divine nature in His own person. God-made-man would show his brother-man how to live the God-life by showing how a God-man lived. No human intellect in wildest fancy ever would have dared to dream the plan divine for the restoration of human kind. Only eternal, creative, frustrated love could have conceived it.

The second Adam, the second head of all humanity, would be the only begotten Son, the Word of God. He would not have been, He could not have been the second Adam, if He had not been

very man, if He had not contained within Himself all human perfections. He would not have been, He could not have been the
restorer of humanity unless he was very God. It was in the divine
plan, wherein justice and mercy would be fully satisfied, the task
for a God. And so the Second Person of the Blessed Trinity would
unite a human nature to Himself, so that the only begotten Son,
God by possession of divine nature, would also be man by the possession of a human nature. There would be no intermingling of
the divine nature and the human. But one and the same divine
person would have two distinct natures united in His own personality. His actions by His human nature would be actions of
God for they would be the actions of a divine person. Thus the
solidarity of human nature with God would be forged anew by
an unbreakable link. As all men were potentially included in Adam
by the law of solidarity, all men would be potentially included in
the second Adam by the solidarity of His redemptive action. Man
asked to be as God. The God-man would teach him the *way* to
walk, the *truths* to think, the *life* to live, to be as God. The second
Adam would establish his right as prophet and king, as priest and
mediator, as sanctifier and Emmanuel. He would begin to do and
teach. He would establish His credentials as in very truth the Son
of God by His unlimited control over nature, by His miracles. The
blind would see, the deaf would hear, the lame walk, the dead rise.
The winds would obey Him, the surging sea would grow calm
at His word, the very devils would be subject to Him. That He
was very man, like unto man in all things, sin excepted, He would
manifest by His all too human tears of infancy and manhood, by
hunger and thirst, by tender sympathy and faithful love, by suffering and by death. As King and Prophet, He would lead and
teach. He would be man's way and truth and life.

*   *   *   *

And then, because as man, as priest and victim, He needs must
die, He would show how in a new mystical body He would live

on in His faithful, as sanctifier and Emmanuel: "Behold, I am with you all days even to the consummation of the world." . . .

Thus the great supernatural solidarity of man with God and man with man, destroyed by Adam would be restored through the second Adam, Jesus Christ.

DANTE ALIGHIERI   (*1265–1321*)

TRIES TO PROVE CHRIST SANCTIONED ROMAN EMPIRE

Translated by F. J. Church

I say, then, that if the Roman empire did not exist by right, Christ in being born presupposed and sanctioned an unjust thing. But the consequent is false; therefore the contradictory of the antecedent is true; for it is always true of contradictory positions, that if one is false the other is true. It is not needful to prove the falsity of the consequent to a true believer: for, if he be faithful, he will grant it to be false; and if he be not faithful, then this reasoning is not for him.

I prove the consequence thus: wherever a man of his own free choice carries out a public order, he countenances and persuades by his act the justice of that order; and seeing that acts are more forcible to persuade than words (as Aristotle holds in the tenth book of his *Ethics*) therefore by this he persuades us more than if it were merely an approval in words. But Christ, as Luke who writes His story, says, willed to be born of the Virgin Mary, under an edict of Roman authority, so that in the unexampled census of mankind, the Son of God, made man, might be counted as man: and this was to carry out that edict. Perhaps it is even more religious to suppose that it was of God that the decree issued through Caesar, so that He who

had been such long years expected among men should Himself en-
roll himself with mortal man.

Therefore Christ by His action, enforced the justice of the edict of
Augustus, who then wielded the Roman power. And since to issue a
just edict implies jurisdiction, it necessarily follows that He who
showed that He thought the jurisdiction under which it was issued
just: but unless it existed by right it were unjust.

And it must be noted that the force of the argument taken to destroy the consequent, though the argument partly holds from its
form, shows its force in the second figure, if it be reduced as a syl-
logism, just as the argument based on the assumption of the antecedent is in the first figure. The reduction is made thus: all that is
unjust is persuaded to man unjustly; Christ did not persuade us unjustly; therefore he did not persuade us to do unjust things. From
the assumption of the antecedent thus: all injustice is persuaded to
men unjustly; Christ persuaded a certain injustice to man, therefore
He persuaded unjustly.

And if the Roman empire did not exist by right, the sin of Adam
was not punished in Christ. This is false, therefore its contradictory
is true. The falsehood of the consequent is seen thus. Since by the
sin of Adam we were all sinners, as the Apostle says: "Wherefore, as
by one man sin entered into the world, and death by sin, and so death
passed upon all men, for that all have sinned,"—then, if Christ had
not made satisfaction for Adam's sin by his death, we should still by
our depraved nature be the children of wrath. . . .

If, therefore, Christ had not suffered by the sentence of a regular
judge, the penalty would not properly have been punishment; and
none could be a regular judge who had not jurisdiction over all mankind; for all mankind was punished in the flesh of Christ, who "hath
borne our griefs and carried our sorrows," as saith the prophet Isaiah.
And if the Roman empire had not existed by right, Tiberius Caesar,
whose vicar was Pontius Pilate, would not have had jurisdiction over
all mankind. It was for this reason that Herod, not knowing what
he did, like Caiaphas, when he spoke truly of the decree of heaven,

sent Christ to Pilate to be judged, as Luke relates in his gospel. For Herod was not the viceregent of Tiberius, under the standard of the Senate; but only a king, with one particular kingdom given him by Tiberius, and ruling the kingdom committed to his charge under Tiberius.

JONATHAN EDWARDS   *(1703–1758)*

"CHIEF OF TEN THOUSANDS"

I have sometimes had a sense of the excellent fullness of Christ, and His meetness and suitableness as a Saviour; whereby He has appeared to me, far above all, the chief of ten thousands. His blood and atonement have appeared sweet, and His righteousness sweet; which was always accompanied with ardency of spirit; and inward strugglings and breathings, and groanings that cannot be uttered, to be emptied of myself, and swallowed up in Christ.

Once as I rode out into the woods for my health, in 1737, having alighted from my horse in a retired place, as my manner commonly has been, to walk for divine contemplation and prayer, I had a view that for me was extraordinary of the glory of the Son of God, as Mediator between God and man, and His wonderful, great, full, pure and sweet grace and love, and meek and gentle condescension. This grace that appeared so calm and sweet, appeared also great above the heavens. The person of Christ appeared ineffably excellent with an excellency great enough to swallow up all thought and conception—which continued, as near as I can judge, about an hour; which kept me the greater part of the time in a flood of tears, and weeping aloud. I felt an ardency of soul to be, what I know not otherwise how to express, emptied and annihilated; to lie in the dust, and to be full of Christ alone; to love Him with a holy and pure love; to trust in Him; to live upon Him; to serve and follow Him;

and to be perfectly sanctified and made pure, with a divine and heavenly purity. I have, several other times, had views very much of the same nature, and which have had the same effects.

FREDERICK WILLIAM FABER   (*1814–1863*)

THE AGONY IN THE GARDEN

Long years have passed since that New Year's Day of the guiltless Babe of Bethlehem; and now another scene opens to our view. It is the Agony in the Garden. Jesus kneels there. He is now a grown-up man. Three and thirty years have passed over Him. They have been the longest, because the fullest years that earth has ever known. His weary ministry of three years has drawn to its close. He has been often weary. He was weary when He sat by Jacob's well and asked the Samaritan woman for an alms of the fresh cold water which He Himself had created. He has been weary on the mountain sides, when He prayed instead of sleeping, while the moon shone tremulously on the limestone rocks, as if it hardly dared to light up the furtive figure of its Creator keeping watch among the crags. But His love of souls has never yet been tired. His weariness has never yet reached the yearnings of His Sacred Heart. This Thursday night amidst the olives we find Him still unchanged. To-morrow men will crucify His blessed body and pour out His Blood like water. But to-morrow is not soon enough. To-night His adorable soul, that King among creatures, that royalest of all the works of God, will itself crucify His Body. He will suffer a martyrdom to-night even more mysterious than that Martyrdom on Calvary. . . . That soul . . . gathers round it all the sins of men, manifold, multitudinous, ponderous. Never on earth was there such mortal heaviness, such aching sadness, such a drying up of life's fountains, such a tormenting languor, such an exceeding sickening of soul. Then it lifts up its hands that mighty soul, as if with more than Samson's strength it were about to pull down

the big heavens upon itself; and it draws down upon itself the huge
storm of God's eternal Justice, and overwhelming wrath, and then
lies crushed beneath it, a plaintive Human Life almost extinguished,
and only not extinguished because it is a Divine Life as well.

CUNNINGHAM GEIKIE (*1824-1906*)

HIS WORDS LIKE LEAVEN

The freshness and interest of the name of Jesus, and its power as a
great factor in the spiritual history of the world, increase with each
generation. The influence of His life, His words, and His death, have,
from the first, been like leaven cast into the mass of humanity. He
made religion spiritual instead of ceremonial and external; universal,
instead of local. He gave us the magnificent dowry of a faith in One
Common Father of the whole human race, and, thus, of a world-
wide brotherhood of all mankind. He confirmed the doctrine of our
immortality, and scattered abroad the germs of a heavenly life by
His fundamental requirements of love to God and our neighbour.
All reforms of individual and public life lie veiled in these principles,
awaiting the advance of our moral sense, to apprehend and apply
them. They have already given freedom to the slave; raised woman;
purified morals; mitigated war; created liberty; and made humanity
a growing force, in things private, civil, and political. All that love to
our fellow-man can prompt finds itself only a copy of that Life which
was spent in continually doing good, and the noblest self-sacrifice
for others finds itself anticipated by Calvary.

To the individual Christian, Jesus is the Divine Saviour, to believe
in Whom is life everlasting: to know Whom is to have peace with
God. Love has no diviner emblem than the Good Shepherd: Beneficence no ideal so perfect, as that "it is more blessed to give than to
receive": Fidelity to duty no loftier standard than a life laid down

at its command; Self-sacrifice no dream so perfect as the record of His death on the Cross.

Alban Goodier, S.J.   (*1869–1939*)

IDEAL MAN OF SORROWS

If, then, we see in Jesus Christ the Model of Manhood, this, too, will be conspicuous in him, and that in its highest form; the Model of Man will in some way be the Model Man of Sorrows. And it is so. We speak not only of the Passion, though that alone, its cause; its cause, and its issue, voluntarily undergone, for no other reason but that other men might be the gainers, their burthen shouldered that they might be set free, would of itself suffice to win for him, *par excellence,* the title of the Ideal Man of Sorrows. But we speak also of his whole career, of all that life which, from the day when he came among men to the end, was one of self-annihilation and subjection, of injustice and mental agony, of contempt and failure and lonely struggle against ingratitude and hatred, of interior trial whose mere shadow, flitting from time to time across the surface, gives us no more than an idea of that which was endured within.

We speak, moreover, of one who alone of all men had no occasion to suffer; who, from the very nature of his being, knew what suffering and sorrow were more than any other man could know them; who from the very first foresaw all that was to come to him, and yet at every step deliberately chose it for himself; who at any given moment might have said, with more than justice on his side, that what he had thus far endured was enough and the rest would have been spared him; who, nevertheless, in ways we can see for ourselves and in ways we cannot hope to discover, took into his soul every barb of sorrow that was hurled at him, every grief that it falls to the lot of man to bear.

THOMAS HUGHES   (*1822–1896*)

"MOST TENDER AND SENSITIVE OF MEN"

It is this most tender and sensitive of the sons of men—with fibres answering to every touch and breath of human sympathy or human hate—who has borne with absolutely unshaken steadfastness the distrust and anger of kinsfolk, the ingratitude of converts, the blindness of disciples, the fitful and purblind worship, and hatred, and fear, of the nation of the Jews. So far, we can estimate to some extent the burden and the strain, and realize the strength and beauty of the spirit which could bear it all. Beyond and behind lie depths into which we can but glance. For in those last hours of his life on earth the question was to be decided whether we men have in deed and in truth a brotherhood, in a Son of Man, the head of Humanity, who has united mankind to their Father, and can enable them to know Him.

C. E. M. JOAD   (*1891–   *)

WHAT HIS DEATH HAS TAUGHT

We are told by Mr. Lewis that Christ's death upon the Cross was an event of unique importance in the history of man, because every man who ever lived after that event has a better chance in the next world, or perhaps, I should say, *of* the next world, than any man who had lived before it. Christ, we are told, was sent into the world by God to redeem mankind and in fulfilment of that design He died upon the Cross. This conception, the conception of the Atonement, has been developed and embroidered by Christian writers in such a great variety of surprising ways that it is difficult to understand all the meanings, historical, symbolical, supernatural and transcendental, which have been read into it. But that there is one meaning which may be legitimately ascribed to it nobody can, I think, deny, and that is that because of Christ's life and death upon the Cross existence upon this planet is a different thing for men and women from what it would have been if He had not died, and from what it was before He died. Let me try to analyze the content of this difference. It might be said, in the first place, that men have been given a truer view of man's nature and of his destiny; it has been intimated to them in plainer terms than ever before, that man's nature is that of an immortal soul made in God's image and that his destiny is to achieve eternal life.

Secondly, it might be insisted, they have been offered a better chance of realizing their nature and achieving their destiny than they had before. It is, of course, for them to determine whether they will take advantage of this chance. If, having been given the chance, they do not take advantage of it, they are to that extent more culpable.

George Johnson   (*1889–1944*)

"A TERRIBLE, AN AWESOME PERSON"

"Unto as many as received him, he gave the power to become the sons of God." Christ came to regenerate us, to make us over, to constitute us some beginning of a new creature. He did not come to leave us a memory, or to charm us with a bit of sentiment as fragile and as tenuous as the tinsel on a Christmas tree. He is not a carol to be sung by one lonesome for his childhood, not an escape from reality by means of a sprig of holly stuck in a neatly wrapped Christmas package. The Babe of Bethlehem is a terrible person, an awesome person, if we keep in mind what he means. He means death, death to selfishness, death to sin, death to meanness, death to always having your own way, death to pride and gluttony and covetousness, to anger and envy and lust and sloth. He means a cross to be taken up daily. He wants to live, to live in all men and women, to live in the poor and the rich, to live in the weak and the strong, to live, above all, in the hearts of little children, and he can live only if you and I are willing to die. To the degree that we cling to ourselves, to the degree that we go on living as though we were the arbiters of our own destiny, to the degree that we are perfectly satisfied with ourselves and see no reason for change, to the degree that we serve God with our lips and keep Him far, far from our hearts, to the degree that we are different from the children of the world only on Sunday, to that degree His swaddling clothes become as fetter to bind Him to the manger and prevent Him from going forth on His mission of salvation to the world of men.

Toyohiko Kagawa   (*1888–*   )

"THE MOST SUCCESSFUL MAN"

Translated by Helen F. Topping

The ministry of Jesus had one peculiar feature: He limited his religious mission to the sick, the weak, the poor, the wanderers and the sinners. That is, Jesus, penetrated into the essence of the universe from the pathological aspect. . . .

What definition did Jesus give to "success"? He said that true success is to complete one's life. It is to attain to eternal life; all else is failure.

Napoleon called Jesus of Nazareth a success. But truly Jesus Christ was a failure of failures. When He died He had nothing but a coat, a girdle and a seamless gown; and the Roman soldiers divided these and cast lots for the gown. His end was the Crucifixion. Today we glory in the Cross, but in those days it was the worst form of capital punishment.

Jesus Christ was crucified as a failure, and His disciples all ran away from Him. But, nevertheless, Jesus Christ did not call Himself defeated. Jesus was a success, though apparently a failure. There are many who think themselves successful and do not realize that actually they are failures.

Jesus Christ spent His life in destitution and had nothing to the last moment. But nevertheless the Crucified One was the most successful man that ever lived. True success is to succeed in, to inherit life. The truly successful man is the one who can enjoy the life of God.

Jesus Christ spent all He had for His movement. He said to a rich young man, "Go, sell all that thou hast, and come!" Jesus seems to have been a very successful carpenter. In the apocryphal gospels it is written that Jesus made the throne for Herod's palace. He might have become a *nouveau riche* if He had not given it up for a religious movement. But Jesus chose not this way to so-called success, but the road which led to poverty and the Cross. And there he gained true success.

CHARLES KINGSLEY   (*1819–1875*)

"THE WRATH OF THE LAMB"

All the little that is great or noble in man or woman is perfected in Christ: he only is perfectly great, perfectly noble, brave, meek. He who to save us sinful men, endured the cross, despising the shame, till he sat down at the right hand of the Majesty on high, perfectly brave he is, and perfectly gentle, and will be so forever; for even at his second coming when he shall appear the Conqueror of hell, with tens of thousands of angels, to take vengeance on those who know not God, and destroy the wicked with the breath of his mouth, even then, in his fiercest anger, the scripture tells us his anger shall be "the anger of the Lord." Almighty vengeance and just anger, and yet perfect gentleness and love all the while—Mystery of mysteries!— the wrath of the Lamb.

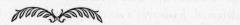

Jean Baptiste Henri-Dominique Lacordaire   (*1802–1861*)

"HE IS KING, HE IS GOD!"

Translator Anonymous

I find in Jesus Christ a threefold perpetuity: perpetuity in his
life, perpetuity in the exclusive irradiation of his life, perpetuity in
the superiority of his life. I also find in him a threefold progress:
progress in the territorial state, progress in the numerical state, progress
in the moral state. Jesus Christ has then overcome time; he has overcome the great enemy, and, beholding him upon the summit of ages
in all the serenity of his imperturbable youth, I remember what St.
Paul said of him in another sense: *Christ risen from the dead, dieth
no more.* Once he descended into the tomb; but the human race, for
which he died, bent towards him, and, raising him up with a love
which has never grown cold, bears him in its hands, risen again to
life. Behold him, gentlemen, examine him well, he lives! Look again,
he dieth no more, he is young, he is King, he is God.

Pope Leo XIII   (*1810–1903*)

HEAVEN'S WRATH APPEASED

Translator Anonymous

Never to have known Jesus Christ in any way is the greatest of misfortunes, but it involves no perversity or ingratitude. But, after having known to reject or forget Him, is such a horrible and mad crime
as to be scarcely creditable. For He is the origin and source of all
good, and just as mankind could not be freed from slavery but by
the sacrifice of Christ, so neither can it be preserved but by His
power. "Neither is there salvation in any other. For there is no other

name under heaven given to men, whereby we must be saved" (Acts
iv, 12). . . .

There would not be so many alienated by pride or buried in sloth if
they recollected what benefits they had received from God, what
Christ has rescued them from and to what He has brought them. Disinherited and exiled, the human race for ages was hurrying to destruction, enthralled by those dreadful evils which the sin of our
first parents had begotten and by other woes beyond the power of
man to remedy, when Christ our Lord came down from Heaven
and appeared as our Redeemer. In the first dawn of the world's history, God Himself had promised Him to us; as the victor and conqueror of "the serpent"; succeeding ages looked forward to His
advent with eager longing; holy prophets had long and plainly foretold that on Him all our hopes depended; nay, the various fortunes of
the Chosen People, their history, their institutions, their laws, their
sacrifices and ceremonies, had clearly and distinctly prefigured that
the salvation of humanity would be wrought and completed in Him,
who it was declared should be at once the High Priest and propitiatory
Victim, the Restorer of human liberty, the Prince of Peace, the
Teacher of all nations, founding a kingdom which should endure for
ever. By these titles, and under these images and prophetic utterances, various in kind, but agreeing in sense, He was designated as the
one who for the exceeding love wherewith He loved us should one
day give His life for our salvation. Accordingly, when the time of the
divine counsel was ripe, the Only-Begotten Son of God, being made
man, offered an abundant and complete satisfaction for men to His
offended Father, and by so great a price redeemed and made the
human race His own. "You were not redeemed with corruptible
things as gold and silver . . . but with the precious blood of Christ,
as of a lamb unspotted and undefiled" (I Peter, i, 18, 19).

Accordingly, all men without exception were already subject to
His power and sway, because He is the Creator and Preserver of all.
He made them His a second time by redeeming them in the truest and
most literal sense. "You are not your own, for you are bought with
a great price" (I Cor. vi, 19, 20). Hence all things are reestablished

in Christ by God. "The mystery of His will, according to His good pleasure, which He hath purposed in Him, in the dispensation of the fulness of time, to re-establish all things in Christ" (Eph. i, 9, 10). So that when Jesus had blotted out the handwriting which was contrary to us, and fastened it to the Cross, the wrath of Heaven was immediately appeased; the disordered and erring race of man had the bonds of their ancient slavery loosed, the will of God was reconciled to them, grace restored, the way to eternal happiness opened, and the title to possess and the means of attaining it both given back, Then, as though awakened from a long and deadly lethargy, man beheld the light of truth so long desired, but for generations sought in vain; he recognized, in particular, that he was born for much higher and more splendid things than the frail and fleeting objects of sense, to which he had formerly confined his thoughts to pursuits, and that this was in fine the constitution and supreme law of human life, and the end to which all must tend, that as we came from God so we should one day return to Him. From this beginning, and on this foundation consciousness of human dignity was restored and lived again; the sense of a common brotherhood took possession of men's hearts; their rights and duties in consequence were perfected or established anew and virtues beyond the imagination or conception of ancient philosophy were revived. So men's purposes, tenor of life, and characters were changed, and the knowledge of the Redeemer having spread far and wide, and His power having penetrated into the very life-blood of nations, expelling their ignorance and their ancient vices, a marvellous transformation took place, which, originating in Christian civilization, utterly changed the face of the nation.

C. K. MAHONEY   (*1884–1932*)

REDEMPTION HIS MISSION

Jesus was direct in his thinking. He had no time to be otherwise. He had a great message of vital truth to deliver. He could not stop to argue about it, and arguing about it would not have been wise. It was mainly truth to be tested by practice. He was dealing with life as he found it. He was offering men new and different ideals that would transform life. His business was the redemption of human beings that needed new spiritual life. He came that men might have life and have it more abundantly. He could not, therefore, express his purpose in a gospel of repression. He must preach doctrines of positive promise and furnish a program of positive actuality. There was a sense in which his whole program was a criticism of his age and of the past, but it was a criticism which offered a new view of life and furnished a new doctrine of existence. It did not so much contradict the religion of the past as transcend it.

JACQUES MARITAIN   (*1882–*)

LEVELING THE BARRIER OF ENMITY

Translated by Harry Lorin Binsse

The growing solicitude in Israel's heart for the Just Man crucified through the error of the high priests is a symptom of unquestionable importance. Today in America representative Jewish writers like Sholem Asch and Waldo Frank are trying to reintegrate the gospel into the brotherhood of Israel. While not yet recognising Jesus as the Messiah, they do recognise Him as the most pure Jewish figure in human history. They themselves would be disturbed to be considered as leaning toward Christianity. Yet while remaining closer than ever to Judaism, they believe that the gospel transcends the Old Testament and consider it a divine flower issuing from the stem of the Patriarchs and the Prophets. . . .

"Jesus Christ is in agony until the end of the world," said Pascal. Christ suffers in every innocent man who is persecuted. His agony is heard in the cries of so many human beings humiliated and tortured, in the sufferings of all those images and likenesses of God treated worse than beasts. He has taken all these things upon Himself, He has suffered every wound. "Fear not, my child, I have already travelled that road. On each step of the abominable way I have left for you a drop of my blood and the print of my mercy." . . .

Jesus Christ suffers in the passion of Israel. In striking Israel, the anti-Semites strike Him, insult Him and spit on Him. To persecute the house of Israel is to persecute Christ, not in His mystical body as when the Church is persecuted, but in His fleshly lineage and in His forgetful people whom He ceaselessly loves and calls. In the passion of Israel, Christ suffers and acts as the shepherd of Zion and the Messiah of Israel, in order gradually to conform His people to Him. If there are any in the world today—but where are they?—who give heed to the meaning of the great racist persecutions and who try to understand that meaning, they will see Israel as drawn along the road to Calvary, by reason of that very vocation as stimulus of history which I have described, and because the slave merchants will not pardon it for the demands it and its Christ have implanted at the heart of the world's temporal life, demands which will ever cry "no" to the tyranny of force. Despite itself Israel is climbing Calvary, side by side with Christians—whose vocation concerns the Kingdom of God more than the temporal history of the world; and these strange companions are at times surprised to find each other mounting the same path. . . .

The central fact, which has its deepest meaning for the philosophy of history and for human destiny—and which no one seems to take into account—is that *the passion of Israel today is taking on more and more distinctly the form of the Cross.*

Christ crucified extends His arms toward both Jews and Gentiles; He died, Saint Paul says, in order to reconcile the two peoples, and to break down the dividing barrier of enmity between them. "For He is our peace, He that hath made both one, and hath broken down the dividing barrier of enmity." . . .

If the Jewish people did not hear the call made to them by the dying Christ, yet do they remain ever summoned. If the Gentiles indeed heard the call, now racist paganism casts them away from it and from Him who is our peace. Anti-Semitic hatred is a directly anti-Christic frenzy to make vain the blood of Jesus and to make void His death. Reconciliation, breaking down the barrier of enmity —these, which the madness of men prevented love from accomplishing, and the frustration of which is the most refined torment in the sufferings of the Messiah—these, agony now is the way of achieving, a universal agony in the likeness of that of the Saviour, both the agony of the racked, abandoned Jews and of the racked, abandoned Christians who live by faith. More than ever, the mystical body of Christ needs the people of God. In the darkness of the present day, that moment seems invisibly to be in preparation, however remote it still may be, when their reintegration, as Saint Thomas puts it, will "call back to life the Gentiles, that is to say the lukewarm faithful, when 'on account of the progress of iniquity, the charity of a great number shall have waxed cold' (Matt. xxiv: 12)."

C. C. Martindale, S.J.   (1879–   )

EXAMPLES SET MANKIND

When Christ upon the Cross refused to drink the cup "mingled with Myrrh," He did so, not because it was bitter, but because it was drugged. You would have thought it impossible that anyone to-day should be ignorant that Christ during his life amongst us suffered much; yet I have known many who were perfectly unaware of what "Good Friday" commemorated; and during the war many soldiers did not know what crucifixes meant, and were astounded when they were told. They had not known that the "Christ" whose name appeared so lightly on their lips was one who had suffered at least as much as they were called upon to suffer, and had died as they, at any moment, might be called upon to die. I am told that by many a road overseas, and I know how (again and again) in hospitals, the sight of the dying Christ, or the story of His death, transformed for very simple men an experience that was about to break them.

It is no use to think about Christianity if we eliminate the memory that Christ suffered much. I remind you that theology teaches, and our intelligence anyhow makes clear, that God could have imparted His revelation and salvation to us men in a variety of ways. A resplendent apparition in the clouds, an all-quelling voice exhorting us to repentance, could have sufficed. Such never has been God's method, if I dare so to speak. Not for me here to ask why God should have created man at all; why He should have done so, knowing that man would sin; why, in all things, God should pursue the paths He does towards the rectification of the world's manifest wrong. Enough to-day to observe the ways that God in fact does take.

His Son came into our world, proposing in no manner to exempt Himself from the full experience of life. Born, like ourselves, from a human mother, he traversed the whole of our human existence till He died. Born, again, not in exceptional conditions—unless you say that the conditions of His birth were indeed exceptional in that they were of a poverty and anxiety indescribable—born, I mean, in no soft circumstances such as only the very rich or powerful can command, He lived the life of work which is the lot of most men; and you will recall that the "sensational" part of Christ's life (if I may so call it) was very short, and that the invisible, normal, laborious, wage-earning part of His life was nearly all of it. And when He left His workshop He became poorer still; for He set the example of permitting only spiritual gifts—voluntary alms He did not refuse, but when they did not come, He with His friends had so little to eat that (as custom explicitly allowed) they picked the ears of corn by the path's side, rubbed them between their hands, and ate the grain;

as for roof, He Himself said that the foxes had their holes, the birds their nests, but that He had not so much as where to lay His head.

*   *   *   *

Anything, then, that the Christian thinks of suffering has to be shot through with what he thinks of Christ; and what he thinks of Christ cannot possibly exclude the perception that in Christ's life was much pain, that He never shirked pain though He might have avoided it, that even by His words He allowed us to know that He suffered, and that His body is an evidence to us of what His soul was.

FRANÇOIS MAURIAC   (*1885–*)

HIS PREFERENCE FOR SIMPLE HEARTS

Translated by Julie Kernan

All Jesus' words, during the last weeks of his life, betrayed this preference for simple hearts, capable of excess. He who was so harsh with the doctors and the Pharisees, allowed himself to unbend with the humble. It was not by humility nor the spirit of sacrifice that he remained in their midst. He preferred them, or rather he hated the world and gave himself to those who were not of the world. Herod, whom he called "that fox", was the only being of whom he spoke with contempt. It was but a game for him to fight the wise men on their own ground; but he cared nothing about reducing the foolish dialecticians to silence! His real joy was to reveal himself to the poor men crushed under their habitual sins and to open under their feet an abyss of mercy and of pardon.

Thus he compared himself to the shepherd of the sheep who abandons ninety-nine to go after the hundredth which is lost; and who brings it back in his arms. In listening to this parable, everyone must have thought: "He is speaking of me."

JOHN HENRY (CARDINAL) NEWMAN   (1801–1890)

HIS NO TALE OF HUMAN WOE

Say not, my brethren, that these thoughts are too austere for this season, when we contemplate the self-sacrificing, self-consuming charity wherewith God our Saviour has visited us. It is for that reason that I dwell on them; the higher He is, and the more mysterious, so much the more glorious and the more subduing is the history of His humiliation. I own it, my brethren, I love to dwell on Him as the Only-begotten Word; nor is it any forgetfulness of His sacred humanity to contemplate His Eternal Person. It is the very idea, that He is God, which gives a meaning to His sufferings; what is to me a man, and nothing more, in agony, or scourged, or crucified? there are many holy martyrs, and their torments were terrible. But here I see One dropping blood, gashed by the thong, and stretched upon the Cross, and He is God. It is no tale of human woe which I am reading here; it is the record of the passion of the great Creator. The Word and Wisdom of the Father, who dwelt in His bosom in bliss ineffable from all eternity, whose very smile has shed radiance and grace over the whole Creation, whose traces I see in the starry heavens and on the green earth, this glorious living God, it is He who looks at me so piteously, so tenderly from the Cross. He seems to say, —I cannot move, though I am omnipotent, for sin has bound me here.

REINHOLD NIEBUHR   (*1892–*   )

"THE PERFECT MAN, THE SECOND ADAM"

In Christian thought Christ is both the perfect man, "the second
Adam" who had restored the perfection of what man was and ought
to be; and the Son of God, who transcends all possibilities of human
life. It is this idea which theology sought to rationalise in the doctrines of the two natures of Christ. It cannot be rationalised and yet
it is a true idea. . . . Christ, who expresses both the infinite possibilities of love in human life and the infinite possibilities beyond
human life, is . . . a true revelation of the total situation in which
human life stands. . . . Men . . . may seek to explain the dogma
of the Incarnation in terms which will make it an article in a philosophical creed. Such efforts will lead to varied deceptions; but the
deceptions cannot destroy the truth of the Incarnation.

Yet the revelation of God in the Incarnation is not of itself the
redemption. Christianity believes that Christ died to save men from
sin. It has a gospel which contains a crucifixion as well as an incarnation, a cross as well as a manger. This doctrine of the atoning
death of the Son of God upon the cross has led to many theological
errors, among them to theories of substitutionary atonement which
outrage the moral sense. There is in fact no theory of the atonement
which is quite as satisfying as the simple statements of the vicarious
death of Christ in the Gospels.

*   *   *   *

The atoning death of Christ is the revelation of ultimate reality
which may become the principle of interpretation for all human
experience. It is not a principle yielded by experience, but it is applicable to experience and validated by it. . . .

Most profoundly the atonement of Christ is a revelation of what
life actually is. It is tragic from the standpoint of human striving. Human striving can do no better than the Roman law and the Hebraic
religion, both the highest of their kind, through which the Lord was

crucified. Yet this crucifixion becomes the revelation of that in human history which transcends human striving. . . . The message of the Son of God who dies upon the cross, of a God who transcends history and is yet history, who condemns and judges sin and yet suffers with and for the sinner, this message is the truth about life. It cannot be stated without deceptions; but the truths which seek to avoid the deceptions are immeasurably less profound. Compared to this Christ who died for men's sins upon the cross, Jesus, the good man who tells all men to be good, is more solidly historical. But he is the bearer of no more than a pale truism.

MARTIN NIEMÖLLER   (*1892–*   )

WHENCE COMES HIS POWER?

Translated by Jane Lymburn

The Church *speaks* once again, and there is no doubt about the fact that by her words she bears witness to Jesus of Nazareth as her deliverer from the power of the devil; and "the people wonder" and once again the question arises: "Who *is* this man really? And where exactly does he get his power?" Or is that power which closed the Church's mouth not to be taken so seriously after all? Do we speak here of the devil and of Jesus of Nazareth as his conqueror only in order to give what we say greater weight and greater emphasis, whilst in reality the Church's silence could be put down to a very natural laziness and the fear of possible unpleasantness? . . .

The truth is, we need only to open our eyes to see, and we need only to open our ears to hear. The hostility around us is not aimed at the Church, its members and its shepherds at all, it is aimed at the Church's Lord. The hatred which is beating against us is not meant for us poor contemporaries; no, it is meant for the Lord Jesus Christ, whose name we bear. Here men are not striving with men

—though it is a matter of life and death, and that is serious enough!
—no, friends, the devil is here wrestling with the Redeemer for
damnation and salvation.

And that is why Jesus of Nazareth is the best-hated and most
slandered man in our generation; that is why everything He does
must become highly obnoxious and devilishly suspect; for the methods of the devil, who has ever been a murderer and a liar, have
always been the same, and will always be the same. He pretends to
be the angel of light, God's representative, and the Son of God must
be called a servant of the devil. And so to-day we are once more ex-
periencing what the disciples had to experience at that time; the
devil hides behind men; and as Jesus' miracle cannot possibly be
denied, the only thing is to throw doubts upon His divine mission.

Martin J. O'Malley   (*1889–*   )

A FORMULA OF SOCIAL PEACE

The Gospel of Jesus Christ is a message of love. The record of His
Church on earth is a chronicle of love. Love is God and love is the
great force that rules the universe. . . .

And "God so loved the world, as to give his only begotten Son."
In the fulness of time came the world's Redeemer. His commandment
was a "new commandment"—the commandment of love. "This,"
said He, "is the greatest and the first commandment." "Thou shalt
love the Lord thy God with thy whole heart, and with thy whole
soul, and with thy whole mind . . . And the second is like to this:
Thou shalt love thy neighbour as thyself." The promised "Peace to
men of good will," was to be realized in the fellowship of charity.
The Father's kingdom would come on earth as it is in heaven by love
of neighbor through the love of God. And in this divine teaching is
found the formula of social peace.

The Incarnate Savior came not upon this earth as a social reformer.

He came to redeem the world from sin. He came bringing light and life, regeneration and redemption by love. And the function of Christianity is not to reform or devise economic or social systems. Her function is to reform and transform men—to reform and transform the economists and sociologists themselves. . . .

Love, of course, supposes justice. *"Opus justitiae pax,"* says the Prophet Isaias. Peace is the work of justice. And what the Scripture affirms is the sense of mankind itself. Peace is inconceivable apart from justice. And in a world unsettled as ours is today, with injustices rife in the social, economic, and political spheres, the necessity of correcting injustices as necessary aid to peace is obvious to all. Render to each what is due, is the precept of justice; and this is patently linked with the tranquility of order. . . . "Charity cannot take the place of justice unfairly withheld."

Yet the love that Christ taught is more than justice; and it is necessary to the permanence of social peace. . . . Reject the Christian commandment of love and you have no other choice but selfishness and egoism and hatred. But egoism and hatred have never established anything on this earth. They are of their natures powers of destruction. . . . Love brings brotherhood, unity, and social harmony. For love is the unitive force of the universe. . . .

The makers of true social peace in the world are the saints of Christ. They heard the Master say: "As long as you did it to one of these the least my brethren, you did it to me"; and thus inspired, their lives are records of tremendous human activity.

KIRBY PAGE (*1890–*)

THE POWER OF HIS PRESENCE

The chief impression we get from the records of Jesus' life is that he was so high above his contemporaries in the quality of his character and conduct as to be in a class by himself. So profoundly impressed were the early disciples that in spite of the fact they were rigid monotheists, they regarded Jesus as having a unique relationship with God. Even on a basis of the lowest possible estimate, he was an extraordinary individual with amazing vitality. Now if life is continuous and death only opens up illimitable opportunities for more complete living, and if mind can communicate with mind, why should it be regarded as impossible for Jesus to be in constant communication with those who are in tune with his spirit. The record of history bears important testimony concerning this point. Multitudes of Christians in every age and in all lands, including many of the keenest minds and most consecrated spirits, have been dominated by the certain conviction that the living presence of Christ was the greatest power in their lives.

This is the way Jesus saves us; by revealing the nature of God and by creating within us the desire for fellowship with Him; by exhibiting life as it ought to be and may be and thus inspiring us to nobler conduct; by showing the hideous results of estrangement by enmity and by producing penitence and aspiration; by creating a consciousness of God's forgiveness and loving concern; and by prompting us day by day to higher thinking and more courageous living.

POPE PIUS XI   (*1857–1939*)

PROMISE OF THE REDEEMER

Translator Anonymous

The promise of a Redeemer brightens the first page of the history of mankind, and the confident hope aroused by this promise softened the keen regret for a paradise which had been lost. It was this hope that accompanied the human race on its weary journey, until in the fullness of time the expected Saviour came to begin a new universal civilization, the Christian civilization, far superior even to that which up to this time had been laboriously achieved by certain more privileged nations.

POPE PIUS XII   (*1876–*   )

A MEDIATOR OF SALVATION

Translator Anonymous

It is the same Apostle who portrays for us mankind in the unity of its relations with the Son of God, image of the invisible God, in whom all things have been created: "In Him were all things created" (Colossians 1, 16); in the unity of its ransom, effected for all by Christ, Who, through His Holy and most bitter Passion, restored the original friendship with God which had been broken, making Himself the Mediator between God and men: "For there is one God, and one Mediator of God and men, the man Christ Jesus" (Timothy 2, 5).

And to render such friendship between God and mankind more intimate, this same Divine and universal Mediator of salvation and of peace, in the sacred silence of the Supper Room, before He consummated the Supreme Sacrifice, let fall from His divine Lips the words which reverberate mightily down the centuries, inspiring heroic charity in a world devoid of love and torn by hate: "This is my commandment that you love one another, as I have loved you" (St. John 15, 12).

MONSIGNOR FULTON J. SHEEN   (*1895–*   )

A SAVIOUR OF MEN, NOT HIMSELF

Of course, He could not save Himself. No man can save himself who saves another. The rain cannot save itself, if it is to bud the greenery;

the sun cannot save itself if it is to light the world; the seed cannot
save itself if it is to make the harvest; a mother cannot save herself
if she is to save her child; a soldier cannot save himself if he is to save
his country. It was not weakness which made Christ hang on the
Cross; it was obedience to the law of sacrifice, of love. For how could
He save us if He ever saved Himself? Peace he craved; but as St.
Paul says, there is no peace but through the blood of the Cross. Peace
we want; but there is none apart from sacrifice. Peace is not a passive,
but an active virtue. Our Lord never said: "Blessed are the peaceful," but "Blessed are the Peacemakers."

UPTON SINCLAIR   (*1878–*   )

THE GREATEST ART THEME OF THE AGES

Some of these days—the last thing that I can see on the horizon of
my future—I am going to write a tragedy called Jesus. The time is
past, it seems to me, when an artist must leave alone the greatest art
theme of the ages.

Is it not the greatest? Is there any story in history more sublime
than the story of this man? A humble, ignorant peasant he was, and
out of the faith of his soul he made the future of the world for centuries. It is a thing that makes your brain reel.

I write it casually, but I have shuddered over it far into the deep,
deep night. I have dreamed of two acts—one of them Gethsemane,
and the other Calvary.—Poor fool, perhaps I shall never write them!

I have burrowed into that soul, seeking out the truth of it; the
truth, as distinguished from the ten thousand fancies of men. When I
write that drama I shall deal with those truths.

The climax of the scene in the garden of Gethsemane will be a
vision in which looms up before him the whole history of Chris-

tianity; that will be the last agony. It will be then that he sweats blood.

That will be something, I think.

PIERRE VAN PAASSEN   (*1895-*)

WHEN THE CROSS RETURNS

There is a storm coming up. I can hear its distant roar gathering strength as a wail that travels over wide fields. The waves roll on, uniform, equal in height and shape. With the waves pass the armies of slaves. There is struggle but no hope of victory. Chained together, they march to the end of the earth. . . .

Now I feel the air growing colder. A Cross comes into sight. I hear the groans of the Man on the Cross. I see the blood on His face. He turns His head from side to side in nameless pain. His lips move. Hear! He speaks: *"Eli, Eli, lama sabachtani!"* A dark mist descends. The song of the birds is silenced, and the forests cease their rustling. The moon's rays are frozen, and the earth stands still. There is nothing but the wood and the Man who suffers on the Cross in eternal torment. The river moves on, but the Cross remains, now as a vague vision that recedes in the night, then moving forward in stark reality.

When the strong torture the weak, when the poor cry for bread, when the innocent languish in dungeons, when mothers go insane because they see their children die, when the outcasts roam in the wilderness, when the soldiers go to battle, when those who sit in darkness pray for light, the Cross returns, and the head of the Man on the Cross sinks deeper on the tired breast.

JOHN J. WALDE　　　　　　　　　　　　　　　　　(*1900*–　　)

NO WELCOME THEN OR NOW

With hearts filled with sadness we recall the day when Christ made
His entrance into the world. Instead of a welcome for Christ—for
which the prophets had prepared the people, telling them when they
might expect Him, informing them from what family He would
come, in which town He would be born—the inhabitants of Bethlehem greeted Him with closed doors and with even more tightly
closed hearts. What a tragedy that the Son of God should have come
"unto his own, and his own received him not" (*John* 1: 11). Because
of love for comfort, many homes in that little town lost immortality
that night. They lost the chance of being the home in which Christ
was born. The tragedy is not so much that Christ was not accorded
the privilege of an open door, not so much that He had to be born
in a stable—the tragedy is that selfishness blinded human hearts to
the extent that they locked out God from their homes and hearts. . . .

Over and over history repeats the story of the inhabitants of Bethlehem. But with this great difference: Those of our day deserve the
greater blame. On the cross Christ prayed: "Father, forgive them,
for they do not know what they are doing" (*Luke* 23: 34). The citizens of Bethlehem and those who nailed Christ to the Cross had
only the promise of the Prophets while today we have had the miracle
of Christianity for nineteen hundred years.

PETER WUST　　　　　　　　　　　　　　　　　(*1884*–　　)

"LOVE THAT IS NOT LOVED"

I have often sat meditating before an Italian bookmarker, which I discovered between the leaves of a Dante. On this bookmarker there
is a very original little picture. In the midst of a flowery spring land-

scape stands a tall cross. Christ hangs upon it, His downward glance movingly expressive of the anguish He suffers. At the foot of the cross sits a man wearing a cowl, his face supported in his hands, and softly sobbing to himself. He is Francis. Everywhere around him and around the cross there is loneliness—dreadful, terrible loneliness—for all men have fled, and he alone has remained. Beneath the picture are the words, *L'amore che non é amato,* "Love that is not loved." Further comment is unnecessary. *L'amore che non é amato.*

LEADER

A TRIUMPHING KING

We are marching to victory, and we are followers of a triumphing King. The joy of his life should be in our hearts and the light of his life on our faces. Because we are Christ's, we must deny ourselves all pleasures and joys? No! Because we are Christ's, all things are ours . . . for if we are Christ's, death is our servant, not our master.

Christ's secret of happiness is character. Each quality or attribute of character has its own peculiar blessedness.

* * * *

Jesus pities not all those who laugh, but those who do nothing else but laugh. He who compared himself to one playing in the market-place that the children might dance to his music, does not denounce merriment. "A merry heart doeth good like medicine." But he looks with pity upon those to whom life is only a stage on which nothing but comedy is enacted. Those who make a jest of everything and who shut their eyes to everything of which they cannot make a jest; those who have no tears for sorrowing, no heartaches for the afflicted; those who take nothing seriously, not even themselves; those who play the part of a king's jester in life's court, satisfied to be amusing and to be amused, Christ pities. . . .

Jesus pities the popular man, the man of whom all men speak well.

JAMES TRUSLOW ADAMS   (*1878-*   )

AN APPEALING ETHICAL DOCTRINE

Confucius, Buddha, Plato, and Christ would have understood one another perfectly in their ideals. Christ, of course, should not be confused with the Christians any more than Plato with the Platonists. It must be remembered that an ethical system is different from the religious system to which it may or may not be bound. In an age of faith the latter may give powerful support to the former as a sanction, but the two are different. These ethical systems—the outgrowth of racial wisdom—are closely fitted to the needs of the races among which they arise.

The needs of the Western European civilization, springing largely from Greece, have been fed by Greek philosophy, the teachings of Christ, and the Roman Stoics. Taken together, these form a great body of ethical doctrine, of which, for the great mass of people, the most appealing is that derived from Christ. *Some* body of such doctrine is essential if we are not to drift into moral anarchy. To say that a great mass of hundreds of millions can dispense with the old ethics and rule themselves according to science is, if I may say so, the sheerest drivel. Whatever may be said of some sciences, those of man and society still have to have their diapers changed every hour or so. To expect the mass of our populations to guide their lives according to the latest pronouncements of a Freud or any single "modern" is to have lost all contact with reason.

PETER AINSLIE   (*1867–1934*)

HIS MISSION TO REVIVE SOUL OF LOVE

Jesus came to blaze the way to the holiness of His inner sanctuary. There must be harmony or the music cannot be at its best. The discords of Christendom have drowned the finest strains of music in the human soul and the Disciples have attempted to clear the dust from the pages of the Scriptures that the chords of the human heart may again vibrate in perfect harmony with the heart of Christ, who is the only solution to discord.

SAMUEL ANGUS (*1881–*)

HIS ETHICS DEFY CHALLENGE

Ideas must be incorporated in a person before they can effectively move mankind. Christianity could boast of a founder of unique holiness and power. Its sturdy competitors, the Mystery-Religions, could offer only myths which called for constant purification and allegorization to meet the moral needs of the day. The ethics of Jesus defied challenge; His character required no burnishing. He was and remained Leader and Captain to His followers: no modernization nor allegorization was necessary to remove offense to the moral consciousness.

ANONYMOUS *

ONE SOLITARY LIFE

Here is a man who was born in an obscure village, the child of a peasant woman. He grew up in another obscure village. He worked in a carpenter shop until he was thirty, and then for three years he was an itinerant preacher. He never went to college. He never put his foot inside a big city. He never traveled two hundred miles from the place he was born. He never did one of the things that usually accompany greatness. He had no credentials but himself. He had nothing to do with this world except the naked power of his divine manhood.

While still a young man, the tide of public opinion turned against him. His friends ran away. One of them denied him. He was turned over to his enemies. He went through the mockery of a trial. He was nailed upon a cross between two thieves. His executioners gambled for the only piece of property He had on earth while He was dying,

* Sometimes attributed to Phillips Brooks.

and that was His coat. When He was dead He was taken down and laid in a borrowed grave through the pity of a friend.

Nineteen wide centuries have come and gone, and today He is the centerpiece of the human race and leader of the column of progress.

I am far within the mark when I say that all the armies that ever marched, and all the navies that ever were built, and all the parliaments that ever sat, and all the kings that ever reigned, put together, have not affected the life of man upon this earth as powerfully as that One Solitary Life!

Bruce Barton   (*1886–*   )

HIS QUALITIES AS A LEADER

First of all he had the voice and manner of the leader—the personal magnetism which begets loyalty and commands respect. The beginnings of it were present in him even as a boy. John felt them. On the day when John looked up from the river where he was baptizing converts and saw Jesus standing on the bank, he drew back in protest. "I have need to be baptized of thee," he exclaimed, "and comest thou to me?" The lesser man recognized the greater instinctively. We speak of personal magnetism as though there were something mysterious about it—a magic quality bestowed on one in a thousand and denied to all the rest. This is not true. The essential element in personal magnetism is a consuming sincerity—an overwhelming faith in the importance of the work one has to do. . . .

He invited frail bewildered humanity to stand upright and look at God face to face! He called upon men to throw away fear, disregard the limitations of their mortality, and claim the Lord of Creation as Father. It is the basis of all revolt, all democracy. For if God is the Father of all men, then *all* are his children and hence the commonest is equally as precious as the king. No wonder the authorities trembled. They were not fools; they recognized the implications of the teaching. Either Jesus' life or their power must go. . . .

It is said that great leaders are born, not made. The saying is true to this degree, that no man can persuade people to do what he wants them to do, unless he genuinely likes people, and believes that what he wants them to do is to their own advantage. The secret of Jesus' success was an affection for folks which so shone in his eyes and rang in his tones, that even the commonest man in a crowd felt instinctively that here was a friend. . . .

Jesus was notably tolerant of almost all kinds of sinners. He liked the companionship of the rough and ready folk who were entirely outside the churches; he was tender toward unfortunate women; he had a special fondness for James and John whose ungovernable tempers had given them the title of "Sons of Thunder"; he forgave the weakness of Peter who denied him; and was not resentful of the unbelief of his near relatives and his native town. But for one sin he had no mercy. He denounced the *insincerity* of the Pharisees in phrases which sting like the lash of a whip. They thought they had a first mortgage on the Kingdom of Heaven, and he told them scornfully that only those who become like little children have any chance of entering in.

Ernest Sutherland Bates   (*1879–1939*)

JUDAS' TESTIMONY OF JESUS

He was a buckler of strength unto the weak, and unto the poor he was a tower of joy.

They were like oxen beneath the yoke, they lay like worms upon the ground; he made them to run like young colts in the pasture, he sent their spirits on errands through the sky.

He lifted them up with the right hand of fellowship; with the right hand of fellowship he rescued their souls.

His touch upon the sick was soft as the summer waves of Galilee; calm as the waters of Magdala were the words of comfort that he spoke; and deep as the depths of Capernaum was the depth of his love for man.

The snows of Lebanon were not whiter than his soul; and as the dew of Hermon was the coolness of his hands.

He took men into his heart as into a cup; he wiped away their tears with a word.

Such was Jesus in the days when first I knew him, surpassing the nightingale in sweetness, surpassing the lion in strength.

Other men might speak the same words, but they were no longer the same. Because Jesus was Jesus and no other, but to look upon him made men strong in themselves.

I, Judas, that later betrayed him, bear this witness of him.

JOHN SUTHERLAND BONNELL   (*1893–*   )

"STANDS ABOVE THEM ALL"

The advent of Jesus marked a turning point in human history. Our calendars reckon time from that event. This is all the more remarkable in view of His lowly birth and the limitations which circumstances imposed on Him. He belonged to a race which, in his lifetime, was noted for its narrow-mindedness, intolerance, and fanaticism. He had little opportunity for education and culture. So far as we know He never once set foot outside of Palestine. His life was spent within a geographical area equal to the State of Connecticut.

* * * *

But the impact of Jesus upon history is altogether out of proportion to the brevity of the records and unexplainable by the circumstances in which He lived and died. . . .

We must go beyond the records of His life for an explanation of the profound influence of Jesus upon the world. In the few years allotted to Him, He gathered around Him a little group of men and endeavored to impress on their minds His principles, and to inspire them with His own wondrous spirit. He planted a few seeds, he kindled a few fires, and then looked to those men to carry on after He had gone. But far more powerfully than the records of His life, the spirit of Jesus has reached across the centuries, transforming men and women. He cannot be identified with any particular race or age or civilization—He stands above them all, appraising them, judging them, ennobling and inspiring them.

WALTER RUSSELL BOWIE   (*1882-*   )

A LIGHT SET UPON A HILL

Jesus trusted to the power of the spirit which he himself knew and which others were to learn from him. He moved through Galilee with no outward authority. He knew that the ruling classes were hostile to him. He seemed to have nothing on his side,—except the invisible influence of a colossal faith. But that was enough. He went serene and confident through the midst of opposition. He stood untroubled when others were afraid. He and those who learned his secret, should be the makers and the masters of the future. "Ye are the salt of the earth," he said. "Ye are the light of the world. A city set on a hill cannot be hid."

The astonishing thing is that nineteen centuries have not been able to obliterate that light he set upon a hill. This man out of Nazareth, with a calmness which still seems incredible, said that the fundamental assumptions which the whole human race had lived by were leading life down a wrong road—a road which could lead only to disaster and to doom. His own contemporaries were blind to this conception which he set before them. They were in the grip of a growing passion of hatred against the rule of Rome—a hatred which they thought to satisfy presently in some great day of vengeance, but which in fact was hurrying them blindly on to the horror that was presently to come in the siege of Jerusalem and its destruction. They thought that they could conquer evil by the sword, and prevail over old violences by setting up a new one. But Jesus saw that this returning path of blood which the world had been following so long could never lead to any end. He would show another road—he in his own spirit would be that road. Men could only triumph over their enemies as they included their enemies also in a new vision of redemption for all the earth.

MARION JOHN BRADSHAW   *(1886–   )*

HIS MEANING INEXHAUSTIBLE

The ablest minds of a past century remind us that the continued influence of Jesus in the world does not depend upon the acceptance of some one opinion about him. While there is an understandable sense in which he is the same yesterday, today, and forever, it is historically true that altered concepts of Jesus Christ follow from changes in social structure, in intellectual fashion, and in economic organization. There is no Christology adequate to portray him. There is no age which exhausts his meaning. There is no class which controls his influence. There is no institution which monopolizes his Power. There is no portrait of the Lord Jesus which is final. He can be Lord and Saviour for men of divergent philosophies. Representatives of philosophy's major viewpoints may still join in thinking that each new insight gained by men will reveal in him a more uplifting tragedy and a sublimer love. That is some foundation for a Christian's faith that a portrait of Jesus will adorn future humanity's inmost shrine.

ARTHUR BRISBANE   (*1864-1936*)

OF SUCH IS THE KINGDOM

Jesus gave to the child its place in society.

With all the power of divine authority He built around the feeblest among us a wall that has protected them through the ages.

Before His day the child existed only by sufferance. It had no rights.

It was but a counter, an infinitesimal atom. It was considered simply the property of the parent. Its father had power of life and death over it. The homeless dog that roams the streets to-day is more effectively shielded from cruelty than was the friendless child before Jesus came to live and die for the weak and poor. The law had said:

"The parent is ruler of the child, and may dispose of it as he sees fit."

But Jesus said—and these are the most beautiful and affecting words in all the moral law of the world:

"Take heed that ye despise not one of these little ones; for I say unto you, that in heaven their angels do always behold the face of my Father which is in heaven." (Matthew xviii, 10)

*   *   *   *

It is impossible now to conceive the horrid indifference to childhood's rights which preceded the birth of Christianity.

Infanticide was not the exception, but a settled custom. So much so, that in Rome the "exposure" of children in desert places was almost a virtue, since it gave the child some slight chance of surviving.

Not a few, but thousands and tens of thousands of children were thus "exposed." They fell a prey to wild beasts, or to the human beasts, still more ferocious, who took the children to make slaves or criminals of them.

Jesus came and a miracle was worked—a miracle that no man will deny.

Jesus spoke, and thousands of millions of men, through nineteen centuries, have believed, and obeyed the command.

*   *   *   *

It was this childless, homeless Man that ever used His marvelous power to protect children.

It was He who gave to children their definite share in the Kingdom of God.

*   *   *   *

Wherever Jesus went children followed Him and the tiniest little soul, in its mother's arms or tottering along in wide-eyed curiosity, could arrest His loving attention.

THOMAS A. CARNEY

HIS INCONTESTABLE CREDENTIALS

The Christian era dawned. Then came the *Splendor Patris,* that Exceeding Brilliancy from the Father of Lights, Jesus Christ, sent by the Father to reilluminate and illuminate completely the paths of men with truth, and to show them the way to happiness both on earth and in Heaven.

This Leader presented to the world the incontestable credentials of His miracles as a testimony of His divine claims and mission. But the pagans, steeped in sensuality, were slow to recognize Him, and the Chosen People, stiff-necked and proud, would not receive Him and in jealous frenzy took Him to Calvary and nailed Him to a cross. Only a handful recognized and followed the Light!

And, through the centuries, though countless millions in increasing numbers have recognized and followed the leadership of Jesus Christ and have found the promised happiness, a sensual world has been blind to this Light, notwithstanding its exceeding brilliancy, and stiff-necked and proud worldlings have striven to keep Christ, their Saviour, nailed helplessly to the cross!

Oh, indeed, we need to turn to the *Splendor Patris,* the Light that Illumines the world! We need the light of truth that shines forth resplendent in the teachings and example of Jesus Christ! We need the spiritual leadership of Christ the King!

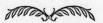

DOROTHY DAY   (*1899–*   )

GOD OR AN IMPOSTOR

Many Christians have lost sight, to a great extent, of the communal aspect of Christianity, so the collective ideal is the result. They have failed to learn a philosophy of labor, have failed to see Christ in the worker. So in Russia, the worker, instead of Christ, has been exalted. They have the dictatorship of the proletariat maintained by one man, also a dictator. The proletariat as a class has come to be considered the Messiah, the deliverer.

A mystic may be called a man in love with God. Not one who loves God, but who is *in love with God.* And this mystical love, which is an exalted emotion, leads one to love the things of Christ. His footsteps are sacred. The steps of His passion and death are retraced down through the ages. . . .

When we suffer, we are told to suffer with Christ. We are "completing the sufferings of Christ." We suffer His loneliness and fear in the garden when His friends slept. We are bowed down with Him under the weight of not only our own sins but the sins of each other, of the whole world. We are those who are sinned against and those who are sinning. We are identified with Him, one with Him. . . .

Christ is God or He is the world's greatest liar and impostor. How can you Communists who claim to revere Him as a working class leader fail to see this? And if Christ established His Church on earth with Peter as its rock, that faulty one who denied Him three times, who fled from Him when He was in trouble, then I, too, wanted a share in that tender compassionate love that is so great. Christ can forgive all sins and yearn over us no matter how far we fall.

THOMAS DE QUINCEY   *(1785–1859)*

HIS LEADERSHIP MANIFESTED

The supreme qualifications for leadership manifested and emblazoned in the person of Jesus Christ were evident to all parties in the Jewish community, and not merely to the religious body of his own immediate followers. These qualifications were published and expounded to the world in the facility with which everywhere he drew crowds about himself, in the extraordinary depth of impression which attended his teaching, and in the fear as well as hatred which possessed the Jewish rulers against him. Indeed, so great was this fear, so great was this hatred, that, had it not been for the predominance of the Roman element in the government of Judea, it is pretty certain that Christ would have been crushed in an earlier stage of his career. . . .

Once announcing himself, and attesting by daily cures his own mission as a *hakim,* Christ could not be rejected as a public oracle of truth and heavenly counsel to human weakness. This explains what else would have been very obscure, the undue emphasis which Christ allowed man to place upon his *sanitary* miracles. His very name in Greek presented him to men under the idea of the *healer,* but then, to all who comprehended his secret and ultimate functions, as a healer of unutterable and spiritual wounds.

Lloyd C. Douglas   (*1877-*)

"A STRANGE CATALYZING ENERGY"

An hour came in the Master's career when even his sworn friends
considered the new cultis a lost cause. Surely, if anything was ever
to be judged by purely circumstantial evidence, the mission of Jesus
came to an inglorious end. But when he went to the cross—by all
human reckoning defeated—it was with martial step; for however
appearances that day were unfavorable to his cause, he knew that
he had planted something in the soil of society that nobody would
ever be able to dig up! Like leaven in a meal, a strange catalyzing
energy had been introduced into the spiritual chemistry of civilization. It was his soul, his mind, his life! He was confident, even as
death filmed his eyes, that this indestructible element was already at
its task of transformation. That catalysis had already set in! Nothing
could ever stop it!

It mattered very little to him that he had been whipped and slapped
through the streets of Jerusalem; that he had been manacled and
reviled; for every added indignity that day only brought forth increasing evidence that he had succeeded in presenting a highly potential energy to the world. . . .

When the crowds along the Via Dolorosa shed bitter tears as he
passed, staggering under his shameful load, he said: "You need not
weep for me!" Nor was his refusal to be pitied accounted for as a sudden flare of martyr's valor. He meant it, in very truth. He knew that
he had finished his work. To all seeming, the total results of his
message could be called nothing less or else than complete failure;
but Jesus knew that he had laid hold upon life at its most sensitive
neural plexus; that he had gripped humanity's trunk nerve! . . .

Religion and government had put him to death as a disturber of
the peace. No man then living survived long enough to realize just
how great a disturber of the peace he was; but he knew. He knew
the world would never be the same after that day. He knew that he

had set in motion certain forces so dynamic that any man who tried to thwart them would do so at his peril. . . .

Whoever finds these statements a mere rhetorical exuberance, can give himself an interesting hour of making an attempt to delete Jesus from our present life. If it is suspected that the poets and prophets have sentimentally overrated the Master's importance to civilization, let the critic put this overestimated teacher where he belongs by dropping his name and all allusions to his career from our own speech. Let him resolve that he will consistently refuse to enter any building in which there is an ascription of honor to this teacher; that he will not again look upon any statue or painting which has to do with this man or his message; that he will avoid hearing any music which involves this theme; that he will not read any more history in which the cause of Christianity is at issue. Let him proceed further and discontinue the use of any benefits, inventions, or energies produced as a direct result of education fostered by Christianity.

He will discover that long before he has finished deleting Jesus from his life he has jeopardized everything he holds in esteem. Pontius Pilate in an uncomfortable moment of perplexity, enquired of the crowd that sought Jesus's life: "What, then, will ye do with Jesus?" This query seems to echo through the centuries. Of course, any individual who stolidly refuses to recognize the question can continue to live his whole life without giving it his attention; but only as a pensioner upon the people who do recognize it as worthy of a reply.

PAUL GALLICO   (*1897–*   )

CHRISTMAS EVE FOR PRIVATE BILL

"Gee, it's Christmas Eve back home. I wonder if it snowed. They'll be having a tree, Mom and Pop and Sis and young Jimmy. Maybe after supper Mary'll come over for a while and help Mom wrap presents. I guess they're thinking of me as I am of them. . . .

"Wouldn't they be surprised if they knew where I am tonight—right where it all started. Funny, when you're back home you don't think about it so much—Christmas Eve, the night Christ was born. It happened right here, maybe not far from where I'm standing. I'd like to be back home with them, but maybe I'm lucky to be here where everything began. It makes you think—all kinds of things you never thought before. . . .

"This is the night when Christ was born . . . He lived right here. Men saw Him and heard Him talk. Maybe He once stood where I stand. . . .

"I used to think they made up those pictures of Bethlehem I used to see around Christmas, but they looked just like it looks here now, just the same as it was a couple of thousand years ago when Christ first saw it, the same hills and sheep and trees, the same kind of old plow. Christ could have walked under the same moon. . . .

"He was a good guy. He wanted everybody to be on the square and give his neighbor a decent break. I guess maybe that's really what we're fighting for, why I'm here. This is where it started. Maybe He walked right in these hills one night, thinking those kind of thoughts. What a long way it is from Centreville to here, and yet back home we've never forgotten those thoughts He had and the words He spoke. That's what they taught us to live by, and I guess if you learn to live by something you'll fight and, if you have to, die for it too. . . .

"He had enemies in those days too, all the guys who weren't on the level, but full of pride and power. Funny, how it's the same guys who are His enemies today. You got to be on one side or the other. The guys we're fighting are against everything He stood for. All He wanted of folks was to be decent and act decent towards one another; for the strong to look after the weak, not to rob, or cheat, or get puffed up with money or power. . . .

"The guys we're fighting say He was all wrong, that the strong were meant to steal from the weak and persecute and torture them, and that's what they're going to do. I guess that just about puts us in His Army, and on His side. . . .

*   *   *   *

"I wish I was home tonight, with Mom and Pop and Sis and Jimmy and Mary, but maybe I'm glad I can be here, too. There'll be a lot of my kind of Christmases again, after we've won. And when I'm there with . . . Mary, and maybe my own kids, I guess maybe I'll understand a whole lot more, what it means, because of my being here tonight. I don't guess I'll ever forget being here on Christmas Eve looking at it just the way it was when Christ lived here, and came and walked at night and thought His thoughts about us, and living together with other men, and how we ought to be . . . square and decent towards one another . . ."

WILLIAM EWART GLADSTONE   (*1809–1898*)

HE CAME NOT AS A CONQUEROR

No more in the inner than in the outer sphere did Christ come among us as a conqueror, making His appeal to force. We were neither to be consumed by the heat of the Divine presence, nor were we to be dazzled by its brightness. God was not in the storm, nor in the fire, nor in the flood, but He was in the still small voice. This vast treasure was not only to be conveyed to us, and to be set down as it were at our doors; it was to enter into us, to become a part of us, and that part which should rule the rest; it was to assimilate alike with the mind and heart of every class and description of men. While, as a moral system, it aimed at an entire dominion in the heart, this dominion was to be founded upon an essential conformity to the whole of our original and true essence. It therefore recognised the freedom of man, and respected his understanding, even while it absolutely re-

quired him both to learn and to unlearn so largely; the whole of
the new lessons were founded upon principles that were based in
the deepest and best regions of his nature, and that had the sanction
of his highest faculties in their moments of calm, and in circumstances
of impartiality. The work was one of restoration, of return, and of
enlargement, not of innovation. A space was to be bridged over, and
it was vast: but where all the piers, and every foundation-stone of
the connecting structure, were to be laid in the reason and common
sense, in the history and experience, of man.

T. R. GLOVER   (*1869*–   )

THE LIBERATOR OF MEN'S MINDS

If Jesus was another Apocalyptic dreamer, what had he to offer a
wide-awake, anxious and disillusioned world that the other Apocalyptic dreamers did not offer it? For it is plain that the world was
not interested in Apocalypses at all; there were too many of them
altogether, and the world of Horace and Tacitus, of Dio Chrysostom
and Dio Cassius, had great traditions of intellectual daylight, which,
it is plain, the early Christians did not ask them to forsake. If Christ
had an essentially Apocalyptic mind, it is plain that his early followers did not share it. . . . There is no despair in Christ's mind,
and no sense of hurry, no nervous jogging of the Father's elbow. . . .
Long before the whole world was won, the Last Things and the
Second Advent had a secondary place; they had become pictures of
a final victory; they were not munitions of war. It was other things
that conquered the world for the Galilean.

. . . Jesus came to the world as a liberating force, at once in virtue of the factors he was to teach men to recognize and of the personality that he was. . . .

Even in the early Roman Empire Jesus Christ proved to be the liberator of men's minds. He was not like Muhammad a legislator, and therein lay much of his power to liberate.

MAURICE GOGUEL   (*1880–*   )

GOSPEL AND CHURCH LINKED

Translated by Frederick Stephens

If in the course of events Christianity absorbed elements foreign to the thought of Jesus and to Judaism, it was, nevertheless, born out of the preaching of Jesus and the impression He had made upon the few men who had grouped themselves around Him.

Christianity is not the religion of Jesus; it is that of the worshipers of Jesus. It was the personality of the Master which linked together the Gospel preached in Galilee and the religion of the primitive Church, and which explains the organic unity of the entire movement initiated by Jesus.

Not only did the thought of Jesus exercise on the Church (especially in the moral sphere) a decisive influence as the source of her inspiration, but still more was it the impression left by the personality of Jesus which gave the impulse through whose activity the whole system of Christian thought was developed. Between the preaching of the Kingdom of God by Jesus and the doctrine of salvation elaborated and developed in the Church there is more than a simple coincidence in time; there is an organic relationship. It is through the impression produced by Jesus that the Church professed her doctrine of redemption. If this doctrine has some kinship with the Mystery Religions, it is differentiated from them and cannot be reduced to them. While the worshipers of Mithra, Attis and Adonis knew perfectly well that the redemptive story of their heroes plunged into such fabulous antiquity that all reality was lost to it, the Christians were persuaded that it was not at the beginning but at the end of the age that their Christ had lived. His life, for them, could be fitted in a very intimate manner into the reality of history.

EDWARD EVERETT HALE (1822–1909)

A LEADER FROM GOD

It is a very curious observation that the Saviour himself was so indifferent as to men's questions or thoughts about him. He once asked his apostles what the multitude thought about him. On this occasion he does not even speak of himself. He asks a general question as to the Messiah whom all expected. Whose son shall the Messiah be? Must he be David's son? "Whose son is he,—the son of David or the son of God?" For the rest he said squarely, "It is my Father who does the works. It is the Holy Spirit who speaks the word. If any man blasphemes me, he may be forgiven." He even chides his disciples because they can do nothing without him. He sinks his own personality. As Paul says so well, "He makes himself of no reputation. He takes upon himself the form of a servant." You might say he is quite indifferent how men define his nature or his position if only they will follow him. . . .

What think ye of the Christ, then? The gospel answer to this question is, that the Christ is the Son of God.

Thou art the Christ, the Son of the living God, is indeed the motto for the cornerstone of the church, as he said it was.

And any effort to make it out that more was concealed behind this phrase than it expresses, is an effort which re-acts against him who makes it. . . .

There are thirty different texts in which the Saviour more or less distinctly defines Christian discipleship. Such is the statement to Nicodemus, the earliest of them: "Except a man be born again he cannot see the Kingdom of God." I need not read them. It will be a better exercise for you to copy them from your own Bibles yourselves. In those thirty texts he speaks three times of their believing on him. In all of them he speaks as to those who love him enough to believe him and to follow him. But in not one of them does he lay the least stress on any intellectual process. In not one of them does he open the question as to what they think of him, or what honor they shall pay him. He offered himself as our Master, and left us his unfinished work. He says to us, "If you obey me, you will follow me." He proved his affection in his death. And he says, "If you believe in me, you will love me." He means that we shall unite in such love, and he says: "If you love me, you will love each other." In all these statements he speaks as one who would bring in the Kingdom of the Living God. Of himself he says almost nothing. But when he does speak, it is to say that he represents that living God as his anointed and well-beloved Son. . . .

Whoever will take the Saviour of men, in his work of saving them from their sins, whoever will try the great experiment of prayer, and the other experiment of sacrifice, as this Leader of men bids him try one and the other, comes to the certainty that here is a Leader who knows what he is talking about, and who shows the way. Whoever follows, though with trembling foot and fickle faith, follows each day more hopefully and strongly, and knows that this is no finite guess that he is working on; he knows that he has God's law for the affairs of men; this time he is sure of his Leader. This Leader is from God, commissioned by him, inspired by him, and sustained by him. He who follows that Leader, comes to believe that Leader, and to live in his Life.

A. Eustace Haydon   (*1880*-   )

THE GOD OF CHRISTIANITY

When the early Christian missionaries began to preach the gospel of their Jewish Savior, the shores of the inland sea were the gathering place of a multitude of deities, embodying the cultural experiences of

Egypt, Babylonia, Syria, Palestine, Asia Minor, Persia, Greece and Rome. . . .

To this multitude of gods the early Christians added their Savior, the resurrected, heavenly Christ, associated with the jealous Yahweh of Israel. Neither they nor their gentile contemporaries realized that from their movement would emerge a new god to claim the lordship of the earth, before whose majesty all the elder, pagan deities would abandon their thrones . . .

Jesus had no thought of introducing a new god to the world. He remained true to the God of his people Israel—the one, only Lord of heaven and earth, the all-wise, almighty creator and ruler of the world. He knew that as a supreme judge, Yahweh could be hard and severe, but at the same time kind and merciful. His forgiveness went out to meet the man who forgave his fellows and turned toward righteousness. All nature and all men were enfolded in his goodness and providence. His eye swept creation. Not a sparrow could fall to earth without his knowledge. He was not an absentee God, but a near-at-hand, personal presence, dealing directly with earthly affairs. His tender care was especially over those who were faithful to the ideal of the kingdom. He was a father ruling his household with authority; a generous master of his servants, but doing what he pleased with his own. His sovereign will, molding the centuries, gave security to the lowly lovers of righteousness patiently awaiting the coming of the Kingdom of God.

It was not the teaching of Jesus about God, but the teaching of Christians about Jesus that gave the Christian God the qualities which distinguished him from all the other gods of the Graeco-Roman world. Like Jesus himself, the early disciples and Jewish Christian churches recognized no God but Yahweh of Israel. If Christianity had remained within the boundaries of Judaism, interpreting Jesus as the Messiah whom God rescued from the realm of the dead, exalted to heaven and, on some fateful day, would send again in power to establish the perfect kingdom on earth, there would have been no need of a distinctive Christian God.

HENRIK IBSEN   (*1828–1906*)

"GREATEST REBEL THAT EVER LIVED"

Translated by William Archer

Maximus. Were Constantius and death your worst terrors? Think.

Julian. No, you are right. The priests—! My whole youth has been one continuous dread of the Emperor and of Christ. Oh, he is terrible, that mysterious—that merciless god-man! At every turn, wherever I wished to go, he met me, stark and stern, with his unconditional, inexorable commands.

Maximus. And these commands—were they within you?

Julian. Always without. Always "Thou shalt." If my soul gathered itself up in one gnawing and consuming hate towards the murderer of my kin, what said the commandment: "Love thine enemies!" If my mind, athirst for beauty, longed for scenes and rites from the bygone world of Greece, Christianity swooped down upon me with its "Seek the one thing needful!" If I felt the sweet lusts of the flesh towards this or that, the Prince of Renunciation terrified me with his: "Kill the body, that the soul may live!"—All that is human has become unlawful since the day when the seer of Galilee became ruler of the world. With him, to live means to die. Love and hatred, both are sins. Has he, then, transformed man's flesh and blood? Has not earth-bound man remained what he ever was? Our inmost, healthy soul rebels against it all;—and yet we are to *will* in the very teeth of our own will! Thou shalt, shalt, shalt!

Maximus. And you have got no further than that? Shame on you!

Julian. I?

Maximus. Yes, you, the man of Athens and of Ephesus.

Julian. Ah, those times, Maximus! It was easy to choose then. What were we really working at? A philosophic system, neither more nor less.

Maximus. Is it not written somewhere in your Scriptures "Either with us or against us"?

Julian. Did not Libanius remain the man he was, whether he took the affirmative in a disputation, or the negative? This lies deeper. Here is action that must be faced. "Render unto Caesar the things that are Caesar's." In Athens I once made a game of that;—but it is no game. You cannot grasp it, you, who have never been under the power of the god-man. It is more than a doctrine he has spread over the world; it is an enchantment, that binds the soul in chains. He who has once been under it,—I believe he can never quite shake it off.

Maximus. Because you do not wholly *will.*

Julian. How can I *will* the impossible?

Maximus. Is it worth while to *will* what is possible?

Julian. Verbiage from the lecture-hall! You can no longer cram my mind with that. And yet—oh, no, no, Maximus! But you cannot understand how it is with us. We are like vines transplanted into a new, strange soil; transplant us back again, and we die; yet in the new soil we cannot thrive.

Maximus. We? Whom do you call we?

Julian. All who are under the terror of the revelation.

* * * *

Maximus. Friend—if delusion be a necessity to you, return to the Galileans. They will receive you with open arms.

Julian. You know well that is impossible? Emperor and Galilean! How reconcile that contradiction?

Yes, this Jesus Christ is the greatest rebel that ever lived. What was Brutus—what was Cassius, compared with him? They murdered only the man Julius Caesar, but he murders all that is called Caesar or Augustus. Is peace conceivable between the Galilean and the Emperor? Is there room for them both upon the earth? For he lives on the earth, Maximus,—the Galilean lives, I say, however thoroughly both Jews and Romans imagined that they had killed him;— he lives in the rebellious minds of men; he lives in their scorn and defiance of all visible authority.

"Render unto Caesar the things that are Caesar's—and to God the things that are God's!" Never has the mouth of man uttered a more crafty saying than that. What lies behind it? What, and how much, belongs to the Emperor? That saying is nothing but a bludgeon to strike the crown from off the Emperor's head.

*   *   *   *

Julian. And what does the conqueror win? Is it worth while to conquer? What has the Macedonian Alexander, what has Julius Caesar won? Greeks and Romans talk of their own renown with cold admiration,—while the other, the Galilean, the carpenter's son, sits throned as the king of love in the warm believing hearts of men.

Where is he now?—Has he been at work elsewhere since that happened at Golgotha?

I dreamed about him lately. I dreamed that I had subdued the whole world. I ordained that the memory of the Galilean should be rooted out on earth, and it was rooted out.—Then the spirits came and ministered to me, and bound wings on my shoulders, and I soared aloft into infinite space till my feet rested on another world.

It *was* another world than mine. Its curve was vaster, its light more golden, and many moons circled around it.

Then I looked down at my own earth—the Emperor's earth, which I had made Galileanless—and I thought that all I had done was very good.

But behold, Maximus—there came a procession by me, on the strange earth where I stood. There were soldiers, and judges and executioners at the head of it, and weeping women followed. And lo!—in the midst of the slow-moving array, was the Galilean, alive, and bearing a cross on his back. Then I called to him, and said, "Whither away, Galilean?" But he turned his face toward me, smiled, nodded slowly, and said: "To the place of the skull."

Where is he now? What if that at Golgotha, near Jerusalem, was but a wayside matter, a thing done, so to speak, in passing, in a leisure hour? What if he goes on and on, and suffers, and dies, and conquers, again and again, from world to world?

DEAN W. R. INGE, K.C.V.O., D.D.   (*1860*–   )

"HIS CHARACTER STILL LIVES"

No real biography of Jesus Christ can ever be written and much that we should like to know remains uncertain. But the figure of the Saviour is not shadowy; His character lives; the Gospels give us a genuine portrait. The obvious *naïveté* and uncritical simplicity of the Evangelists forbid us to imagine that they could have created such a picture. If their object had been merely the apotheosis of the founder of a cult, the human traits which we find in the Gospels would have been suppressed or overlaid with honorific legend. I do not say that there is no tendency of this kind in the Synoptics; they contain a few things which we feel to be quite incongruous; but these are not numerous and do not blur the clear impression of a real likeness. I will venture, though with much diffidence, to enumerate the features which seem to me to stand out most plainly.

The traditional portraits of Jesus Christ, in illustrated books and pictures, express only a serene and gentle dignity, sometimes even with a slightly effeminate look. The Gospels do not give this impression of Him. He is described as deeply moved by compassion, by anger, perhaps even by fear. But His was a commanding personality; no one ever dared to take liberties with Him.

Nor was gentleness the chief attribute of His teaching. He spoke of God as our Father; but was fatherhood associated with good-natured forbearance at this time? I think not. He did not shrink from making the severest demands on His followers—sometimes to "leave all," home, work and possessions. Even when no such external renunciation is required, Christianity is the sternest of all creeds, because it claims the whole man, his words and thoughts as well as his actions. . . .

The immediate effect of His teaching was an impression of power, of authority and mastery, the commanding dominance of a leader of men. Again and again the word "power" is used in connexion with His personality. Those who, like Paulsen, have found that His character is marked by renunciation of life; those who, like Renan, have spoken only of "infinite sweetness, vague poetry, universal charm"; and those who, like Hase, say that "never did a religious hero shun so little the joys of life," give impressions so one-sided as to be misleading. He appeals mainly to the will, and not in emotional language. He calls for a moral decision. This appeal is made with a royal independence of traditional authority, as is proved by His language about the Sabbath, about the wine-skins, in the story of the adulteress which has found its way into manuscripts of St. John, and in the treatment of the Ten Commandments in the Sermon on the Mount.

He was not a fanatic, an anarchist, a socialist, a dreamer, or an Essene ascetic. His discourses display, not only perfect sanity and balance, but (if one may say so without presumption) great intellectual power. We have to remember that His reporters were not intellectually gifted men; they were inadequate to their task and probably missed many examples of His irony, that weapon of the misunderstood, and the playfulness with which He half expressed truths which they could not grasp.

COUNT HERMAN A. VON KEYSERLING   (*1880–*   )

A CHILD OF THE SUN

Translated by J. Holroyd Reece

If children of the sun like Jesus appear on the horizon, humanity reveres them, perhaps also believes their promise, but is hardly encouraged, for the distance seems too great and the road to them not clear. If, however, some one arises from their midst, a man like the rest, who, as it were, works himself beyond humanity, then humanity is filled with joy, gains wings and follows him, full of hope. It was ever thus. Through the example of Christ, as such, Western humanity would never have been stimulated to make the ascent; He was too immeasurable; nor is He the father of Christianity. If St. Paul had not appeared, a man who, being a child of the world, was intelligible to every one, yet finally grew to be a saint, we would know nothing of Jesus any more. And that Christianity developed into a world religion, into glad tidings for the whole of the West, is the desert of St. Augustine. This most powerful of all ethical natures the West has produced gave the human example thanks to which only Christ Himself could become one. His life proved that sin implied not only an obstacle but also assistance, that it is precisely the barriers of nature which make it impossible to overcome her; that imperfection is the very substance of which God stands in need in order to take shape in man. Thus his example applies really to every one.

Frank Kingdon (1894–   )

A MOST MOVING INCIDENT

Any withdrawal from the world . . . that means discarding responsibility for the shaping of actual events is not mere self-denial in the ordinary sense but is actually a denial of the self which can know itself only through action. One of the most moving incidents in the life of Christ is that in which He is reported to have stood on the Mount of Olives and to have looked on Jerusalem from the outside, weeping over it, and saying: "O Jerusalem, Jerusalem, how often would I have gathered thee as a hen gathereth her chickens under her wing, and ye would not." But he did not stop there. He called His disciples and went down the hill and across the brook into the city. He mingled with the crowds and put into the turmoil of Jerusalem's life all the power and eloquence that He had. He did not avoid the clash that He must have known was coming. He deliberately walked into it. And this, not simply because He was courageous but because He knew that in the very struggle itself He was to find the clearer sense of companionship with the Father whom He served.

GEORGE M. LAMSA *(1892–   )*

NEVER MAN MORE WORSHIPPED

Kings and realms bow in prayer to him and crowns are surmounted with his Cross. The world has never worshipped any other man more than Jesus. In heaven and on earth humanity knows no sweeter name. He has received worship through many forms, yet he never sought worshippers, nor did he ever attempt to inaugurate a new system of worship to supplant that of Judaism. He discounted honors and publicity. He refused to be called Rabbi. He instructed his disciples not to call anyone Master, or to seek high places at feasts and weddings. He wanted nothing from men but to do the will of his Father. He came, not that men should sacrifice to him, but that he might be sacrificed for them. . . .

We know less about Jesus now than his followers did in the first century. Yet he was not a philosopher or a magician. He was born in a humble town of humble parents, reared among a simple people, to whom simplicity and poverty were the highest realities in life, and who never spoke or thought in abstruse ways.

Jesus was inspired by the promises which God had made to the people of his faith: the sacred covenant established with Abraham, Isaac and Jacob. As a patriotic Jew, he cherished the great hope for the fulfilment of this covenant. He preached a gospel with simple words, derived from daily language, illustrated with stories which were common to all—a gospel acceptable only to the poor of his time. He chose simple men as his companions. They were regarded as the outcasts of ignorance by the accepted religious teachers who would not think of training such to be leaders. He, moreover, spoke in parables characteristic of all Oriental teachers, in a manner that these unlearned men and the public could understand and grasp. . . .

Jesus, no doubt, is a mystery and he will never be fully understood. But we needlessly multiply difficulties by taking him out of his Oriental context and thinking of him in terms of modern Occidental Christianity and wholly in the light of our complex social life. The stimulus to our rapid transformation during the past nine hundred years has made us like a clock which moves only forward. We think for the future and forget the past. Our religion and worship have grown side by side with our social and economic life; our churches are organized on the same business principles as our industrial institutions. Our schools, colleges and universities graduate lawyers, doctors and politicians, as well as preachers.

In the olden days prophets were called by God, and religious men were selected only from the ranks which represented the moral concerns of the people. In these modern days, instead of raising ourselves above our material interests, we try to make religion fit our social order. We live in a scientific age with an artificial social order; yet we want miracles like those that happened two thousand years ago, to a people who believed in them and who lived close to nature. And because they do not happen now, we question their reality in the past. Why do we need miracles in an age of airplanes, radio, and railroads? Why do we need healers, with all our doctors and hospitals? Do our religious geniuses believe in healing? Have they ever really tried it? The fact is that some who have tried it with success have been condemned as fanatics. And yet the healing ministry of Jesus was one of his conspicuous achievements. . . .

The amazing fact about Jesus is that he, a simple peasant, free from any political and religious backing, was able to formulate a religion which appealed to the souls of all mankind, and to leave behind an unconquerable influence which still abides and will so abide forever, regardless of all political, social and economic changes throughout the world.

WILLIAM H. LECKY   (*1838–1903*)

AN IDEAL CHARACTER

It was reserved for Christianity to present to the world an ideal character, which through all the changes of eighteen centuries has inspired the hearts of men with an impassioned love; has shown itself capable of acting on all ages, nations, temperaments and conditions; has been not only the highest pattern of virtue but the strongest incentive to its practice; and has exercised so deep an influence that it may be truly said that the simple record of three short years of active life has done more to regenerate and to soften mankind than all the disquisitions of philosophers and all the exhortations of moralists. This has indeed been the well-spring of whatever is best and purest in the Christian life. Amid all the sins and failings . . . it has preserved, in the character and example of its Founder, an enduring principle of regeneration.

ROGER LLOYD   (*1900–*   )

CHRIST OR CHAOS

With the point of view of one who is bewildered, and even made contemptuous, by the suggestion that Christ can save our world, and that no one else can, we have much sympathy. But however impracticable it may seem to some, to others it seems a statement of quite terrifyingly obvious fact that Christ or Chaos is a true choice for humanity. Such a point of view is more than legitimate. It needs to be put, and it is worth the attention even of those who are temperamentally disinclined to think that there is much in it.

No one can doubt that chaos, with its attendant miseries, is one of the possible alternatives which the facts of our world hold out to us. If it is not believed that allegiance to Christ is alone capable of rescuing us, by what other force can we be saved? . . .

Humanity is not so adult that it can do without hero-worship. Those who are plagued by the arid kind of intellectualism, which is wholly out of touch with the realities of life and human nature, may disparage and despise the aptitude of mankind to find heroes to worship and serve, and may spend their spare time in the pleasant, profitable, though rather ignoble occupation of debunking the great names of the past. But ordinary men and women need someone to revere and follow. The dictatorships realize that clearly enough, and the first result of Totalitarianism in every state where it comes to power, is that a leader is erected to whom is paid honours which are not far from those proper to the august dignity of Deity itself. But if the Nazi worships the Fuehrer, if the Russian appeals always to the need of preserving the safety of the glorious Stalin, and if the Japanese Imperialist virtually worships his Emperor, Christians at least have a hero and a king who is worthier of a greater honour, and whose power to attract the best of men never wanes nor ceases. The power of the name of Christ, is, on any showing, a power greater than that lying behind the name of Hitler or Mussolini, or even of the greatest and best of authoritarian statesmen, Masaryk. It has proved itself capable of attracting the loyalty of men and women of all ages, all races, all levels of spiritual and mental capacity, and all tongues. To-day, there is no sign of the waning of that power. Whatever men may think of the Church, Christ Himself is more than ever seen to be the only power making for social righteousness, international justice, and decency. Millions all over the world are haunted by their belief of what He has it in His power to do for a world desperately in need of Him.

He is the actor from outside who breaks the vicious circle and sets the captives free. That office He performed for the vicious circle in which the overwhelming success of Roman Imperialism had bound the world, and that office He can perform for us in our own generation, and no one else can. Our problems and difficulties may be more intricate, more profound, and more dangerous than any of those which troubled the last of the Caesars, but the power is there, and His own diagnosis remains accurate and unchallenged still. The day must come when distresses, perplexities, dangers and tumults over-shadow the world, with "Men's hearts failing them for fear, and for looking after those things which are coming on the earth." It is pre-cisely then that He bids us look for salvation, "When these things begin to come to pass, then look up, and lift up your heads; for your redemption draweth nigh." The Redeemer is Christ. The power illuminating and sustaining freedom is to-day what it has always been, the Christian Faith, alone powerful to understand and defeat the new idolatry which is fast making a desert of the heritage of man-kind.

ALOYSIUS McDONOUGH   (*1902–*   )

HIS HUMANITY A MAGNET

It is fascinating to realize how well adapted Christ's humanity was, as a *fit instrument* of divinity, in the furthering of our salvation. But, just as it is difficult to take in at one glance, the full beauty of a many-faceted gem, so it is not easy to appreciate at one brief mental glance, the many phases of Christ's humanity, as a *human* instru-ment *divinely* attuned.

Let us begin by resort to an illustration. Suppose we place a strong magnet upon a table. Then, bring a number of iron particles within the radius of this magnetic influence. What happens? By a law of natural attraction, the particles are drawn to the source of influence as to a goal. Lift the magnet from the table, move it here or there, and the particles cling fast, are lifted and moved with it.

Making due allowance in the application of our analogy, we may liken ourselves to the particles, the humanity of Christ to the magnet, the divinity of Christ to the one who made the magnet, and placed it on the table as an instrument of attraction.

In the example resorted to, we find the particles are drawn to the magnet irresistibly. We are brought under magnetic influence of Christ by His teaching, His example, the grace that He proffers—but we are free to resist. Though He "reacheth from end to end mightily," yet He "ordereth all things sweetly." As long as we are on probation and in our "earning" capacity, we may refuse Him, even though to do so is to thwart ourselves. We may spurn His mercy, if we prefer to incur His justice. We may flaunt this independence of ours, as crazily as the suicide. Any human being who can boast of sanity, owes it to himself to choose not only freely, but *wisely*. To choose the eternal in preference to the temporal, the spiritual before the material, the supernatural rather than the natural, is dictated by well-ordered selfishness. An honest man admits this and is brave enough to face the issue. The sinful man is a dishonest fool—too mean to pay the price—even "the price of Him that was prized."

We have likened the humanity of Christ to a magnet. How does this part of the comparison apply? The humanity of Christ is a magnet in the mighty hand of God—that is to say, an attractive force that draws men of good will by means of wisdom, kindness, and power. This magnet was presented to men that they might adhere to it and cling fast, and finally be withdrawn together with it, from earth to heaven.

In the stupendous work of restoring man to his heavenly estate, God could have dealt with us in many ways. But He chose to deal with us in as "human" a way as possible, though without detriment to the divine success of His plans. And so "the Word was made flesh and dwelt amongst us." God came among us in Person, but so to speak—clothed in humanity. In general, this was an ingenious accommodation on His part, whereby He deigned to "adapt His pace" to frail man, whose soul must falter through this life, leaning upon five crutches of bodily sense. Thus, He Who is divine also, became visible to human eyes, audible to human ears, tangible to human contact—even vulnerable by man-made weapons! But this is not all.

Besides being a delicate instrument adapted to our frailty, the humanity of Christ was divinely attuned to the high purposes of God.

We find this especial efficiency at work in two spheres. . . . For the moment, let us consider the sphere of nature.

To arrest the attention of men, to secure their recognition of His leadership, Christ did many miracles. He healed the dying, recalled the dead to life, He expelled demons. Only divine power can work a miracle, but God can empower an agent as His instrument. When God does so, He bestows upon the agent a share of His own omnipotence. In all the miracles of Christ, God made use of His human nature as an instrument of divinity, transmitting divine power through the agency of His human body and soul, to the patients who were cured. "Virtue went out from Him, and healed all." Sometimes a human word, sometimes a gentle touch of His hand—and divine results followed. "And Jesus said: Somebody hath touched me, for I know that virtue is gone out from me."

Christ the God taught us, and died for us, through the instrumentality of Christ the Man. During thirty-three years, Christ preached an uncompromising war in behalf of God and men, against the powers of darkness—a war of virtue against vice. He led the way, bidding others—He still does—to come after Him. "Follow Me. I am the way, the truth, and the life." His doctrine was attractive in itself, but with the endorsement of divine miracles, Christ's influence over men was magnetic to the highest possible degree. The magnetism of Christ was athrob with divine power.

Of those who came under the influence of Christ, some clung steadfast: "Lord, to whom shall we go? Thou hast the words of eternal life." Others shied away: "And (they) walked no more with Him." Christ the man was the magnetic instrument of Christ the God, Who would draw His adherents with Him through a struggle unto death, waged for heaven in the arena of this earth. Just as today, so on that Friday, some men thought only of the few hours of Christ's weakness, forgetting the many years of His magnetic strength. Christ's faithful believe firmly, hope bravely and serve lovingly, because they realize that when Christ emerged triumphant from the tomb of death, He justified the divine boast uttered beforehand, "And I, if I be lifted up from the earth, will draw all things to Myself!"

SHAILER MATHEWS   (*1863–*   )

TWO INSEPARABLE GIFTS

The outstanding element in the character of Jesus is obviously sacrificial love. He gave men what he had to give, himself and his service. The two cannot be separated from each other. His was not a life of acquisitiveness either of material goods or of honor. He cheered those who were poor and outcast, and served them, sacrificing what must have seemed as good to them as they do to us—family fortune, friendships, comfort, life. He did not attempt to enforce his rights, nor does he seem to have been particularly concerned to have them recognized. He was more interested in giving justice than in acquiring it, and he died a victim to the enmity of those who would perpetuate their privileges at the expense of the unprivileged.

Another striking thing in the life of Jesus is that he brought personality into semi-personal or depersonalized groups. He was poor, despised, forsaken. The common people, the poor, the criminal, were his followers. He spoke his blessings to the hungry, the sorrowful, the poor. He himself partook in the struggle of these depressed classes. He gave personal value to the despised masses. He took upon himself the form of a servant and died the death of a criminal.

The contrast between his inner supremacy and his outer humiliation, however, is more apparent than real, because humiliation was his way of bringing personal values to life. Without it his life might have been interesting, but it would not have been important. It was because he recognized the worth of the human soul even in its least respected state that he has been worshiped as the savior of the world rather than of classes.

With him there was no room for bond or free, male or female, national aggressions or class consciousness. The more one studies society, the more one feels that the future will belong either to Jesus Christ or to coercive mechanism. Wherever one turns one finds the same issues dominant. Is the world to progress only by the enforced surrender of rights, or will it move forward under the inspiration of those free and Christlike spirits who are willing to share their privileges with others? . . . The real hope for the future lies in the faith of those who believe that the example and the spirit of Jesus are the keys to unlock social difficulties.

ROBERT ANDREWS MILLIKAN   (*1868-*   )

THE ESSENCE OF THE GOSPEL

The first idea—namely, that one's own happiness, one's own most permanent satisfactions are to be found through trying to forget oneself and seeking, instead, the common good—is an altruistic ideal so contrary to the immediate promptings of the animal within us that it is not strange that it found little place in the thinking or acting of the ancient world, or, for that matter, in the acting of the modern world either, in spite of the professions of Christianity. There will be common consent, however, that the greatest, most consistent, most influential proponent of this idea who has ever lived was Jesus of Nazareth. Buddha, Confucius, Socrates, all had now and then given voice to it, but Jesus made it the sum and substance of his whole philosophy of life. When he said, "All things whatsover ye would that men should do to you, do ye even so to them: for this is the law and the prophets," I take it that he meant by that last phrase that this precept epitomized in his mind all that had been commanded and foretold—that it embodied the summation of duty and of aspiration.

Now, when the life and teachings of Jesus became the basis of the religion of the whole Western World, an event of stupendous importance for the destinies of mankind had certainly taken place, for a new set of ideals had been definitely and officially adopted by a very considerable fraction of the human race—a fraction which will be universally recognized to have held within it no small portion of the world's human energies and progressive capacities, and which has actually determined to no small degree the direction of human progress. The significance of this event is completely independent even of the historicity of Jesus. The service of the Christian religion and my own faith in essential Christianity would not be diminished one iota if it should in some way be discovered that no such individual as Jesus ever existed. If the ideas and ideals for which he stood sprang up spontaneously in the minds of men without the stimulus of a single great character, the result would be even more wonderful and more inspiring than it is now, for it would mean that the spirit of Jesus is actually more widely spread throughout the world than we realize. In making this statement, I am endeavoring to say just as positively and emphatically as I can that the credentials of Jesus are found wholly in his teachings and in his character as recorded by his teachings, and not at all in any real or alleged historical events.

And in making that affirmation, let me also emphasize the fact that I am only paraphrasing Jesus' own words when he refused to let his disciples rest his credentials upon a sign.

My conception, then, of the essentials of religion, at least of the Christian religion, is that they consist in just two things: first, in inspiring mankind with the Christlike ideal—that is, the altruistic ideal which means, specifically, concern for the common good as contrasted with one's own individual impulses and interests, wherever in one's own judgment the two come into conflict; and second, inspiring mankind to do, rather than merely to think about, its duty, the definition of duty for each individual being what he himself conceives to be for the common good. In three words, I conceive the essential task of religion to be "to develop the *consciences,* the *ideals,* and the *aspirations* of mankind." . . .

First, that if the basis of Western religion is to be found in the element that is common to all its branches, then the one indispensable element in it now is just that element which formed the center of Jesus' teaching, and which I have above called the essence of religion. . . .

Now, looking to the influence of religion in the future, I have in the preceding paragraphs found the essence of the gospel of Jesus in the Golden Rule, which, broadly interpreted, means the development of a sense of social responsibility in the individual. In the last analysis, civilization itself is primarily dependent upon just this thing. . . . The amazing insight of Jesus is revealed in his having kept himself free from creedal statements, particularly statements that reflected the state of man's knowledge or ignorance of the universe that was characteristic of his times. In spite of our enormously increased knowledge of the universe, a large part of his sayings seem to us to be just as true now as they seemed to be then. The things that a man does not say often reveal the understanding and penetration of his mind even more than the things he says. The fact that Jesus confined himself so largely to the statement of truths that still seem to us to have eternal value is what has made him a leader and teacher of such supreme influence throughout the centuries.

Sir William Osler   (1849–1919)

HIS MESSAGE TO THE WORLD

Do you remember the most touching of all incidents in Christ's ministry, when the anxious ruler Nicodemus came by night, worried lest the things that pertained to his everlasting peace were not a part of his busy and successful life? Christ's message to him is His message to the world—never more needed than at present: "Ye must be born of the spirit." You wish to be with the leaders . . . know the great souls that make up the moral radium of the world. You must be born of their spirit, initiated into their fraternity, whether of the spiritually-minded followers of the Nazarene or of that larger company, elect from every nation, seen by St. John.

JOSEPH PARKER (*1830–1902*)

"ALONE AMONG ALL MEN"

Many false Christs have gone out into the world. The Christ that was born in Bethlehem has now to compete with the Christ born in the poet's fancy, carved out of an ideal humanity, or developed out of a benevolent sentiment. The noble, simple Nazarene has been left behind somewhere, probably in the Temple, or has passed through so many guises that the characteristic lineaments have been lost. This circumstance is a significant feature of the spiritual civilization of the day. Deepest and truest among its lessons is the doctrine that men must have a Christ. There has ever been a motion, a gravitation, more or less palpable, towards a man who should be the complement of every other man; and who, by the perfectness of his manhood, should be able to restore and preserve the equipoise which universal consciousness affirms to have been disturbed or lost.

The Incarnation is the radical mystery in the life of the Christ accepted by the Church. Without following the theologian into doctrine, we are bound to follow the historian into matters of fact. The historian introduces a man, under the name of Jesus, who was begotten as no other man was ever begotten. He does not represent the usual conditions of human birth, but stands alone among all men. The mysteriousness of his origin, even if it be but a supposition, will supply an easily available test of his entire life and teaching; the Man who begins as no other man ever began must continue as no other man ever continued.

WILLIAM LYON PHELPS   (*1865–1943*)

A MAN OF SORROWS

The true teacher has inexhaustible patience. He looks for no sudden miracle. He will sow and another will reap. This is the marked difference between physicians of the body and physicians of the mind. The surgeon performs an operation, and in a short time he has the satisfaction of seeing his patient strong and healthy. The teacher and the preacher can only hope that perhaps in later years some of his work on some minds may possibly bear good fruit. The eternal obstacle is human nature.

There is a tone of unutterable sadness in these words:

I must work the works of him that sent me, while it is day: the night cometh, when no man can work.

Jesus was compelled to leave his disciples, as a dying mother leaves little children, at the mercy of strangers.

He was a man of sorrows, and *acquainted with grief*. Grief and not joy is the universal language; if you talk the speech of hilarity and cheerfulness, there are many who do not understand you, for there is so little in their lives corresponding to your mood. But everyone knows pain; everyone knows sorrow. Of all the realities in the world, there is no reality more evident than grief. Jesus was acquainted with it. He knew.

*   *   *   *

Jesus never promised his disciples immunity from pain; but he gave them the inner fortitude necessary to bear it.

Healthy pessimism to the right mind is a challenge. For there is a healthy pessimism, which we should all feel; it is simply the honest, clear-sighted recognition of the facts of life.

*   *   *   *

It is the way of the world to belittle and to destroy the beneficent influence of those who wish only to be of service. Nature is almost always directed against virtue, almost never against vice. Jesus knew all this; he knew that his golden words would arouse malicious opposition, deliberate misrepresentation, and that at best they would often be received with complete indifference. . . .

But Jesus spoke freely with everybody, high and low, rich and poor; he ate and drank what was set before him. He came to save; he knew that he could not be infected with sin, that his virtue was more contagious than disease. He therefore accepted invitations to dine with the tax-gatherers, with the well-to-do, and with the poorest of the poor. Evil companions could not hurt him and he cared not at all what hostile critics might say. Let them make of it what they pleased. He went on his way, willing to stop, dine, and talk with anyone. No one ever denounced some of the Pharisees more uncompromisingly than Jesus; but he did not hesitate to accept an invitation to dinner in a Pharisee's house.

* * * *

It would seem at first sight that even those who refused and refuse to believe in Jesus would not be offended in him; that is, could not be made worse by him, could not be made to stumble and go wrong. But history proves that Jesus knew that not only would there be many who would be angered, that is "offended" in the common modern meaning, by his teaching, but that many would actually be led astray. "The time cometh, that whosoever killeth you will think that he doeth God service." What happened? Enemies sought his life and finally succeeded in crucifying him. Today he has numerous and powerful antagonists whom he seems to goad into ever more active opposition.

* * * *

Jesus foresaw not only the malignant opposition of his foes, but the internal jealousies and tragic quarrels among his followers. The twelve disciples fought among themselves as to who should be the greatest in the new kingdom; the mother of two made the preposterous demand that her sons sit respectively on the right and on the left, which I think must have caused our Lord actual amusement.

* * * *

Some of the parables and the sayings of Jesus at first sight seem positively cruel, but upon reflexion we see that they are no more cruel than life. They represent to his disciples and followers the facts of life, so that they may not be taken unawares, not thrown into confusion by a surprise attack.

* * * *

Unlike most reformers, who work for the passage of new laws that shall restrain men from vice, and who seek to put their own personal opinions into the constitution of their country, Jesus paid little attention to laws and none at all to politics. He knew that under any government the poor would always be with us, that sin and disease would abound. Jesus refrained from political activity, and can be claimed by no political party. He was sufficiently pessimistic to know that under a monarchical or under a Bolshevist régime, sorrow and pain would everywhere meet the eye. He dealt not with governments, laws, and parties, but solely with the human heart.

* * * *

Before his death and resurrection, Jesus looked into the future. He saw the long centuries of sin, oppression, greed, selfishness and war. Amid this circle of hostility, his disciples must keep the faith with steadfast hearts; they would suffer, but they would have that inward peace of mind which enables one to withstand enmity and pain. "I pray not that thou shouldst take them out of the world, but that thou shouldst keep them from the evil." "These things I have spoken unto you, that in me ye might have peace. In the world ye shall have tribulation; but be of good cheer; I have overcome the world."

Michael Pupin (1858–1935)

CREATED SPIRITUAL DYNAMICS

The testimony of Christ is, according to our Christian belief, by far the most convincing of all the testimonies relating to the co-ordinating action of the spiritual forces. The arguments supporting this belief appeal to our reason with the same force as the arguments supporting a well-established physical theory. Our Christian knowledge of the spiritual forces revealed by Christ is deeply rooted in the solid ground of human experience of nearly two thousand years; it is built upon the hard rock of experience, and not upon the shifting sands of arbitrary hypothesis. This knowledge, like scientific knowledge, is the extract of innumerable observations and experiments recorded in the history of human lives; it is, therefore, just as carefully tested and as trustworthy as our knowledge of physical forces. Dealing as it does with the laws of actions and reactions of spiritual forces, it may be called spiritual dynamics. Christ created it long before Newton had announced his dynamics of matter in motion, Maxwell his electrodynamics, and Carnot his thermodynamics. These dynamical sciences deal with the physical world; Christ's dynamics deal with the spiritual world. The dynamical sciences of the physical world are naturally incomparably simpler than the dynamics of the spiritual world, but their mutual resemblance both in form and in evolutionary growth is obvious. This resemblance finds the simplest and most striking illustration in the efforts of the spiritual forces to transform the life of humanity into a cosmos, a living structure of simple law and beautiful life. It is here that the mode of operation of the co-ordinating spiritual forces reminds us most vividly of the mode of operation of the co-ordinating physical forces, and this exhibits the most obvious resemblance between physical and spiritual realities.

Our Christian faith sees, in the life and the teaching of Christ the highest spiritual reality which our belief in God, the fountainhead of all spiritual realities, planted in the soul of man. This reality, we believe, endowed our souls with the spiritual forces which guide us in the spiritual co-ordination of each individual life and of the life of humanity. Love, according to Christ, is the most powerful of all these co-ordinating forces. Its co-ordinating action in the spiritual world is very similar to the co-ordinating action of the gravitational force in the physical world. Christ discovered it and revealed it to us in His two commandments:

Thou shalt love thy God, with all thy heart, and with all thy soul, and with all thy mind.

Thou shalt love thy neighbor as thyself.

These commandments are the fundamental law of Christ's spiritual dynamics. It is obvious that under the guidance of this law we can liberate ourselves from the dominating love of purely material things and thus rescue our own individual lives and the life of humanity from the threatening chaos, and transform it into a cosmos, a life of simple law and beautiful order.

BISHOP WILLIAM A. QUAYLE   (*1860–1925*)

A TERRIFIC POWER REVEALED

"Which of you convinceth me of sin?"—John 8:46

This saying always makes me afraid. I think it is as terrible as the resurrection, and I know nothing that will make the face white so soon as the resurrection morning. And the reason it does is because it displays out in the open a terrific power we did not know existed. And this calm saying of the calm Christ to the effect that he is sinless, and consequently impenitent, makes a man halt and grow silent. It is hard to talk about so mighty a matter as this; and the solitary defense I offer in my own behalf is that it is the solemn service a preacher is bound to render to talk sometimes when he would love to be silent, and to talk oftentimes about things that are sky heights above his little stature.

Now, this calm assumption of Jesus that he is not a sinner will take hold of the wrists of any thoughtful mind and twist them till it must come to your knees. We have known egotists in history. There are not a few of them. Their voices are easily detected. They always talk about themselves. It is often not a large talk, but they rejoice in it. And we know the egotists frankly well. But there never has been an egotist so colossal out of all them, great as they are, that would have claimed that he never was a sinner. I think representative egotists, so far as a moment's observation of them may be concerned, may be named as follows: Goethe, Napoleon, and Herbert Spencer. These men seem to be simply masters of art in the unvaried realm of egotism. . . .

Well, supposing, then, we say, for argument's assumption, that possibly and probably Christ was an egotist. Let us mark some egotists. Coleridge was an egotist. Sam Johnson was an egotist. Byron was an egotist. Rousseau was an egotist. We know the egotist's manner—sometimes less passionate and sometimes more, all times a personality who thought he had something in himself to divulge and didn't mind talking about it, though it is nothing much, and then keeps reiterating it, and who makes us very weary before the day is out, so much so that he puts us sick abed. But the quality of the egotist, as we know, is this—he is always thinking of himself and always talking about what he is thinking about. Jesus was always thinking about others and himself as related to the rehabilitation of others and the world. Now, that is a matter of observation any readers of the gospel can certify to. That Jesus talked about himself no one can deny. He had to, because he was the center; and he had to fix a center in order that life might know how to revolve. The sun, if it talked at all besides the talking of the daylights and noons and ruddy skies and glorious heights of air filled with flashing whiteness, would have to talk about itself. Why? Because it is full of itself? No; because the solar system is full of it. If the sun were to say anything to this earth of ours, it would have to say, "Keep close to me." Why? Why, because if the earth gets out of range of the sun, it will rush to ruin. The sun would have to talk about itself because itself is central, significant and compelling.

Now, Jesus is here to get the world up to where the world should be and where the world must feel the tug of him. O sun, what doest thou? And the answer of the sun is, "Getting my hands upon my planets." There is no safety in the planetary system except the sun have his hand upon the shoulder of each and all. And Jesus is to bring life back, uphill, to God. And he talks that. But I defy anybody here who has the thoughtful mood to read the sayings of Jesus, even a minute, to mistake what he hears as being the bickerings and the rasping voices of an egotist. Jesus never smoothed his garments down and glanced at himself in a glass and looked to see how he looked. He looked to see how the earth looked. Do you calmly think that anybody who ever heard Jesus talk would think that he was egotist or egotistical? Think you John thought it? Think you Peter thought it? Think you Judas Iscariot thought it, or Mary of Magdala thought it, or Martha the sister of Lazarus thought it, or Lazarus, coming out of the grave, thought it? Think you that? Didn't you know that while he spoke of himself he spoke of himself as related to us? "I am the light of the world; therefore, people who want daylight, here it is." He wasn't inviting people to look at him, but authentically inviting people to live in him; and he said people who want death rather than life stay far from me, but such as want life rather than death stay near to me; and his arguments were never for self-gratulation, but his arguments were eternally for the heartening of the world and that dark valleys might have daylight, and that those who ran might read when the book was far from their eyes.

M. Raymond, O.C.S.O.

HE WORKED THROUGH HUMAN NATURE

Jesus Christ called twelve to his side personally, the thirteenth he struck from his horse; but for the nineteen hundred years since then, every vocation that I know of has been the most natural of supernatural works. No longer does Christ appear personally. No longer does He strike people from their horses. But He calls thousands and thousands to His side by working in, on, and through their natures. Just as He worked in Palestine, so does He work today. Do you remember how He appeared to Peter and Andrew, to James and John, who were fishermen? He said to them, "Come, and I will make you fishers of men." Have you never known why the twelve were so attached to Him? They wanted to be great, so great that they were even squabbling as to who was going to be the greatest. Do you not recall how James and John played on his sympathies? That is an intensely natural and human story. These "sons of thunder" were so greedy for the glory of being first in His Kingdom that they got their mother to plead for them. They knew the sensitive heart of their Master, so they played on it, and played on it with the most delicate of instruments—the tenderness of a mother's prayer. Yes, every Apostle of Christ was drawn to the supernatural by the natural, and every follower of Christ, if he is to be a real follower of Christ, must want to be great, must be greedy for glory, must be a self-seeker; for there is a selfishness that is salutary and a pride that is praiseworthy.

Despite what certain books say, which are rhapsodies and romances rather than revelations and biographies, every vocation is ultimately founded on the salutary selfishness by which an individual, despite the whole world, seeks to save his own immortal soul. Every vocation has been followed, because those who were called really wanted to be great. Nature and the natural are never to be despised. On them is built the supernatural! . . .

Hold fast to the fact that nature comes from God, and that when

God wanted to work His miracle of miracles, and His greatest work of love, He assumed a human nature!

It is a good thing to know our own limitations, but not unless we also know our potentialities. For while a "superiority complex" is a disgusting, a deadly, and a dangerous thing, it is not nearly so dangerous or so deadly as an "inferiority complex" where things spiritual are concerned. We must become divine, and the only foundation on which we can build is what so many writers decry . . . our human nature. They call it humility to consider oneself lower than the earthworm and to revile one's body. But that is not humility, that is "humbug." Half-truths are always more dangerous than whole lies, and the lopsided view of human nature taken by some writers is at best a half-truth. They have forgotten their human psychology, much of their logic, and all of their life of Christ. He always worked on, in, and through human nature; and today, with His gifts of grace, He works the same way.

ERNEST RENAN   (1823–1892)

HE WILL NOT BE SURPASSED

Translated by Charles Edwin Wilbour

Shall originality be born anew, or shall the world henceforth be content to follow the paths opened by the bold creators of the ancient ages? We know not. But whatever may be the surprises of the future, Jesus will never be surpassed. His worship will grow young without ceasing; his legend will call forth tears without end; his sufferings will melt the noblest hearts; all ages will proclaim that among the sons of men there is none born greater than Jesus.

DEAN HOWARD CHANDLER ROBBINS (*1876–*)

EVER MOVED WITH COMPASSION

"When Jesus saw the multitudes, he was moved with compassion." How often, as we read the New Testament, we meet that phrase, or something like it! One of the things brought out most clearly and sharply in the Gospels is the appeal which great companies of men and women had for Jesus. They stirred his sympathy; they aroused his compassion; they engaged his interest. One takes the impression that what chiefly moved him was their passivity, their want of leadership, their dim outstretchings after unknown beliefs. He speaks of them on more than one occasion as sheep having no shepherd. He felt keenly what might be termed the pathos of a crowd.

Sometimes the circumstances of his relations with these unshepherded folk are very touching. One thinks, for instance, of the time when word was brought to him of the murder of his cousin, John the Baptist. John was a beloved kinsman, a boyhood playmate of Christ, but he was more than that. He was the forerunner of Christ's ministry, the voice of one crying in the wilderness, Prepare ye the way of the Lord. He was the man who had baptized Jesus, the man who had recognized him as the Christ and given him eager welcome, the man who had given his heart to him in high loyalty and unswerving allegiance. This great prophet of righteousness, this beloved friend and kinsman had been butchered in prison, butchered to gratify the dissolute and revengeful woman whom he had reproached for her adulterous union with King Herod. News of the outrage must have come to the Saviour as a profound shock; probably it was one of the keenest personal bereavements of his life. He wanted to be alone with his grief. But the crowds would not have it so. They found out where he had gone and followed him, and we read that when they did so, Jesus came forth and welcomed them. Welcomed them, and under such conditions: what a miracle of self-forgetful kindness!

Or one thinks of another occasion when Christ and his disciples were wearied by long-continued ministrations and found it necessary to get away for a little while from the incessant and exhausting demands upon them. They entered into a fishing-boat and sailed across the Lake of Galilee to seek rest and seclusion in a desert place on the uninhabited side of the lake. But the crowds again found out where he had gone, and went around the lake on foot to overtake him. Their coming defeated the purpose for which he sought retirement, and yet we read of no sign of regret, no expression of disappointment. Instead, we are told again that Jesus was moved with compassion, and began to make immediate provision for their needs. "Whence shall we buy bread, that these may eat?"

That question shows an interesting feature of Christ's compassion for the multitude. It was, as we put it, exceedingly "practical." It took into account and reckoned with physical and material as well as moral and spiritual needs. There is a so-called spirituality which finds the needs and pains of the body so distasteful that it takes refuge, ostrich-like, by burying its head in the sands of metaphysics and denying the existence of matter. Suggestion is powerful, and many real as well as fancied ills have undoubtedly been cured by this simple process of lopping off their heads, but it is to be noticed that metaphysics of this order is not conducive to the spirit of compassion. It does not drive men and women to take their place in the front ranks of the pitiful, desperately engaged in the war against pestilence and famine and plague. The heroes and martyrs of our civilization are bred on sterner views of life than that. Our Lord's compassion for the multitudes is at one and the same time idealistic and practical; idealistic in its faith in them, its far-flung aims, its glowing hope, but practical in its concern for their physical wants and needs. There is thought for their weariness and for their hunger. There is solicitude, fear that if they are not fed they will faint by the way on their long homeward journey around the lake.

Benjamin W. Robinson   (*1883–1942*)

HIS AUTHORITY RECOGNIZED

The positive impression which Jesus made upon his friends and observers is everywhere recognized. At the close of the Sermon on the Mount the multitude felt that he had been teaching as one that had authority. . . . He made the impression upon the Roman centurion of being a man in the habit of being obeyed by subordinates, even when the obedience meant making a "withered palsy cease to shake." Even the wind and the sea "obeyed" him and were "muzzled" into silence. When once we begin to listen to them, the assertions are numerous and insistent. He revised the Bible of his day, "You have heard that it has been said . . . but I say unto you." His sway is universal. "All things have been delivered unto me of my father." In the Fourth Gospel he is the eternal bread, the living water. He sent word to the Baptist that it was blessed not to find any occasion of stumbling in him and declared on a memorable occasion that if acknowledgment were withheld by his disciples the stones in the roadway would become vocal in his honor.

Perhaps it is not as sufficiently noticed that with equal emphasis Jesus, on the other hand, disclaims any personal authority or dignity and utterly renounces those miracles by which law-givers and prophets in Israel had asserted themselves. He would not ask the sun and moon to stand still, nor the manna to descend, nor the pillar of fire to glow. He declared that he was meek and lowly of heart. . . . With wonderful charm of modesty he called his flock a little one, or likened his kingdom to a mustard seed that, when grown, scarcely attained the rank of a tree or to leaven that spread through some domestic batch of meal. . . .

There is a paradox here but no self-contradiction. Jesus' self-assertion and his self-effacement belong side by side. Just before saying that he is meek and lowly of heart he insists that all things have been delivered to him by his father and asks that men take upon themselves the yoke of obedience and service to himself. Jesus, in a word, lives a life of modesty and humility, a life of self-sacrifice devoted to the unspectacular service of others and to the fearless and heroic assertion that God is a father who loves the children of men as his own sons. His self-effacement and modesty are part of the ideal life he actually lives; his self-assertion belongs to his insistence that this very life, meekness and lowliness included, is one with the life of God, that to love it is to be in union with him and that to fail of it is the one irreparable calamity. Hence Jesus affirms himself whenever the necessity of this life or of its eternity or glory, as shown in himself, is at stake. Some doubted his personal authority and commission as an individual man. He waived the point. He did not insist upon himself. But at the same time he insisted, with an affirmative and positive force to which nothing could be added, that the principle which his life embodies was as eternal as God and the continuous violation of it involved a ruin without remedy.

* * * *

At the close of his life Jesus more openly and clearly identified himself with the life and principles which he asserted. This is the meaning of the triumphal entry. The end was near and the union of eternal quality and historic personality must be clearly asserted. He therefore affirms himself openly and plainly. He insists that the stones of the pathway are in league with him. The untrained beast of the field submits to his reign. The children's hosannas pay him their natural homage and the general multitude carpet the roadway with their garments and join in his praise. The scripture is fulfilled and he is exhibited as the King of Israel.

ARCHBISHOP JOSEPH F. RUMMEL   (*1876*-   )

A BEAUTIFUL LEGACY

One of the most beautiful legacies bequeathed to us by Jesus Christ and elaborated with much care and insistence by St. Paul is the doctrine of the Mystical Body. According to this doctrine the Church instituted by Christ is not just another religious system or organization but a living, active organism, having, like the human body, many members with diversified functions and capacities. This living organism St. Paul in fact repeatedly compares to the human body: "Being compacted and fitly joined together, by what every joint supplieth, according to the operation in the measure of every part" (Eph. IV, 16). The Head of this organism or body, which we call mystical to distinguish it from the historic or natural body of Christ, is Christ Himself. It is He who animates it, invigorates it, directs its operations, and gives to each member the power to function according to its proper end and capacity. In the words of St. Paul to the Colossians: "He (Christ) is the head of the body, the church" (Col. I, 18); and to the Ephesians: "Doing the truth in charity, we may in all things grow up in him who is the head, *even* Christ: from whom the whole body . . . maketh increase of the body, unto the edifying of itself in charity" (Eph. IV, 15-16).

Albert Schweitzer   (*1875-*)

HIS SPIRIT STILL AT WORK IN THE WORLD

Translated by W. Montgomery

Jesus means something to our world because a mighty spiritual force streams forth from Him and flows through our time also. This fact can neither be shaken nor confirmed by any historical discovery. It is the solid foundation of Christianity.

The mistake was to suppose that Jesus could come to mean more to our time by entering into it as a man like ourselves. That is not possible. First because such a Jesus never existed. Secondly because, although historical knowledge can no doubt introduce greater clearness into an existing spiritual life, it cannot call spiritual life into existence. History can destroy the present; it can reconcile the present with the past; can even to a certain extent transport the present into the past; but to contribute to the making of the present is not given unto it. . . .

But the truth is, it is not Jesus as historically known, but Jesus as spiritually arisen within man, who is significant for our time and can help it. Not the historical Jesus, but the spirit which goes forth from Him and in the spirits of men strives for new influence and rule, is that which overcomes the world. . . .

The abiding and eternal in Jesus is absolutely independent of historical knowledge and can only be understood by contact with His spirit which is still at work in the world. In proportion as we have the Spirit of Jesus we have the true knowledge of Jesus.

MONSIGNOR FULTON J. SHEEN   (*1895–   *)

DISCIPLES HIS POSTHUMOUS SELF

Our Lord's earthly life was not long, as we reckon a human life. He completed His Father's business while still in His early thirties. He knew that His footprints would soon fade away from the sands of the seashore and the dust of Jerusalem's streets. He knew furthermore that Peters and Johns of the twentieth century would stand in just as much need of His teaching, His power, and His sanctification, as the Peters and Johns of His Own Day. Knowing all this, He would therefore not be an architect who lays a foundation and then disappears. He vowed His life to all men at all times and all places, to be their Teacher, their King, and their Priest unto "the consummation of the world."

But how could He be with us as Teacher, King, and Priest to the consummation of the world? He told us how. He said He would be with us in a new body which He would take from humanity as He took His physical body from His Blessed Mother. The new body would not be a physical body, which He was taking to heaven, but rather a social body, like a kingdom or a spiritual corporation.

And He assumed it on Pentecost when He sent the Holy Spirit upon the Apostles. They were the nucleus or germ of His new body, for they had been told that they were to represent Him when He was gone; to stand before princes and governors and speak the truths His Spirit would give them to speak. They were to evangelize the world, because they are His posthumous Self, His prolonged Personality, the scattered reapers of His harvest, the lights kindled as His great Light, the broken syllables of Him Who is the Word.

CHARLES M. SHELDON   (*1857–1941*)

FOLLOWING IN HIS STEPS

It is the personal element that Christian discipleship needs to emphasize. "The gift without the giver is bare." The Christianity that attempts to suffer by proxy is not the Christianity of Christ. Each individual Christian, business man, citizen, needs to follow in His steps along the path of personal sacrifice for Him. There is not a different path to-day from that of Jesus' own times. It is the same path. The call is . . . for a new discipleship, a new following of Jesus, more like the early, simple, apostolic, Christianity when the disciples left all and literally followed the Master. Nothing but a discipleship of this kind can face the destructive selfishness of the age, with any hope of overcoming it. There is a great quantity of nominal Christianity to-day. There is need of more of the real kind. We need a revival of the Christianity of Christ. We have, unconsciously, lazily, selfishly, formally, grown into a discipleship that Jesus Himself would not acknowledge. He would say to many of us, when we cry, "Lord, Lord," "I never knew you."

JEREMY TAYLOR   (*1613–1677*)

A LIFE GLORIOUS IN DARKNESS

However the person of Christ was depressed with a load of humble
accidents, and shadowed with the darkness of poverty and sad con-
tingencies, so that the Jews, and the contemporary ages of the Gentiles, and the apostles themselves, at first, could not discern the bright-
est essence of divinity; yet as a beauty artificially covered with a thin
cloud of cypress transmits its excellency to the eye, made more
greedy and apprehensive by that imperfect and weak restraint; so
was the sanctity and holiness of the life of Jesus glorious in its dark-
nesses, and found confessors and admirers even in the midst of those
despites which were done him upon the contrariant designs of malice
and contradictory ambition. Thus the wife of Pilate called him "that
just person"; Pilate pronounced him "guiltless"; Judas said he was
"innocent"; the devil himself called him "the Holy One of God."
For however it might concern any man's mistaken ends to mislike the
purpose of his preaching and spiritual kingdom, and those doctrines
which were destructive of their complacencies and carnal securities,
yet they could not deny but that he was a man of God, of exemplary
sanctity, of an angelical chastity, of a life sweet, affable, and com-
plying with human conversation, and as obedient to government
as the most humble children of the kingdom. And yet he was Lord
of all the world.

And certainly very much of this was with a design that he might
shine to all the generations and ages of the world, and become a
guiding star, and a "pillar of fire" to us in our journey. For we who
believe that Jesus was perfect God and perfect man, do also believe
that one minute of his intolerable passion, and every action of his,
might have been satisfactory, and enough for the expiation and recon-
cilement of ten thousand worlds; and God might upon a less effu-
sion of blood, and a shorter life of merit, if he had pleased, have accepted human nature to pardon and favour; but that the Holy
Jesus hath added so many excellent instances of holiness, and so

many degrees of passion, and so many kinds of virtues, it is that he might become an example to us and reconcile our wills to him, as well as our persons to his heavenly Father.

FRANCIS THOMPSON   (*1859–1907*)

"UNDER WHICH KING?"

'Under which king?' For under a king it must be, not merely a flag. No common aim can triumph, till it is crystallized in an individual, at once its child and ruler. Man himself must become incarnate in a man before his cause can triumph. Thus the universal Word became the individual Christ; that total God and total man being particularized in a single symbol, the cause of God and man might triumph. In Christ, therefore, centres and is solved that supreme problem of life—the marriage of the Unit with the Sum. In Him is perfectly shown forth the All for one and One for all, which is the justificatory essence of that substance we call Kingship; and from which, in so far as each particular kingship derogates, it forfeits justificatory right. When the new heavens and the new earth, which multitudinous Titans are so restlessly forging, at length stand visible to resting man, it needs no prophecy to foretell that they will be like the old, with head, and form, and hierarchic memberment, as the six-foot bracken is like the bracken at your knee. For out of all its disintegrations and confusion earth emerges, like a strong though buffeted swimmer, nearer to the unseen model and term of all social growth; which is the civil constitution of angeldom, and Uranian statecraft of imperatorial God.

HENRY VAN DYKE (*1852–1933*)

CENTRAL WORD OF HIS OWN PREACHING

The person of Jesus Christ stands solid in the history of man. He is indeed more substantial, more abiding, in human apprehensions, than any form of matter, or any mode of force. The conceptions of earth and air and fire and water change and melt around Him, as the clouds melt and change around an everlasting mountain peak. All attempts to resolve Him into a myth, a legend, an idea,—and hundreds of such attempts have been made,—have drifted over the enduring reality of His character and left not a rack behind. The result of all criticism, the final verdict of enlightened common sense, is that Christ is historical. He is such a person as men could not have imagined if they would, and would not have imagined if they could. He is neither Greek myth, nor Hebrew legend. The artist capable of fashioning Him did not exist, nor could he have found the materials. A non-existent Christianity did not spring out of the air and create a Christ. A real Christ appeared in the world and created Christianity. . . .

He Himself was the central word of His own preaching. He offered Himself to the world as the solution of its difficulties and the source of a new life. He asked men simply to believe in Him, to love Him, to follow Him. He called the self-righteous to humble themselves to His correction, the sinful to confide in His forgiveness, the doubting to trust His assurance, and the believing to accept His guidance into fuller light. To those who became His disciples He gave doctrine and instruction in many things. But to those who were not yet His disciples, to the world, He offered first of all Himself, not a doctrine, not a plan of life, but a living Person. . . .

An aura of wonder and mystery surrounded Jesus of Nazareth in His earthly life. All who came in contact with Him felt it; in love, if they desired to believe; in repulsion, if they hated to believe. In His presence, faith in the invisible, in the soul, in the future life, in God, revived and unfolded with new bloom and colour. In His presence hypocrisy was silenced and afraid, but sincere piety found a voice and prayed. This effluence of His character breathes from the whole record of His life. It was not merely what He said to men about the eternal verities that convinced them. It was something in Himself, an atmosphere surrounding Him, and a silent radiance shining from Him, that made it easier for them to believe in their own spiritual nature and in the Divine existence and presence. He drew out of their fallen and neglected hearts, by some celestial attraction, spontaneous, gentle, irresistible, a new efflorescence of faith and hope and love. Where He came a spiritual springtide flowed over the landscape of the inner life. Blossoms appeared in the earth and the time for the singing of birds was come.

HUGH WALPOLE   (1884–1941)

"A MAN LIKE NO OTHER MAN"

First the personality and character of Jesus Christ Himself. I had read that He had never existed. Georg Brandes, whom I had known once in Denmark, had written a book to prove it. I had been told and read again that there was nothing new in His doctrine, that He was a commonplace obscure rebel, that His divinity was a myth. I didn't know about His divinity, but I did know that, increasingly through my life, had I never been told a word about Him and had chanced upon the Lord's Prayer, the Sermon on the Mount, the sayings and the Parables, His tenderness to little children and all the lost, His anger and indignation, the details of the Last Supper and the Crucifixion, I would have cried out: "Here is a Man like no other man who has ever been, and in realizing Him I go beyond all earthly physical things into the world of the spirit. If He is true then the life of the spirit is true."

REBECCA WEST   (*1892*–   )

WHAT THE WORLD NEEDED

The spectacle of the rise of Fascism, and some contact with the Eastern Church, which is many centuries nearer primitive Christianity than the Western Church, have made it clear to me that the life of Christ should have been an incomparable blessing to man and a revelation of the way he must follow if he is not to be a beast, and a failure at that. Christ was an incarnate denunciation of cruelty. He was sinless, he was full of love, he was ingenious in devising prescriptions of mercy; he was what the world needed, he could have taught us how to make life a perpetual pleasure. Society could find nothing better to do with him than kill him. Here was a man who could have saved his life if he had dissimulated his virtue. He unveiled it, knowing that he made himself a target for man's arrows. Just as a great artist finds the perfect myth to symbolize the truth he has discovered, that shall sum it up in a form that is acceptable by the human faculty of attention, so his crucifixion demonstrated exactly what the assault of cruelty on the innocent means; and the subsequent services devised by the early Church commemorated the beauty of the virtue that was slain and the beastliness shown by the slayer, and reiterated the warning that this was the kind of crime man was inherently likely to commit unless he watched himself. There could be no more proper medicine for the human disease.

P. W. WILSON   (*1875*–   )

"HE CLAIMED THE HEARTS OF MEN"

Two thousand years ago He came, conquering and to conquer. Think first of His ambitious humility, His kingly and imperial modesty. Go to the British Museum and count the statues of Rameses, how many they are and in how hard a stone. See how every Roman Emperor has his bust. Note the faces of monarchs on coin and postage stamp. Trace the ciphers of Louis XIV on window and portal of his chapel at Versailles. How familiar are the moldened features of Napoleon. But the countenance of Christ, which did not see corruption—although instantly recognized by Paul, who never saw Him in the flesh—rose above this world, unrecorded by any sculptor or painter. Not a photograph remains of Him who made the sun. Yet who, of all rulers of men, was as ambitious as He? The potentates of history built cities and destroyed them, changed the names of provinces and lorded it over the map. He claimed the hearts of men. And because He was of no reputation among the classic artists of His day, whose dim frescoes still adorn what is left of pleasure places, like Pompeii, long desolate, He has since been highly exalted. The reverent brush of supremest genius has labored to reveal the glorious lineaments of the Son of Man. His countenance, faint or clear, is known, as if by instinct, to us all. The crude coloring of the Armenian altarpiece is one with the glowing splendors of Holman Hunt or Rubens, and no artist, whether of the brush, the chisel, the pen, or of daily life, can honestly endeavor to show Him forth without rising nobler from the effort. . . .

The historian of Rome, like Dio, ignored Him, and He was content to come without their observation. Knowing the fallibility of man, He yet entrusted His message to the memory of those who loved Him through death. He took no visible precautions to secure what the Speaker of the House of Commons call "the greater accuracy" of their reminiscences. He applied no critical safeguards. He wished nothing to survive that had not helped someone who needed help. And His confidence in the generation that slew Him was incredibly justified.

ESMÉ WINGFIELD-STRATFORD   (*1882–*)

A KINGDOM OF THE SPIRIT ALONE

When a leader of supreme spiritual genius did at last arise, in the person of Jesus of Nazareth, He found His message by no means acceptable to the majority of His countrymen. For Jesus had, in the highest sense, come to fulfil the task of the prophets. They had looked forward to a Prince of Peace who should establish a new and better order of things, but the invisible Kingdom that Jesus sought to found was of the spirit alone, and had its seat in the soul of every believer. God is a spirit, and to be a partaker of that spirit is the only thing that matters. No prophet had ever dared to push the claims of the spirit to such revolutionary extremes as this young enthusiast from Galilee. Worldly considerations were allowed to go by the board. His followers would not resist evil or oppression, would not even trouble to put by for a rainy day, because those who had become free of the Kingdom of Heaven would be too much absorbed in their new life to trouble about such things. There is something almost naive in the friendly advice proffered to a rich young man, to disencumber himself promptly of his fortune—but it is the naivete of genius. Just because the spiritual nature of man was really all in one to Jesus, and spiritual standards the only ones that he dreamed of applying, His personality acquired a force that proved irresistible.

He would have been an ideal candidate for the role of patriotic Messiah, had He condescended to fill it. But nothing was further from His thoughts than to prevail by violence, though His naturally fiery temper did once betray Him into clearing the temple courts with a whip. He avoided the least suggestion of turning aside from His spiritual quest to political or nationalistic aims. To one whose treasure was in Heaven, the payment of taxes to Caesar was no grievance. As He explained to the Roman governor, His kingdom was not of this world, for then His followers would have fought. Indeed when the staunchest of them, Peter, had shown fight at His arrest, Jesus had promptly commanded him to sheathe his sword, adding His final verdict upon methods of violence:

"All they that take the sword shall perish by the sword."

It is no wonder that the little band of disciples, who had perhaps cherished, up to this last moment, some forlorn hope of their Leader's invincibility, were seized with a sudden panic and fled for their lives into the darkness.

It was, had they only known it, this very refusal of Jesus to rely on any but spiritual weapons that rendered Him invincible. The combined forces of Church and State might unite to crush the obscure and deserted Evangelist. But as the Chinese sage, Lao Tse, had long ago divined, the man who has the secret of life is immune to violence.

VIRGINIA WOOLF   (*1882–1941*)

MADE RELIGION KNOWN

What the Christian religion is has been laid down once and for all by the founder of that religion in words that can be read by all in a translation of singular beauty; and whether or not we accept the interpretation that has been put on them, we cannot deny them to be words of the most profound meaning. It can thus safely be said that whereas few people know what medicine is, or what law is, everyone who owns a copy of the New Testament knows what religion meant in the mind of its founder. Therefore, when in the year 1935 the daughters of educated men said that they wished to have the profession of religion opened to them, the priests of that profession, who correspond roughly to the doctors and barristers in the other professions, were forced not merely to consult some statute or charter which reserves the right to practice that profession professionally to the male sex; they were forced to consult the New Testament. They did so; and the result, as the Commissioners point out, was that they found that "the Gospels show us that our Lord regarded men and women alike as members of the same spiritual kingdom, as children of God's family, and as possessors of the same spiritual capacities. . . ." In proof of this they quote: "There is neither male nor female: for ye are all one in Christ Jesus" (Gal. iii, 28). It would seem then that the founder of Christianity believed that neither training nor sex was needed for this profession. He chose his disciples from the working class from which he sprang himself. The prime qualification was some rare gift which in those early days was bestowed capriciously upon carpenters and fishermen, and upon women also.

MESSIAH

MATTHEW ARNOLD   *(1822–1888)*

"HERE WAS A VERY GREAT SPIRIT"

Jesus came, calling himself the Messiah, the Son of Man, the Son of God; and the question is, what is the true meaning of these assertions of his, and of all his teaching? It is the same question we had about the Old Testament. Is the language scientific, or is it, as we say, *literary?*—that is, the language of poetry and emotion, approximative language, thrown out, as it were, at certain great objects which the human mind augurs and feels after, but not language accurately defining them? Popular religion says, we know, that the language is scientific; that the God of the Old Testament is a great Personal First Cause, who thinks and loves (for this too, it seems, we ought to have added), the moral and intelligent Governor of the universe. Learned religion, the metaphysical theology of our bishops, proves or confirms this by abstruse reasoning from our ideas of cause, design, existence, identity, and so on. Popular religion rests it altogether on *miracle.* . . .

The bringer of light and happiness, the calmer and pacifier, or invigorator and stimulator, is one of the chiefest of doctors. Such a doctor was Jesus; such an operator, by an efficacious and real, though little observed and little employed agency, upon what we, in the language of popular superstition, call the *unclean spirits,* but which are to be designated more literally and more correctly as the *uncleared, unpurified spirits,* which came raging and madding before him. This his own language shows, if we know how to read it. *"What does it matter whether I say, Thy sins are forgiven thee! or whether I say, Arise and walk!"* And again: *"Thou art made whole; sin no more, lest a worse thing befall thee."* His reporters, we must remember, are men who saw thaumaturgy in all that Jesus did, and who saw in all sickness and disaster visitations from God, and they bend his language accordingly. But indications enough remain to show the line of the Master, his perception of the large part of moral cause in many kinds of disease, and his method of addressing to this part his cure.

It would never have done, indeed, to have men pronouncing right and left that this and that was a judgment, and how, and for what, and on whom. And so, when the disciples, seeing an afflicted person, asked whether this man had done sin or his parents, Jesus checked them and said, "Neither the one nor the other, but that the works of God might be made manifest in him." Not the less clear is his own belief in the moral root of much physical disease, and in moral therapeutics; and it is important to note well the instance of miracles where this belief comes in. For the action of Jesus in these instances, however it may be amplified in the reports, was real; but it is not, therefore, as popular religion fancies, thaumaturgy,—it is not what people are fond of calling the *supernatural,* but what is better called the *non-natural*. It is, on the contrary, like the grace of Raphael, or the grand style of Phidias, eminently natural: but it is above common, low-pitched nature; it is a line of nature not yet mastered or followed out.

Its significance as a guarantee of the authenticity of Christ's mission is trivial, however, compared with the guarantee furnished by his sayings. Its importance is in its necessary effect upon the beholders and reporters. This element of what was really wonderful, unprecedented, and unaccountable, they had actually before them; and we may estimate how it must have helped and seemed to sanction that tendency which in any case would have carried them, circumstanced as they were, to find all the performances and career of Jesus miraculous. . . .

The more we convince ourselves of the liability of the New Testament writers to mistake, the more we really bring out the greatness and worth of the New Testament. For the more the reporters were fallible and prone to delusion, the more does Jesus become independent of the mistakes they made, and unaffected by them. We have plain proof that here was a very great spirit; and the greater he was, the more certain were his disciples to misunderstand him. The depth of their misunderstanding of him is really a kind of measure of the height of his superiority. And this superiority is what interests us in the records of the New Testament; for the New Testament

exists to reveal Jesus Christ, not to establish the immunity of its writers from error.

Jesus himself is not a New Testament writer; he is the object of
description and comment to the New Testament writers. As the
Old Testament speaks about the Eternal and bears an invaluable
witness to him, without yet ever adequately in words defining and expressing him; so, and even yet more, do the New Testament writers
speak about Jesus and give a priceless record of him, without adequately and accurately comprehending him. They are altogether on
another plane from Jesus, and their mistakes are not his. It is not
Jesus himself who relates his own miracles to us; who tells us of his
own apparitions after his death; who alleges his crucifixion and sufferings as a fulfilment of the prophecy; *The Eternal keepeth all the
bones of the righteous so that not one of them is broken;* who proves
salvation to be by Christ alone, from the promise to Abraham being
made to *seed* in the singular number, not the plural. If, therefore,
the human mind is now drawing away from reliance on miracles,
coming to perceive the community of character which pervades
them all, to understand their natural laws, so to speak,—their loose
mode of origination and their untrustworthiness,—and is inclined
rather to distrust the dealer in them than to pin its faith upon him;
then it is good for the authority of Jesus, that his reporters are evidently liable to ignorance and error. . . .

Now, the more we regard the reporters of Jesus as men liable to
err, full of the turbid Jewish fancies about "the grand consummation" which were then current, the easier we can understand these
men inevitably putting their own eschatology into the mouth of
Jesus, when they had to report his discourse about the kingdom of
God and the troubles in store for the Jewish nation, and the less
need we have to make Jesus a co-partner in their eschatology.

Again, the futility of such demonstrations from prophecy as those
of which we have given examples, and generally of all that Jewish
exegesis, based on a mere unintelligent catching at the letter of the
Old Testament, isolated from its context and real meaning, of which
the New Testament writers give us so much, begins to disconcert

attentive readers of the Bible more and more, and to be felt by them as an embarrassment to the cause of Jesus, not a support. Well, then, it is good for the authority of Jesus, that those who established it by arguments of this sort should be clearly men of their race and time, not above its futile methods of reasoning and demonstration. The more they were this, and the more they were sure to mix up much futile logic and exegesis with their presentation of Jesus, the less is Jesus himself responsible for such logic and exegesis, or at all dependent upon it. He may himself have rated such argumentation at precisely its true value, and have based his mission and authority upon no grounds but solid ones. Whether he did so or not, his hearers and reporters were sure to base it on their own fantastic grounds also, and to credit Jesus with doing the same.

In short, the more we conceive Jesus as almost as much over the heads of his disciples and reporters then, as he is over the heads of the mass of so-called Christians now, the more we see his disciples to have been, as they were, men raised by a truer moral susceptiveness above their countrymen, but in intellectual conceptions and habits much on a par with them, all the more do we make room, so to speak, for Jesus to be a personage immensely great and wonderful; as wonderful as anything his reporters imagined him to be, though in a different manner.

SHOLEM ASCH   (*1880–*   )

"THE TONGUE OF THE POWER"

Translated by Maurice Samuels

It was in the days when Tiberius was Emperor in Rome, Vitellius proconsul in Syria, Pontius Pilate procurator of Judaea, Herod Antipater ethnarch of Galilee, and Joseph Kaifa (better known as Caiaphas) High Priest in Jerusalem, that a man (shall we use that designation?) went out from one of the ravines which enclose the modest little town of Nazareth. He left behind him the hill country and descended into the Valley of Jezreel, threading his way on foot past the settlements and farms which dotted the level stretches, till he came to the shore of the Sea of Gennesaret, and the town of K'far Nahum, or Capernaum. It was that time of the year which follows on the rainy season. The earth was heavy with dampness, as it always is there in the early spring, but, again as always, its renewal was already evident to the senses. A tender, grassy carpet was stretched out from the lower reaches of the hills of Gilead, and on this the man trod, leaving behind him the imprint of his footsteps. But it was not only on the soil which sustained him that he left his imprint; with every footstep he impressed himself upon the form of all the earth, imparting to it the aspect which it presents to this day.

What was it that constituted the coming of this incomprehensible personality, which has become for the entire Christian world the symbol of the coming of the Messiah? He himself divided his advent into two parts: in the first he came to prepare man and the world for the Kingdom of God; in the second he would come upon the clouds in heaven as judge and ruler of the Kingdom of Heaven when it should have begun on earth.

What was the substance of his activity in his first coming? It may be divided, again into three parts: to bring the tidings of the authority which had been given into his keeping by the father in heaven: to make of his sojourn among men an example of the life which is guided and informed by the authority of the faith; to accept of his own free will a martyr's death, paying this price for his mission and for the authority of the Messiah which had been entrusted to his keeping.

What was the substance of his teaching? It consisted primarily— and this we must bear constantly in mind—in faith in the heavenly father, who was the one and only God of Israel, but Who had spread out His grace upon all mankind and would send His Savior for the redemption of all. . . .

Jesus of Nazareth was not merely a Rabbi of his time; had he been that, he would have been nothing more. If we seek to evaluate the full significance of the message and life of Jesus, who has become the most important single factor in our civilization, we must gather up the strength to leap across the frightful barriers—seas of blood and bitterness, the ashes of autos-da-fé, and the bones of slaughtered martyrs—which separate the two religions; and, standing side by side, we must then examine the purely religious values which are involved. With all its fidelity to the spirit and style of the Jewish scholars of his time, the teaching of Jesus did nevertheless pass beyond the boundary, to stand in a place of its own. Had it not done so it would most probably have remained within the framework of Jewish interpretation, and would not have created a world religion. What was quite new in the teaching of Jesus was that for the first time there appeared in Israel a teacher who, while in agreement with the law of Moses, did not derive his authority from that law, merely interpreting it according to his own lights, as others had always done. But instead he appealed to an authority which had been entrusted to his keeping.

"Ye have heard that it hath been said, Thou shalt love thy neighbor, and hate thine enemy. *But I say unto you,* love your enemies, bless them that curse you, do good to them that hate you, pray for them which despitefully use you, and persecute you; that ye may be the children of your father which is in heaven: for he maketh his sun to rise on the evil and the good, and sendeth rain on the just and on the unjust." Now the whole of this passage, without those words *But I say unto you* could, without much difficulty, be fitted into the moral aphorisms of the Ethics of the Fathers, as the independent view of a Rabbi, and as an acceptable rule of right conduct. But the "I say unto you" changes the passage in that one essential character, placing upon it the stamp of the mandate. "For," Matthew reports, "he spoke as one having authority." This, then, is not exposition of the Law of Moses as given on Sinai; it is "the tongue of the power." He had heard this from the lips of God. And new again in the history of all Jewish doctrine was the fact that a teacher or lawgiver included himself in the article of faith. "Whosoever shall confess me before men, him will I confess before my father which is in heaven."

The element of authority in the teaching of Jesus became the cornerstone of the Christian faith, the foundation of the Pauline theology. In it Paul found justification for the creation of the new religion and for compromises with the law. For it was only by means of the authority which Jesus claimed to have in his keeping that the Pauline theology was able to open new sources of religious values and spread them over new areas of the human race.

We may even put it thus: Jesus not only thought of himself as carrying the mandate; he considered himself part of the mandate. He included himself in the substance of the faith. He is a significant part of it by "the flesh and blood of the new covenant." He is, moreover, able to distribute the authority among his own messengers. "Verily I say unto you, whatsoever ye shall bind on earth shall be bound in heaven: and whatsoever ye shall loose on earth shall be loosed in heaven." And again: "For wherever two or three are gathered in my name, there am I in the midst of them." Are not these like words which God Himself has spoken: "There where my name is mentioned I shall come to bless you." . . .

Everything else that is comprised in the life, the acts, the sayings, and the death of Jesus, however necessary it may have been for the manifestation of his mission, however important a role it played in the subsequent theology, ritual, and mysticism of Christianity, and however creative it may have been in the field of faith, was not a specific factor of his Messiahship; it was only given standing, and strengthened in its influence, by being associated with the first principle of his Messiahship, namely his special authority, deriving direct from God, to fulfill the first part of his mission and prepare the world for the Kingdom of Heaven. The birth of Christianity is not to be attributed to the fact that its founder, Jesus, was a high, ethical personality. There were in his time many high, ethical personalities. The submission of his life to the strict law (we must not forget that it was Paul who laid the foundations of the separate faith of Christianity; Jesus stood, like every other Jew, "under the law") was self-understood. Nor was it for the healing of the sick, the restoring of the dead, and the performance of other miracles, that Jesus was accepted by his followers as the Messiah. There were in his day many, many others who performed the same wonders. Every Jewish scholar who was a member of the Sanhedrin had to be a practicable magician, so that he might not be taken in by the practices of other magicians. In his days wonders were so natural that no one "wondered" at them. In every city which the Apostles visited they encountered magicians, soothsays and star-gazers who performed miracles. No Messiah had ever been proclaimed for the miracles he had performed; and there is a specific statement in the law, or Torah: "Miracles are not the signs of a prophet." Nor was it in the magnificence of his martyr's death, which has become such a source of religious inspiration to the civilized world, that Jesus demonstrated his Messiahship to his disciples. There were many in his day who died magnificently for their convictions and ideals, and were not proclaimed Messiahs. The deeds of Jesus of Nazareth acquire their religious value and become factors of high importance in the new faith, through the proclamation that he holds in his hand the authority of God—as the Messiah; through Peter in Caesarea Philippi; through the declaration of Jesus that he "will sit on the right hand of the power and will come with the clouds of heaven," made at the trial before the High Priest; and through many other indications that he is the "Son of man"; in short, through the claim that he holds in his hand the authority of the Messiah, given to him by his father in heaven. . . .

This is not the place for the rehearsal of the material in which scholars, basing themselves on careful historical research, have proved that in any event, whoever did happen to be the instrument of the death of Jesus, it was not historic Jewry. With that aspect of the question I cannot deal here at length, but as a Jew I may permit myself what the devout Christian may not: I may speculate on the place which Jesus of Nazareth would have occupied in the spiritual life of the Jewish people, by virtue of his teaching, his acts, and his martyr death, if he had not proclaimed that he carried with him the authority of the Messiah.

Such a one, had he lived in the time of the first Temple, or in the Babylonian interlude, or even in the early days of the Return, when the people was still in the condition to accept prophets, would undoubtedly have been placed in their ranks. His life would have been an inspiration, like that of Elisha or Jeremiah, and his death would have been sanctified like that of the Ten Martyrs of Hadrian. In his own day, when the people was no longer in the condition to accept prophets, he would have been included among the Rabbis. His sayings, his parables and his doctrine would have been among the pearls of the Ethics of the Fathers; his prayer would have been included in our psalter; his life would have been crowned with the crown of the martyr in the pages of the Agadah. We have lost a Prophet. We miss, even to our own day, the golden page of the sayings of Jesus; that, however, was the price we paid in order that the Jewish genius might give the world a redeemer who brought it under the authority of God.

JACQUES BÉNIGNE BOSSUET   (1627–1704)

THE TRIUMPH OF THE KING

Translator Anonymous

I shall not dwell upon the mistaken notion which even the Apostles affixed to the character of the Messiah, but shall endeavor to explain the sentiments which the holy Jesus entertained upon that subject. I cannot observe without an emotion of astonishment, the conduct of the Son of God in this particular! I see him through the course of his ministry displaying, even with parade, the lowliness of his condition; and when the hour approaches which is to terminate in his death, the word Glory dwells on his lips, and he discourses with his disciples of nothing but his greatness. On the eve of his ignominious death, when the traitor Judas had just gone from him big with his execrable intention, it was then that the Saviour of the world cried out with a divine ardour, "Now is the Son of Man glorified." Tell me in what manner is he going to be glorified? What means the emphatic word *now?* Is he to rise above the clouds, and thence to launch vengeance on his foes? or is the angelic hierarchy, seraphs, dominations, principalities, and powers! to defend him from high, and pay him instant adoration? Ah, no! he is going to be degraded, to submit to excruciating pain, and to expire with malefactors. This is what he denominates his glory; this is what he esteems his triumph. Behold him as he makes his entrance into Jerusalem, riding on an ass. Ah, Christians! let us not be ashamed of our Heavenly King; let the sceptic, the deist deride, if they please, this humble appearance of the Son of God; but I will tell human arrogance, this lowly exhibition was worthy of the King who came into this world, in order to degrade, to crush beneath his feet all terrestrial grandeur! . . .

The last time he entered Jerusalem, it was in order to die; and in consonance with the sentiments of the Messiah, to die is to reign. How dignified was his conduct through the whole process of his passion! how august his deportment at the tribunal of Pilate! Did he not humble the majesty of the Roman fasces by the dignity of silence? Let Pilate return into the pretorium, for the purpose of interrogating our Saviour; he will make no reply, but to one question: the Roman president says, "Art thou a King?" The Son of God, who had disdained to utter any answer to the other questions of his judge, no sooner heard his title to royalty mentioned, than he abruptly replies, "Thou sayest that I am a King; to this end was I born; and for this cause came I into this world, that I should bear witness unto the truth."

. . . If then Jesus is your King, pay to him the homage of your actions, as well as your words; and if the prince of darkness is your king, add, without constraint, the homage of your words to your actions. But heaven and earth forbid we should ever make this sacrilegious choice. Let us conclude with renewing our vow of allegiance to our celestial King. Oh, Jesus! Royal Master, to whom we so justly and exclusively belong, who has redeemed us with the price of unutterable love and unbounded charity, we acknowledge thee to be our Sovereign; we offer thee this day a solemn dedication of ourselves; thy law shall be the law of our hearts. I will sing thy praise; I will never cease proclaiming thy mercies; I vow to thee eternal fidelity; and in this entire consecration of myself to thy service, may I live, and may I die.

GEORG BRANDES   (*1842–1927*)

HIS HISTORICITY QUESTIONED

Translated by Edwin Bjorkman

Every student of ancient religious rites knows full well . . . the ideal image of one unjustly tortured and martyred; of one tormented for the very reason that he is good and righteous; of one chosen as a victim by human malice and bearing his sufferings for the sake of the rest . . . that this image had been drawn long before the time when the historical Jesus is supposed to have come into this world. The figure of the suffering Messiah was the personification of the Jewish people as oppressed and maltreated by their neighbors, and yet as stronger than these because they were the mouthpieces of truth and justice. This ideal of majesty, of undeserved suffering, of superior humanity, is already discernible in the Second Isaiah. In another shape, the same ideal revealed itself to Plato in his contemplation of the spiritual superiority of Socrates, whose reward was an ignominious death.

In other words, the Christ figure as an ideal of spiritual superiority, of love for humanity, of charity and purity, was many centuries older than the noble-minded Galilean man of the people who, nineteen hundred years ago, was said to have given historic embodiment to this prototype. The same figure will survive him for many centuries to come, even if he, as now seems likely, should never have existed.

In the last analysis, therefore, it is of no importance how his life on earth is said to have shaped itself. We no longer ask whether Jesus was born by a miracle, whether he wrought miraculous cures, or whether he drove out evil spirits by miraculous means . . . we no longer know what a devil is any more than we know what is meant by a virgin birth or any other miraculous event.

LEWIS BROWNE   (*1897–*   )

A WONDROUS LOVE PREACHED

Whether Jesus himself was convinced he was the Messiah is a problem still unsolved. His refusal to make the claim in public, the almost too astute way in which he avoided a direct answer whenever the question was put to him, presents to this day a dilemma to the faithful. But it is certain that many of those who followed Jesus believed him to be the Messiah. The sight of that ragged young Jew hurrying beneath the hot sun of Galilee, poor, unlearned, yet able to breathe a perfect frenzy of hope and cheer into vast throngs of forlorn derelicts, must have seemed proof indisputable that he was indeed the "Anointed One." There was a wondrous love in his preaching and, coupled with it, an air of certainty, of authority. For five hundred years some Messiah had been awaited, and more than once it had been men of the basest stuff that had been mistaken for Him. Charlatans and madmen, arrant knaves and driveling fools, had time and again been hailed by the hysterical mob as the Awaited One. Is it any wonder, therefore, that an exalted person like this young carpenter, Jesus, should have been hailed likewise? . . .

That Jesus was indeed an exalted person is hardly to be doubted. Even when one has discounted all the legends . . . one still is left with an extraordinary personality to explain. It must be remembered that Jesus was not the only preacher of kindness or worker of miracles that ever had been known among the Jews. Many such men had preceded him; many there were in his own day; and many more came after him. But none other succeeded in so impressing his character on his followers.

MARY BAKER EDDY   (*1821–1910*)

HIS MESSIANIC MISSION

To the senses, Jesus was the son of man: In Science, man is the son of God. The material senses could not cognize the Christ, or Son of God: it was Jesus' approximation to this state of being that made him the Christ-Jesus, the Godlike, the anointed.

*   *   *   *

The only record of our Master as a public benefactor, or personal Saviour, opens when he was thirty years of age; owing in part, perhaps, to the Jewish law that none should teach or preach in public under that age. Also, it is natural to conclude that at this juncture he was specially endowed with the Holy Spirit; for he was given the new name, Messiah, or Jesus Christ,—the God-anointed; even as, at times of special enlightenment, Jacob was called Israel; and Saul, Paul.

The third event of this eventful period,—a period of such wonderful spiritual import to mankind!—was the advent of a higher Christianity.

From this dazzling, God-crowned summit, the Nazarene stepped suddenly before the people and their schools of philosophy; Gnostic, Epicurean, and Stoic. He must stem these rising angry elements, and walk serenely over their fretted, foaming billows.

Here the cross became the emblem of Jesus' history; while the central point of his Messianic mission was peace, good will, love, teaching, and healing.

* * * *

Three years he went about doing good. He had for thirty years been preparing to heal and teach divinely; but his three-years mission was a marvel of glory; its chaplet, a grave to mortal sense dishonored—from which sprang a sublime and everlasting victory!

* * * *

Only three years a personal Saviour! yet the foundations he laid are as eternal as Truth, the chief cornerstone.

MICHAEL, CARDINAL VON FAULHABER   (*1869–*)

"THE ONE SUPERMAN OF HISTORY"

Translated by George D. Smith

Christ is the fulfilment of the Old Covenant. In a messianic prophecy (Gen. xlix, 26) he is hailed from afar as "the desire of the everlasting hills." From the tents of the Patriarchs, those hills on the horizon of antiquity, from the scrolls of the prophets, from the messianic types, from the Psalms, from the whole liturgy of the early Bible comes a greeting and a foreshadowing of the Lord's Anointed. From the third to the sixth hour, from the sixth hour to the ninth the cry of longing becomes louder still. And at the eleventh hour a mood lay over the Promised Land rather like that of the whole of created nature, when it seems to hold its breath as the red of dawn appears over the eastern mountains with the rising of the sun. When the last of the prophets, John the Precursor, preached his Advent sermons on the banks of the Jordan, all the people went forth to hear him, and the authorities asked him the official question: "Art thou He that art to come, or look we for another?" (Luke vii, 19 *seq*.) And when the first Apostles were called, they ran one to another with the joyous news: "We have found Him of whom Moses in the law and the prophets did write" (John i, 45). Striking proofs, these, of the intensity with which men longed for the expected Saviour. The prophet Isaias makes the Messias say: "The Spirit of the Lord is upon me, because the Lord hath anointed me. He hath sent me to preach to the meek, to heal the contrite of heart, and to preach a release to the captives and deliverance to them that are shut up; to proclaim the acceptable year of the Lord" (Is. lxi, 1–3). In the fullness of time Jesus read out this passage in the synagogue of His own village; then He handed back the scroll and said: "This day is fulfilled this scripture in your ears" (Luke iv, 16–21). With these words He publicly announced: "I am the fulfilment, the Omega of the messianic prophecies."

Christ is the redemption of the Old Covenant. Men are able even after their death to prolong their activity for a while in their children or their schools, in their books and their works. Perhaps even a monument to their memory may for a long time cast its shadow on some strip of earth. But never has a man been heralded for centuries before his birth, as the child of Bethlehem was heralded by the prophets. Some men have been honored in history by the name of Great; but not even a cock-crow has foretold their birth. The Child of Bethlehem, the greatest of the great, was greeted for centuries before His birth by the welcome of the Messianic prophecies. This fact alone is a proof of the Divinity of Emmanuel; it is itself a piece of the Gospel, a unique privilege, an indication that Christ is the one Superman of history. He is superhuman because millenniums after His death the traces of His blessings cannot disappear. Superhuman because long before His birth as the "angel of the covenant" He was guiding the chosen people, and Himself decided in what people and of what mother He should be born.

Christ is the Saviour of the world in the widest sense of the word; He is the Redeemer for every world, for pre-Christian as well as for post-Christian humanity. "It hath well pleased the Father through Him to reconcile all things to Himself, making peace through the blood of His cross, both as to the things that are on earth and the things that are in heaven" (Col. i, 19 *seq*.). Our vision would be short-sighted and incomplete if we thought only of the period after Christ. . . .

Christ is the absolute Alpha of the New Covenant. In the Gospel of His public life the fundamental truths of Christianity for all time are revealed. The truth of truths, that of the Divinity of Christ, shines out from every page of the Gospel; from His words and from His miracles, from His ethical teaching and from the ethical greatness of His personality. He and the Father are one. He who sees Him sees the Father also.

ABBÉ CONSTANT FOUARD   (*1837–1904*)

PROPHET, KING, MESSIAH

Translated by George F. X. Griffiths

In the very hour of man's fall God had declared to Adam that One should be born of the seed of the woman; and thereafter He set apart from the race of Sem one people, of the stock of Abraham, and from that people one tribe,—the tribe of Juda,—from which was to be born the Messiah.

That mysterious Figure stands forth still more clearly, more perspicuously, as the years hasten on toward the realizing of all expectation of Him. As Moses sees Him, He is a Prophet, his equal in power: in David's eyes He is a King, His Son, heir to his glories, as well as his misfortunes. His very Name is discovered to the Psalmist; this King of all times to come and of the timeless Eternity is to be called the Anointed of God, the Christ, the Messiah. One after another the Prophets added each a line to the limning of this portraiture which foreshadowed the advent of Divinity. Bethlehem is to be His birthplace, Galilee his native land, a Virgin His Mother. He will preach the Good News to the pure and humble of heart. He will enter Sion mounted upon the foal of an ass. He shall be despised and rejected, led to the slaughter as a Lamb; His vestments shall be parted, lots shall be cast for His tunic, His hands and His feet pierced; vinegar shall moisten His lips. Yet shall He become subject to the malefactor's death only that He may show forth the glory of His Resurrection; His soul snatched from the deep pit, and His body from corruption, that He may seat Himself upon the right hand of Jehovah, henceforth to reign forever in the world of human hearts.

Such was the Messiah for Whom all true Israelites waited in expectation.

JULIUS KATZENSTEIN   (*1890–*   )

A MESSIAH IN A SPECIAL SENSE

Translated by Huntley Paterson

Jesus . . . was so completely the child of the Jewish life of his age, that it would only be necessary to write a history of the period, the country, and the people in it, in order to marshal all the details of his personality and fate. His peculiar tragedy lay in the part of his *personality* which failed to strike the right note in those whom he wished to serve and to save. The overemphasis of his personality, and the failure of the expectations, which he himself has awakened, led and could not help leading to the hopeless and tragic disillusionment of his followers. When the Messiah ceases to be a leader, a fulfiller, and a herald, and moved by exaggerated egoism aims at being an example and a reformer, his office falls to pieces in his hands. This constituted the tragedy of Jesus, and the turning point in his career.

For Jesus, the whole gravity of the conditions in the age in which he lived were implicit in his meeting with John the Baptist. There in front of his very eyes stood the forerunner of the Messiah, the first or possibly even the last step towards fulfilment! The advent of the Messiah was a matter of days or at most a few years. The great day was at hand and it was high time for those whom it might concern to examine themselves with a view to discovering whether they had done all that lay in their power, or whether still further efforts might not be expected of them. It was incumbent on every man to look into his own heart and decide whether he was a rabbi, a teacher, or a fulfiller, a Messiah. This is what Jesus did. And to carry out his tests he withdrew into the wilderness. . . .

The man who was to be the Messiah was expected at that time to have a threefold qualification. He was to be the King-Messiah, the destroyer of the pagan world. . . . The terrible fate of those who had fought in the War of Liberation did not encourage Jesus to choose this path, and it would perhaps have been unreasonable to expect him to do so, seeing that, like the moderate Pharisees, he believed in spiritual and not material resistance. The second qualification of the Messiah was that he should be a great student of the Torah. . . . If it was not modesty that made Jesus repudiate the possession of this quality, it was at all events his recognition of the fact that the age in which he lived required understanding rather than knowledge. . . . Thirdly, the Messiah was expected to establish a rule of peace and happiness on earth and to free mankind from sorrow for evermore. Implicit in this expectation was a firm conviction that unrelieved distress was an unfavourable basis for the free development of the soul. But to the thoughtful Galilean, brought up in poor and humble circumstances, with the example of John the Baptist, a penniless and ascetic recluse, before his eyes, such an idea did not appeal in the light of a life mission.

*   *   *   *

But it very soon became clear that he confessed himself to be the Messiah in a very special sense, that is to say, he was a Messiah who had given up all idea of gratifying the longings of his people, but came forward with claims of his own. True, in the wilderness Jesus had at first repudiated and then accepted the call. But that first act of repudiation was really a refusal, a failure, a denial.

* * * *

The final failure and misunderstanding took place before Pilate. The famous question was put: "Art thou the King of the Jews?" At this time the concept King-Messiah conveyed a very different meaning to the Jew from what it did to the Roman. The latter regarded the title as one which in any case laid claim to an office, and a position of authority, which was directed against the Roman imperium, and was therefore high treason. The reply: "Thou sayest," given by Jesus, amounted at once to a confession and an evasion; but in any case it was a reply which sealed his fate and delivered him up to it.

And thus fate struck him down. It was a Jewish fate, the fate of a particular period, and of a man of that period, who, to the best of his ability, had tried to serve his people. . . . But after his death fate dealt kindly by him, and, in the minds of those who called themselves his followers, he was endowed with immortality in other worlds and other spheres.

JOHN LOCKE   (*1632–1704*)

MADE THE TRUE GOD KNOWN

In this state of darkness and error, in reference to the "true God," our Saviour found the world. But the clear revelation he brought with him, dissipated this darkness; made the "one invisible true God" known to the world: and that with such evidence and energy, that polytheism and idolatry have nowhere been able to withstand it; but wherever the preaching of truth he delivered, and the light of the gospel hath come, those mists have been dispelled. And in effect, we see that since our Saviour's time, the "belief of one God" has prevailed and spread itself over the face of the earth. For even the light that the Messiah brought into the world with him, we must ascribe the owning and profession of one God. . . . This light the world needed, and this light is received from him: that there is but "one God" and he "eternal, invisible": not like to visible objects nor to be represented by them. . . .

Only those who have believed Jesus to be the Messiah, and have taken him to be their King, with a sincere endeavor after righteousness, in obeying his law; shall have their past sins not imputed to them; and shall have that faith taken instead of obedience, where frailty and weakness made them transgress and sin prevailed after conversion, in those who hunger and thirst after righteousnes (or perfect obedience) and do not allow themselves in acts of disobedience and rebellion, against the laws of that kingdom they are entered into.

He did not expect, it is true, a perfect obedience, void of slips and falls: he knew our make, and the weakness of our constitution too well, and was sent with a supply for that defect. Besides, perfect obedience was the righteousness of the law of works; and then the reward would be of debt and not of grace; and to such there was no need of faith to be imputed to them for righteousness. They stood upon their own legs, were just already, and needed no allowance to be made them for believing Jesus to be the Messiah, taking him for their king, and becoming his subjects. But that Christ does require obedience, sincere obedience, is evident from the law he himself delivers (unless he can be supposed to give and inculcate laws, only to have them disobeyed) and from the sentence he will pass when he comes to judge.

These two, faith and repentance, i.e. believing Jesus to be the Messiah, and a good life, are the indispensable conditions of the new covenant, to be performed by all those who would obtain eternal life.

To this, it is likely, it will be objected by some, that to believe only that Jesus of Nazareth is the Messiah is only an historical, and not a justifying or saving faith.

To which I answer, that I allow to the makers of systems and their followers to invent and use what distinctions they please, and to call things by what names they think fit. But I cannot allow to them or to any man an authority to make a religion for me, or to alter that which God has revealed. And if they please to call the believing that which our Saviour and his apostles preached, and proposed alone to be believed, an historical faith; they have their liberty. But they must have a care how they deny it to be a justifying or saving faith, when our Saviour and his apostles have declared it so to be; and taught no other which men should receive and whereby they should be made believers unto eternal life: unless they can so far make bold with our Saviour, for the sake of their beloved systems, as to say that he forgot what he came into the world for; and that he and his apostles did not instruct people right in the way and mysteries of salvation. For that this is the sole doctrine pressed and required to be believed in the whole tenor of our Saviour's and his apostles' preaching, we have showed through the whole history of the evangelist and the Acts. And I challenge them to show that there was any other doctrine, upon their assent to which, or disbelief of it, men were pronounced believers or unbelievers; and accordingly received into the church of Christ, as members of his body; as far as mere believing could make them so: or else kept out of it.

JOHN MASEFIELD   (*1878–*   )

THE DREAM OF PROCULA

PROCULA

Dear, forgive me, if I come again
About this Jesus, but I long to know
What Herod said. Did he dismiss him?

PILATE

No.

He sent him back for me to try,
The charge being local.

PROCULA

Have you tried him?

PILATE

Ay,

Henceforth he will be kept outside the walls,
Now, listen, wife: whatever dream befalls,
Never again send word to me in Court
To interrupt a case. The Jews made sport
Of what you dreamed and what you bade me fear
About this Jesus man. The laws are clear.
I must apply them, asking nothing more
Than the proved truth. Now tell me of your dream:
What was it? Tell me then.

PROCULA

I saw a gleam
Reddening the world out of a blackened sky,
Then in the horror came a hurt thing's cry
Protesting to the death what no one heard.

PILATE

What did it say?

PROCULA

A cry, no spoken word
But crying, and a horror, and a sense
Of one poor man's naked intelligence,
Pitted against the world and being crushed.
Then, waking, there was noise; a rabble rushed
Following this Jesus here, crying for blood,

Like beasts half-reptile in a jungle-mud.
And all the horror threatening in the dim,
In what I dreamed of, seemed to threaten him. . . .
So in my terror I sent word to you,
Begging you dearly to have nought to do
With that wise man.

PILATE

I grant he says wise things.
Too wise by half, and too much wisdom brings
Trouble, I find. It disagrees with men.
We must protect him from his wisdom then.

PROCULA

What have you done to him?

PILATE

Made it more hard
For him to wrangle in the Temple yard
Henceforth, I hope.

[Enter Longinus]

PROCULA

You have not punished him?

PILATE

Warned him.

LONGINUS

The envoy from the Sanhedrim
Is here, my Lord.

PILATE

Go. I must see him. Stay.
You and your women, keep within to-day.
It is the Jewish Feast and blood runs high

Against us Romans when the zealots cry
Songs of their old Deliverance through the land.
Stay, yet. Lord Herod says that he has planned
To visit us to-night, have all prepared.

PROCULA

I would have gone to Herod had I dared,
To plead for this man Jesus. All shall be
Made ready. Dear, my dream oppresses me. *Exit.*

PILATE

It is this earthquake weather: it will end
After a shock. Farewell.

[*Enter Chief Citizen*]

CHIEF CIT.

       Hail, Lord and friend.
I come about a man in bonds with you,
One Jesus, leader of a perverse crew
That haunts the Temple.

PILATE

       Yes, the man is here.

CHIEF CIT.

Charged with sedition?

PILATE

       It did not appear
That he had been seditious. It was proved
That he had mocked at rites which people loved.
No more than that. I have just dealt with him.
You wish to see him?

CHIEF CIT.

No, the Sanhedrim
Sends me to tell you of his proved intent.
You know how, not long since, a prophet went
Through all Judea turning people's brains
With talk of One coming to loose their chains?

PILATE

John the Baptizer whom old Herod killed.

CHIEF CIT.

The Jews expect that word to be fulfilled,
They think that One will come. This Jesus claims
To be that Man, Son of the Name of Names,
The Anointed King who will arise and seize
Israel from Rome and you. Such claims as these
Might be held mad in other times than ours.

PILATE

He is not mad.

CHIEF CIT.

But when rebellion lowers
As now, from every hamlet, every farm,
One word so uttered does unreckoned harm.

PILATE

How do you know this?

CHIEF CIT.

From a man, his friend,
Frightened by thoughts of where such claims would end.
There had been rumors, yet we only heard
The fact but now. We send you instant word.

PILATE

Yes. This is serious business. Would I had known.
But none the less, this Jesus is alone.
A common country preacher, as men say,
No more than that, he leads no big array:
No one believes his claim?

CHIEF CIT.

At present, no.
He had more friends a little while ago,
Before he made these claims of being King.

PILATE

You knew about him then?

CHIEF CIT.

His ministering
Was known to us, of course.

PILATE

And disapproved?

CHIEF CIT.

Not wholly, no; some, truly; some we loved.
At first he only preached. He preaches well.

PILATE

What of?

CHIEF CIT.

Of men, and of escape from hell
By good deeds done. But when he learned his power
And flatterers came, then, in an evil hour,
As far as I can judge, his head was turned.
A few days past, from all that we have learned

He made this claim, and since persists therein.
Deluders are best checked when they begin.
So, when we heard it from this frightened friend,
We took this course to bring it to an end.

PILATE

Rightly. I thank you. Do I understand
That friends have fallen from him since he planned
To be this King?

CHIEF CIT.

They have, the most part.

PILATE

Why?

What makes them turn?

CHIEF CIT.

The claim is blasphemy
Punished by death under the Jewish laws.

PILATE

And under ours, if sufficient cause
Appear, and yet, if all the Jews despise
This claimant's folly, would it not be wise
To pay no heed, not make important one
Whom all contemn?

CHIEF CIT.

His evil is not done.
His claim persists, the rabble's mind will turn.
Better prevent him, Lord, by being stern.
The man has power.

PILATE

That is true, he has.

CHIEF CIT.

His is the first claim since the Baptist was,
Better not let it thrive.

PILATE

It does not thrive.

CHIEF CIT.

All ill weeds prosper, Lord, if left alive.
The soil is ripe for such a weed as this.
The Jews await a message such as his,
The Anointed Man, of whom our Holy Books
Prophesy much. The Jewish people looks
For Him to come.

PILATE

These ancient prophecies
Are drugs to keep crude souls from being wise.
Time and again Rome proves herself your friend,
Then some mad writing brings it to an end.
Time and again, until my heart is sick.
Dead prophets spreading madness in the quick.
And now this Jesus whom I hoped to save.
Have you the depositions?

CHIEF CIT.

Yes, I have.

PILATE

Give me.

CHIEF CIT.

This is the docquet.

PILATE

This is grave.

Chief Cit.

I thought that you would think so.

Pilate

               I will learn
What he can say to this and then return.
Wait. I must speak. Although I shall not spare
Anyone, man or woman, who may dare
To make a claim that threatens Roman rule,
I do not plan to be a priestly tool.
I know your Temple plots; pretend not here
That you, the priest, hold me, the Roman, dear.
You, like the other Jews, await this King
Who is to set you free, who is to ding
Rome down to death, as your priests' brains suppose.
This case of Jesus shows it, plainly shows.
He and his claim were not at once disowned;
You waited, while you thought "He shall be throned,
We will support him, if he wins the crowd."
You would have, too. He would have been endowed
With all your power to support his claim
Had he but pleased the rabble as at first.
But, since he will not back the priestly aim,
Nor stoop to lure the multitude, you thirst
To win my favor by denouncing him.
This rebel does not suit the Sanhedrim.
I know. . . . The next one may.

CECIL ROTH   (*1899–*   )

MESSIAH AND REFORMER

In Jesus of Nazareth there was a double strain. On the one hand, he claimed (so, at least, many of his followers believed) to be the promised Messiah who was to deliver his people from sovereign bondage. On the other, he followed the tradition of the moral and social reformers who had always been so characteristic a feature in Hebrew history. In his wanderings through the country he urged the people to amend their manner of life. His utterances were not entirely original. He quoted and elaborated the teachings of contemporary Rabbis as he had heard them repeated in the synagogue of his native place. It was in the spirit of the ancient prophets of Israel that he censured the exploitation of the poor by the rich and the stranglehold which formalism could establish upon religion.

Under such circumstances, no man could have failed to concentrate upon himself an overwhelming degree of opposition—from the Romans whose rule was threatened by his political aspirations, from the fashionable religious leaders whose example he condemned, from the priesthood, on account of his attempt to reform the Temple worship, and from the moneyed classes whom he reviled with all the poor man's virulence. When he died on the cross, it was to be imagined that his influence would have died with him, as was the case with so many of his contemporaries. However, his personal magnetism must have been amazingly great. The group of disciples who had followed him continued to cherish his memory and to look forward to a second coming which would achieve all that had been left undone at the time of his death. Gradually new adherents gathered round them. Their opponents in Greek-speaking Antioch referred to them contemptuously as "Christian," after the *Christos* or "Anointed one" (Messiah) whose teachings they followed. The name, like so many others first applied in contempt, became generally adopted, and under it the Hebraic ideals which the new faith embodied were to become part of the common heritage of the Western world.

BURNETT H. STREETER (*1874–1939*)

CLIMAX IN SERIES OF PROPHETS

There is the fact that Jesus was Himself convinced that He was the Christ, the Messiah for whose coming the prophets had for centuries been looking. The fact has been questioned by a few, but only a very few, competent scholars. But the most eminent of these seem to me to have unconsciously allowed their purely critical judgment to be warped by their respect for the person of Jesus—a respect so profound that they would gladly think Him incapable of entertaining a belief which to them appears intrinsically absurd. They have been tempted to belittle the evidence that Jesus thought He was the Messiah by the feeling that it would have been discreditable in Him to think so. But the weight of historical evidence is overwhelmingly against them. The exact significance that Jesus attached to the term Messiah may reasonably be disputed; what is not disputable is that to the mind of any Jew the appearance of the Messiah was an event not merely of national but of world significance, and that it was the climax in God's dealing with mankind. Had Jesus been a person of low intelligence and mean ideals, or had His influence on human history in point of fact turned out to be of little moment, His personal belief that He was the Christ is a thing we should dismiss with a wave of the hand as a mere delusion. The facts being what they are, many will think such a gesture a little too light-hearted.

In the majesty and tenderness of the figure depicted in the Gospels we are conscious of something august—as of One whose being is rooted in immensities. This is not a thing that can be argued about; it can only be felt. Yet a scientific analysis of the historical facts goes some way to justify this impression that in Christ we are in contact with a personality of a quality which, in a sense, we may call "absolute"; that He is not just one (not even the greatest) of a series of prophets, but, as He Himself supposed, its climax.

REFORMER

FOREMOST AMONG TEACHERS

Jesus came to seek and save the lost. His friends were among the lowliest. "He spake as never man spoke before," but the unlearned, the ignorant, and the beggars and sinners understood Him and flocked about Him. He was misunderstood by the wise. Those who confronted him with philosophical and metaphysical doubts were set right by practical illustrations which pointed the way of service for humanity. Jesus was a teacher but His teaching was interrupted constantly by His service in behalf of His fellowmen. He came into the world not to glorify God primarily, but to save fallen men and the world itself. "God so loved the world that He gave His only begotten Son, that whosoever believeth in Him should not perish, but have everlasting life." He was one of the great religious teachers who illustrated His teachings with such simple stories that the people knew exactly what He was trying to say.

The man who fell among the thieves on the road to Jericho was rescued by the good Samaritan. Jesus, in the story, did not have the Samaritan go and hunt up a companion and philosophize over the conditions and then run away from his duty. The Samaritan would certainly have had ample excuse to have felt that in determining where his love to his neighbor should begin and end, it was not with the Jew. A young man came to Jesus and said: "What must I do to inherit eternal life?" Jesus did not give him a hard stone in philosophical abstractions but at once set for him a practical task, and when he sent out his disciples it was to heal, to teach, and to baptize. These disciples were the "feet of the Gospel." "The Kingdom of Heaven," said Jesus, "is a man traveling to a far country who called his servants and delivered unto them his goods. Unto one he gave five talents; to another two; and to another one; to each according to his several abilities. And straightway took his journey. Then he that had five talents went and traded with the same and made them into another five talents, and likewise he that had received two talents, he also gained another two, but he that had received one talent went and digged it into the earth and hid his lord's money. After a long time the lord of those servants cometh and reckoned with them. To the servant who had made five talents, as well as the one who had gained two, he said, well done." Now suppose Jesus had taken the other viewpoint. Suppose that Christianity is just a philosophical system and that if you apply it, you destroy it. He would have said then to these men who had increased their talents: "You have been enthusiastic and altogether too much interested in worldly affairs; by your zeal and optimistic attitude you indicate that you are no longer entitled to the place of honor." And to the servant who hid his talent he would have said: "Thou knewest that I reap where I sow not and gather where I have not strewn. Therefore, thou hast done well to be quiet and wait until I return to claim my own. Therefore, enter thou into the joy of thy Lord." . . .

Jesus demanded service. He based the reason for that service on the conversion of the individual, the transformation of character, so that the disciple of Jesus does what he does and acts as he does because as a "new man in Christ Jesus" he can do no other. . . . It is this compulsion that is making the Church strong where it is strong to-day. Jesus is the way of truth and the light. He stands foremost among those who have pointed out the path to a better life for mankind. His love and its compulsion is one of the strongest forces that can be utilized in eradicating war and bringing about permanent peace. He should be first in the counsel chamber of the nations. If His will and His example and His influence have their way, war will cease.

HENRI BARBUSSE   (1874-1935)

THE CRUCIFIXION EVE

Translated by Solon Librescot

All day nothing was done against me.

The sky was blue and the fields were radiant. But it was too late for me to enjoy them.

And the evening came as before. And when it was there, I said to myself, "It is tonight that all will be consummated."

As I walked heavily, not knowing what to do, for I had too little time before me, I saw Judas Iscariot.

He was in a gloomy mood, full of rancor, grinding his teeth.

As soon as he saw me, he said:

"I have something against you.

"I am annoyed by something you said in your sermon in the Temple, and before that in your sermon on the mount; I mean by what you said about the people's having to fight their own battles.

"Lord, you would have done better to keep silent, or to talk of something else. See here, I have been thinking the matter over, and it is just as I say. For your own good, listen to my words and reflect on them, Rabbi.

"Do not mix Caesar with your gospel. Speak of the spirit and let Caesar alone."

I said, "Friend, it is not fitting to speak of one and be silent about the other."

He said, "What of it? It will not be noticed at first. Let us take a middle course, or at least keep safely on the side."

I understood more fully than before that the gravest temptations are those which do not appear as such, and that this man was far away from me and against me, though not ill-disposed.

Because he is concerned with the small affairs of the moment, and always seems to be right.

When he stands there, it seems to me that the whole world is gathered there against me.

I said once that it was like running against a tree.

No, it is as if, in the night, I ran against the forest.

My anguish increased a hundredfold, a thousandfold.

Then, in despair, I became like a child, and called for my mother, and my steps led me in search of her.

She was with some friends in Bethany.

In the village, the tranquil life of the day was ending. They had all been busy since dawn. Now they were returning, each man into his own place, content with his toil. The odor of their gardens came out to meet them. They said to the evening wind, Give!

Evening is the best season of the day.

And each thing is lovelier than the next.

I love it all.

But I was the winter and carried the winter with me; for each man, every hour, remakes the world in his own image.

All things seemed clothed with beauty. But their beauty was only the charity of the passerby.

And night is to close your eyes.

And nevertheless, it would require many calm years to age the light which bathes these households.

But everything they enjoy is ended for me.

I shall not walk here again, nor there. I have reached the moment when every step says, Good-bye!

And there I saw an old man come slowly down a stairway. He will go up again. He who descends into the grave will not rise up again.

In one house, behind the curtain of the door, a happy song was spreading its perfume of immortality.

The deep house, with all its openings closed. For those who live inside, it is a thing. For those who pass, is it not a creature? And, because it has rained, this wall has wept.

A young girl came to meet me. But because I went away, she also went away.

Here, where some one was working lately I could see a light burning. It made the square house and the palm tree seem blue.

How blue was all the world!

I love.

My God, my God!

Thinking of my days, which will have passed so soon, I childishly let slip the words, "My God!"

It was my mouth and my regret which spoke, in spite of myself.

*   *   *   *

I found my mother sitting at her work, and spoke to her of great matters. "Listen; I have pitted myself against the world."

She put off, with painful efforts, the humbleness of her nature, and finding herself embarrassed by speaking of such things, she blushed.

She even dropped the vessel in which she was preparing food.

And she said, "One shouldn't be different from the others. People are beginning to find it strange that you complain of everything which takes place.

"Doubtless, when people are listening to you and shouting Hosanna, you are proud.

"But there are others who say you aren't a good Jew."

As I said nothing and the moments passed, she took a pot she had placed on her knees and began rubbing it with her roughened fingers, so as not to lose time, because evening was here and the meal must be made ready.

She said, "It would be nice if people would say, Mary, you are the mother of Jesus, an honest carpenter whom nobody talks about.

"Instead of this, my son, they say, That fellow Jesus is a man without a country. He has no respect for rank and property. He is a communist.

"I don't know personally, but this is what they say.

"Let things be as they are. They are all right, I assure you on my word. Obey your elders."

She looked at me, to convince me, with shining tears on her eyelids.

And I was helpless, because of my great anguish, before the woman who gave me all I have.

I did not choose my mother. What have we in common, she and I?

She is the woman whom I have seen face to face, and this is all we have in common.

My mother bows her frail shoulders.

The patience of her kisses would soften the stones.

Instead of replying I thought of passing the garden of Ananias, and of seeing the graven Ashtoreh with its little gilded child that had tempted her one day.

And, drawing a comparison between the frail artificial beauty of the goddess, perfect in its immobility, and the poor maternity of my mother, with her drowned eyes where the stars had taken root, I began to murmur, "The goddess Mary"; and in my anguish I smiled very faintly.

When I said good-bye, her face was already stained with the night. I took the road to Gethsemane, and the people of the village faded away, died, and the cry which a little while since had begun to well from my throat was completed: "My God, my God, why hast thou forsaken me?"

. And this was a temptation that came from the Great Books.

It was breaking the bonds of a fatherhood which we cannot escape seeing: my Father . . .

My Father, who art in Heaven, thou echoest back the sound of our sorrows.

And I know why we believe in God.

If I were mad, I should believe in God.

MARY BORDEN   (*1886*-   )

JESUS TELLS HIS MOTHER OF HIS MISSION

How dim the light was. Even the courtyard seemed to be in shadow. Hark! What was that sound of fluttering? Was it only the children's pigeons come flying over the roof to the pigeon house? Once long ago, she had heard a rush of wings not very different from this soft sound and a voice had called her by name saying, Fear not, Mary, He shall be great. He shall be born of the Holy Ghost. He shall be called the Son of God.

Oh, why had he gone after the dangerous wizard of the waste land who cursed Herod the king and stirred even the soldiers of Judea to rebellion? What had he done? What had she done that all her hopes for him should come to nothing and worse than nothing? Where had she failed him? How could she have kept him safe at home? What awful spirit of unrest had driven him to defy the holy authority of the synagogue and abandon his family to follow this strange man who proclaimed the end of the world?

She saw his figure receding swiftly in the morning twilight, seemed to hear his footsteps growing fainter while his voice rang again in her ears.

I must go. We must be ready. Great events are preparing. The people are in peril. They have fallen asleep on the eve of the end of the world and there is no one to wake them, for their watchmen too are asleep. They are dumb dogs who cannot even bark. Now there is this one man. Like the prophets of old, he has arisen to warn the nation. He is a voice crying alone in the wilderness.

What are you saying, Jesus? Of whom do you speak? How do you know that this man is a prophet come from God? The prophets are dead. There has been no prophet in Israel for three hundred years.

He had begged her to endeavour to understand and believe. But how could she understand him or lend herself to this terrible talk against the holy rabbis? And how could she believe that the world was coming to an end suddenly? Did he mean that all in a moment, in the twinkling of an eye, this house, these tables and chairs and Bathsheba the children's goat who was nibbling a bunch of leaves, and all the town she knew so well with its busy market and its trumpet summoning the people to prayer, would vanish, be as if it had never been? She had always known that some day there would be an awful judgment when all the dead would rise from their graves, but she had never thought of it as coming in her life-time, nor did she know what Jesus meant by being ready.

I love the Lord God with all my heart and all my strength, Jesus. Isn't that enough?

He had looked at her a long moment.

Yes, he had said. It is enough. It is more than all the teachings of the rabbis. But it is not true of the people. The people are led by schoolmasters who have lost the key to the knowledge of God. The rabbis can teach them nothing for they know nothing.

They know and teach the holy Law.

No, they have forgotten the Law. They have made it a dead thing and buried it under their dead tradition. They know nothing but the rules they themselves have invented. Rules cannot save a nation in peril.

But what peril do you mean, Jesus? Has anything happened? I know that Pilate——

The danger will not come from Pontius Pilate. I'm not speaking of war or rebellion or the danger of another massacre. The danger is in ourselves and our faithlessness. We are a small people and very weak as the world counts weakness. We have no army, no power over our own land, no voice in the councils of the nations. But we are the people whom God chose out of all the world to be a kingdom of priests. He did not choose us because we were many or because we were braver than other men, for we were fewest of all. He chose us because He loved us. And that was our destiny, to make known to the world the love of God and found the Kingdom of Heaven.

Who remembers? Who cares for God now, to-day in Nazareth? Who knows Him and loves Him and lives with Him as children do

in the house of their Father? But that, I say to you, was our peculiar
duty in the world, and if we do not do that, we are nothing.

Don't you understand? We have lost our way. We are no better
than blind, helpless sheep, stumbling on the edge of a precipice, and
not one of our masters is a good shepherd, for not one speaks the
truth.

Do you make the Master of Nazareth a liar?

She had spoken sharply, so shocked by his words that her mind
was suddenly stiffened against him, and she had thought, if Joseph
were alive he would not dare to talk so. I must use my authority.
I must rebuke him as his father would have done. I must not let
his strange power overcome me. He has been led astray by some
foreigner. Some evil Greek has put a doubt in his soul, and she cried
out:

What has come over you, Jesus? Have you forsaken the faith of your
people? Your father taught you to rever the elders of the synagogue.
You know that the Rabbi of Nazareth is a good and holy man,
learned in the word of God.

His mind is dark, Mother.

Dark with the word of God?

Dark with tradition. . . .

Words. One hears nothing but words in the synagogue. Written
words that once were the living word of God, they are empty now.
And spoken words endlessly repeated till they sound without meaning. And the scribes argue in the schools as to the sense of these
dead words and between words of wisdom and words of foolishness
none can choose.

They debate all night, I have heard them, as to whether an egg laid
on a holy day can be eaten by a pious man; and I have seen them
in a frenzy over the length of fringes on a night-gown, and when,
roaring like bears over the matter, they have split the strong law of
good and evil into a million hairs, weightless as thistledown, they
decree that a man who forgets one single word of their wisdom will
be cast into the burning pit of Gehenna for ever.

How could she not be terrified? He would talk sometimes far into the night, striding up and down the room with the candle throwing his huge shadow on the wall. She would hear James stirring, hear him mount to the room where he kept his books, and her heart would break between the two of them. James upstairs bending his weary, unkempt, haggard head over the sacred books of the Law, and Jesus who defied the Law, pacing the room like a lion.

It is all lies, and they know in their hearts it is lies.

Hush, I pray you, Jesus, be quiet.

I cannot be quiet, Mother. I cannot be dumb any longer or listen any more to the dry rustle of their words. We are lost if we listen to them. Our people will perish. Can a dry wind among dead leaves save a nation that is dying of thirst? . . .

She had listened trembling, her hands clasped tight together and her heart sick within her. He was her glorious eldest son. Once she had known that he was chosen by God for a great destiny and she had given him to God when he was only a few weeks old, just as Hannah, the other mother in ancient Israel, had given her son Samuel. And she had often thought of that mother of long ago whose son had judged Israel. Jesus could never be a priest, he was not of the sons of Aaron, but he could be a holy rabbi; and when he was a child and she had taught him his first lesson, that had always been her dream. . . .

Now suddenly this Jesus was become a stranger, a man on fire with a terrible doctrine, who recognised no authority on earth but the authority of an unknown wizard who had appeared in the desert and was stirring up all the people of Judea. She dared not rebuke him, but she cried out:

What sign has John given of being a prophet of God?

He speaks the truth. He is calling on the people to repent of their sins.

Do you know the truth better than the learned men of the synagogue?

I know God. . . .

I have no master here, Mother. I know no one in this place with power to forgive me my sins and I have no time to wait for the approval of the neighbours.

James had interrupted them. He had come down for a candle and a cup of warm milk. His lamp had gone out, he was shivering with cold, and while she was heating the milk, Jesus had left the house, though it was still many hours before dawn, and when he came back in he was silent. Nor had he talked to her again before he went away.

Then the rabbi had come. The good Master had knocked on her door asking to see Jesus, and she had had to tell him that he had gone down into Judea.

JEROME DAVIS   (*1891–*   )

A SOCIAL GOSPEL PREACHED

It is becoming clear that the old distinction between the individual and the social gospel is largely meaningless, for the individual is the social problem and the social problem is a network of interpenetrating individuals. To ask the individual to follow Christ in much of the business world to-day is almost like asking a man to live Christ while employed in a gambling house. Individual salvation demands social salvation. . . .

The question of whether capitalism can ever be harmonized with the teachings of Jesus demands clear analysis. To some at present capitalism spells the prosperity and culture of contentment, the system under which large fortunes come to those who deserve them. . . .

It is obvious that competition has rarely transmuted selfishness into consistent public service, as the record of the rise of railroads, of oil, of steel, public utilities, and other natural monopolies has abundantly indicated.

The Sermon on the Mount seems to contradict this teaching of competition as the law of life. Seeking first the righteousness of God and His Kingdom and doing unto others what we would wish them to do to us are spoken in another language. Loving one's neighbor as oneself in business to-day is irony. The spiritual by-products of competition are far from the spirit of Christ: insincerity, suspicion, hatred, legalism, ruthless denial of the supreme worth of personality. To co-operate in a friendly brotherhood so that all may secure the more abundant life would utilize personality values great and small. Friendly competition in scientific discovery and in production for use may be beneficial, but modern business competition is another matter. . . .

The Christian ethic teaches the infinite worth of each human personality. Each has the right to follow the highest inner light which God and his own search for truth gives him. Private property for power gives one man the right to throw workers, many or few, out of employment at a mere command. It enables him to blacklist a union man. It can dictate starvation or happiness to the individual and his family. Such powers used in the struggle for material goods (which may demoralize the possessor) can hardly square with the Golden Rule, much less with Jesus' insistence on placing spiritual values first. . . .

To one who reads the teachings of Jesus without any preconceptions it is abundantly clear that the self-sacrificing love demanded in the Gospels is antithetical to the profit system and to property for power.

Jesus believed in a Father God, "And all ye are brothers." Consequently if industrial enterprise could view its objective as the production of necessary goods through the democratic working relationships of brothers and sisters in a family, that would suggest the "Co-operative commonwealth." There are few business men to-day who would maintain that this is now being done. The fact is that the texture of our economic order is interwoven with selfishness and crass materialism, although here and there one finds reflections of the brighter colors of unselfishness. The entire structure is covered with a veneer of beautiful platitudes and pious declarations of service. The devil always dresses beautifully, for if we could see the stark-naked ugliness of his reality all would be repelled. *Profit* is the real God, which is competing to-day with Jesus' concept of a Father God.

G. R. ELLIOTT   (*1883–*   )

MODERNIST VIEWS ANALYZED

Today many persons who religiously swallow the authority of science, who religiously believe that Einsteinism is true and wish they could understand what it means, reject all authority in religion.

They say that Jesus himself rejected it, and patronise Him as the first of the moderns. They isolate Him from the religious organism to which he was deeply attached: which shaped his principles no less than his images: and through which indeed, during the long preceding centuries of Hebrew history, his sublime nature itself had been (if this may be said without irreverence) gradually "evolved." Thus they affix to Him a singularity no less miraculous, no less disruptive of the laws of human nature and history, than that attributed to him by popular orthodoxy: but far better calculated to debauch with blind pride the souls of his worshippers or, as the case may be, his modern rivals or superseders. They have learned from Him, not wisely but too well, that the Sabbath was made for man and not man for the Sabbath. They hug the false inference which he so sternly and constantly rejected, namely, that man was made to disuse instead of to use the Sabbath, to win spiritual maturity by discarding institutional religion, Jesus discarded revolution. He continued and reformed a great religious tradition. He made it capable of feeding itself—and us—upon the best of Greek as well as Hebrew thought. He made it nobly catholic in the very process of nourishing his individual soul upon it. He was crucified because he was more deeply true to it than the modernists, as well as the loyalists, of his day. Our modernists, however, deem that his hand was raised and pierced to direct us to bite the hand that fed us.

The gnawing pride of religious individualism cloaks itself in the assumption that the individual has transferred his reverence *entire* from the traditional deity to "the present God" as Emerson called Him, or to the present Reality as successors of Emerson often prefer to call it. But actually that transfer is never accomplished. The reverence never arrives entire. Always some of it, often most of it, leaks away unnoticed during the transshipment. Therefore this exchange is never attempted by the greatest men of religion, nor advocated by the truest realists or humanists. Jesus and Socrates both found the "Father's business" in the Temple, in the moral and imaginative organism of orthodox religion, and never more so than when they were doing their best to cleanse it of thieves. They were wrongly accused of an intention for which some of our modern spiritual leaders have been wrongly praised, the intention of destroying the Temple in order to rebuild it on their own insights, as it were in three days. No doubt all men of deepest insight are strongly tempted, in their first maturity, by this pseudo-divine impatience with tradition. They yearn to show immediately that the Power within them is more reliable than the "pinnacle of the Temple." But they perceive the spiritual pride of this yearning, its tempting of God, and they forthwith school themselves to the divine patience. They recognise that the Temple is essential for *their own* fullest development.

George Walter Fiske   (*1872–*   )

A BASIC PRINCIPLE

The quibblers who discard Jesus' social teachings as irrelevant to the modern age, because he never heard of elevator wells and sprinkler systems or even shoe factories, are more rabbinical than Christian. We can imagine Christ's retort to their quibbling: "What matters it whence the peril, or how human life is slain, or in what form the property is held, *is not a man of more value than a sheep?"* And there is a glorious democracy of that word of his, "A MAN"—any man, any person, regardless of race, sex, sect, or color. It suggests Burns's noble line: "A man's a man for a' that."

Jesus' teaching of the preciousness of a single human soul was a basic principle in his religion. It comes out in this familiar question, "What doth it profit a man, if he gain the whole world and lose his own soul?" A man's life is worth more than all the world's possessions, at least to himself, and to all who love him. Yet countless people are still as reckless of their own lives as others are for them. Failure to respect personality, whether of ourselves or others, is the basic social sin, and the cause of most crimes of social injustice. No prophet of the past had taught how fundamental this principle is until the keen discernment of Jesus discovered it.

ALBERT FIELD GILMORE   (*1868*–   )

THE EVILS OF HIS TIME

The notion that Jesus was constricted in his years of preparation, that he was merely a rustic lad, that he lacked contact with humanity in its various aspects, is wholly dispelled when the true picture of his environment is envisioned. He was gaining an understanding of humanity and its needs that would be invaluable to him in the great work that lay ahead. Not in Rome, not in Alexandria, not in Athens, but here on the edge of the great plain was he observing humanity in its varied aspects, its needs, its aspirations, its worth, its failures and its triumphs. Surely, nothing was lacking in the experiences he was undergoing, experiences that gave him both a broad and an intimate outlook upon life.

Other influences beside the geographical and physically environmental bore in upon Jesus' youth. Coupled with the glamour of the

Roman authority exercised by Pontius Pilate and other officials of the Empire, living in splendor regarded as in keeping with their positions, was the insidious infiltration of the Greek culture. The language of their forefathers, the ancient Hebrew, was gradually giving place to the liquid cadences of the Greek tongue.

*   *   *   *

In this atmosphere Jesus was reared. It was a period of tension. The restless spirit of the masses was for the time held in suspense. But it was the calm before the storm. Jerusalem itself was in the path of the mighty tornado of imperial might that in a few decades swept it into ruin and, its destroyers believed, into oblivion.

The flow of commerce along the great highways, together with the enterprise of Roman merchants, had brought extensive wealth to the upper classes. And this flow of wealth reached beyond the secular group, into the pockets of the priestly class. An intricate system of taxes for various phases of worship, together with the exorbitant prices charged for the creatures gathered for sacrifice at the great festivals, aggregated a vast sum, for the most part extracted falsely from the people. This was another condition that Jesus confronted when he began his ministry. It was not new to him, for, reared in the very midst of it, he was thoroughly familiar with the hypocrisy and dishonesty involved.

One can hardly wonder at the vehemence with which Jesus denounced these evils. Thoroughly imbued with the spirit of honesty, of justice and mercy, he was deeply stirred; and with him witness of a wrong was the signal to attack it, not in the spirit of hatred and malevolence, but rather to heal it, to remove its weight from the shoulders of the people. No man was ever so courageous in attacking evil; no man was ever so little afraid of consequences. He sought no worldly honor. He served no purpose but service to God, to establish a Kingdom of good, or righteousness, in which every mortal could become a citizen and beneficiary of its blessings by fulfilling the conditions of citizenship, exchanging material beliefs for spiritual understanding, for knowledge of God and His universe; that is, by forsaking the god of mammon, of materiality, for the Christ, the Comforter, the everpresent Truth.

FRANCIS J. HAAS   (*1889-*   )

HE RAISED MAN'S NATURE

When Jesus Christ, the Son of God, came into the world, He did more than merely visit man. He became man. By this act He vested the human race with a new dignity; He raised man's nature to a higher order of nobility. And He made no exceptions: every child of Adam, by virtue of birth, was thenceforth to be admitted to brotherhood with Jesus Christ, and to sonship to God the Father. None was to be barred from sharing the privileges and rights of inheritance. All were to enjoy the prerogatives of heavenly citizenship, and none was to be denied the opportunity of using the goods of the earth to realize his eternal destiny. One person might not justly stand in the way of another's normal development, for in the divine democracy, no one essentially was more important than another. This basic truth, the Divine Master taught, is to be the controlling rule of law in the court of final judgment. The "least" of mankind is as great as the greatest. If you did a kindness "to one of these my least brethren," he said, "you did it to me," your Judge (MATT. xxv, 40).

The Saviour further insisted that the life, not only of the individual is sacred; that of the race is equally inviolable. Not alone those now on earth, but also those of generations yet to come must be protected. He reaffirmed the original commandment that husband and wife shall be "two in one flesh." More than that, He made the marriage contract a holy undertaking, a sacrament, to be dissolved for no cause whatsoever, to be sundered only by death.

ADOLF VON HARNACK (*1851–1930*)

THE GOSPEL A SOCIAL MESSAGE

Translated by Thomas Bailey Saunders

Jesus laid down no social programme for the suppression of poverty and distress, if by programme we mean a set of definitely prescribed regulations. With economic conditions and contemporary circumstances he did not interfere. Had he become entangled in them; had he given laws which were ever so salutary for Palestine, what would have been gained by it? They would have served the needs of a day, and tomorrow would have been antiquated; to the Gospel they would have been a burden and a source of confusion. We must be careful not to exceed the limits set to such injunctions as "Give to him that asketh thee" and others of a similar kind. They must be understood in connection with the time and the situation. They refer to the immediate wants of the applicant, which were satisfied with a piece of bread, a drink of water, an article of clothing to cover his nakedness. We must remember that in the Gospel we are in the East, and in circumstances which from an economical point of view are somewhat undeveloped. Jesus was no social reformer. He could say on occasion, "The poor ye have always with you," and thereby, it seems, indicate that the conditions would undergo no essential change. He refused to be a judge between contending heirs, and a thousand problems of economics and social life he would have just as resolutely put aside as the unreasonable demand that he would settle a question of inheritance. Yet again and again people have ventured to deduce some concrete social programme from the Gospel. Even evangelical theologians have made the attempt, and are still making it—an endeavour hopeless in itself and full of danger, but absolutely bewildering and intolerable when people try to "fill up the gaps"—and they are many—to be found in the Gospel with regulations and programmes drawn from the Old Testament.

The Gospel is a social message, solemn and over-powering in its force; it is the proclamation of solidarity and brotherliness, in favour of the poor. But the message is bound up with the recognition of the infinite value of the human soul, and is contained in what Jesus said about the kingdom of God. We may also assert that it is an essential part of what he there said. But laws or ordinances or injunctions bidding us forcibly alter the conditions of the age in which we may happen to be living are not to be found in the Gospel.

JOSEPH K. HART   (*1876*-   )

ALL MEN HIS BROTHERS

Jesus . . . urged the ending of the old group hatreds against the alien groups and the outsider. He said, "Ye have heard it said by them of old that ye must love your neighbor but hate your enemies. But I say unto you, love your enemies." . . . This meant that the ancient hostilities between particular groups, whatever values these may have had in the past, were no longer endurable. They must be overcome in a larger group pattern, and the erstwhile enemy must become the personal friend.

Jesus claimed all men for his brothers. This was an especially difficult point of view for the members of an exclusive group like the Hebrews to understand. He rejected patriotisms and nationalisms which maintained themselves by keeping alive group antagonisms, blocking the way to that inclusive humanity which was eventually to fill the earth. He denounced wealth and private possessions in so far as these obstructed the development of this larger social cooperativeness among all men; and he taught that this eventual humanity was to be the Kingdom of God on earth, within which all men should feel themselves members of the only human group, all of them citizens of humanity and children of the universal God.

To demonstrate what these things would mean, Jesus broke the old Hebrew sabbath. That is to say, he denied the finality of the folkways of the Jews, and he taught, what we can now see to be historically true, that institutions were developed in the first place to serve the needs of men, else men became prisoners of their own pasts. Men must make ever new relationships until finally they achieve universal humanity.

WALTER MARSHALL HORTON   (*1895-   *)

HE SAW WITH LUMINOUS CLARITY

It seems to be an inescapable law that all religious systems consciously designed to preserve civilizations prove unable to do so; while those that spring from some fresh, disinterested apprehension of superhuman Reality prove ultimately most powerful as social restoratives.

It is for this very reason that we must reject John Macmurray's suggestion that Jesus consciously and clearly "foresaw" the consequences of His new religious movement: "the destruction and scattering of his own people, the persecution of his own disciples . . . by the Roman Empire, their multiplication in numbers in spite of persecution, the failure of every effort to stamp them out, the ultimate dissolution of the Roman Empire by its own inherent contradiction, and the creation of medieval Christendom upon its ruins by the Christian Church." I cannot believe that Jesus looked ahead upon world history and world civilization with any such clear and calculating gaze. He was not trying, like Augustus, to draft a religion which would have desirable sociological consequences. Indeed, we may grant without qualms or embarrassment that His sociological vision was probably inferior to that of His imperial contemporaries; yes, inferior even to our own. We, looking back upon subsequent events, can clearly see that it was only a radically reformed Judaism—Judaism shorn of its archaic ritualism, its cumbersome law-codes, its national peculiarities, and beautified with many elements of Graeco-

Roman culture not incompatible with its essential genius—that only such a religion was fitted to become the social cement that would reunite and preserve the best elements in Roman civilization. But if our Lord's vision was blurred and foreshortened on the human and historical plane by lack of information easily accessible to the Roman Emperor in his palace, and to every schoolboy today, it was not so limited on the transcendent and superhistorical plane. There, He saw with a luminous clarity that makes him forever the Light of the World. . . . In and through Jesus and His little band of followers, the divine intention to create a universal family and comprehensive world culture among men, typified by the Jewish religious community, but transcending its local and national peculiarities, for the first time became an incarnate actuality, a working force in the very midst of human affairs.

Whatever may have been the conscious intention of its Founder, there can be no doubt that the early Christian community had no conscious intention of undermining and conquering the Roman Empire. It looked to see it destroyed from above, for its many sins, on that great Day when all the elements would melt with fervent heat; it never dreamed of the possibility of transforming it inwardly by gentle warmth. Yet that was just what the new warmth of Christian charity and fellowship was in God's providence destined to accomplish.

ELBERT HUBBARD   (*1856–1915*)

WHERE HE GREATLY SURPASSES

Jesus was not an educated man in our sense of the word, and this is most fortunate. Learning tames and dilutes a man; he grows to reverence authorities and things that are dead, and so he gradually loses his own God-given heritage of self-reliance. A reformer must of necessity be more or less ignorant. In fact, the finest nobility is only possible in a man who has never had a teacher—who acknowledges no authority but the God within. As a general proposition, ignorance and isolation are both necessary in the equipment of the supremely great who are to mold the minds of men and break up the firm ankylosis of social habit, fixed thought and ossified custom. . . .

With such thinkers as that other great Jew, Spinoza, Jesus does not for an instant compare in point of intellect. . . . Where he greatly surpasses . . . is in his sublime faith in both himself and his divine mission. He believed that he was in absolute communion with the living God, the Creator of the World. And this great welling heart that went out to all humanity, seeking to bring all men into a relation of brotherhood, was at once his supreme virtue, and his fault. For such faith as his there is no fulfillment.

VICTOR HUGO   (*1802–1885*)

"THE WAR OF JESUS CHRIST"

Translation, London Times, *May 31, 1878*

To combat Pharisaism, to unmask imposture, to overturn tyrannies, usurpations, prejudices, falsehoods, superstitions—to demolish the temple in order to rebuild it—that is to say, to substitute the true for the false, attack the fierce magistracy, the sanguinary priesthood; to scourge the money-changers from the sanctuary; to reclaim the heritage of the disinherited; to protect the weak, poor, suffering, and crushed; to combat for the persecuted and oppressed—such was the war of Jesus Christ!

E. Stanley Jones *(1884–)*

THE SEDITION OF THE SERMON

The Sermon on the Mount seems dangerous. It challenges the whole underlying conception on which modern society is built. It would replace it by a new conception, animate it with a new motive, and turn it toward a new goal. . . . This Sermon strikes at the whole selfish competitive idea underlying modern economic life and demands that men cooperate in love or perish in strife. . . .

The Sermon on the Mount was and is seditious. It finally put Jesus on the cross, and it will do the same for his followers who follow it in modern life. But it would not end there. There would be a resurrection so great, so transforming in human living that we would know by actual experimentation that it is the only way for us to live. . . .

Our present-day Christianity, anaemic and weak from the parasites that have fastened themselves on its life through the centuries, needs a blood transfusion from the Sermon on the Mount in order to renew radiant health within it that it may throw off these parasites and arise to serve and save the world.

Rufus M. Jones *(1863–)*

NO DIAGNOSIS FOR SIN

Jesus's approach to men was always one of daring faith in man. He recognized, as every true "curer of souls" does, that lives become sadly warped and twisted by sins, by shams and insincerities, and that a powerful reconstruction and transformation must take place before there can be complete spiritual health. He had no shallow diagnosis for sin and he never expected any man to be made good by a spray of rose water.

But he did expect, as his greatest parables indicate, that when a person truly *comes to himself,* when in a lucid moment he gets down below his follies, his mistakes, his shams and his self-deceits, he will want to go back home to his Father where he belongs and find the inward joy of being a son. He seems everywhere to imply that man essentially "belongs" to God. The basic nature is spiritual, not carnal. The crucial process is coming to oneself. It is his method with diseased souls to bring them back to their deeper original sources of faith. The unwarped child, with his spontaneous faith and confidence in goodness, is the best illustration of that spirit which fits the Kingdom of God. It is impossible to suppose that he believed that the little child was a depraved limb of Satan. It is not easy to interpret his words, "Their angels do always behold the face of my Father," but these words at least mean that the unspoiled child and the Eternal Father have something in common. The preciousness, the infinite worth, of the individual soul forms a luminous atmosphere everywhere in his Gospel. It is, I think, the most unique feature of his message about life. How he *arrived* at this insight is nowhere explained. How he reached such an estimate of the worth of life is never told. It is more wonderful than changing water to wine or than opening a blind man's eyes, but it is never listed among his miracles. His main contention with the Scribes and Pharisees was that they reduced life to rules and regulations, that they made it consist of doing "things that are required" for conformity, and that they turned life into a utilitarian scheme of adjustment, to get or to avoid certain results, here or hereafter.

CHARLES FOSTER KENT   *(1867–1925)*

HIS IMPULSES ALL SOCIAL

Jesus sprang from a race of social teachers. Almost every page of the ancient scriptures which he read and studied intently and eagerly was saturated with social idealism. As a boy at Jerusalem he came into direct contact with the stirrings of the new social awakening inaugurated by Hillel. In his early manhood it was the voice of the heroic social teacher, John the Baptist, that proved irresistible. Thus the strongest influences that from childhood touched and stirred Jesus were distinctly social.

Jesus' own personal inclinations and impulses were all social. There was nothing of the recluse or ascetic in his nature. He himself declared by word as well as by his manner of living that "the Son of Man came eating and drinking" (Mt. 11^{19}). He fully appreciated and even called attention to the wide difference in this respect between John the Baptist and himself. He was a sympathetic friend of all classes and above all of the tax collectors and sinners—the classes that presented in many respects the most difficult and insistent social problem of his day. In the few rare instances in which he defined his mission he declared that he came to save these social outcasts, "the down and outs" of Jewish society. He met his death as a direct result of his attempt to right a great social wrong. . . .

The oldest gospel records make it clear that Jesus inaugurated a great popular, democratic movement. It was the common people who "heard him gladly." The supreme evidence, however, of his interest in social questions is found in the character of his teachings. Fully half of them are distinctly social in their content and application. It was pre-eminently a social gospel which he proclaimed. This new social teaching was the essence of the "good tidings" that arrested the attention of Judaism and of the Graeco-Roman world.

* * * *

Of all the New Testament writers, Luke, the physician, was most keenly alive to the importance of giving a full record of Jesus' social teachings, although, like Paul, he was often inclined to paraphrase them. If it had not been for Luke's social interest we would have known nothing, for example, of Jesus' parables of the Rich Man and Lazarus and of the Good Samaritan. To him alone we owe the priceless record of the social conversion of the grafting tax collector

Zaccheus. Luke's intense social interest possibly led him in one or two cases to heighten the colours. Thus, in 12[33] he makes universal the command to sell all possessions and give to the poor, which, according to Matthew 19[16-22], was addressed simply to a rich young man in whom Jesus saw large possibilities of discipleship. . . .

Even if . . . Luke at one or two points gave Jesus' social teachings a distinctly socialistic interpretation, . . . he, more than any other gospel writer, has pictured Jesus as the friend of sinners and outcasts, of children and women, and of the socially disinherited classes. In this great social gospel are revealed most clearly Jesus' chivalry and his sympathy for the helpless. At the same time it is profoundly significant that in the gospels where the interest is not primarily social there is a wealth of social principles, which indicates how extensive and all-pervading was this element in Jesus' teachings. Undoubtedly in an age which had not as yet awakened to the importance of social questions many of Jesus' important social doctrines were lost.

* * * *

It is probable that the details of Jesus' social aim and plan gradually crystallised in his mind. There are even suggestions that these were not fully complete until late in his public ministry. In any case, it is clear in the light of the oldest records that he was following no preordained social programme. Rather, he was aiming to meet in a way that would be complete and final the universal social needs which were exemplified in the society of his day. It is also evident that he carefully studied the best place and method of realising concretely his social plan.

* * * *

One striking characteristic distinguishes his method as a social teacher from that of the prophets. They appealed primarily to the nation or to classes within the nation. Jesus also in rare instances addressed the nation, or classes like the scribes and Pharisees; but his chief work was done not with the mass, but with the individual. . . .

He appealed to the individual, however, rather than to the mass, not because he followed the wise, but because he realised that only by training citizens, who were governed by the right social ideals, could he lay the foundations for a perfect and stable social order. Hence his first aim was to socialise the individuals with whom he came into personal contact. He trusted in men rather than in institutions. He spent all his time and effort in the endeavour to implant his social ideals in the breasts of certain definite men and women, and then left them to determine the exact methods and agencies by which these ideals were to be realised. History amply demonstrates the eminent wisdom of his method.

* * * *

Jesus went deep into the analysis of the evils which dismember society. Chief among these are the class and national hatreds due to ignorance, unjust suspicion, or hasty incrimination. Hence he sought to check these unsocial crimes at their fountain-source.

* * * *

In the social order which Jesus endeavoured to establish there was absolutely no place for hate, even toward enemies; for he realised that hate is not only unsocial, but that it destroys the peace of mind and weakens the strength of one who cherishes it. His words indicate that he knew that to love enemies and pray for persecutors was one of the chief tests of those who are striving to be in every sense sons of the divine Father. . . . In the great human family which Jesus was endeavouring to reorganise, good will must reign supreme if his ideal is to be attained. He held up no mediating standard. As he in his own experience realised, complete fatherhood demanded complete sonship.

WINIFRED KIRKLAND   (*1872–1944*)

BUILDER OF A NEW FOUNDATION

Jesus, the builder, saw the words Kingdom of Heaven as a seed phrase, destined to inexorable growth. So he went everywhere, up and down the narrow earth confines that constrained his human feet, flinging forth the good news that should grow. Jesus, we are told in the homely earth-words of the ancient record, came preaching the good news of the Kingdom of Heaven. Early and late, and everywhere he preached this gladness ceaselessly. His preaching and his practice were both the announcement of a new motive in all human relationships, for the well-spring of the coming kingdom is the benefit of one's neighbor. Always the other man is the target of aim. What shall best serve that other man's health and happiness and uplifting and upbuilding, that is the incessant shining motivation of the Kingdom of Heaven. Such motivation in human affairs could have but one basis—in order to have the intelligence to build aright for another, one must first love him. To love, if we study the revelation of Jesus' behavior, means to desire for any individual, at any cost to himself or to us, his release to growth. The Kingdom of Heaven therefore is a form of human society where not only children may grow freely but where grown-ups, too, crippled and frustrated though they be, may also lift up glad eyes to their own development. The Kingdom of Heaven is that social order where nobody retards anyone else, where nobody employs anyone else as a stepping-stone. . . . The new order which Jesus came to earth to inaugurate would clean away all desire for advantage. Jesus, the builder, would construct a new foundation. To that end, he offered his own example. "Love men as I can be seen to love them," he enjoined us.

*   *   *   *

The structure Jesus formulated for humanity was for him the inexorable result of his example, long ago planted in human aspiration, an example secure in influence as the growth of the mustard seed. The Kingdom of Heaven means the change in motive by which we shall begin to obey no longer the impulses of the beast, but of the God within us. The level eyes of Jesus of Nazareth are gazing into the eyes of all men of all times and of all races when he pronounces forever, "The Kingdom of Heaven is within you."

POPE LEO XIII   *(1810–1903)*

A CURE FOR SOCIETY

Translator Anonymous

Jesus Christ, when He redeemed us with plentiful redemption, took not away the pains and sorrows which in such large proportion make up the texture of our mortal life; He transformed them into motives of virtue and occasions of merit; and no man can hope for eternal reward unless he follow in the blood-stained footprints of his Savior. "If we suffer with Him, we shall also reign with Him." [II Tim. ii. 2]. His labors and His sufferings accepted by His own free will, have marvelously sweetened all suffering and all labor. And not only by His example, but by His grace and by the hope of everlasting recompense, He has made pain and grief more easy to endure. . . .

Therefore, those whom fortune favors are warned that freedom from sorrow and abundance of earthly riches, are no guarantee of that beatitude that shall never end, but rather the contrary [St. Matt. xix. 23, 24]; that the rich should tremble at the threatenings of Jesus Christ—threatenings so strange in the mouth of our Lord [St. Luke vi. 24, 25]; and that a most strict account must be given to the Supreme Judge for all that we possess.

*   *   *   *

As for those who do possess the gifts of fortune, they are taught by the Church that, in God's sight poverty is no disgrace, and that there is nothing to be ashamed of in seeking one's bread by labor. This is strengthened by what we see in Christ Himself, "Who whereas He was rich, for our sakes became poor" [II Cor. viii. 9]; and Who, being the Son of God, and God Himself chose to seem and to be considered the son of a carpenter—nay, did not disdain to spend a great part of His life as a carpenter himself. "Is not this the carpenter, the son of Mary?" [St. Mark vi. 3]. From the contemplation of this Divine example, it is easy to understand that the true dignity and excellence of man lies in his moral qualities, that is, in virtue; that virtue is the common inheritance of all, equally within the reach of high and low, rich and poor; and that virtue, and virtue alone, wherever found, will be followed by the rewards of everlasting happiness. Nay, God Himself seems to incline more to those who suffer evil; for Jesus Christ calls the poor blessed [St. Matt. v. 3: "Blessed are the poor in spirit."]; He lovingly invites those in labor and grief to come to Him for solace [St. Matt. xi. 28: "Come to Me all you that labor and are burdened, and I will refresh you."]; and He displays the tenderest charity to the lowly and oppressed.

*   *   *   *

Of these things there cannot be the shadow of a doubt; for instance, that civil society was renovated in every part by the teachings of Christianity; that in the strength of that renewal the human race was lifted up to better things—nay, that it was brought back from death to life, and to so excellent a life that nothing more perfect had been known before or will come to pass in the ages that are yet to be. Of this beneficent transformation, Jesus Christ was at once the first cause and the final purpose; as from Him all came, so to Him all was to be referred. For when, by the light of the Gospel message, the human race came to know the grand mystery of the Incarnation of the Word and the redemption of man, the life of Jesus Christ, God and Man, penetrated every race and nation, and impregnated them with His faith, His precepts, and His laws. And, if Society is to be cured now, in no other way can it be cured but by a return to the Christian life and Christian institutions.

HENRY C. LINK $\qquad$ (*1889–*)

INTERPRETER AND REFORMER

Truly no personality who now walks the earth begins to be alive compared with the living influence of Jesus!

Jesus was a great liberal but in a sense quite different from that represented by the popular current liberalism. His liberalism was based on a reaffirmation of the ancient law. . . .

When the rich young man asked Jesus what he must do to have eternal life, Jesus told him to keep the commandments. When he asked, which, Jesus named five of the Ten Commandments and this: "Thou shalt love thy neighbor as thyself." All these, the young man affirmed, he had kept from his youth up. Only then did Jesus say: "If thou wilt be perfect, go and sell what thou hast, and give to the poor, and thou shalt have treasure in heaven: and come and follow me."

Thus Jesus consistently tested the new by the old, rather than the old by the new. Even though he was instigating a radically new social order, it was one more firmly than ever based on the old moral law. He amplified the laws and the prophets much as the rules in competitive sports are developed—not by a process of repudiation or substitution, but by using the foundation already given. His liberalism was like that of the modern scientist: he began with axioms already demonstrated and built upon this foundation. It was the exact opposite of the modern liberalism among jurists who regard the interpretations of lawyers as more important than the law itself.

Jesus was an interpreter, a reformer. He believed that the law was made for man and not man for the law. However, he did not therefore believe that man, not even himself, could twist the law to suit his particular philosophy. To him the Ten Commandments were not the *folklore of capitalism* nor the folklore of any other *ism*. They were the basic axioms of personality under any economic system. They were the guideposts through any period of social reform. They were the very foundation for the brotherhood of man, the very bulwark against the barbaric theory that might makes right.

Jesus' subordination of his own reason and ambitions to the existing law is nowhere better demonstrated than in the stories of the temptation. After Jesus had fasted forty days, Satan tempted him to command that the stones around him be turned to bread. Jesus answered: "It is written: Man shall not live by bread alone but by every word that proceedeth out of the mouth of God." Again Satan tempted him, and again the reply was: *It is written* . . . Finally, Satan took him up on a high mountain and promised to give him all the great kingdoms he could see for the simple act of falling down and worshipping him. The reply was: "Get thee hence, Satan: for it is written, Thou shalt worship the Lord thy God, and Him only shalt thou serve."

The analogy between the story of the temptation and the history of our times is remarkable. Jesus was tempted by a vision of speedy power and popularity if he would but discard tradition for expediency. His answer was: "It is written." Instead of a few disciples trained by laborious teaching, he could have had a whole kingdom of lands and people merely by resorting to a few simple devices. His verdict was: "It is written." Instead of achieving a doubtful success in time, he could have achieved it at once by discarding his old-fashioned ideals for more practical methods. But again his answer was: "It is written."

Jesus is the great liberal of all time, yet his mission was one of fulfilling rather than repudiating the old order. He was a conservative first and a progressive afterward. Instead of deprecating the moral axioms of the Old Testament, he made them the foundation for his new structure. Though he built slowly, he built with a permanence and with a type of values which make him supreme among personalities even today.

His goal was the Kingdom of God, but not by short-cuts which would destroy personality in the process. Indeed, his great contribution to man was a concept of personality far above any yet conceived. Personality was a force that transcended any form of earthly government, any system of economics, any ritualistic or intellectual order. But further, he formulated codes of action by which personality could be achieved, he gave authority to these codes, and he inspired man with the confidence that he could achieve his highest personality under these codes.

Other men have given their lives for their faith, or done great deeds for humanity; but this was Christ's great gift to man: a concept of freedom through the moral law. Christ is the great Liberator of man from his own follies. He is the prophet of the potential greatness in all men!

Bishop Francis J. McConnell   (*1871–*   )

PILLARS OF DEMOCRACY

When the Founder of Christianity declared it to be the duty of every man to love God with all his life he spoke into the existence of the individual that inalienable dignity which is one of the pillars of democracy. By that declaration every man has value in the sight of God, and the love of every man is sought by God. . . .

When the Founder of Christianity declared it further to be the duty of every man to love his neighbor as himself he set up another pillar of democracy. If the first utterance puts upon the separate life a great dignity the second ennobles all impulses toward closer fellowship among men. All that is needed to keep this double doctrine back of the democratic movement as a compelling force is an insistence upon the duty of bringing more and more of the acts of the individual under the conception of divine service and more and more persons under the term neighbor. The efficacy of the religion of Jesus in such progress is beyond all question. . . .

God revealed in Christ—or the Christ-like God—has been the chief theme of Christian students of all ages. The clearest note in all discussion has been that which sounds the love of God. We repeat that this note can be kept clear for social progress only as the love is kept profoundly moral. It is the fashion nowadays to relegate creedal statements as to atonement in Christ to the classrooms of professional theologians, but some common aspects of these great phrasings should be more often brought out into full view. For example, all the more important theories of the redemptive work of God in Christ speak of an "objective" phase in the redemption of the Cross. Without regard to details of doctrinal construction we can easily discern the urgent purpose in this emphasis on the "objective." Men were seeking to guard against making God's work for the race merely a "subjective" or personal affair. They were aiming to link God's work into certain great moral necessities, to prevent its being a merely personal expression of feeling. We are not here concerned with the inconsistencies into which the dogmatists fell as they tried to work the thought through, but the essential purpose is clear and sound. There are inescapable laws for both God and man, and the work of Christ is in harmony with those laws. Criticize some of the theories as out-of-date if we please, but we must concede that in trying to found the work of Christ in holy and loving devotion to fundamental moral verities, the theories were making against arbitrary irresponsibilities which would be out of place in a kingdom of God which men could respect.

*   *   *   *

When Jesus gave his followers the parable of the Good Samaritan he seems to have had in mind the de-humanizing effects of institutions when they are allowed to become ends-in-themselves. The fault with the priest and Levite was that each had been institutionalized into a mere professional. Each was more of a priest or a Levite than a man. All through the career of Jesus runs this protest against the tendency in the religious institutions of his day to become sacred in themselves. As we read the old Mosaic laws their aim at the purification and redemption of human life as such is entirely clear. It is tragic to think of the distortion of perspective by which the later priests came to treat man as if man were made for the Sabbath and not the Sabbath for man. Yet the tragedy is always possible. . . .

The Church enthrones and worships a Creator. How better worship a Creator than by showing a creative spirit? The Scriptures reveal a progressive movement. Is it conceivable that the movement was to come to a standstill at any stage in human affairs? To be sure the revelation in Jesus was made once for all, but the interpretation of that revelation goes on and on. The only adequate revelation of the truth in Jesus is the progressive incarnation of his truth and spirit not only in individuals here and there, but also in individuals knit together in closer and closer social relationships.

* * * *

Ask one non-resistant why he will not fight and he replies that it is a sin to kill one's fellow-man. The voice of conscience is unmistakable. But suppose the fellow-man is himself killing others of our fellow-men. The non-resistant replies that his conscience is at perfect peace, and some observers declare that the Christian joy of the objectors is like the joy of the members of the early church. The argument on the other side takes the form of showing that the joy which attends a self-sacrificing surrender to conscience is no conclusive proof that the concrete commands of conscience are right. The agonized surrender of thousands of other persons to the necessity of war is not without its moral significance. The non-resistant may continue that he is only obeying literally the commands of Jesus. But is he also obeying literally the commands of Jesus in other respects—as to property, as to lending, as to subordination of family interests, as to judging others? And is he certain that he is right in his interpretation of Jesus? Does the word as to a Good Shepherd's giving his life for the sheep mean that a good shepherd passively allows the wolves to devour him? Or, if the robbers had returned while the Good Samaritan was busy at his merciful task how best could the Samaritan have continued his work of neighborliness—by non-resistance or by fighting? Moreover how do we regard Jesus? Is Jesus just a man among other men? But Jesus is regarded by the Church as sustaining such a unique relation to God as to be the revelation of God to man. With such a conception of Jesus it is permissible to maintain that the non-resistance of Jesus shows the spirit of patience and love in which God carries on the universe. For if we start out to prove that God Himself is absolutely non-resistant we land in the bog. If the spirit of Jesus is the spirit of God we find the meaning of the non-resistance of Jesus in its revelation of the spirit in which God uses even the physical forces of the world. But God does not cease to use the forces. If finally the non-resistant declares that his own method is the only one that will break the evil will and win the love of man the reply may be appropriate that methods are not necessarily matters of immediate revelation.

SHAILER MATHEWS   (*1863-*   )

HIS APPROACH TO THE IDEAL SOCIETY

It goes without saying that Jesus does not base his hopes of a new society upon an "enlightened self-interest," or any other hedonist philosophy. That the individual would seek his own good he seems to have assumed, and he never hesitated to appeal to humanity's hopes and fears. But that this in any way needed excuse, or that it was necessary to raise their natural impulse into a philosophy and reduce all social service to terms of a whitewashed selfishness, seems never to have occurred to him. No man ever struck out more manfully against both self-depreciation and self-exaltation than Jesus, but the motive upon which he expected men to act was not that of the improvement of the individual atom. Self-preservation may be the final motive of physical nature, but not with the followers of Jesus. "Whosoever will save his life shall lose it."

Taken altogether, it is obvious that the forces upon which Jesus relied to make his ideal society an actual fact in life, were neither mechanical nor selfish. Whatever approach society as he found it was to make towards that better order which he described would not be the result of external propulsion or calculation. As the kingdom of God is spiritual, so are the forces which bring about its realization; and as it is a family, so are its members to be not self-seekers, but brothers. . . .

Thus Jesus is thoroughly consistent with himself. The new social order which he outlines is not beyond the power of men as he conceives them. It is true that a moral regeneration of the individual is presupposed before society as such can be perfected, but here Jesus is true to human capacities. Religion, just as much as selfish calculation, is one of the motive forces in human life, and to disregard it is to throw away the most powerful source of moral impulse. Therefore it is that while one may perhaps wonder that Jesus should have counted to so small a degree upon other forces that have made forward movements successful, it is quite impossible to say that he has erred in thus centring attention upon the religious side of man's nature and upon that enthusiasm for humanity which is the outgrowth of a perception of the consequent new human fraternity. Life is indeed something more than search for creature comforts. Those men of the past who have marked stages in the march of the race have always so judged. Take from the goodly company of the men who have permanently beautified society, those men whose impulse have not in some way sprung from the sense of God or the sense of fraternity, and how many will be left? In his revelation of divine sonship and the consequent human brotherhood, Jesus has furnished the basis for lasting social progress. For if humanity is to become a family inspired by the love of the divine Father, there is no power in earth or hell that can prevent the realization of the noblest social ideals of which the world has dreamed.

HENRY L. MENCKEN   (*1880*–   )

TAUGHT THE EQUALITY OF MAN

The historicity of Jesus is no longer questioned seriously by anyone, whether Christian or unbeliever. The main facts about Him seem to be beyond dispute: that He lived in Palestine during the reigns of the Roman Emperors Augustus and Tiberius, that He was a pious Jew and a man of great personal dignity and virtue, that He believed the end of the world was at hand and sought to induce His fellow Jews to prepare for it, that He aroused thereby the enmity of the Jewish priests and was put to death at their behest, that certain of His followers after His death believed that He had arisen from the tomb, and that this belief, appealing powerfully to the imagination of the time, carried His ideas from end to end of the Roman world, and so founded what is now called Christianity. The New Testament is thus an historical document of very tolerable authority, needing only to be read with due circumspection. . . .

The egalitarianism that He preached was anything but the political egalitarianism that we know today, and it is thus absurd to call Him, as so many do, the father of Socialism. What He had in mind was not political or economic equality, but simply the equality of man before God. . . . And in His preaching of the fatherhood of God there was ground enough for any egalitarianism imaginable, for a divine Father could hardly be thought of as making some of His children slaves of the rest. Thus the teachings of Jesus fell upon soil that had been long preparing for them, and perhaps it would not be unfair to add that they took vigorous root there largely because they were misunderstood. To poor and miserable men, so misunderstanding them, they must have come as revelations of a new and enormously happier world order. . . . Nor was it only the poor who hearkened to them, and hearkening, rejoiced and gave thanks to God, for among the first to accept them were certain persons of rank and fortune, and especially women, who had long dreamed of a better day.

John · Middleton · Murry   (*1889*–   )

"HE CAME TO DESTROY BY LOVE"

Christ was and is a revolutionary. "The Sabbath was made for Man, not Man for the Sabbath." There never was a more revolutionary utterance than that. But at the same time, he came "not to destroy but to fulfill." Unless we hold these two elements together in our experience and imagination, we pervert Christ to the service of our Selfhood. There is no way of holding those two things together except by the experience and imagination of love: which is the experience and imagination of the living Christ. Christ came to destroy by love: and to destroy by love is to fulfill. It is . . . to destroy Evil by destroying the Selfhood: ultimately, to destroy it in the only place where it can be destroyed—in our Selves. This—and nothing else is—the gospel of Christ.

A. J. Muste   (*1885*–   )

HE REJECTED COMPROMISE

Let us turn now to consider Jesus' wrestling with the same problem that confronted the prophets of the great age. Anyone who thinks of Jesus as a secular revolutionist, socialist, or communist is certainly mistaken. But it is quite as mistaken to think of Jesus as a Barthian who could make distinctions as to the sphere of life in which the law of love is fully operative. He, too, finds his nation ground under the heel of the dictator. Nothing seems to me clearer than that He applied the teachings which we sketched in the preceding chapter to the crucial political and social question of his day, that of the attitudes of his people toward the Roman oppressors, toward Caesar and Caesarism.

He knows himself called to be God's instrument to redeem his people, "to proclaim liberty to the captives." But how to do it? Surely He must achieve influence, power? He must take "the kingdoms of the world and the glory of them?" Then He will be able to use his place and power to establish God's reign. If this means that He must stoop, "bow the knee" a little, surely that could not be helped. If the Messiah is not to base His policy primarily on meeting material needs (making bread out of stones) and if He is not to impose himself by magical means (leaping from the pinnacle of the Temple), then He must in some measure take men as He finds them, must be "practical" and "realistic," a little flexible as to the means He employs. But it was precisely this suggestion of compromise, the idea that evil might overcome evil, that He rejected most decisively. He rejected it as Satanic—"Get thee behind me, Satan"—that is, as contrary to His fundamental conception of God. The God whose Son He knew himself to be was not a heavenly potentate, a celestial general, but the prophets' God of righteousness and love. So his servant could not be an earthly Caesar. He must be "the suffering servant of Jehovah."

If one rejects the method of domination and violence in order to overcome evil and establish the reign of good, what means then can he use? He can live the life of love. He can proclaim it to his fellows and urge them to adopt it. He can expose the hypocrisy of those who have power in Church and state and the evils of their rule. He can organize in peaceful ways to bring about a different order. If a man does all these things, he will meet opposition. If he refuses to fight back, he is likely to be defeated and killed. Jesus accepted that fact. He rejected the way of the sword and knew that He would therefore have to tread the way of the Cross. Peter could not understand that, but when he exclaimed that the Christ whom he had just confessed must not be crucified, Jesus again said, "Get thee behind me Satan!" The idea that there is another way than this of suffering love was for Him the last, most subtle, most Satanic temptation which assails the good man, the man eager to help his fellows. Jesus' other contemporaries did not understand Him at this point either. They stood at the foot of His cross and said: "Let him now come down from the cross, and we will believe on him"—that is to say: "He is good and great, He could be Messiah, our deliverer, but not in this unrealistic, fantastic fashion. Let Him now come down from the cross and—" But Jesus had made His decision.

To His people Jesus in effect said: "Do not hate the Romans; love your enemies. You think the Romans are oppressors, they conscript you, they take your cloaks, they 'rob widows' houses'? But so do you, Pharisees. You too have violated all the canons of social justice, all 'the weightier matters of the law.' And it is worse for you, because you had the light of the great prophets of the past to whom you like to build monuments, whereas the Romans did not. The real reason you do not want the Romans around is because you want to have a monopoly on robbing widows' houses, you do not like those who can teach you lessons in exploitation and cruelty. But the judgments of the Lord which are true and righteous altogether overtake such as you.

"If now you, the chosen people of God, do not repent, change your whole outlook and take first the beam out of your own eye, making yourselves true servants of light and righteousness, then how can we ever get out of this mess into a better world? If even God's people can only join the endless circle of meeting evil with evil, if the salt has lost its savor, its distinctiveness, wherewith shall it be salted?

"Furthermore, if you do not live up to your greater light, if you trample it under foot, how can you honestly claim that you represent more sacred values, a higher order than the Romans, which you must and may defend by any means at your disposal? If war comes under these circumstances, it will not be a war of light against darkness, God's hosts against Satan's. It will be a war of brute force against brute force; or more accurately of one misguided group of God's children called Jews against another misguided group of God's children called Romans.

"A new, distinctive force and technique must be introduced into the situation. Do you, therefore, prove yourselves the sons of prophets, rather than the sons of those who killed the prophets. Do you repent; give up selfish, imperialist ambition; renounce every foolish intention to overcome evil with evil, to stop Caesar with his own weapons. Do you devote yourselves to infusing a spiritual principle, the saving social principle of brotherhood, into this great politico-economic structure which men have succeeded in building and which has such great possibilities.

"Do you do that and by being thus willing to risk your own life as one power-state among many, you will save yourself. And you will save this civilization, this magnificent body which needs a soul. Caesarism will not be able to stand against such faith, righteousness, and love. I shall then be King, a King of a new kind, 'meek and riding upon an ass.' You shall know the peace of God, not the uneasy truces of man.

"If you will not take this way of peace, if in self-righteousness and selfishness and fear, you bring yourself down to Caesar's level, use his weapons, you will join Caesar's representative presently in crucifying me. Then destruction will overtake you, 'there shall not be left here one stone upon another that shall not be torn down.' And since the salt that should have preserved this civilization will have proven savorless, this civilization also will degenerate and perish.

"But," Jesus concluded his religious-political manifesto to his people, "that will not be the end. You will not have defeated my Father-God. Into His hands I shall confidently commend my spirit, that spirit on which every enduring society will have to be built. After three days I shall rise again. You will see the Son of Man coming in his glory."

DAVID SAVILLE MUZZEY   (*1870*–   )

THE SUM OF HIS GOSPEL

We have seen how Jesus subjected the entire religious system of his countrymen, its observances, its authorities, and its dogmas to searching ethical criticism based on the unshakable conviction of sonship with a Heavenly Father. In this we must recognize him as one of the hardiest religious innovators the world has ever seen. Yet so great was his tact and so perfect his balance that he made destruction appear like fulfilment. With a divine consistency and persistency that will be the wonder of humanity through all time he seized on the essential spiritual truth of every situation and every doctrine, and gave it to the world in a form so simple that a child may understand it. He did not allow himself to be drawn aside from his grand purpose and become involved in minor controversies. He was not an ascetic, though he rose above all temptations of the flesh; he was not a preacher of social revolution; though he constantly spoke of the danger of riches; he did not make capital of the world's misery, though he blessed the poor and needy; he did not antagonize culture, labour and property, though he asked what profit there was if one "gained the whole world and lost his own soul." He spoke always as one who has become fully persuaded in his own mind of the supreme good of life and has bartered all else for that good—"the pearl of great price." Nowhere do we find hurry, anxiety, or struggle in his nature. A deep peace, complete trust in a Heavenly Father, a satisfying joy of sonship, and a confident belief in every man's and woman's power and need to turn from selfishness and worldliness, and become, like him, a child of God—these simple but vivifying principles seem to have been all his Gospel. He did not shrink from the furtherest consequences of his Gospel, whether they involved the holiest customs and beliefs of his people; and withal there was nothing of the bitter dialectician or the nagging controversialist in him. He had no anxiety for his doctrine, only a great desire to spread its blessing as far and wide as possible. His enthusiasm was undisturbed by any misgiving that his mission might fail. "Heaven and earth shall pass away, but my words shall not pass away." And this was because his word was not of himself, but of the Father who sent him.

BEVERLEY NICHOLS   (*1899–*   )

EPIGRAMS LIKE STARS

Christ was, after all, by far the greatest wit that the world has ever known. Most men's epigrams are like sparks—they fly up into contemporary skies, light up a tiny fragment of landscape, put out an eye, and then they are as ashes. But Christ's epigrams are like stars. And like the stars, they are as near to eternity as we could want. Consider, for example, that extremely startling statement (which was not saved up for a dinner table, but was casually thrown off in a conversation with some fishermen)—*For he that hath, to him shall be given: and he that hath not, from him shall be taken even that which he hath.* If Christ had said only that one sentence He would have said more than most men in their passage through this world. For this sentence is not only an epigram, and not only a shrewd criticism of the process of contemporary capitalist society. It is also, as Aldous Huxley has pointed out, the formulation of a natural law. Indeed, it might very well have served as a text on the front page of the *Origin of Species*.

DANIEL A. POLING   (*1884–*   )

DEATH THE OPEN DOOR

It was in an hour when the cause of Christ faced disaster, when He, himself, was close to crucifixion, that He said, "Except a corn of wheat fall into the ground and die, it abideth alone; but if it die, it bringeth forth much fruit." The language is of the East and the truth is a parable, but the words mean "the end is the beginning," and Jesus was speaking of Himself.

For Jesus, death was the open door. Before the stone was rolled away from His physical tomb, He had moved into the glory of His new life, into the triumph of His greater career. The end was indeed the beginning. It was the beginning of the Christian church, and of Christian civilization. It was the beginning of modern history and of a new era of human progress. Here was dawn of the first day of a victory that is still in its morning, the victory of man over materials and the emergence of the dignity of human personality.

Democracy in all its modern forms, political and social freedom as well as free religious expression, have risen from the tomb in Joseph's garden. In a few generations, the North American continent has witnessed this flowering. Here all the freedoms and all who would cherish them, have grown together. Now with a unity that sweeps across racial and religious frontiers, the American people rise to protect their heritage and defend their faith. Each must stand in his own place or in the position assigned him with a determination to contribute the maximum of his strength each for all and all for the common cause. It was the Great Teacher, himself, who taught that man is a citizen of two worlds; that he owes allegiance to God first but to the state always. Those who have gone before us . . . have in some measure fulfilled that immortal promise of the Great Teacher: "If a corn of wheat fall into the ground and die, it bringeth forth much fruit."

The end is the beginning. Out of death has come new and greater life. Those who have died have not died in vain.

S. RADHAKRISHNAN   (*1888–*   )

REVEALED CONCEPTION OF GOD

Christian theology . . . takes its stand on the immediate certitude
of Jesus as one whose absolute authority over conscience is self-
certifying and whose ability and willingness to save the soul it is impossible not to trust.

*   *   *   *

The conception of the Holy One who loves mercy rather than sacrifice, who abominates burnt offerings, who reveals himself to those
who yearn to know him asserts itself in the writings of Isaiah and
Hosea. In the revelation of Jesus we have the conception of God as
perfect love.

*   *   *   *

After all, what counts is not creed but conduct. By their fruits ye
shall know them and not by their beliefs. The truly religious never
worry about other people's beliefs. Look at the great saying of Jesus:
"Other sheep I have which are not of this fold." Jesus was born a
Jew and died a Jew. He did not tell the Jewish people among whom
he found himself, "It is wicked to be Jews. Become Christians." He
did his best to rid the Jewish religion of its impurities. He would
have done the same with Hinduism were he born a Hindu. The true
reformer purifies and enlarges the heritage of mankind and does not
belittle, still less deny it.

*   *   *   *

Justice is an attribute of God. The character of God is represented
by Jesus as one "with whom there can be no variation neither shadow
that is cast by turning." Every act, every thought is weighed in the
invisible but universal balance-scales of justice. The day of judgment
is not in some remote future, but here and now, and none can escape
it. Divine laws cannot be evaded. They are not so much imposed

from without as wrought into our natures. Sin is not so much a defiance of God as a denial of soul, not so much a violation of law as a betrayal of self. It is an ineffaceable record which time cannot blur nor death erase.

Walter Rauschenbusch (*1861–1918*)

RAREST SECRET OF ALL

In truth Jesus was not a reformer of the modern type. Sociology and political economy were just as far outside his range of thought as organic chemistry or the geography of America. He saw the evil in the life of men and their sufferings, but he approaches these facts purely from the moral, and not from the economic or historical point of view. He wanted men to live a right life in common, and only in so far as the social questions are moral questions did he deal with them as they confronted him.

And he was more than a teacher of morality. Jesus had learned the greatest and deepest and rarest secret of all—how to live a religious life. . . . Jesus had realized the life of God in the soul of man and the life of man in the love of God. That was the real secret of his life, the well-spring of his purity, his compassion, his unwearied courage, his unquenchable idealism: he knew the Father. But if he had that greatest of all possessions, the real key to the secret of life, it was his highest social duty to share it and help others to gain what he had. He had to teach men to live as children in the presence of their Father, and no longer as slaves cringing before a despot. He had to show them that the ordinary life of selfishness and hate and anxiety and chafing ambition and covetousness is no life at all, and that they must enter into a new world of love and solidarity and inward content. There was no service that he could render to men which would equal that. All other help lay in concentric circles about that redemption of the spirit and flowed out from it.

* * * *

If we want to understand the real aims of Jesus, we must watch
him in his relation to his own times. He was not a timeless religious
teacher, philosophizing vaguely on human generalities. He spoke
for his own age, about concrete conditions, responding to the stirrings
of the life that surged about him. We must follow him in his adjustment to the tendencies of the time, in his affinity for some men and
his repulsion of others. That is the method by which we classify
and locate a modern thinker or statesman.

*   *   *   *

Jesus began his preaching with the call: "The time is fulfilled;
the kingdom of God is now close at hand; repent and believe in the
glad news." The kingdom of God continued to be the center of all
his teaching as recorded by the synoptic gospels. His parables, his
moral instructions, and his prophetic predictions all bear on that.

We have no definition of what he meant by the phrase. His audience needed no definition. It was then a familiar conception and
phrase. The new thing was simply that this kingdom was at last on
the point of coming.

*   *   *   *

When Jesus used the phrase "The kingdom of God," it inevitably
evoked that whole sphere of thought in the minds of his hearers. If
he did not mean by it the substance of what they meant by it, it was
a mistake to use the term. If he did not mean the consummation of
the theocratic hope, but merely an internal blessedness for individuals with the hope of getting to heaven, why did he use the words
around which all the collective hopes clustered? In that case it was
not only a misleading but a dangerous phrase. It unfettered all the
political hopes of the crowd; it drew down on him the suspicion of
the government; it actually led to his death.

Unless we have clear proof to the contrary, we must assume that
in the main the words meant the same thing to him and to his audiences. But it is very possible that he seriously modified and corrected

the popular conception. That is in fact the process with every great, creative religious mind: the connection with the past is maintained and the old terms are used, but they are set in new connections and filled with new qualities. In the teaching of Jesus we find that he consciously opposed some features of the popular hope and sought to make it truer.

For one thing he would have nothing to do with bloodshed and violence. When the crowds that were on their way to the Passover gathered around him in the solitude on the Eastern shore of the lake and wanted to make him king and march on the capital, he eluded them by sending his inflammable disciples away in the boat, and himself going up among the rocks to pray till the darkness dispersed the crowd. Alliance with the Messianic force-revolution was one of the temptations which he confronted at the outset and repudiated; he would not set up God's kingdom by using the devil's means of hatred and bloodshed. With the glorious idealism of faith and love Jesus threw away the sword and advanced on the intrenchments of wrong with hand outstretched and heart exposed.

He repudiated not only human violence, he even put aside the force which the common hope expected from heaven. He refused to summon the twelve legions of angels either to save his life or to set up the kingdom by slaying the wicked.

* * * *

The popular hope was all for a divine catastrophe. The kingdom of God was to come by a beneficent earthquake. Some day it would come like the blaze of a meteor, "with outward observation," and they could say: "Lo, there it is!" We have seen that the prophetic hope had become catastrophic and apocalyptic when the capacity for political self-help was paralyzed. When the nation was pinned down helplessly by the crushing weight of the oppressors, it had to believe in a divine catastrophe that bore no causal relation to human action. The higher spiritual insight of Jesus reverted to the earlier and nobler prophetic view that the future was to grow out of the present by divine help. While they were waiting for the Messianic cataclysm that would bring the kingdom of God ready-made from heaven, he saw it growing up among them.

*   *   *   *

Like the old prophets, Jesus believed that God was the real creator of the kingdom; it was not to be set up by manmade evolution . . . He certainly believed in a divine consummation at the close. But the more he believed in the supreme value of its spiritual and moral blessings, and in the power of spiritual forces to mould human life, the more would the final act of consummation recede in importance and the present facts and processes grow more concrete and important to his mind. It was an act of religious faith for John the Baptist to assert that the long-desired kingdom was almost here. It was a vastly higher act of faith for Jesus to say that it was actually here.

*   *   *   *

Jesus, like all the prophets and like all his spiritually minded countrymen, lived in the hope of a great transformation of the national, social, and religious life about him. He shared the substance of that hope with his people, but by his profounder insight and his loftier faith he elevated and transformed the common hope. He rejected all violent means and thereby transferred the inevitable conflict from the field of battle to the antagonism of mind against mind, and of heart against lack of heart. He postponed the divine catastrophe of judgment to the dim distance and put the emphasis on the growth of the new life that was going on. . . . The old intent gaze into the future was turned to faith in present realities and beginnings, and found its task here and now.

ECONOMICS OF HIS TEACHINGS

What did Christ teach those who actually listened to Him, concerning the economic life? There are those who hold that what He said held good for them and for those also who live centuries after in a different kind of world. But I do not know anyone who declares that He spoke *only* to generations unborn, and that His teaching had no application to the lives of those who heard His words. . . . There is no ground for assuming either that His words had *no* application to the facts of His day, or that He said many unrecorded things which His chroniclers thought fit for their own reasons and interests to suppress. . . .

Christ commented often upon the contrast between rich and poor, and unequal distribution of wealth. But He dwelt most emphatically upon the moral risks of wealth to the individual owner. . . . The act of material accumulation was contrasted with spiritual wealth. . . . He did not suggest that the rich man, as such, was an economic or even a moral evil in his environment. . . . The home in Bethany that meant so much to Him was certainly "well off". . . . Different lessons have been drawn from the incident of the rich young ruler. It was certainly personal to his case, and some think the injunction was only for his own good; others conclude that he could not, with wealth, have really become one of the circle of followers. . . .

He also showed that riches were sometimes gained by inexcusable means and that restitution was proper . . . , but beyond that did not specifically condemn the *process* of acquiring wealth. But He placed very high the proper *disposal* of wealth, when made, by individual volition, not by compulsion. And the value of the act of charity lay in its *initiative*—it was not a social process. . . .

The disuse of all gifts was punished by loss. . . .

Undue preoccupation not merely with wealth, but even with modest material accessories of life, was reproved. . . . It is not clear that

He promised *material* satisfactions to those who themselves ignored the methods of securing them. . . . He assumed that carelessness about one's possessions was not creditable. . . . Possessions are assumed as a social process without condemnation. . . . But Christ went a long way towards suggesting that poverty in the things of this world might receive comparative adjustment in the things of the next . . . or in *spiritual* counterweight now. . . . He indicated that in spiritual matters there should not be too nice a calculation of material sacrifice. . . .

There was no suggestion that poverty was *socially* curable . . . though much of the intention in the references to the poor seems to be more consistent with poverty of *spirit*. . . .

Economic forethought and planning is a reasonable act . . . though excessive thought for the morrow is deprecated. Cause and effect are often referred to, extending the analogy from nature to the moral sphere. . . .

When Christ frequently asserts the place of spiritual cares as against, or superior to material goods . . . He does not of course condemn the "meat that perishes." There must be an economic system alongside the spiritual kingdom.

The clearest fact that emerges from this survey is that Christ did not condemn the institutions and relationships of His day; He accepted them with a rather astonishing acquiescence—the priestly taxation and the Roman yoke. What he insisted on was that the measure of personal authority actually given to each person in the system by higher authority must not be exceeded or abused, and the duty imposed must not be shirked. . . . How popular Christ would have been if He had even given a hint that the oppressive system was wrong, and the Roman yoke burdensome—and both could rightfully have been urged—but He was not a political revolutionary, or anything but law-abiding, calling for the highest personal morality *within the system*. . . . While Jesus was not a social revolutionary, He was no *laissez-faire* optimist. He was vehement against abuses and false ideas such as the hypocritical legalism of Corban, or the one-sided obligations of marital fidelity, in the Jewish law, which took account of adultery only of the wife.

HARRIET BEECHER STOWE   (*1811–1896*)

THE CALM OF THE DIVINE REFORMER

What impresses us most in the character of Jesus, as a reformer, is the atmosphere of peacefulness that surrounded him, and in which he seemed to live and move and have his being.

Human beings as reformers are generally agitated, hurried, impatient. Scarcely are the spirits of the prophets subject to the prophets. They are liable to run before the proper time and season, to tear open the bud that ought to enfold. They become nervous, irascible, and lose mental and physical health: and if the reform on which they have set their heart fails, they are overwhelmed with discouragement and tempted to doubt Divine Providence.

*   *   *   *

In our Saviour's public career we are surprised at nothing so much as his calmness. He was never in haste. His words have all the weight of deliberation, and the occasions when he refrains from speech are fully as remarkable as the things he says.

There seems to be about him none of the wearying anxiety as to immediate results, none of the alternations of hope and discouragement that mark our course. He had faith in God, whose great plan he was working, whose message he came to deliver and whose times and seasons he strictly regarded. So, too, did he regard the mental and spiritual condition of the imperfect ones by whom he was surrounded. . . . When their zeal transcended his, and they longed to get hold of the thunderbolts and call down fire from heaven, his grave and steady rebuke recalled them: "Ye know not what manner of spirit ye are of."

DAVID FRIEDRICH STRAUSS   (*1808–1874*)

HIS LEADERSHIP IN IDEALS

Translator Anonymous

Among these improvers of the ideal of humanity Jesus stands at all events in the first class. He introduced features into it which were wanting to it before, or had continued undeveloped; reduced the dimensions of others which prevented its universal application; imported into it, by the religious aspect which he gave it, a more lofty consecration, and bestowed upon it, by embodying it in his own person, the most vital warmth; while the Religious Society which took its rise from him provided for this ideal the widest acceptance among mankind. It is true, indeed, that the Religious Society originated in quite other things than the moral significance of its founder, and did anything but exhibit this in its purest form—in the only writing of our New Testament which perhaps comes from an immediate disciple of Jesus, the Revelation of John, there lives a Christ from whom little is to be gained for the ideal of humanity; but the features of patience, gentleness, and charity which Jesus made predominant in that image have not been lost to mankind, and are exactly those from which all we now call Humanity might germinate and grow. . . .

It cannot be overlooked, that in the pattern exhibited by Jesus in his doctrine and in his life, some sides being finished to perfection, others were only faintly sketched, or not indicated at all. Every point is fully developed that has reference to Love towards God and our neighbour, to purity in the heart and life of the individual; but even the life of man in the family is left by the Teacher, himself childless, in the background; his relation toward the body politic appears simply passive; with trade he is not only by reason of his calling unconcerned, but even visibly averse to it, and everything relating to art and enjoyment of the elegancies of life is absolutely removed from his range of view.

ARCHBISHOP SAMUEL A. STRITCH   (*1887*–   )

GAVE MAN A NEW DIGNITY

Too often in our past men have talked about their rights and on them built up a selfish individualism and forgotten the rights of others in the recognition of which justice is complemented by charity. Certainly the second of these concepts, human dignity, has its roots in our very rational nature and free will, but as a clear social concept it broke upon the world from the Cross of Calvary. When in His Human Nature all men won the victory over sin and the privilege of incorporation into His Body, there came a new sacredness, a new dignity to human nature. As a social concept it broke the shackles of the slave, exalted women from the condition of a chattel, clothed the weak and the helpless with an immunity from exploitation. The pagans dimly saw the truth of human rights, but they never envisioned the fact of human dignity. And the last of these concepts I have called neighborliness. It too came to us from the Cross where men see Christ become as St. Augustine says, "our neighbor." In this concept we are asked to give more than mere justice to others, we are asked to give them charity. There must be a trying to understand the problem of others, an appreciation of their individual gifts, a mutual helpfulness. These three social concepts which call to God and to Christ are strikingly absent in the totalitarian and fascist and communist systems, but they must not be forgotten in the peace if there is to be a better day for the world when our victory comes.

Norman Thomas   (*1884*–   )

SOURCE OF HIS ETHICAL PRINCIPLES

Christianity has no economics or political service for our guidance; it has certain great ethical principles perhaps more explicitly and clearly stated and exemplified in the Jesus of the Gospels than in other religions. But if we can tell anything at all about the mind of Jesus it is clear that for him these ethical principles were derived simply and directly from his sense of God. Whatever one may think of the learned discussions of the "apocalyptic hope" and the "interim ethic" in the teachings of Jesus, it seems to me clear that his way of life, his exhortations to forgiveness, to mercy, to brotherhood, in short to an unworldly perfection, were based on his belief in One who forgives us as we forgive others, whose mercy is everlasting, whose Fatherhood is the ground of human brotherhood and who is Himself perfection.

There are dozens of more powerful reasons for a decent code of social ethics or for a new economic order than Christianity in the more extreme of its modern versions can give us. If Jesus was mistaken about God we may admire him as we admire many another of the prophets and saints of all religions and of none; we cannot reasonably accept his ethics as authoritative.

On the other hand, if a man does accept in any sincerity a faith in Jesus and Jesus' God, whether he calls himself orthodox or modernist, it is impossible to see how he can be at peace with the present social order whose God is profit and whose largest loyalty is the inadequate and divisive loyalty of nationalism.

Count Lyof N. Tolstoi   *(1828–1910)*

FORMULATOR OF THE NEW LAW

Translator Anonymous

I now understand the words of Jesus: *"Ye have heard that it hath been said, An eye for an eye, and a tooth for a tooth; but I say unto you, That ye resist not evil."* Jesus' meaning is: You have thought that you were acting in a reasonable manner in defending yourself by violence against evil, in tearing out an eye for an eye, by fighting against evil with criminal tribunals, guardians of the peace, armies; but I say unto you, "Renounce violence; have nothing to do with violence; do harm to no one, not even to your enemy." I understand now that in saying *"Resist not evil,"* Jesus not only told us what would result from the observance of this rule, but established a new basis for society conformable to His doctrine and opposed to the social basis established by the law of Moses, by Roman law, and by the different codes in force to-day. He formulated a new law whose effect would be to deliver humanity from its self-inflicted woes. His declaration was: "You believe that your laws reform criminals; as a matter of fact, they only make more criminals. There is only one way to suppress evil, and that is to return good for evil, without respect of persons. For thousands of years you have tried the other method, now try mine,—try the reverse."

John J. Walde   *(1900–   )*

SOME GLOWING PROMISES

When Christ preached His memorable Sermon on the Mount he made some glowing promises. He told hungry hearts that they would have their fill of happiness but nowhere did He say, "Blessed are the rich. Blessed are the comfortable." By this He did not exclude the moneyed man or the moneyed woman from His Kingdom, but he did mean that they must be poor in spirit and that they must always realize that they are only the stewards of this world's goods. Besides, if one has wealth or power, he must always hunger for justice; he must be filled with mercy and always anxious for peace. Blessedness was promised to the poor, the meek, the mourning, to the hungry and thirsty after justice, to the merciful, the pure, and the peaceful, and very specially to those persecuted for justice sake. All these counsels go counter to wordly ambitions, and yet these are the guiding lights of Christian living. They savor very much of the Cross, and so they have been rejected.

H. G. WELLS   (*1866–*   )

TAUGHT A REVOLUTIONARY DOCTRINE

In the reign of Tiberius Caesar a great teacher arose out of Judea who was to liberate the intense realization of the righteousness and unchallengeable oneness of God, and of man's moral obligation to God, which was the strength of orthodox Judaism, from that greedy and exclusive narrowness with which it was so extraordinarily intermingled in the Jewish mind. This was Jesus of Nazareth, the seed rather than the founder of Christianity.

We are left . . . with the figure of a being, very human, very earnest and passionate, capable of swift anger, and teaching a new and simple and profound doctrine—namely, the universal loving Fatherhood of God and the coming of the Kingdom of Heaven. He was clearly a person—to use a common phrase—of intense personal magnetism. He attracted followers and filled them with love and courage. Weak and ailing people were heartened and healed by his presence.

This doctrine of the Kingdom of Heaven, which was the main teaching of Jesus, . . . is certainly one of the most revolutionary doctrines that ever stirred and changed human thought. . . . For the doctrine of the Kingdom of Heaven, as Jesus seems to have preached it, was no less than a bold and uncompromising demand for a complete change and cleansing of the life of our struggling race, an utter cleansing, without and within. . . .

God, he taught, was no bargainer; there were no chosen people and no favourites in the Kingdom of Heaven, God was the loving father of all life, as incapable of showing favour as the universal sun. And all men were brothers—sinners alike and beloved sons alike—of this divine father. . . . All whom God takes into the kingdom, he taught, God serves alike; there is no distinction in his treatment, because there is no measure to his bounty. From all, moreover, as the parable of the buried talent witnesses, and as the incident of the widow's mite enforced, he demands the utmost. There are no privileges, no rebates, and no excuses in the Kingdom of Heaven.

And not only did Jesus strike at patriotism and the bonds of family loyalty in the name of God's universal fatherhood and the brotherhood of all mankind, but it is clear that his teaching condemned all the gradation of the economic system, all private wealth, and personal advantages. All men belonged to the kingdom; all their possessions belonged to the kingdom; the righteous life for all men, the only righteous life, was the service of God's will with all that we had, with all that we were. Again and again he denounced private riches and the reservations of any private life.

It was not merely a moral and social revolution that Jesus proclaimed; it is clear from a score of indications that his teaching had a political bent of the plainest sort. It is true that he said his kingdom was not of this world, that it was in the hearts of men and not upon a throne; but it is equally clear that wherever and in what measure his kingdom was set up in the hearts of men, the outer world would be in that measure revolutionized and made new.

The whole tenor of the opposition to him and the circumstances of his trial and execution show clearly that to his contemporaries he seemed to propose plainly and did propose plainly to change and fuse and enlarge all human life. But even his disciples did not grasp the profound and comprehensive significance of that proposal. They were ridden by the old Jewish dream of a king, a Messiah to over-throw the Hellenic Herods and the Roman overlord, and restore the fabled glories of David. They disregarded the substance of his teach-ing, plain and direct though it was; evidently they thought it was merely his mysterious and singular way of setting about the adven-ture that would at last put him on the throne of Jerusalem. They thought he was just another king among the endless succession of kings, but of a quasi-magical kind, making quasi-magical professions of an impossible virtue.

He was too great for his disciples. And in view of what he plainly said, is it any wonder that all who were rich and prosperous felt a horror of strange things, a swimming of their world at his teaching? Perhaps the priests and the rulers and the rich men understood him better than his followers. He was dragging out all the little private reservations they had made from social service into the light of a uni-versal religious life. He was like some terrible moral huntsman dig-ging mankind out of the snug burrows in which they had lived hitherto. In the white blaze of this kingdom of his there was to be no property, no privilege, no pride and precedence; no motive in-deed and no reward but love. Is it any wonder that men were dazzled and blinded and cried out against him? Even his disciples cried out when he would not spare them the light. Is it any wonder that the priests realized that between this man and themselves there was no choice but that he or priestcraft should perish? Is it any wonder that the Roman soldiers, confronted and amazed by something soaring over their comprehension and threatening all their disciplines, should take refuge in wild laughter, and crown him with thorns and robe him in purple and make a mock Caesar of him? For to take him seriously was to enter upon a strange and alarming life, to abandon habits, to control instincts and impulses, to essay an incredible hap-piness. . . .

Is it any wonder that to this day this Galilean is too much for our small hearts?

Paul Austin Wolfe (*1898–*)

HIS MODERATION A CHARACTERISTIC

He was once asked whether it was lawful to pay tribute to Caesar. It was a penetrating question. Jesus was a Jew and his first allegiance was to God. Caesar was from Rome and his allegiance was to force. How could a man who was loyal to God pay tribute to force?

You remember how Jesus answered that question. He asked for a piece of money, and when he had received the coin he asked his hearers whose image and superscription was on it. They told him, "Caesar's." Jesus said, "Render therefore unto Caesar the things that are Caesar's." He seems to say, "If Caesar made this coin, if he is responsible for it, then by all means give it to him. Render unto force that recognition and support which an orderly society requires." And he added, "Render unto God the things that are God's."

What we ought to mark in those words is the balance, the moderation of Christ. He was not a fanatic. He was not an extremist. He dealt with life as it is. He understood that the State is a necessity. That is what Caesar represented. Caesar stood for law, for the orderly processes of social life, of trade and commerce by which the bodies and spirits of men are kept alive. Jesus recognized that order was necessary.

PROPHET

THE KINGDOM HE PROCLAIMED

The dull, stagnant, blighting ecclesiasticism in which the religion of Israel languished during our Lord's earthly ministry afforded no suitable environment for any servant of God. The dissertations of Scribes and Pharisees, who usurped the seat of Moses and hedged about the law with traditions that obscured its meaning and obstructed its operation, were entirely antagonistic to the mission and message of Jesus. Yet there were also protagonists of the Messianic hope who were not fettered by the lifeless formalism of that day: vigilant and prayerful souls who, though few in number, clung to the purer ideals of their ancestors, and waited for the consolation of Israel. Our Lord went beyond both these groups and heralded the Kingdom for what it was, and, as we have seen, had always been, a present, living, growing reality. He showed that the same fundamental principles underlay and created all changing phenomena, which were adapted to the particular stage of evolution in which they occurred. Now that the fullness of the time had come, it was not by specific Mosaic legislation, still less by the erroneous and acrid teachings of its latest commentators, but by the ethical and spiritual truths, which from the beginning had found their amplest expression in the prophets, that the Kingdom would be brought in and prove victorious. Injunction, code and ordinance were honored by being absorbed in its great law of love to God and one's neighbor. The realization of its essential character and aims was in Himself; its fulfillment belonged to His future. For this fulfillment He instructed His disciples to pray, and to believe that their prayers would be answered when all men should know and do the Father's will. Crowns and thrones were not abolished: they were etherealized into symbols of the reward of the saint and the martyr. They reigned in His kingdom who best served truth and the brotherhood, and He became its King because He alone exalted His divine ideal by a divine sacrifice. . . .

The path which he trod from Nazareth into His public ministry can be clearly traced. He was a rabbi who gathered around Him a few disciples of His own locality and social condition, to whom He conveyed the truths they could assimilate. He was an evangelist who itinerated among the shepherdless multitudes, healing their bodies and their souls. He was also the prophet who proclaimed the purposes of Heaven in terms that indicated His perfect intimacy with the Father and His perfect obedience to the Father's will.

SIR HALL CAINE   (*1853–1931*)

A PROPHET TAUGHT BY GOD

He was born poor, lived poor, and died penniless. Like all great men he loved humanity with a deep love. Especially he loved the poor, the weak, the oppressed and the sinful, and he passed the few years of his life among them with a tenderness of sympathy for their sufferings which it is often difficult to think of without tears. He became a man of great wisdom, perhaps of great learning, certainly of great genius. As far as we can see he was a prophet taught by God. . . .

By a small group of persons in Palestine, the prophet of the Galilean hills was in his last days, or soon after them, believed to be the Son of God in the special sense that he was the Christ who had been promised by the wisest of His people, and had to die to save the world from its sins. Because he believed the same, himself, and openly proclaimed his belief, he was put to death on a different accusation, at the instigation of an obscure high priest of his own people.

RALPH WALDO EMERSON   (*1803–1882*)

OF THE TRUE RACE OF PROPHETS

Jesus Christ belonged to the true race of prophets. He saw with open
eye the mystery of the soul. Drawn by its severe harmony, ravished
with its beauty, he lived in it, and had his being there. Alone in all
history he estimated the greatness of man. One man was true to what
is in you and me. He saw that God incarnates himself in man, and
evermore goes forth anew to take possession of his World. He said,
in this jubilee of sublime emotion, 'I am divine. Through me, God
acts; through me, speaks. Would you see God, see me; or see thee,
when thou also thinkest as I now think.' But what a distortion did
his doctrine and memory suffer in the same, in the next, and the
following ages! There is no doctrine of the Reason which will bear
to be taught by the Understanding. The understanding caught in this
high chant from the poet's lips, and said, in the next age, 'This was
Jehovah come down out of heaven. I will kill you, if you say he was
a man.' The idioms of his language and the figures of his rhetoric
have usurped the place of his truth; and churches are not built on
his principles, but on his tropes. Christianity became a Mythus, as
the poetic teaching of Greece and of Egypt, before. He spoke of
miracles; for he felt that man's life was a miracle, and all that man
doth, and he knew that this daily miracle shines as the character
ascends. But the word Miracle, as pronounced by Christian churches,
gives a false impression; it is Monster. It is not one with the blow-
ing clover and the falling rain.

He felt respect for Moses and the prophets, but no unfit tenderness at postponing their initial revelations to the hour and the man
that now is; to the eternal revelation in the heart. Thus was he a true
man. Having seen that law in us is commanding, he would not
suffer it to be commanded. Boldly, with hand, and heart, and life,
he declared it was God. Thus is he, as I think, the only soul in
history who has appreciated the worth of man.

WILLIAM ELLERY LEONARD   (*1876–1944*)

NO WEAKNESS IN HIMSELF

Jesus was a sublimely discontented soul. What might be on earth, what he felt should be on earth filled him with grief and dismay before what he saw was upon earth. He preached glad tidings—tidings of the fatherhood of God, of the brotherhood of man, and of a coming day of righteousness; he bade men rejoice and be exceeding glad; sometimes he sang with triumph and joyousness; but how often we hear the undertones of quiet sadness. . . . And this was inevitably deepened by his personal afflictions, by the abuse and isolation he endured; for he was from the beginning the rejected of men, and while even the foxes had their holes, the Galilean prophet had not where to lay his head. . . .

The Nazarene's, as we know, was a supreme vision of righteousness, but he found naught like it in Galilee, or in Judea, or in the regions beyond the Jordan. This is the tragedy of his life, of which the tears of Gethsemane, the scourge, the crown of thorns, were but the last eventful scenes. It was the discontent of the poet; his pain was "the pain of genius": he was crucified many times before Calvary.

But one pain at least, let us trust, was spared him. Legend has loved to dwell upon Jesus as among men alone the sinless one; but, though we have little warrant from the fragmentary facts of the *Synoptics* and from Jesus' explicit words in making him a perfect being, nothing can impugn the essential sublimity of his character. Thus one pain was spared him: he had not to suffer the pain of mocking his own visions by any disloyalty or weakness in himself.

James Martineau   (*1805–1900*)

THE APPOINTED EMBLEM

Jesus Christ of Nazareth, God hath presented to us simply in his inspired humanity. Him we accept, not indeed as very God, but as the true image of God, commissioned to show what no written doctrinal record could declare, the entire moral perfections of Deity. We accept, not indeed his body, not the struggles of his sensitive nature, not the travail of his soul, but his purity, his tenderness, his absolute devotion to the great idea of right, his patient and compassionate warfare against misery and guilt, as the most distinct and beautiful expression of the Divine mind. The peculiar office of Christ is to supply a new *moral* image of Providence; and everything, therefore, except the *moral* complexion of his mind, we leave behind as human and historical merely, and apply to no religious use. . . . The universe gives us the scale of God, and Christ, his Spirit. We climb to the infinitude of his nature by the awful pathway of the stars, where whole forests of worlds silently quiver here and there, like a small leaf of light. We dive into his eternity, through the ocean waves of time, that roll and solemnly break on the imagination, as we trace the wrecks of depraved things upon our present globe. The scope of his intellect, and the majesty of his rule, are seen in the tranquil order and everlasting silence that reign through the fields of his volition. And the spirit that animates the whole is like that of the Prophet of Nazareth; the thoughts that fly upon the swift light throughout creation, charged with fates unnumbered, are like the healing mercies of One that passed no sorrow by. The government of this world, its mysterious allotments of good and ill, its successions of birth and death, its hopes of progress and of peace, each life of individual or nation, is under the administration of One, of whose rectitude and benevolence, whose sympathy with all the holiest aspirations of our virtue and our love, Christ is the appointed emblem. A faith that spreads around and within the mind a Deity thus sublime and holy, feeds the light of every pure affection, and presses with omnipotent

power on the conscience; and our only prayer is, that we may walk
as children of such light.

Thomas Garrigue Masaryk   (*1850–1937*)

NO THEOLOGIAN, BUT A PROPHET

Translated by M. and R. Weatherall

*I have noticed one: whenever you mention your own faith you quote
Christ and the Apostles.*

Yes. Jesus—I usually do not say Christ—for me he is the example
and teacher of religiousness; he teaches that love towards a kind
God, love of one's neighbour and even of one's enemy, and thus a
pure, unstained humanity, is the substance of religion. Religiousness
and morality for Jesus are the chief elements of religion. Notice that
in the Gospels—in comparison with the Old Testament, or with
Greek mythology—there is almost no mythology, almost no cos-
mology, and eschatology, almost no history; there you do not find
detailed regulations concerning cult and ritual; nor ecclesiastical organization. Jesus gives almost nothing but moral instructions, he
turns continually to practical questions as he is forced by the life
around him; he manifests himself his love towards his neighbour by
effective help in spiritual and physical misery. Just look again into
the Gospels; how discreet are Jesus' theological prescriptions, and
his references to the transcendental! God is father to him, to Him
he is in an intimate personal relation, but he does not speak of this
relation much, he lives it, and he does not lay down any system of
theology. Jesus was a living example; he did not preach love merely
with words, but he continually put it into practice, he associated with
the poor, and lowly, he sought out the sinners, and those morally
outcast, he healed the sick, filled the hungry, he warned the rich. Such

a living faith spreads more by example than with words, like a fire,
like an infection. Jesus gave no proof of his religion, speaking always
as one that had authority; he entered into no theological disputes,
but he confuted the Scribes and Pharisees by pointing to the false-
ness of their religiousness and morality. He showed that real religion, real religiousness permeates the whole of life, even the daily
one, the ordinary one, and it permeates it always, at every moment;
most people are satisfied with Sabbath-day religion, with an osten-
tatious, and hardly sincere religion—only in exceptional circumstances, especially when things are looking bad, do they remember
the Good Lord, and cry for help and expect signs and miracles. But
eternal life will not be only after death, and in the other world
—we live in eternity already now, and always. Of course, people do
not like to be aware of that, they put eternity a long way from them;
they keep it in reserve for the time after death. Religion can be experienced not only in church, but also in the factory, in the field,
in the cowshed, and in the drawing-room, in sadness, and in joy.
That is Jesus' example.

And do you accept the historical person of Jesus?

In the Gospels, in the old Christian literature as a whole, and in
tradition, the rich and homogeneous personality of Jesus emerges;
that, sir, is difficult to think out, and put together merely from a series
of legends. For me the Gospels, and the old Christian literature are
enough; their contents give a plastic, lively, and fine picture of the
beginnings and development of Christianity, of its doctrine, of the
people and of the church, and for me that seems to be the chief
thing. Above all things the quality of the doctrine, and the character
of the personality to whom this doctrine is ascribed are the things
that count. The doctrine and the personality are unique, tremendous.

The personality is so lifelike that one is tempted to follow it further.

I have read the most important so-called biographies of Jesus; in
none of them do I find so much religious life as in the Gospels. The
Gospels have the very smell of reality. It is impossible to write the
real life of Jesus, there are too many accounts: from Jesus himself we

have not a word that is genuinely authentic, he himself wrote and left nothing. The first accounts come from Paul who died, I believe, about the year 64, and the Gospels were written from about the year 70 onwards. Also the text of the whole New Testament that has come down to us is open to doubt in many and important parts, there have been interpolations, mistakes in copying, mistakes in translation, and so on; but the main doctrine and religious character of Jesus is caught by the Scriptures well and clearly enough.

And what about the other religious geniuses, say Buddha, Lao-Tse. . . .

I do not presume to pass judgment of them, I have not concerned myself with them very much, but this at least I am prepared to say: They do not overshadow Jesus. If some modern Europeans seek in them a religion higher than that of Jesus it is, I think, due to cultural weariness; they need something exotic to excite their jaded religious phantasy. In that as well the modern crisis in religion stands revealed. I have a special appreciation for the oriental wisdom of resignation, but the wisdom of effective love is much higher. . . .

For me, the leader and teacher of religion is Jesus. Jesus was not a theologian, he was a prophet, the greatest of the prophets; what genius is for art, science, politics, and other spheres, the prophet is for religion. A prophet—that doesn't merely mean to prophesy, and foresee, but to proclaim the divine word, to rebuke, and to lead, to lift up to a new and more spiritual life; to be an example, to be the voice of conscience, to be the awakener of life—it is not easy to express it in a word.

According to the teaching of Jesus religion is faith in the only God, Creator, Director of the world, Father; but Jesus does not overstrain transcendentalism, his religion is not solely for heaven, it is for the earth, and for daily, ordinary life. He did not speak much of the beginnings, or of the end of the world, he did not occupy himself with history, like the Old Testament, which in that also was only a national religion and doctrine. Jesus' religion reveals itself in morality and humanity, it is humanitarianism sub specie aeternitatis.

The difference between religiousness and morality we express with the words: holy and good. Holiness is moral life in God.

Giovanni Papini   (*1881–*   )

PROPHET AND FRIEND OF ALL

Translated by Dorothy Canfield Fisher

Here was no prophet of the mountains shouting in waste places, far from men, solitary, distant, forcing others to come to him if they wished to hear him. Here was a prophet living like a man among other men, a friend of all, friendly to the unfriended, an easy-going and companionable comrade, searching out His brothers where they work in the houses, in the busy streets, eating their bread and drinking wine at their tables, lending a hand with the fisherman's nets, with a good word for every man, for the sad, for the sick, for the beggar. . . .

Jesus spent His time with them walking from one region to another, or talking, seated among His friends. Always dear to Him was the sunny shore of the lake, along the curve of quiet clear water scarcely ruffled by the wind from the desert, dotted with a few boats silently tacking back and forth. The western coast of the lake was His real Kingdom; there He found his first listeners, His first converts, His first disciples.

Winwood Reade   (*1838–1875*)

APPEARED AS A SHINING ANGEL

The prophet of Nazareth did not differ in temperament and character from the noble prophets of the ancient period. He preached, as they did, the religion of the heart; he attacked, as they did, the ceremonial laws; he offered, as they did, consolation to the poor; he poured forth, as they did, invectives against the rulers and the rich. But his predictions were entirely different from theirs, for he lived, theologically speaking, in another world. The old prophets could only urge men to do good that the Lord might make them prosperous on earth, or, at the most, that they might obtain an everlasting name. They could only promise to the people the restoration of Jerusalem and the good things of the Gentiles; the reconciliation of Judah and Ephraim, and the Gathering of the Dispersed. The morality which Jesus preached was also supported by promises and threats, but by promises and threats of a more exalted kind: it was also based upon self-interest; but upon self-interest applied to a future life. For this he was indebted to the age in which he lived. . . . Jesus was a carpenter by trade, and was urged by a prophetic call to leave his workshop and to go forth into the world, preaching the gospel which he had received. The current fancies respecting the approaching destruction of the world, the conquest of the Evil Power, and the reign of God had fermented in his mind, and had made him the subject of a remarkable hallucination. He believed that he was the promised Messiah or Son of Man, who would be sent to prepare the world for the kingdom of God, and who would be appointed to judge the souls of men, and to reign over them on earth. He was a man of the people, a rustic and an artisan: he was also an imitator of the ancient prophets, whose works he studied, and whose words were always on his lips. Thus he was led as man and prophet to take the part of the poor. He sympathised deeply with the outcasts, the afflicted, and the oppressed. To children and to women, to all who suffered and shed tears; to all from whom men turned with loathing and contempt; to the girl of evil life, who bemoaned her shame; to the tax-gatherer, who crouched before his God in humility and woe; to the sorrowful in spirit and the weak in heart; to the weary and the heavy laden Jesus appeared as a shining angel with words sweet as the honey-comb, and bright as the golden day. He laid his hands on the heads of the lowly; he bade the sorrowful be of

good cheer, for that the day of their deliverance and their glory was
at hand.

UPTON SINCLAIR   (*1878–*   )

A PRINCE OF THE SOUL

Half that I love in my soul's life I owe to the prophet of Nazareth.
The other half I owe—not to Nietzsche, but to the new Dispensation
of which he is a priest. . . .

When I speak of Christ let no man think of Christianity. I speak
of a prince of the soul, the boldest, the freest, the noblest of men that
I know. With the thousand systems that mankind has made in his
memory, I have simply nothing in any way to do.

To me all morality is one. Morality is hunger and thirst after
righteousness. Morality is a quality of will. The differences that there
are between Christ and Nietzsche are differences of the intellect—
where no man is final.

The doctrines of each is a doctrine of sacrifice; with one it is a
sacrifice of love, with the other it is a sacrifice of labor. . . .

Moral sublimity lies in the escape from self. The doctrine of Christ
is a negation of life, that of Nietzsche an affirmation; it seems to me
much easier to attain to sublimity with the former.

NICHOLAS P. T. CARDINAL WISEMAN   (*1802–1865*)

HIS HOLD ON PEOPLE

We can easily conceive how this familiarity with the proverbial forms
of speech in use among the Rabbins and learned men of His nation,
this apt and elegant use of their favorite expressions, and this power
of giving them new and peculiar beauties, gained Him at once the

respect and confidence of the people; associated Him, of right, with their admitted teachers; shut the jealous mouths of these men, and delighted and charmed all; till they would remain whole days, regardless of food, in His society. Hence even in that very place where He was no prophet, the people "all gave testimony to Him: and they wondered at the words of grace that proceeded from His mouth, and they said, Is not this the son of Joseph?"

ACKNOWLEDGMENTS

The editor and the publisher are grateful to the following copyright owners and their publishers for their generous cooperation in granting permission to reprint selections from the copyrighted works mentioned:

ABINGDON-COKESBURY PRESS, for permission to use passages from Henry Sloane Coffin's "Religion Yesterday And Today", copyright 1940; Halford E. Luccock's "Christianity And The Individual In A World of Crowds"; E. Stanley Jones' "Is The Kingdom Of God Realism?", copyright 1940; Luther Allan Weigle's "Jesus And The Educational Method", copyright 1939; William A. Quayle's "The Healing Shadow"; E. Stanley Jones' "The Christ Of The Mount".

AMERICA, for permission to use Editorial by Reverend John La Farge, S.J., in the issue of April 18, 1936.

D. APPLETON-CENTURY COMPANY, for permission to use passages from Maurice Goguel's "Jesus The Nazarene—Myth Or History?"; Will Irwin's "Christ Or Caesar?"; Felix Adler's "Ethical Philosophy Of Life"; Thomas L. Masson's "Ascensions".

ASSOCIATION PRESS, of the National Council of the Y.M.C.A.'s of the U.S.A., for permission to use passages from Harry Emerson Fosdick's "The Manhood of the Master".

HARRY ELMER BARNES, Cooperstown, N.Y., for permission to use passages from his "The Twilight of Christianity".

BLACKIE AND SON, LTD., England, for permission to use a passage from F. C. Burkitt's contribution to "Christianity In The Light Of Modern Knowledge".

BLOCH PUBLISHING COMPANY, for permission to use passages from H. G. Enelow's "A Jewish View Of Jesus".

THE BOBBS-MERRILL COMPANY, for permission to use passages from "The Man Nobody Knows" by Bruce Barton, copyright 1924, used by special permission of the Publishers, The Bobbs-Merrill Co., and from "The Sky Is Red" by Jean S. Milner, copyright 1924, used by special permission of the Publishers, The Bobbs-Merrill Co.

ALBERT AND CHARLES BONI, INC., for permission to use a passage from Edwin Bjorkman's translation of Georg Brandes' "Jesus A Myth".

DR. JOHN SUTHERLAND BONNELL, Fifth Avenue Presbyterian Church, New York, for permission to quote from his sermon "Christ's Appeal To Human Hearts".

THE BRUCE PUBLISHING COMPANY, for permission to use passages from Herbert Ellsworth Cory's "The Emancipation Of A Free-Thinker" and M. Raymond's "The Man Who Got Even With God".

CHURCH OF JESUS CHRIST OF LATTER DAY SAINTS, Office of the First Presidency, Salt Lake City, Utah, for permission to use passages from "The Journal Of Discourses" by Brigham Young.

COLUMBIA UNIVERSITY PRESS, for permission to use a passage from Marion John Bradshaw's "Philosophical Foundations Of Faith", 1941, page 222.

THOMAS Y. CROWELL COMPANY, for permission to use passages from Lyman Abbott's "Christ's Secret Of Happiness".

CROWN PUBLISHERS, for permission to use a passage from Joseph K. Hart's "Mind In Transition".

CURTIS BROWN, LTD., New York, for permission to use passages from H. G. Wells' "The Outline Of History".

THE JOHN DAY COMPANY, for permission to use a passage from Lin Yutang's "My Country And My People".

THE DIAL PRESS, INC., for permission to use 216 words from Pierre Van Paassen's "That Day Alone", published by Dial Press, Inc., copyright by Pierre Van Paassen.

DR. JOHN H. DIETRICH, for permission to use a passage from "The Humanist Pulpit", a volume of addresses.

DODD, MEAD AND COMPANY, for permission to use passages from G. K. Chesterton's "The Everlasting Man"; "Golden Tales Of Anatole France".

DOUBLEDAY DORAN AND COMPANY, INC., for permission to use passages from Hall Caine's "Life Of Christ", copyright 1938, by Doubleday Doran and Co., Inc.; Beverley Nichols' "The Fool Hath Said", copyright 1935, 1936, by Doubleday Doran and Co., Inc.; David Saville Muzzey's "Spiritual Heroes", copyright 1902 by Doubleday Doran and Co. Inc.; Mary Borden's "Mary Of Nazareth", copyright 1933 by Doubleday Doran and Co. Inc.; Hugh Walpole's "Roman Fountain", copyright 1940; "Faith For Today" by Stanley High, Frank Kingdon, Gerald Groveland Walsh, S.J., Louis Finklestein, Ph.D., Swami Nikhilananda, copyright 1941 by Doubleday Doran and Co., Inc.; Basil King's "The Conquest Of Fear", copyright 1921 by Doubleday Doran and Co. Inc.; Don Marquis' "The Dark Hours", copyright 1924 by Doubleday Doran and Co., Inc.

E. P. DUTTON AND CO. INC., for permission to use passages from Phillips Brooks' "The Light Of The World"; Sir Francis Younghusband's "The Sum Of Things"; W. E. Orchard's "The Necessity Of Christ"; Nicholas of Cusa's "The Wisdom Of God", translated by Emma Gurney Salter.

FARRAR AND RINEHART, INC., for permission to use passages from "Humanism And America", edited by Norman Foerster, copyright 1930; Carl

G. Jung's "The Integration Of The Personality", translated by Stanley Dell, copyright 1939.

DOROTHY CANFIELD FISHER and the INTERNATIONAL COUNCIL OF RELIGIOUS EDUCATION, Chicago, Ill., for permission to use a passage from Mrs. Fisher's statement prepared for the Council for use in connection with Youth Week, Jan. 30, 1944.

PAUL GALLICO, for permission to use Paul Gallico's "Christmas Eve For Private Bill", from *Esquire,* January 1944, copyright 1944 by Esquire, Inc.

HARCOURT BRACE AND COMPANY, for permission to use passages from the translation by Dorothy Canfield Fisher of "The Life Of Christ" by Giovanni Papini, copyright 1923 by Harcourt Brace and Co.; "Three Guineas" by Virginia Woolf, copyright 1938, by Harcourt Brace and Co.; "The Condition Of Man", copyright 1944, by Lewis Mumford, by permission of Harcourt Brace and Co.; "The Travel Diary Of A Philosopher" by Count Hermann Keyserling, copyright, 1925, by Harcourt Brace and Co.; "The Letters Of Lincoln Steffens", copyright, 1938, by Harcourt Brace and Co.; "Collected Edition Of Heywood Broun", copyright, 1941, by Heywood Hale Broun, by permission of Harcourt Brace and Co.

HARPER AND BROTHERS, for permission to use passages from Sherwood Eddy's "Jesus Christ—What Is His Significance?"; James Moffatt's "Everyman's Life Of Jesus"; Kirby Page's "Jesus Or Christianity"; A. J. Muste's "Non-Violence In An Aggressive World"; Walter Marshall Horton's "Can Christianity Save Civilization?"; Henry A. Atkinson's "Prelude To Peace"; Roger Lloyd's "Revolutionary Religion"; George M. Lamsa's "My Neighbor Jesus"; C. E. M. Joad's "God And Evil"; Ralph W. Sockman's "Morals Of Tomorrow"; Albert Jay Nock's "Memoirs of A Superfluous Man"; J. Middleton Murry's "Jesus Man Of Genius"; John MacMurray's "The Clue To History"; Aldous Huxley's "An Encyclopedia Of Pacifism"; "In After Days" by Julia Ward Howe and Others; Charles Reynolds Brown's "Have We Outgrown Religion?"; "Christ The King" by Bishop William T. Manning and Others; Albert Payson Terhune's "The Son Of God"; Willard L. Sperry's "Rebuilding Our World"; J. B. Priestley's "Rain Upon Godshill"; Everett Dean Martin's "The Mystery Of Religion"; Jerome J. Jerome's "Life And Times"; Mary Austin's "A Small Town Man".

B. HERDER BOOK COMPANY, for permission to use passages from "The Spiritual Exercises of St. Ignatius".

GRANVILLE HICKS, for permission to use a passage from his "Eight Ways Of Looking At Christianity".

LE ROY HODGE, Attorney of Hamilton, N.Y. and Dr. Herman Aude, Executor of the W. H. Crawshaw Estate, for permission to use a passage from William H. Crawshaw's "The Genius Of Christ".

VYVYAN HOLLAND, for permission to use a passage from Vol. 7 of "The Complete Writings Of Oscar Wilde".

JOHN HAYNES HOLMES, for permission to use a passage from one of his sermons delivered at The Community Church, New York, N.Y.

E. G. HOMRIGHAUSEN, Princeton Theological Seminary, for permission to use a passage from his translation of Karl Barth's "God In Action".

HOUGHTON MIFFLIN COMPANY, for permission to use passages from Havelock Ellis' "The Dance Of Life" and the same author's "The Fountain Of Life"; John Burrough's "The Light Of Day"; Sir William Osler's "The Student Life And Other Essays".

ELBERT HUBBARD II, East Aurora, N.Y., for permission to use a passage from Elbert Hubbard's "The Man Of Sorrows".

MONSIGNOR GEORGE JOHNSON, Catholic University of America, for permission to use a passage from his Christmas 1940 sermon.

KEGAN, PAUL, TRENCH, TRUBNER AND CO. LTD., London, England, for permission to use a passage from Hegel's "Lectures On The Philosophy Of Religion".

ALFRED A. KNOPF, INC., passages from H. L. Mencken's "Treatise On The God"; F. W. Nietzsche's "The Anti-Christ" (H. L. Mencken translation); Oswald Spengler's "The Decline Of The West" (Atkinson translation); Maurice Samuel's "The Great Hatred"; D. H. Lawrence's "Assorted Articles"; all by permission of and special arrangement with Alfred A. Knopf, Inc.

DR. FRANK G. LANKARD, Drew University, for permission to use passages from his "Difficulties In Religious Thinking".

J. B. LIPPINCOTT COMPANY, for permission to use passages from Christopher Morley's "Religio Journalistici".

LITTLE, BROWN AND COMPANY and THE ATLANTIC MONTHLY PRESS, for permission to use passages from Robert Keable's "The Great Galilean"; Lord Charnwood's "According To St. John"; and to LITTLE BROWN AND COMPANY for passages from "The Journal Of Bronson Alcott" edited by Odell Shepherd.

LIVERIGHT PUBLISHING CORPORATION, for permission to use passages from their publication, Emil Ludwig's "The Son Of Man".

LONGMANS GREEN AND COMPANY, INC., for permission to use passages from François Mauriac's "Life Of Jesus" (Translated by Julie Kernan); Abbe Constant Fouard's "The Christ The Son Of God", (translated by

F. X. Griffiths); B. W. Maturin's "Some Principles And Practices Of The Spiritual Life"; Peter Finlay's "The Church Of Christ"; James Harvey Robinson's contribution to "Whither Mankind", edited by Charles A. Beard; John La Farge's "The Race Question And The Negro"; Sigrid Undset's "Christmas And The Twelfth Night"; Charles Lewis Slattery's "The Master Of The World".

THE MACMILLAN COMPANY, for permission to use passages from George Moore's "The Brook Kerith"; Lord Stamp's "Christianity And Economics"; Thomas G. Masaryk's "Masaryk On Thought And Life-Conversations with Karl Capek"; S. Parkes Cadman's "Ambassadors Of God; Norman Thomas' "As I See It"; Walter Rauschenbusch's "Christianity And The Social Crisis"; Karl Adam's "Christ Our Brother"; Harry F. Ward's "Which Way Religion"; Cardinal Faulhaber's "Judaism, Christianity, And Germany"; S. Radhakrishnan's "The Hindu View Of Life"; Daniel A. Poling's "A Preacher Looks At War"; Shailer Mathews' "The Social Teachings Of Jesus"; Henry C. Link's "The Rediscovery Of Man"; Winifred Kirkland's "The Man Of The Hour"; Rufus M. Jones' "The Testimony Of The Soul"; George Walter Fiske's "A Study Of Jesus' Own Religion"; John Masefield's "Good Friday—A Dramatic Poem" from Verse Plays; Lewis Browne's "This Believing World"; Henry Van Dyke's "The Gospel For An Age Of Doubt"; Albert Schweitzer's "The Quest Of The Historical Jesus"; Benjamin W. Robinson's "Jesus In Action"; Shailer Mathews' "Is God Emeritus?"; A. Eustace Haydon's "Biography Of The Gods"; Alban Goodier's "Jesus Christ Man Of Sorrows"; John Elof Boodin's "God And Creation"; "Adventure—The Faith of Science And The Science Of Faith" by Streeter, Chilcott, MacMurray and Russell; Ernest F. Scott's "The Ethical Teaching Of Jesus"; Walter Lippmann's "A Preface To Morals"; Joseph Klausner's "Jesus Of Nazareth"; Rufus M. Jones' "The Trail Of Life In The Middle Years"; James Gordon Gilkey's "What Can We Believe?"; C. F. Andrews' "Mahatma Gandhi's Ideas"; Edward Increase Bosworth's "The Life And Teaching Of Jesus"; William Temple's "Christ The Truth"; John A. Mackay's "A Preface To Christian Theology"; C. S. Lewis' "The Case For Christianity"; L. P. Jacks' "Confessions Of An Octogenarian"; Constance Garnett's translation of Dostoievsky's "The Brothers Karamazov"; George Bernanos' "The Diary Of A Country Priest"; Joseph R. Sizoo's "On Guard"; AE's (George William Russell) "Imaginations And Reveries"; Joseph Klausner's "From Jesus To Paul"; Charles Guignebert's "Christianity, Past And Present"; George Holley Gilbert's "The Student's Life Of Jesus"; "The Epistle To Diognetus", translated by L. B. Radford.

A. C. McClurg and Company, for permission to use a passage from J. L. Spalding's "Religion, Agnosticism And Education".

Bishop Francis J. McConnell, for permission to use passages from his "Democratic Christianity".

Julian Messner, Inc., for permission to use passages from John Middleton Murry's "Heroes Of Thought".

William Morrow and Company, Inc., for permission to use a passage from Esme Wingfield-Stratford's "They That Take The Sword", copyright 1931 by William Morrow and Co., Inc.

The New Jersey General Corporation and Engel, Judge and Miller, of New York, N.Y., for permission to use passages from Arthur Brisbane's "Editorials From The Heart Newspapers".

W. W. Norton and Company, for permission to use two passages from John Cowper Powys' "The Meaning Of Culture".

Alfred Noyes, for permission to use a passage from his "The Unknown God".

The Open Court Publishing Company, La Salle, Ill., for permission to use passages from George R. Montgomery's translation of G. W. Leibniz's "Discourse Of Metaphysics", copyright 1902; Theodore M. Greene and Hoyt H. Hudson translation of Immanuel Kant's "Religion Within The Limits Of Reason Alone", copyright 1934.

Our Sunday Visitor, Publishers of The Catholic Hour Radio Programs, for permission to use passages from radio addresses by Francis J. Haas, Fulton J. Sheen, Joseph F. Rummel, Thomas A. Carney, John J. Walde, Martin J. O'Malley, Ignatius W. Cox, Ignatius Smith, John B. Delaunay, Herbert F. Gallagher.

Oxford University Press, New York, N.Y., for permission to use passages from Arthur C. Headlam's "The Life And Teaching Of Jesus".

Oxford University Press, London, England, and the family of Gerard Manley Hopkins, for permission to use a passage from "The Notebooks And Papers Of Gerard Manley Hopkins" edited by Humphrey House.

The Paulist Press, for permission to use passages from Rev. James A. Gillis' "The Divinity Of Christ"; Paul Schanz's "Did Christ Rise Again?"; Aloysius McDonough's "Jesus Christ—The Divine Bridge-Builder".

Prentice-Hall, Inc., for permission to use passages from Albert Field Gilmore's "Christ At The Peace-Table".

The Preservation Press, Silver Springs, Md., for permission to use passages from Dorothy Day's "From Union Square To Rome".

Princeton University Press, for permission to use a passage from Paul Elmer More's "The Christ Of The New Testament".

G. P. Putnam's Sons, for permission to use passages from Adolf Harnack's "What Is Christianity?"; Sholem Asch's "What I Believe", translated by Maurice Samuel; W. E. Inge's "Christian Ethics And Modern Problems"; Oscar Wilde's "De Profundis".

Mrs. W. S. Rainsford, Garrison-on-the-Hudson, N.Y., for permission to quote from Dr. W. S. Rainsford's "The Story Of A Varied Life".

The Remainder Book Company, for permission to use a passage from Henri Barbusse's "Jesus".

Fleming H. Revell Company, for permission to use passages from William Jennings Bryan's "The Prince Of Peace"; Robert E. Speer's "The Principles Of Jesus"; Peter Ainslie's "The Message Of The Disciples For The Union Of The Churches"; P. W. Wilson's "The Christ We Forget".

The Roundtable Press, for permission to use a passage from Karl Barth's "God In Action", translated by E. G. Homrighausen and Karl J. Ernest.

Mrs. Josiah Royce, Cambridge, Mass., for permission to use passages from the late Josiah Royce's "The Problem Of Christianity".

St. Anthony's Guild, Paterson, N.J., for permission to use a passage from Bishop O'Hara's Foreword to Isadore O'Brien's "The Life Of Christ".

Charles Scribner's Sons, for permission to use passages from Samuel Angus' "The Mystery-Religions And Christianity"; Charles Foster Kent's "The Social Teachings Of The Prophets And Jesus"; Howard Chandler Robbins' "Simplicity Toward Christ"; Michael Pupin's "The New Reformation"; William Lyon Phelps' "Human Nature And The Gospel"; Lloyd C. Douglas' "These Sayings Of Mine"; Walter Russell Bowie's "The Master: A Life Of Jesus Christ"; Reinhold Neibuhr's "Beyond Tragedy"; Jacques Maritain's "Ransoming The Time"; V. F. Calverton's contribution to "America Now" edited by Harold Stearns; Robert Louis Stevenson's "Lay Morals And Other Papers"; Arthur Cushman McGiffert's "The God Of The Early Christians"; Eugene William Lyman's "The Meaning And Truth Of Religion"; George A. Buttrick's "Jesus Came Preaching"; Francis J. Spellman's "The Road To Victory"; Igor Sikorsky's "The Message Of The Lord's Prayer"; George Santayana's "Realms Of Being"; Dmitri Merejkowski's "Jesus The Unknown".

Sheed and Ward, for permission to use passages from Alfred Noyes' "The Unknown God"; C. C. Martindale's "Christianity Is Christ"; Paul Claudel's "Ways And Crossways" translated by John O'Connor; Robert Hugh Benson's "Christ In The Church"; Peter Wust's "Crisis In The West".

THE SIGN, for permission to use an Editorial and a passage from an article in the issue for February 1944.

SIMON AND SCHUSTER, INC., for permission to use passages from John Cowper Powys' "Enjoyment Of Literature"; contributions by Rebecca West and Hendrik Willem Van Loon to "What I Believe" edited by Clifton Fadiman; contributions by James Truslow Adams and Robert Andrew Millikan to "Living Philosophies"; Ernest Sutherland Bates' "The Friend Of Jesus"; Will Durant's "The Mansions Of Philosophy".

UPTON SINCLAIR, Monrovia, California, for permission to use passages from his "The Journal Of Arthur Stirling".

THE STRATFORD COMPANY, Boston, Mass., for permission to use passages from John W. Wayland's "Christ As A Teacher".

STUDENT CHRISTIAN MOVEMENT PRESS, LTD., London, England, for permission to use a passage from Toyohiko Kagawa's "The Religion Of Jesus".

TRUSTEES UNDER THE WILL OF MARY BAKER EDDY, and The First Church Of Christ, Scientist, in Boston, Mass., for permission to use passages from "Miscellaneous Writings", by Mary Baker Eddy, Copyright 1896 by Mary Baker Eddy, copyright renewed, 1924, (from page 161).

UNION OF AMERICAN HEBREW CONGREGATIONS, Cincinnati, Ohio, for permission to use a passage from Cecil Roth's "A Bird's-Eye View Of Jewish History".

THE UNIVERSITY OF CHICAGO PRESS, for permission to use passages from Shirley Jackson Case's "Jesus—A New Biography".

THE VIKING PRESS, INC., for permission to use passages from Francis Yeats-Brown's "Lancer At Large", copyright 1937 by Francis Yeats-Brown; Julius Katzenstein's "History And Destiny Of The Jews", translated by Huntley Paterson, copyright 1933 by The Viking Press, Inc.; William Ellery Leonard's "The Poet Of Galilee", copyright 1909, 1928 by The Viking Press, Inc.

DR. HAROLD BLAKE WALKER, First Presbyterian Church, Oklahoma City, Okla., for permission to quote from one of his sermons.

A. P. WATT AND SON, London, England, for permission to use a passage from Sir Oliver Lodge's "Raymond Or Life And Death", copyright 1916 by Geo. H. Doran and Co.

WILLETT, CLARK AND COMPANY, for permission to use a passage from the Marquis of Lothian's contribution to the symposium "The Universal Church And The World Of Nations".

MRS. WOODROW WILSON, for permission to quote from an address by Woodrow Wilson.

DR. PAUL AUSTIN WOLFE, Brick Presbyteriaι Church, New York, for permission to use a passage from his sermon "Christ And Caesar".

YALE UNIVERSITY PRESS, for permission to use passages from T. R. Glover's "The Influence Of Christ In The Ancient World".

The following authors were kind enough to refer me to passages on Christ in their works: Pierre Van Paassen, Lewis Browne, Sherwood Eddy, Irvin S. Cobb, Shirley Jackson Case, Granville Hicks, Christopher Morley, John La Farge, S.J., Dr. Frank G. Lankard, Dr. Harold Blake Walker, James A. Gillis, C.S.P., Dorothy Canfield Fisher, Norman Thomas, Upton Sinclair, Dr. John Sutherland Bonnell, Dr. Paul Austin Wolfe, Rev. George Johnson. A number of others referred me to passages in their works which, for varying reasons, could not be included in this collection. The editor is equally grateful to them for their cooperation.

The editor is also thankful to the following for suggesting possible sources of material: William C. Smith of the National Council of Catholic Men; Elizabeth W. Lott, Librarian of the Board of Missions and Church Extension of the Methodist Church, New York, N.Y.; Henry S. Brown of the Vice President's Office, Princeton Theological Seminary; Harry Schneidermann, Director, Library of Jewish Information, American Jewish Committee, New York, N.Y.; John La Farge, S.J.; Rev. W. H. Russell of The Catholic University; Frank G. Lankard of Drew University; Dr. John Haynes Holmes; Fred. E. Baer; Miss Florence S. Garing, Librarian of N.Y. Mercantile Library and Miss Carrie Walz, Mrs. Norma Nobles and Miss Ray Hurst of her Staff. The Staff of the excellent Library of The Union Theological Seminary, New York, was most courteous and cooperative. The facilities of The New York Public Library and The Port Washington, N. Y., Public Library were also of great help.

A special debt of appreciation is due Henry F. Woods for considerable research assistance and innumerable suggestions.

R. L. De Wilton and Ellen F. Shippen of The Macmillan Company Editorial Department provided me with expert editorial guidance out of their large experience in the religious book field. Harold Matson tossed in occasional editorial suggestions while quietly handling the business end of the book.

My daughter, Patricia Joan Woods, and my wife, Lillias Watt Woods, helped check manuscript, proofs and the index.

R. L. W.

INDEX OF AUTHORS AND SOURCES

A

ABBOTT, LYMAN (*Christ's Secret of Happiness*), 373

ADAM, KARL (*Christ Our Brother*), 3, 227, 325

ADAMS, JAMES TRUSLOW (*Living Philosophies*), 373

ADAMS, JOHN QUINCY (*Memoirs, Vol. 7*), 115

ADLER, FELIX (*An Ethical Philosophy of Life*), 228

AINSLIE, PETER (*The Message of the Disciples for the Union of the Church*), 374

ALCOTT, BRONSON (*The Journal of Bronson Alcott*), 230

AMIEL, HENRI FREDERIC (*Journal of Amiel*), 327

ANGUS, SAMUEL (*The Mystery-Religions and Christianity*), 375

ANONYMOUS (*Epistle to Diognetus*), 115; (Editorial in *The Sign,* February 1944), 327; (*Osteopathic Magazine,* Vol. 24, no. 12), 375

ARNOLD, MATTHEW (*Literature and Dogma*), 439

ASCH, SHOLEM (*What I Believe*), 442

ATKINSON, HENRY A. (*Prelude to Peace*), 475

AUGUSTINE, SAINT (*Sermons on Selected Lessons of the New Testament*), 116; (*Confessions of St. Augustine*), 328

AUSTIN, MARY (*A Small Town Man*), 4

B

BARBUSSE, HENRI (*Jesus*), 475

BARNES, HARRY ELMER (*The Twilight of Christianity*), 5

BARTH, KARL (*God in Action*), 330

BARTON, BRUCE (*The Man Nobody Knows*), 376

BATES, ERNEST SUTHERLAND (*The Friend of Jesus*), 377

BEECHER, HENRY WARD (*The Name Above Every Name*), 117

BENEDICT XV, Pope (Encyclical—*International Reconciliation*), 230

BENSON, ROBERT HUGH (*Christ in the Church*), 118, 331

BERNANOS, GEORGE (*The Diary of a Country Priest*), 119

BESANT, ANNIE W. (*On The Deity of Jesus*), 121

BEVERIDGE, ALBERT J. (*The Bible as Good Reading*), 7

BLAKE, WILLIAM (*Poems*), 332

BONAPARTE, NAPOLEON (*Napoleon's Argument for Divinity of Christ and the Scriptures*), 122

BONNELL, JOHN SUTHERLAND (*Christ's Appeal to Human Hearts*), 378

BOODIN, JOHN ELOF (*God and Creation*), 332

BORDEN, MARY (*Mary of Nazareth*), 479

BOSSUET, JACQUES BÉNIGNE (*Select Sermons and Funeral Orations*), 447

BOSWORTH, EDWARD INCREASE (*The Life and Teaching of Jesus*), 232

BOWIE, WALTER RUSSELL (*The Master: A Life of Jesus Christ*), 124, 379

BRADSHAW, MARION JOHN (*Philosophical Foundations of Faith*), 380

BRANDES, GEORG (*Jesus a Myth*), 449

BRISBANE, ARTHUR (*Editorials From the Hearst Newspapers*), 381

BROOKS, PHILLIPS (*The Light of the World*), 125, 333

BROUN, HEYWOOD (*Collected Edition of Heywood Broun*), 125

BROWN, CHARLES REYNOLDS (*Have We Outgrown Religion?*), 233

BROWNE, LEWIS (*This Believing World*), 450

BROWNE, SIR THOMAS (*Religio Medici*), 127

BROWNSON, ORESTES A. (*The Mediatorial Life of Jesus*), 334

BRYAN, WILLIAM JENNINGS (*The Prince of Peace*), 128

BUNYAN, JOHN (Author's Preface to *The Pilgrim's Progress*), 129

BURKITT, FRANCIS CRAWFORD (*The History of Christianity in the Light of Modern Knowledge*), 130

BURROUGHS, JOHN (*The Light of Day*), 336